Taxation of
Financial Intermediation

Taxation of Financial Intermediation

Theory and Practice for Emerging Economies

Edited by
Patrick Honohan

A copublication of the World Bank and Oxford University Press

© 2003 The International Bank for Reconstruction and Development / The World Bank
1818 H Street, NW
Washington, DC 20433
Telephone 202-473-1000
Internet www.worldbank.org
E-mail feedback@worldbank.org

A copublication of the World Bank and Oxford University Press.

Oxford University Press
198 Madison Avenue
New York, NY 10016

The findings, interpretations, and conclusions expressed herein are those of the authors and do not necessarily reflect the views of the Board of Executive Directors of the World Bank or the governments they represent.

The World Bank does not guarantee the accuracy of the data included in this work. The boundaries, colors, denominations, and other information shown on any map in this work do not imply any judgment on the part of the World Bank concerning the legal status of any territory or the endorsement or acceptance of such boundaries.

ISBN 0-8213-5434-5

Library of Congress Cataloging-in-Publication Data

Taxation of financial intermediation : theory and practice for emerging economies /
   edited by Patrick Honohan.
      p. cm.
   "A co-publication of the World Bank and Oxford University Press."
   Includes bibliographical references.
   ISBN 0-8213-5434-5
   1. Financial services industry—Taxation—Developing countries.   I. Honohan,
Patrick.

HG195.T39 2003
336.2'783321'091724—dc21   2003050061

Contents

v

TABLES AND FIGURES

FIGURES

Foreword

An impressive body of research now supports the proposition that improving the efficiency and effectiveness of domestic financial systems has an important role in accelerating long-term growth. Furthermore, avoiding financial crashes through well-designed and implemented regulatory policy has a demonstrable and substantial effect in preventing short-term surges in poverty. These two results justify the focus which the World Bank has placed on financial sector research in recent years, and which has greatly enlarged the empirical knowledge base on these matters and enhanced the analysis and formation of policy.

The research continues, as we deepen our understanding of how this complex and adaptable sector functions and how public policy can best be crafted to ensure that it increases its contribution to the economies of our client countries. Taxation is high on the list of the relevant public policy dimensions.

Deciding just how much the domestic financial sector should be taxed, and in what way, is a complex problem for policymakers. On the one hand, governments need revenue and the financial sector is an administratively convenient source. On the other hand, given the central role of finance achieving sustained economic growth, policymakers should not repress the sector's development by an onerous tax burden.

This is clearly a very live topic at present. Quite apart from the Tobin tax—which is outside the scope of this volume, with its focus on domestic tax issues—the financial transactions taxes that have been adopted in Latin America in the last few years have been highly controversial. They have generated a substantial flow of much-needed revenue: revenue that is vital for expenditures that can offer opportunities and support for poor people. But has the cost in terms of distortions been too high?

Striking a balance requires a good understanding of how finance works and how the system is likely to adapt to the taxes that are imposed. This volume provides a valuable toolbox for this purpose. Moving beyond the simplistic mantra that distortions must be avoided, the authors recognize that the financial system should bear its share of taxation, and seek to define criteria for ensuring that the distortions are limited.

A firm theoretical foundation, with several chapters devoted to modeling the behavioral impact of taxation and its potential use as a corrective device, is supplemented by descriptive material on current practice in advanced economies and some case studies illustrating how problems can arise. Perhaps most useful to policymakers, each of the main types of financial sector tax has a chapter of its own, highlighting the options and pitfalls.

In normal times, finance typically makes a sizable contribution to tax revenue, though failing financial systems often involve costly fiscal outlays. Improved arrangements for explicit and implicit taxation of the sector offer the double prospect of a more stable net contribution to the exchequer combined with a pro-growth strengthening of finance.

This is an impressive group of contributors, from a diversity of research and policy institutions. I am particularly glad to welcome several contributions from the International Monetary Fund. Remarkably close and productive Bank–Fund cooperation in the Financial Sector Assessment Program (FSAP) over the past four years has been a hallmark of financial sector work, and I am happy to see further evidence of that cooperation in several dimensions of our research activity.

Nicholas Stern
Senior Vice President and Chief Economist
The World Bank
March 2003

Preface

Taxation of financial intermediation receives surprisingly little analytical attention, despite its practical importance both for national budgets and for the efficient functioning of the financial system. This volume is an attempt to provide a coherent overview of the policy issues involved.

The volume opens with a general survey by Patrick Honohan (chapter 1) of the major issues in financial sector tax reform, characterizing the main styles of reform that have been advocated. Drawing freely on the remainder of the volume, the first chapter proposes some broad recommendations that should guide policy.

The remainder of the volume is organized in three parts. The first part presents the main issues at a theoretical and system-wide level. It leads off with a discussion by Robin Boadway and Michael Keen (chapter 2) of the theory of optimal taxation as it applies to taxation of capital income and financial services. The chapter pays special attention to the implications for tax policy of recent innovations in financial intermediation. Ramon Caminal focuses on banking and presents a simple but powerful model (chapter 3) from which the impact of different forms of taxation on equilibrium behavior can be predicted. The chapter presents some new results on the contrasting impact in competitive and monopolistic environments. Inducements to saving have been a motivation for many tax initiatives affecting financial intermediation. In chapter 4, Tullio Jappelli and Luigi Pistaferri survey theory and experience regarding the effectiveness of such incentives and provide some new cross-country evidence. The use of prudential and other forms of financial regulation as a sort of corrective tax, and their interaction with deposit insurance, is considered in chapter 5. Philip Brock provides some new results on the interaction between these. The chapters in Part I are more technical than those in the remainder of the volume.

The second part of the volume includes three contrasting chapters on empirical experience. Chapter 6, by Mattias Levin and Peer Ritter, reviews recent trends in relevant tax design in industrial countries, highlighting the limited degree of convergence in approach that has occurred. Chapters 7 and 8 describe the rather extreme recent experiences of Brazil and Russia, with quasi-taxes affecting financial intermediation, including inflation and unremunerated reserve requirements. These two case studies, by Eliana Cardoso and Brigitte Granville, respectively, serve as cautionary tales.

The final part contains five essays on specific tax issues. Chapter 9, by Emil Sunley, discusses the principles of loan-loss provisioning and related matters. The following two chapters by Andrei Kirilenko with Victoria Summers and Karl Habermeier, respectively, look at financial transactions taxes. Chapter 10 assesses the recent experience with bank debit taxes in Latin America, providing estimates of deadweight losses. Chapter 11 illustrates the way in which even small securities transactions taxes can have large affects on the volume of trading of related financial instruments. The practical case for applying a form of value-added tax to financial services is assessed by Satya Poddar in chapter 12. Finally, in chapter 13, Patrick Honohan provides new empirical evidence on the inflation tax and discusses its interaction with other taxes in influencing the scale and profitability of financial intermediation.

Much of the underlying research for this volume was funded by the World Bank's research support budget. In addition several chapters have been contributed by officials of the International Monetary Fund. The draft chapters were discussed at a workshop in Washington, D.C., in April 2002. Special thanks are due to the discussants at that workshop: Alan Auerbach, Ricardo Bebczuk, Gerard Caprio, Stijn Claessens, Liam Ebrill, Roger Gordon, Harry Huizinga, Kyung Geun Lee, Alberto Musalem, and Klaus Schmidt-Hebbel. Their comments greatly contributed to the quality of the final product.

Authors also wish to acknowledge additional comments and assistance on individual chapters from: Giacinta Cestone and Jorge Rodriguez (chapter 3); Tea Trumbic (for research assistance, chapter 4); Ilan Goldfajn, Eustáquio Reis, Sergio Schmukler, Altamir Lopes, Eduardo Luís Lundberg, Sérgio Mikio Koyama, and Márcio Issao Nakane (chapter 7); Claudia Dziobek and Victoria Summers (chapter 9); IMF Staff for the data used in chapter 10; Stefan Ingves, Richard Lyons, and participants at the 2001 Australasian Finance and Banking Conference (chapter 11).

Thanks are also due to Agnes Yaptenco for excellent administrative support.

Patrick Honohan
March 2003

Contributors

Robin Boadway
Queen's University, Kingston, Ontario

Philip L. Brock
University of Washington, Seattle

Ramon Caminal
Institut d'Anàlisi Econòmica, CSIC, Barcelona, and CEPR

Eliana Cardoso
Georgetown University, Washington, D.C.

Brigitte Granville
The Royal Institute of International Affairs, London

Karl Habermeier
International Monetary Fund

Patrick Honohan
The World Bank and CEPR

Tullio Jappelli
Universita di Salerno and CEPR

Michael Keen
International Monetary Fund

Andrei Kirilenko
International Monetary Fund

Mattias Levin
Centre for Economic Policy Studies, Brussels

Luigi Pistaferri
Stanford University and CEPR

Satya Poddar
Ernst & Young, LLP

Peer Ritter
Centre for Economic Policy Studies, Brussels

Victoria Summers
International Monetary Fund

Emil M. Sunley
International Monetary Fund

1

Avoiding the Pitfalls in Taxing Financial Intermediation

Patrick Honohan

Because the financial sector keeps systematic accounts and acts as a gatekeeper of liquid resources, it provides many useful tax "handles" for the fiscal authorities. In many countries, a distorted structure of financial sector taxation has evolved, reflecting both inertia and opportunism. Inertia, in that some very old taxation and administrative practices have survived in the financial sector, reflecting the convenience of collection and the fact that those liable to comply are a small and privileged group of regulated intermediaries that are unlikely to be politically vocal and that can, in any event, pass on much of the tax to their customers. Opportunism, in that a sudden need for budgetary revenue can trigger an increase in reliance on this quick and reliable source.

Growing awareness of the strategic importance of the financial sector in catalyzing economic growth, combined with the increasing global competition in financial services, has led to a substantial reconsideration of the domestic financial sector's potential as a cash cow for the budget.[1] Indeed, in some instances the pendulum may have swung to the other extreme, with special interests successfully arguing for exaggerated fiscal concessions in the name of improved financial sector performance.

This volume provides the basis for considering proposals for financial sector tax reform in a comprehensive light. The focus takes account of empirical realities in middle-income developing countries, though many of the principles have wider application. The discussion is confined to *domestic* financial intermediation (thus excluding issues of international cooperation or harmonization), though recognizing that application needs to take account of the international environment.

Financial sector taxation is complex both in theory and practice and it needs to evolve in response to financial innovation and wider economic changes.[2] The volume does not propose or attempt to offer a simple blueprint, but the discussion of theoretical, empirical, and practical considerations does lead to a number of guidelines for developing what would constitute a good financial sector tax system.

Proposals for financial sector tax reform typically come from one of two powerful perspectives. The reformer may be an enthusiast for a big simplification, usually some form of "flat tax," including VAT on financial services, zero taxation on capital income, or a universal transactions tax. Or the reformer may be an advocate of subtle corrective taxation designed either to offset some of the many market failures to which the financial sector is prone or to achieve other targeted objectives.

In practice, just like the perennial conflict between simplicity in tax administration and economic efficiency of the tax rates, the two perspectives can conflict rather severely. Information and control requirements of much of corrective taxation tend to be poorly accommodated by the big simplifications. This tension has remained unresolved over the years. Elements of each approach have become embodied in the taxation, explicit and implicit, of the sector. At the same time, the ever-pressing demands of revenue intrude as a further influence on policy design. As a result, the tax systems in most countries often end up as a complex mixture defying any straightforward rationalization. The big flat-tax ideas are diluted and modified; the corrective taxes may misfire by conflicting with others introduced for different reasons.

Meanwhile, even as simplification and correction continue their tug of war, policy design can all too often neglect the two distinctive traps into which financial sector taxation can fall: namely, the sector's unique capacity for arbitrage and its sensitivity to inflation and thus to non-indexed taxes. This chapter argues that the practical design of financial sector taxation should be guided by a *defensive approach* in which proposed taxes are assessed relative to their ability to resist arbitrage and their degree of inherent indexation. Although the defensive approach does not provide an adjudication between simplification and correction, it will protect against many of the worst distortions that have been observed.

As a working standard, a tax system is considered to be good for the financial system if it meets three main criteria. It minimizes the distortions it imposes, for a given amount of revenue collected, especially by causing the formal financial sector to be bypassed through disintermediation to untaxed or differently taxed competitors. It is corrective of known distortions, such as those that result from imperfect and asymmetric information. Finally, it does not push tax collection from the sector beyond the point where marginal distorting costs exceed those elsewhere in the economy. With these criteria in mind, the theory and experience described in the remaining chapters of this study do suggest some key practical guidelines.

First, while reformers should not expect to find a complete and practical solution in any of the "big ideas," each has lessons for a good system.

• The notion of a value-added tax (VAT) on financial services— even if practicalities impede its introduction as such—represents a useful benchmark against which existing and proposed indirect taxes can be compared for their burden and impact.

• Significant financial transactions taxes are hard to justify on theoretical grounds and should be resorted to only as a transitory device when fiscal revenue is under particular pressure.

• Heavy emphasis on the taxation of income from capital should be avoided.

Second, attempts at corrective taxation should be undertaken with extreme caution. History suggests that unintended side effects or deadweight losses may dominate the results. This implies that special tax-based schemes to encourage stock exchange listing, household saving, and the like should be viewed with caution, bearing in mind the substantial opportunity cost in terms of lost revenue and the questionable gains.

Third, while tax shifting is common throughout the economy, the potential for arbitrage is very high in finance. All financial sector taxes need to be designed in as arbitrage-proof a way as possible (the first defensive criterion).

Fourth, inflation generally has a more pervasive effect in finance on the impact of taxation. All financial sector taxes need to be designed to be as inflation-proof as possible (the second defensive criterion).

Fifth, approximating taxation of the financial sector to that of other sectors is a reasonable goal. The challenge lies in mapping the somewhat distinctive institutions and concepts of financial intermediation to that of the remainder of the economy, and distinguishing between its role as an intermediary and manager of the funds of others from those of a true principal. This allows one to relate or "map" the various tax rates and tax bases affecting financial firms to the more familiar concepts most closely corresponding, such as sales taxes, corporate income tax, and collection on account of customer income taxes.

The remainder of this chapter discusses the background to each of these guidelines, referring as appropriate to the remaining chapters of the volume. The next section reviews the main forms of tax that are relevant. The section that follows describes the thrust of reform ideas. The chapter then examines the effectiveness of the several corrective taxes that have been employed. After highlighting the two most distinctive relevant features of the financial system for designing tax structures, the discussion comes to the practical question of tax rates and how to calibrate these for comparability with nonfinancial taxes. The chapter concludes with a call for moderation in tax design and advocacy of the defensive approach, which should be the guiding principle in policy design.

The Main Types of Explicit and Implicit Tax

Governments have used financial intermediaries to relieve their budgetary pressures in three main ways. First, they have applied a variety of *explicit taxes*. Some are common to firms in other sectors of the economy. Some are special to the financial sector, such as financial transactions taxes, unremunerated reserve requirements, and deposit insurance premia. Some seem similar to those applied to other sectors, but in practice have a qualitatively different impact even if imposed at the same nominal rate. Additionally, differential application of mainstream explicit taxation to financial intermediaries, including different rates of tax, can be important, as in the treatment of loan-loss provisions in calculating taxable income, or in the application of sales taxes to interest received by banks. Second, they have imposed *reserve requirements*, which have had the effect of boosting the net revenue of the central bank and hence indirectly the government. Third, they have made regulations channeling funds to government or favored sectors and borrowers in ways that involve *implicit subsidies*, notably by imposing interest rate ceilings.

Explicit Taxes

Taxes may be levied on many different elements of a financial intermediary's business. Net corporate income (profits), gross revenue (interest and fees), and the value of payments made or received through the intermediary are the most important types. Interest paid by the intermediary to its creditors are also often taxed, and the intermediary may be obliged to withhold this tax, thus making only net-of-tax payments to the creditors. Less commonly, elements of the balance sheet of the financial institution (assets, liabilities, or net capital) could also form tax bases.

Inasmuch as non-financial corporations are also liable to corporate income tax and to a variety of sales taxes, it is important to identify whether, and in what way, taxation of the financial intermediary often differs sharply from the standard situation. The financial intermediary may be subject to special rules or rates. Or the way in which the standard tax is applied may have a distinct incidence on financial intermediaries because of characteristic ways in which their business differs structurally from that of non-financial businesses.

For instance, the total value of payments made and received by a bank (credits and payment to customer accounts) is a large multiple of the total value-added of a bank. Furthermore, the value of payments bears no stable relationship to the value-added or profits of a bank. As with the value of goods carried by shipping or airline companies, a tax on such payments, even at a low rate, could not be regarded as an approximation to a value-added tax on other companies. The same would be true of taxes levied on securities market transactions.

On the other hand gross interest, insurance premium income, and fee receipts in a non-inflationary environment could be of the same order of magnitude: perhaps twice the value-added. Such a ratio would be equally characteristic of many non-financial companies. However, in contrast to these, and unlike net interest, the gross interest is highly sensitive to the nominal level of wholesale interest rates and to expected inflation. In a volatile inflationary environment, this too becomes a rather arbitrary tax base.

The calculation of appropriate reserves against loan losses is an issue for the accounting of any company with receivables or other claims in its balance sheet. But it looms much larger for financial intermediaries, where annual loan-losses even in good years can often be much larger than the profits earned. Therefore the tax treatment of loan-loss provisioning is relatively much more important for financial intermediaries, in that the timing of sizable tax payments can be at stake.

The inertial element in explicit taxation of finance is reflected in stamp and registration duties. These have a long history in taxation, having been applied to the formal registration of legal documents, including those recording transfers of property ownership. They have their legacy in taxes on payments transaction and transactions in securities exchanges. Modern tax systems depend to a large extent on approximations to a comprehensive income tax or expenditure tax. Stamp duties are poor approximations of either concept.

Withholding taxes on interest paid to depositors and other forms of special treatment of income received by the customers of financial intermediaries can also be distorting. This is especially the case when they apply at different rates to different categories of income, such as on local currency and dollar-denominated deposits.[3]

Reserve Requirements and Seigniorage

The inflation tax and related taxes[4] deserve a section by themselves because of their historical importance, the scale of potential revenue, and the ease with which they can be collected.

Requirements that banks should hold a certain fraction of their deposits in the form of liquid reserves, whether in cash, at the central bank, or at some analogous institution, dates at least to the early part of the 19th century. Initially, it represented a convenience to ensure the smooth completion of the daily clearing and to reduce the recourse of banks to central bank borrowing. Since reserves placed with the central bank were often unremunerated, reserve requirements boosted net income of the central bank, which is usually passed to the fiscal authority as a dividend payment in due course and recognized as a nontax revenue item in the budget. In this way the banks were implicitly taxed and the budget relieved. The fiscal element was at first not considered especially important, but it became so as bank margins narrowed, especially where nominal interest rates were rising. Some central banks responded by introducing remuneration on required reserves; others tolerated avoidance through substitution by banks of nonreservable categories of instrument.

Nowadays, reserve requirements are generally seen as an extension of the base of seigniorage, inasmuch as substitution of deposits for cash holdings had reduced the base of seigniorage as a tax.

Secondary liquidity reserve requirements have also been imposed in several countries. Often, secondary reserves have had to be held in the form of designated government securities. Sometimes the securities were sold directly to the banks with off-market yields, and as such embody a fairly obvious implicit tax. Such requirements have often also been imposed on insurance companies and other nonbank intermediaries. These types of requirements thus shade into directed credit and interest ceiling arrangements.

Directed Credit and Interest Ceilings

Governments seek control over where the loanable funds mobilized by the financial system will be applied for somewhat different reasons to those motivating reserve and liquidity requirements, but again there is a clear fiscal dimension. This kind of mechanism has been operated in nearly all countries over the years and takes many forms. Sometimes there is a requirement to place a special deposit amounting to a specified proportion of the bank's mobilized resources in the central bank or another public agency charged with on-lending these to borrowers in preferred sectors. Sometimes there is a requirement to lend a certain fraction of the bank's resources to specified sectors, or failing that, to deposit an equivalent amount with a specialized bank that can do the lending. Whether or not there is an explicit interest rate ceiling on these sectoral requirements, the diversion of funds has the effect of lowering the market-clearing rate for them. This will act as if there were a tax on the interest income from this part of the lending (partly compensated by a higher market-clearing rate on non-favored sectors). Except where the government is the borrower, the benefit of this tax does not directly go to it. Nonetheless, it is appropriate to see the budget as a hidden beneficiary, in that, absent the directed credit, subsidization of the preferred borrowers would have to have been done through other means, including direct budgetary allocations.

System-wide interest rate ceilings, much rarer now than in the past, and capital controls have the effect of lowering local interest rates and this too can be seen as a tax affecting financial intermediation. The government's budget is almost always the largest single borrower, and as such the biggest direct beneficiary of system-wide interest ceilings and their equivalents.

The Big Reform Ideas

One general approach to financial sector taxation is to attempt a great simplification on the theory that low rates and a wide base with few exemptions are likely to generate relatively low distortions. This approach holds out the prospect not only of minimizing the incentive for complex schemes of financial engineering designed to avoid tax, but also of making such schemes relatively difficult to develop.

The three main handles for taxation—income, expenditure, and transactions—have each been the subject of prominent and extensively discussed grand and simple schemes. These are: the proposition that capital income should not be taxed at all; the proposal that value added by the financial services industry should be subject to a uniform tax; and the idea that a tax on all financial transactions at a very low rate could generate large revenues with negligible distortion. These are considered one by one in the sections that follow.

Capital Income: Should It Be Taxed at All?

The underlying basis for the argument that it might be optimal not to tax income from capital at all is the insight that this involves a form of double taxation on future consumption. Shifting the perspective from the statutory base of the tax, capital income, to a variable more closely relevant to economic policy, namely utility based on household consumption, raises serious questions. A constant nominal or statutory tax rate on capital income implies an effective rate on consumption that may increase without bound for consumption far into the future. Because future consumption depends on the reinvestment of after-tax capital income, the more remote the date of future consumption, the higher the effective tax rate; and this effective tax rate may increase without bound. Optimal tax policy can improve on a situation with infinitely high effective tax rates. Accordingly, this reasoning points to the optimality of capital income taxation converging to zero (see chapter 2).

Many subtle qualifications can be made to the implicit models of utility, income, and consumption underlying this analysis, and the precise prescription for zero taxation is not very robust. Nonetheless, it retains some force and serves as an important counterweight to proposals for high rates of capital income taxation designed to achieve other goals. One such goal is that of ensuring the socially optimal rate of national saving (since private markets cannot generally be relied upon to do this and may result in over-saving). Another is redistribution. Yet even if households differ in their wage-earning capacity and tax policy is being used for redistributional goals, these can best be achieved by a tax on wage income alone— at least in simple models of intertemporal preferences. Once again the use of capital income taxation would be suboptimal because of the compound interest effect.

If income from capital is not to be taxed, then it might seem to follow that the income of financial intermediaries ought not to be taxed either. But in practice some corporate income—perhaps a large portion—represents pure profit or economic rent. Neglected in the models that generate the result of no tax on capital income, pure profit may be taxed without distortion, and this argument is another important qualification. Where financial markets are uncompetitive—

and the scale economies that are involved in parts of finance make this relevant, especially in financially closed economies—this could be an empirically important factor.[5]

A stronger line of attack on the zero capital income tax proposition comes from practical issues of enforcement and informational deficiencies. If capital income goes completely untaxed, this may provide an easy loophole for high-earning households to camouflage their earnings by transforming or laundering them into capital income. A tax on capital income may be an important practical expedient to close such loopholes.[6] If so, withholding the tax at source, or taxing corporate income as a form of implicit withholding, may further help to overcome the tax authorities' informational disadvantage and administrative collection costs. However, these considerations tend to be swamped in many developing countries by the need to consider the impact on foreign-owned firms. Given the fact that many capital exporting countries allow credit to their residents for tax paid in the host country, this can pave the way for host countries to tax foreign-owned companies in the knowledge that they will not be discouraged from investing to the extent that the tax paid to the host country simply reduces their home country tax.

The elegant simplicity of the theoretical argument against capital income tax thus ultimately fails, though it points to a need to justify such taxation—and the taxation of the income of financial and other companies—on grounds other than those of simple consistency with taxation of wage income.

Taxing Financial Services: Can a VAT Work?

About 70 percent[7] of the world's population live in countries with a VAT and the tax is a key source of government revenue in more than 120 nations (Ebrill and others 2001). So if a VAT is the way forward for the bulk of (indirect) taxation on expenditure, to what extent should it also be the model for financial services?

The first observation has to be that in practice, most financial services are "exempt" in virtually all countries employing a VAT. This does not mean that these financial services wholly escape the VAT, as the status of "exempt" does not allow financial service providers to recover VAT paid by their taxable suppliers and built into the price of their inputs. Indeed, taxable firms that use financial services as inputs cannot recover the VAT paid by the suppliers of financial service firms either, with the result that there is tax "cascading." But value that has been added by the exempt financial sector firms is not directly captured in the tax. Whether aggregate tax receipts would increase or fall if the exemption were removed is an unresolved empirical issue, which depends not only on the degree to which financial services are used by tax-liable firms, but also on the different rates of VAT that may be in effect.

The exemption of most financial services from VAT appears to be a historical inheritance without much political or economic rationale. While it is not difficult to measure the value-added of a bank (profits plus wages), there is the practical difficulty of deciding how much credit taxable firms that use financial services would be entitled to claim. The charge for many financial services is an implicit one bundled with others in, for example, the spread between deposit and lending rates. Determining how much of the spread should be attributed to depositor services and how much to borrower services is not straightforward. Thus it is not obvious how much credit each should receive for VAT already paid on inputs.

Yet it is not impossible to devise simple rules of thumb that can provide a reasonable approximation. Thus, for example, the cash flow method where VAT is paid on all net cash receipts (including capital amounts) could be adequate in a static environment. However, start-up problems and treatment of risk may not be adequately resolved by this method, and changing tax rates also presents difficulties for the approach. A variant of the cash flow method, using suspense accounts and an accounting rate of interest to bring transactions at different dates to a common standard, could help ease the transition problems and has been shown to be workable by detailed pilot studies in the European Union (see chapter 12).

The lack of any clear potential revenue gain, and fears about the practical complexity and possible hidden distortions or loopholes, have inhibited any significant move to bringing financial services into the VAT net.[8] The resulting distortions are quite serious in some cases. For one thing, there is a clear incentive to self-supply inputs. Second, there are distortions at the margin. Financial services such as factoring, which can represent a particularly effective form of lending to small- and medium-scale enterprises—low cost and low risk— could be severely tax-disadvantaged by falling within the VAT net in many jurisdictions for which other forms of lending are exempt.

The grand simplification offered by the VAT thus fails, not on theoretical grounds, but on the grounds of administrative and practical difficulties or uncertainties. Nevertheless, it does point in the direction of what might be desirable for substitute indirect taxes.[9]

Transactions Taxes: Panacea or Pandora's Box?

Because of their loose connection with consumption and utility, and their potential for generating significant distortions in the organization of production and distribution, transactions taxes (including trade taxes) have lost favor as a tool of general tax policy over the years relative to income and expenditure taxes. But the vast scale of financial sector transactions has presented itself to some scholars and some governments as a convenient base for rapidly generating substantial revenue.

There is a paradox here. Critics of transactions taxes point to the potentially serious distortions that it causes, while advocates argue that, because of the large base, sizable revenues can be realized with low nominal tax rates. To the extent that the deadweight cost of a tax is often supposed to be proportional to the *square* of the tax rate, introducing a low-rate financial transactions tax in order to reduce the much higher rates of labor income or other taxes might reduce total deadweight in the tax system as a whole.

At the most extreme, a recent proposal suggests that what seems at first sight to be an administratively trivial and quantitatively tiny 0.15 percent rate of tax on all automated payments could raise enough revenue (in the United States) to replace the entire existing tax system (Feige 2000). Feige shows that existing automated payments amounted (in 1996) to somewhere in the region of US$300–500 trillion, or of the order of 50 times the value of GDP. How, he asks, could anyone argue that a tax rate of 0.15 percent, even applied to such a large base, be considered seriously distorting by comparison with the existing tax regime?

Analysis of the payments that would be affected reveals that about 85 percent relate to financial transactions (purchase or sale of stocks, bonds, foreign exchange or other money changing transactions, and so on). To a large extent, then, the initial burden of a universal payments tax would fall on the financial sector.

Of course, if the perspective shifts (as before, with the capital income tax) from the statutory or nominal base to the more economically relevant concept of consumption, this argument takes on a different light. Then it becomes clear that the average good or service in the typical consumption bundle must be "hit" by the tax not once, but dozens of times, as it works its way through financing, design, production, and distribution.

Criticisms of this proposal fall into two main groups. First, the tax would not collect as much revenue due to the sizable elasticities involved.[10] Financial sector transactions in particular would be arbitraged in such a way as to drastically reduce the number of recorded transactions. What are now sequences of linked transactions carried out for little more than bookkeeping convenience at negligible cost would be collapsed into a single more complex transaction. Portfolio readjustments would be made with reduced frequency without substantially altering expected return and risk. Microeconomic studies of the precise mechanisms that are at work to generate gross transactions of such a high multiple of GDP in wholesale financial markets are not plentiful so that reliable estimates of these effects are not yet available.[11] Furthermore, the scope for avoiding such a tax through offshore financial transactions must be taken seriously.

The second main objection is that, even if the tax did collect the expected revenue, the distortion costs would not necessarily be any smaller than with the existing system. This objection relies on either of two observations. First, the financial system would bear the main brunt, and as such that the tax would in fact be more concentrated, not less. Or second, in terms of final consumption, the tax would effectively cascade to cumulative rates comparable to those observed at present.

No country has seriously considered replacing its tax system with a universal payments tax, but there are numerous examples of partial transactions taxes, applying for example to bank debits or to securities transactions.[12] Bank debit taxes introduced in half a dozen Latin American countries in the past 15 years or so in a bid to raise revenue have been successful in that goal, at least for a while, with revenues ranging from about 0.5 percent of GDP to as much as 3.5 percent in one case for one year. It is fair to say that revenue from these taxes held up unexpectedly well over three to four years. That revenue would fall off after the first year was predicted by many, and it did occur on average, though the effect did not prove to be statistically significant in regression of the available data. Nevertheless, many of the schemes had to be adapted administratively in the course of their operation, to exempt some transactions that would otherwise have been too distorting (and probably also to capture others that had escaped the net). The distortions of these and of securities transactions taxes have been discussed in the literature. They certainly are distorting, yet applied in moderation, these transactions taxes have been less distorting than many observers expected (see chapters 10 and 11, this volume).

Thus such transactions taxes have been surprisingly resilient—despite expectations that they would not only distort financial markets and drive out capital but would quickly lose their revenue-raising ability. But they are far from being a panacea, and indeed have little to recommend them beyond their ability to deliver revenue speedily and with low direct administrative costs.

Corrective Taxes

It is not just taxation that distorts financial markets. Information deficiencies, monopoly power, and other factors push most financial

markets away from the ideal of the atomistic market with fully informed participants competing on a level basis. Under these circumstances, the nonrevenue side effects of taxes and tax-like measures
can be turned to advantage and form part of the corrective policy
structure in this area.

Indeed, many measures of this type may have regulation and
market efficiency as their primary objective, with revenue seen as a
side effect.[13] But as discussed below, the effectiveness of many such
measures in their supposedly corrective role has been challenged
and remains controversial.

Deposit Insurance

The most complex and contentious of these debated corrective quasi-
taxes is deposit insurance. That it is a tax is fairly clear from the
contributions or levies that are generally imposed on participating
banks, especially given that these are typically compulsory and that
the rate of tax usually bears at best an imperfect relation to the "fair
premium."

Indeed, the anticipated gross revenue from the levy is typically
small and in many cases is calculated to be insufficient to cover even
the *expected* payout costs as calculated using option-pricing formulae (Laeven 2002). Furthermore the probability distribution of net
payout costs is severely skewed. Systemic banking crises entailing
fiscal costs of up to 50 percent of a year's GDP are never matched
by a corresponding deposit insurance fund accumulation in lucky,
crisis-free countries.[14]

For many advocates, the perceived corrective role of deposit insurance is essentially one of reducing the likelihood of depositor
panic. By protecting depositors against the risk that their deposits
will be unpaid if a bank proves to be insolvent, it is hoped that a
self-fulfilling panic—including contagion to other banks triggered
by the insolvency of one bank—can be avoided.[15] On the other
hand, by lowering the vigilance of potentially informed depositors,
the moral hazard of heightened risk-taking by the bankers, unpun-
ished by market discipline, could in theory result in heightened risk
to the system as a whole.

Although early deposit insurance schemes entailed a uniform insurance premium per dollar of deposit, there have been moves in
several countries to differentiate the rate of premium in accordance
with some measure of the perceived riskiness of the participating
bank's portfolio. This dimension of such taxes is designed to reduce
the moral hazard potential, but it depends to some extent on the information available to the deposit insurer as to the accuracy of the
ex ante risk assessment (Honohan and Stiglitz 2001). About a quar-

ter of schemes have some risk-differentiation, but the differentials are small and are not always systematically imposed (Demirgüç-Kunt and Sobaci 2001).[16]

Econometric estimates of how financial system performance varies across countries with the existence and characteristics of deposit insurance systems suggest that countries whose socio-political institutions are generally rated as strong need not fear that the moral hazard side effect will outweigh other beneficial effects. Although deposit insurance weakens market discipline even in such countries, the effects seem to be offset by better official oversight. However, for countries with less well-developed institutions (along the dimensions of rule of law, governance, and corruption), the establishment of a formal deposit insurance scheme[17] does appear to present a heightened risk of crisis (Demirgüç-Kunt and Detragiache 2002; Demirgüç-Kunt and Kane 2002) and does not even promote deposit growth (Cull, Senbet, and Sorge 2002). Having risk-based deposit insurance premia does not appear to mitigate the systemic risk, thus the potential for introducing a corrective structure of the deposit insurance tax may be limited.

Deposit insurance, with or without risk-based premia, may not be a very effective corrective mechanism. It clearly needs to be supplemented in this role by strong administrative or other controls, including supervision of minimum capitalization ratios (see chapter 5). Moreover, it may interact with other taxes. For instance, a tax on bank gross receipts will reduce the expected after-tax return to a risky investment, though chapter 5 shows that there would be some offset to this inasmuch as the government (deposit insurer) is coinsuring the risk to a greater extent in the presence of such a tax. On the other hand, chapter 5 also shows that a marginal reserve requirement (see below) could be more likely to reduce the moral hazard effect on bank risk-taking behavior. All in all, though, the uncertain strength and reliability of such effects argue for blunter and more reliable instruments in restraining bank risk-taking, a matter that lies beyond the scope of the current volume.

Provisioning and Capital Adequacy

The amount of loan-loss provisioning that is allowable to banks as a deduction against income for tax purposes can be a very significant factor in arriving at the net tax liability—and is often sufficient to shelter the entire tax bill. By the same token, this can be a matter of considerable revenue significance for the authorities. But it has long been acknowledged that there is a potential corrective role for the treatment of loan-loss provisions. This argument hinges on the arbitrariness that inevitably arises in arriving at a reasonable provision that would ensure that the banks' accounts represent a true and fair picture of the business. If the fiscal rules have the effect of biasing company accounting, this could be damaging for the transparency of the financial system and for good decisions on risk management. Recent accounting scandals have focused attention on the difficulty of seeing through valuation procedures used in nonfinancial company reporting procedures. Bank accounts can be arguably even less clear-cut, especially in times of economic turbulence or change.

To the extent that equity capital represents a cushion protecting depositors and other claimants against the consequences of a decline in the value of the bank's loan portfolio and other assets, the equity holders of a lightly capitalized bank at risk of failure—and the directors, to the extent that they are acting as the equity holders' agents—will have an incentive to minimize the amount of capital that they truly have at risk. In this way, they will transfer risk to other claimants. They will minimize their capital at risk provided they can do this without inducing an increase in the required return on their other liabilities. If the fiscal authority disallows the deductibility of reasonable loan-loss provisions (for example, provisions that can be justified on the basis of a reasonable objective forecasting model), that reinforces the incentive to understate provisions and thereby to overstate capital, potentially misleading regulators and the market.

On the other hand, a well-capitalized bank may be more attracted by the advantages of advancing tax deductibility, and may use the range of uncertainty to increase loan-loss provisioning, thereby reducing revenue.

Balancing the pressures of revenue needs with the risk of losing transparency is thus a constant tug-of-war and different countries adopt different rules (see chapter 9 in this volume and Laurin and Majnoni 2003). The preferred goal here would seem to be a move away from mechanical rules (such as disallowing general provisions but allowing specific provisions) toward a more realistic, forward-looking accounting that allows predictable but not yet identified losses to be adequately provisioned, so long as these are accepted by the institutional regulator.[18]

Promoting Saving

A widespread explicit goal of corrective tax measures affecting the financial sector is the promotion of saving. The goal is driven partly by fiscal needs, in an attempt to ease the financing of government deficits; partly by a perception (colored by an earlier generation of macroeconomic theories and, because of new research findings, no longer generally accepted by economists) that aggregate economic growth is, in the long-run, driven by national saving; and partly by a desire to ensure that households do not under-save, particularly for retirement, but also for housing and education.[19]

In practice, such measures tend not to affect all savings media equally. Hence their sometimes substantial impact on the structure and performance of the financial system, which, in certain cases at least, can far outweigh the net impact of the policy on the goal of increasing household saving (OECD 1994; Honohan 2000).

For practical reasons, measures that operate by modifying income tax schedules tend to be relevant only in middle-income countries, or at least in countries that have achieved a certain minimum level of the effectiveness of the income tax system. Furthermore, there is widespread skepticism among experts as to the effectiveness of mandatory saving for housing in achieving the goal of improving access to housing for the targeted low-income groups. On the other hand mandatory retirement saving programs appear to increase national saving by a significant amount on average, especially perhaps where they are tax-advantaged (chapter 4).

Other Dimensions of Corrective Financial Taxation

In other cases, supposedly corrective financial sector taxation comes more in the form of a vague and unthinking encouragement of what are seen as social "goods." This is not unique to the financial sector: finance ministers are typically bombarded with proposals to exempt from taxation items or activities thought to be meritorious. Except where tax relief appears to be the most effective way of correcting some market distortion that is resulting in an undersupply of the item or activity in question, the ministers are usually advised to resist such special pleading. But lobbying of this type does appear to be notably successful in finance. For example, consistent with the observation that most countries feel that their financial system is unduly bank-dominated, there is constant advocacy of tax concessions targeted at companies with a stock exchange listing.[20] This is at best a crude instrument, especially if the underlying reason for the underdevelopment of the stock exchange lies in an insufficiently developed information and legal infrastructure, as is often the case. It is much better to direct policy attention to correcting these infrastructural deficiencies.

Another much used quasi-tax often thought of as corrective, in a sense, is the unremunerated reserve requirement. The sense in which this might have been thought of as corrective is that it provides a lever on which monetary policy can operate. Actually, as is now acknowledged by authorities on monetary policy, the perceived need for unremunerated reserve requirements was based on a misconception. Monetary policy does not require unremunerated reserve requirements or any other quasi-tax for its effectiveness (see chapter 5).

Two Distinctive Elements for Financial Sector Tax Design

If there are two key features of the financial sector that distinguish it from other sectors when it comes to designing taxation, these must surely be the system's capacity for arbitrage and its sensitivity to inflation and thus to non-indexed taxes.

The System's Capacity for Arbitrage

Whether mainly flat or mainly corrective, the actual impact of most financial sector taxes depends crucially on the extent to which they have been constructed so as to be insulated from the high elasticities that prevail in the sector. Tax design in this area is confounded by arbitrage between functionally equivalent contracts or institutional forms.

One important illustration of this can be seen when one considers how the incidence of bank taxes can be shifted. Because of substitutability and the possibility of arbitrage and near-arbitrage, the full incidence of taxation imposed on one component of the intermediation process (deposits, loans, intermediary profits) may very well be fully shifted to another component. Ramon Caminal (chapter 3, this volume) has developed a formal model of intermediation, taking account of the provision of liquidity as well as intermediation services by banks in order to examine the influence of various bank taxes on the volume and cost of intermediation services provided to depositors by banks. Several striking results are obtained. For instance, the ability of at least some borrowers to substitute alternative sources of funding implies a tendency for the imposition of a VAT on banking services to be passed back to depositors.[21] Furthermore, the conditions under which a tax on bank loans falls not on the cost of funds, but instead on the return to bank shareholders, are also plausible, including a range of assumptions on competitive conditions. (However, if regulatory capital requirements are likely to be binding in the sense that banks hold more capital than they would freely choose to, a tax on banks' profits may in contrast fall wholly on lending interest rates.) In contrast to general models of production, then, plausible modeling of the degree of substitutability in banking involves such high elasticities that predicting the incidence of a tax to fall wholly on a class of agents not directly the subject of the taxation can be plausibly predicted. On the other hand, recognizing that the services provided to savers by investment funds may be highly substitutable for some of the services obtained from bank deposits, Caminal has also shown how, under reasonable circumstances, the presence of untaxed investment funds implies that taxation of deposits will affect only the monitoring and transaction service provision by banks, and not the provision of liquidity.

These contrasting cases suggest the heightened risks involved in imposing taxes under the assumption that the taxpayer who is liable will be the one incurring the incidence of the tax. Just what the incidence will be can be worked out in theoretical cases (to a greater extent than is the case for taxes on non-financial sectors). However, the task of matching these theoretical cases to the real world is a striking challenge for the empirical policy analyst, given the difficulty of estimating many of the relevant behavioral relationships—as is evident from their relative absence from the literature, even for industrial countries.

Along with the shifted incidence can be a large behavioral effect. This may not be socially costly in equilibrium (if the substitute truly is functionally equivalent). However, short-term disruption and costly incurring of new sunk capital to support the substitute activity could be quite severe.

Even more acute problems of the same general type are associated with the taxation of new financial instruments. At the heart of financial innovation is, in the words of Boadway and Keen (chapter 2), the creation of new instruments by repackaging the cash flows generated by others. Arbitrage is here the mechanism, not just an outcome. The reasons for this repackaging are manifold: to better align the instruments with the liquidity and maturity preferences of different classes of investors; or to shift particular risks between investors who have different appetites for them, whether based on information or on correlations with the remainder of their portfolio. If the rebundled instruments are differently treated by taxation, this can block the repackaging and inhibit the risk-sharing that is involved.[22] Furthermore, of course, differential tax treatment (for example of debt and equity, or of income and capital) can be a powerful driver of innovation designed for no better reason than to repackage cash flows into a less heavily taxed form.

Boadway and Keen note that many of these issues have been dealt with in a piecemeal way by tax authorities in advanced economies. Theoreticians have been exploring ways of rationalizing the taxation of new financial instruments, both by devising unambiguous decompositions of the instruments into fundamental components, and by determining the timing at which the amounts are crystallized for the purpose of calculating the tax (accrual versus realization accounting). To date, no general agreement among theoreticians, let alone practitioners in advanced economies, has yet emerged. This rules out, for the present, the possibility that tax authorities in a developing country could piggyback on a pre-packaged solution. Indeed, for market participants, the tax situation is even less satisfactory in developing countries, where the likely tax treatment of new instruments is often undetermined or disputed.

Sensitivity to Inflation

Although inflation has pervasive effects throughout the economy and in particular has been shown to be negatively correlated with growth, at least for sufficiently high rates, banking and other parts of the financial sector that extensively employ nominal financial contracts can be more directly and deeply affected than most. High and variable rates of inflation induce significant substitution away from non–interest-bearing monetary assets in favor of assets offering higher real returns and inflation hedges. This can, on the one hand, shrink the size of the banking system's intermediation. On the other hand, the financial system's capacity to provide the instruments to insulate economic agents from the inflation will tend to expand this side of its activities. Indeed, empirically, the balance sheet size of the banking system is found to shrink with inflation, whereas inflation is found to be positively associated with profitability and the value-added of the banking system (chapter 13).

Inflation also has a strong influence on the government's finances. The term "inflation tax" is well chosen, even though there is no perfect correspondence between the implicit inflation tax rate as measured by the opportunity cost of holding interest-free base money (which will be related to the expected inflation rate) and the flow of financing to the budget from money creation (Honohan 1996).

The interaction between inflation and a non-indexed tax system can have sizable and unexpected effects, even in a country with single-digit inflation (Feldstein 1983, 1999). As inflation increases, the double distortions of inflation and taxation can be multiplicative rather than additive, with severe consequences. For financial sector firms, the impact of inflation on the scale and activity of financial services firms needs to be considered alongside its impact on their tax-inclusive cost structures. The effective tax rate of several commonly employed financial sector taxes, such as taxes on gross interest receipts of banks, or unremunerated reserve requirements, rise almost in proportion to the rate of inflation. In the case of nominal interest rate ceilings, the effective rate of tax rises more than in proportion to the rate of inflation. Given that inflation rates can be high, volatile, and unplanned, this degree of sensitivity to inflation in the effective rate of tax is generally quite undesirable (chapter 13).

Good tax policy needs to take account of these sensitivities. A defensive approach is needed that ensures that the tax structure is not vulnerable to severe distortion along these lines.

Calibrating Different Types of Tax

Where a defensive approach has not been followed, poorly constructed tax systems—whether the consequence of a drive for revenue, or of misdirected sophistication—have often had sizable unexpected side effects. Some of the most dramatic cases are discussed in the companion chapters by Cardoso (chapter 7) and Granville (chapter 8), both of which—not coincidentally—refer to periods of high inflation.

Part of the problem in many difficult cases has been that the financial sector taxes and implicit or quasi-taxes have not been seen for what they are. Thus very high effective tax rates have emerged in cases where legislators would not have conceived of imposing comparable nominal tax rates.[23]

On the other hand, lobbyists are prone to finding ways of exaggerating the tax burden on financial intermediaries by adding up taxes that touch the sector only slightly and expressing these as a percentage of the sector's profits.

Is there some simple way of approximating the burden of a given tax—or better, the impact of reform in a particular tax? This section looks at how this question might be addressed in respect to the main types of tax or quasi-tax that most often raise such questions.

The relevant taxes include unremunerated reserve requirements, tax on intermediary interest receipts, withholding tax on interest payments by intermediaries, stamp tax on bank debits, and stamp tax on bank loans.

One practical approach to calibrating these taxes and judging their appropriateness is to map each tax into its closest non-financial analog. Thus one decides whether the tax is more nearly an income or a sales tax. If an income tax, is it more a tax on the intermediary's shareholders or on the intermediary's fund-providing customers? If a sales tax, what is the product that is being taxed and what is its net-of-tax price?

As with most issues of incidence, these questions cannot always easily be answered. Nevertheless, even an approximate answer can clarify the issues significantly. The discussion in several chapters of this volume can help.

Market power and substitution possibilities are central. In many countries, the market power of banks is being eroded by international competition for depositor services and from alternative sources of industrial funding, as well as by liberalization of entry. Taxes and quasi-taxes that might hitherto have been assumed to fall on the shareholders of banks in a manner analogous to an income tax may now be more likely to be passed on to those customers who have few alternatives, notably small borrowers whose creditworthiness is costly to determine. Caminal (chapter 3) models these issues in some detail and Cardoso (chapter 7) presents interesting evidence that pass-through has been very high in Brazil.

Under such conditions, the taxes described fall into three groups: those that are best seen as a tax on lending services, those on transactions services, and income taxes on suppliers of funds.

Both unremunerated reserve requirements imposed on banks and special taxes on interest receipts of banks are best seen (under these circumstances) as similar to sales taxes on the provision of lending services (such as credit appraisal and monitoring) to small borrowers. The effective tax rate can be approximated by comparing the tax paid (or, in the case of unremunerated reserve requirements,[24] the opportunity cost of the reserved funds) per dollar lent to the net of tax cost of the service. High effective tax rates often result. Official estimates for Brazil in 2001 can be read, in this perspective, as implying an 85 percent effective tax rate on average for lending (chapter 7). Furthermore, because the tax base—the cost of intermediation services—is not sensitive to the nominal rate of interest whereas the tax paid is, the resulting effective rate can be very sensitive to the nominal rate of interest and thus to the rate of inflation (see chapter 13).

The stamp duty on bank loans, typically proportional to the loan size but not to its maturity, can be analyzed in much the same way. In this case the effective tax rate may increase sharply as maturities shorten, allowing the methodology to reveal the obvious technical deficiency in such a tax.[25]

Transactions taxes and the stamp tax on checks likely fall mainly on the user of the transactions involved. The relevant tax rate is thus computed as if it were a sales tax on the relevant service. This allowed the stamp tax on checks in Chile in 2002 to be computed as a sales tax rate of 100 percent, compared to a rate of about 20 percent for a similar tax imposed in Ireland.

Judging the appropriate treatment of the withholding of income tax on deposit interest requires careful consideration of the effectiveness of the remainder of income tax. If income tax on the revenue from competing capital assets is collected effectively, then the fact that tax due on deposit interest is withheld at the source can best be thought of as chiefly an administrative convenience, rather than as an additional imposition affecting the withholding intermediaries and their other customers. The empirical judgment here will often depend crucially on the degree of international capital mobility (see Huizinga and Nicodeme 2001).

Guarding Against Arbitrage and Inflation

It would be hard to justify a dogmatic approach to reforming financial sector taxation on the basis of the review presented here. None of the extreme blueprints that have been proposed for the optimal structure of financial sector taxation can be fully endorsed.

Nonetheless, some important lessons emerge. Both empirical experience and theoretical propositions suggest that some financial sector taxation can have large and damaging effects that were not anticipated. Therefore the main message proposed here is one of moderation. There is no reason why the financial sector should not pay its share of needed tax revenue. However, design should be defensive in the sense of guarding against the two major vulnerabilities to which the sector is prone: sensitivity to arbitrage and sensitivity to inflation.

Starting with the overall question of capital income tax, the case for exempting capital income from all taxation (the first "big idea" floating in the field) is too narrow to justify action. All that we would propose in this regard is to take the literature as a caution against excessively high capital income tax rates, both in absolute terms and in comparison with income tax. Attempting to "soak the rich" through a high capital income tax rate may be an unwise way to proceed.

The second big idea, that of extending VAT to financial services, seems much better based. It certainly seems a more desirable goal than attempts to rely heavily on transactions taxes (whose distorting effects must soon dominate, even if they have shown their rough and ready merits as transitory revenue-spinners in times of fiscal pressure).

Here, too, excessive enthusiasm should be tempered. The VAT might be the way to go in a world where administrative collection costs were low. In practice, there may be less to gain from it than appears at first sight. Pioneering its adoption could be a diversion for a developing economy—unless the authorities are sure of their administrative capacity to be pioneers in the area. For most, the VAT should best be seen as a benchmark against which to compare other indirect taxes in regard to their neutrality and their burden (effective tax rate equivalent on relevant value-added).

Given the propensity for inflation rates to be high and volatile, taxes and quasi-taxes that are super sensitive to inflation should be avoided. Taxes with such features should be replaced with others that are more inflation-neutral.

Above all, each tax proposal should be considered in terms of the possible substitutes that exist for the activity, asset, return, or transaction being taxed and that could both magnify the behavioral effect of the tax and place its incidence far from where it was originally expected. This must be the key defensive mechanism.

In making judgments on the overall burden of taxation on financial intermediation, which inevitably requires some assessment of incidence, particular efforts need to be made to isolate those taxes that, it can reasonably be assumed, are passed through to depositors. Income tax on deposit interest collected at source, for example, is not borne by the interest payer if income tax on other sources of capital income is also efficiently collected.

Notes

1. To be sure, the enormous fiscal cost of banking crises means that in many countries, the financial system has been a net charge on the budget in recent years.

2. The survey of recent developments by Levin and Ritter (chapter 6, this volume) documents the considerable variety that continues to exist among industrial country systems.

3. Differential treatment of taxation of dividends of listed companies can also be seen as an implicit negative tax on the use of formal stock markets.

4. Seigniorage is the term applied to the profit gained by the issuer of currency. A part of it comes from the inflation tax, which arises because

currency holders must constantly increase their nominal holdings of currency in inflationary times.

5. Caminal (chapter 3, this volume) explores the implications for tax incidence of market power in banking. As he and others have noted, though, leaving banks with some untaxed economic rent (or franchise value, as it tends to be called in the banking literature) can reduce the propensity, potentially strong among insured banks, to assume socially excessive risks (Stiglitz 1994; Caprio and Summers 1996). Indeed it has been argued that the credibility of banks as delegated monitors for the depositors depends on their being able to earn profits in most countries (Diamond 1996).

6. Differentiating the rate of withholding tax as between income from high-risk (equity) and low-risk (debt, deposits) assets could help achieve progressivity, even absent information on the income of the recipients, assuming diminishing risk-aversion with wealth (Gordon 2000).

7. The largest countries, by population, without a VAT are India, the United States, Iran, Ethiopia, Congo DR, Myanmar, Afghanistan, North Korea, Iraq, and Malaysia.

8. A few countries have introduced substitute taxes based on applying a rate to the estimated value-added of banks obtained by summing the wage and profits.

9. Compare the Chinese "business tax," which has recently been applied at the rate of 8 percent to the income from a bank's trading portfolio, but is not applied to the income from the bank's investment portfolio. This strongly discourages trading by banks in government securities, thereby sharply diminishing liquidity in that market. A VAT-like tax would not create such a distortion. (A further distortion in China comes from the exemption from income tax of interest from government bonds, but the inclusion of capital gains from trading such bonds at a rate of 33 percent. Such problems are avoided in some other countries by treating capital gains from trading activities of financial intermediaries on par with income for the purposes of direct taxation.)

10. This consideration needs to be kept in mind by those who would see the proposal as socially progressive in that payments in which they are directly or indirectly involved likely represent a much higher multiple of the income of prosperous people than of the poor. After all, if such a tax did not raise the hoped-for revenue, the consequence might have to be cutbacks in public services needed by the poor.

11. See Lyons (2001) for the foreign exchange market.

12. Tobin taxes, imposed at a low rate on international capital flows, are much more focused and do not typically have revenue as the main objective. Instead they are seen as corrective taxes intended to reduce volatile speculative capital flows. They have generated an enormous literature that will not be summarized here.

13. The revenues are not always explicitly accounted for, as when unremunerated reserve requirements augment the central banks *net* revenue but are nowhere accounted for explicitly as a revenue source.

14. Even the relatively much smaller fiscal costs of the U.S. banking crises of the 1980s were more than enough to empty the insurance funds.

15. Protection of the small depositor is another goal. This is quite a distinct role, of course, as runs only by small depositors do not threaten systemic liquidity.

16. For example, the U.S. premia currently vary according to two criteria, capitalization and supervisory assessment, from zero (for a well-capitalized bank that is highly rated by the supervisors) to 0.27 percent of deposits (for an undercapitalized bank, which is seen by supervisors as posing a substantial probability of loss to the insurer unless corrective action is taken). Argentina has charged a basic rate of 0.36 percent, subject to being doubled where banks were paying high interest rates for deposits (and those with very high rates were not covered at all). Cameroon and other francophone African countries impose 0.15 percent *plus* 0.5 percent of net non-performing loans. Other risk-based formulations, including ex post assessments, are levied in other countries.

17. This, despite the consideration that a degree of implicit protection may be assumed by depositors even when no formal scheme exists.

18. Various formulations are possible. One is to have the tax authorities accept provisioning that had been agreed upon by the prudential regulators. A tougher approach would be to require the bank to defend its provisioning on the basis of an objective forecasting method. However, it needs to be recognized that such forecasts are often more an art than a science.

19. Tax incentives are also widely used to favor health and life insurance (chapter 4).

20. In Egypt, very favorable tax treatment of listed firms from the 1980s induced a widespread listing of firms on the Cairo and Alexandria Stock Exchange, to which the lenient listing requirements provided no discouragement. Over 500 companies were listed by 1990; 10 years later, the figure had grown to more than 1,000. However, most of the firms were closely held and the free-float of shares is little more than one-tenth of the total capitalization. The market capitalization of the actively traded free-float was only about 1 percent of GDP. In this case the supposedly corrective tax exemption had a heavy deadweight in that it failed to achieve the presumed objective of a deep and liquid equity market. Recent listing rule reforms are expected to dramatically cut the number of listed firms in 2003.

21. At least under the plausible assumption that the marginal borrower is VAT-liable while the marginal depositor is not (see chapter 3).

22. For example, the existence of withholding taxes on gross interest receipts can stifle the market in interest rate swaps.

23. The case of Russia in the 1990s, described by Granville in chapter 8 of this volume, is a cautionary example.

24. Or reserves remunerated below market rate. A simple break-even calculation implies that an addition of λ to the loan interest rate will be required to recover an interest penalty of ϕ applied to reserve requirements of θ, where $\lambda = \phi\,\theta/(1-\theta)$.

25. In Egypt, the application of a constant stamp tax independent of loan maturity hampered the development of short-term bridging finance.

References

Boadway, Robin, and Michael Keen. 2003. "Theoretical Perspectives on the Taxation of Capital Income and Financial Services" (chapter 2, this volume).

Brock, Philip L. 2003. "Corrective Taxes and Quasi-Taxes for Financial Institutions and Their Interaction with Deposit Insurance" (chapter 5, this volume).

Caminal, Ramon. 2003. "Taxation of Banks: Modeling the Impact" (chapter 3, this volume).

Caprio, Gerard Jr., and Laurence H. Summers. 1996. "Financial Reform: Beyond Laissez Faire." In Dimitri Papadimitriou, ed., *Financing Prosperity into the 21st Century*. New York: Macmillan.

Cardoso, Eliana. 2003. "Seigniorage, Reserve Requirements, and Bank Spreads in Brazil" (chapter 7, this volume).

Corvoisier, Sandrine, and Reint Gropp. 2002. "Bank Concentration and Retail Interest Rates." *Journal of Banking and Finance* 26(11): 2155–89.

Cull, Robert, Lemma Senbet, and Marco Sorge. 2002. "Deposit Insurance and Financial Development." *The Quarterly Review of Economics and Finance* 42(4): 673–94

Demirgüç-Kunt, Aslı, and Enrica Detragiache. 2002. "Does Deposit Insurance Increase Banking System Stability?" *Journal of Monetary Economics* 49 (7): 1373–1406.

Demirgüç-Kunt, Aslı, and Edward J. Kane. 2002. "Deposit Insurance around the Globe: Where Does It Work?" *Journal of Economic Perspectives* 16 (2): 175–95.

Demirgüç-Kunt, Aslı, and Tolga Sobaci. 2001. "Deposit Insurance around the World: A Database." *World Bank Economic Review* 15 (3): 481–90.

Diamond, Douglas W. 1996. "Financial Intermediation as Delegated Monitoring: A Simple Example." *Federal Reserve Bank of Richmond Economic Quarterly* 82 (3): 51–66.

Ebrill, Liam, Michael Keen, Jean-Paul Bodin, and Victoria Summers. 2001. *The Modern VAT*. Washington, D.C.: International Monetary Fund.

Feige, Edgar. 2000. "Taxation for the 21st Century: the Automated Payment Transaction Tax." *Economic Policy* 31: 473–511.

Feldstein, Martin. 1983. *Inflation, Tax Rules, and Capital Formation.* Cambridge, Mass.: National Bureau of Economic Research.

———. 1999. "Capital Income Taxes and the Benefit of Price Stability." In Martin Feldstein, ed., *The Costs and Benefits of Price Stability.* Chicago: University of Chicago Press.

Gordon, Roger H. 2000. "Taxation of Capital Income vs. Labour Income: An Overview." In Sijbren Cnossen, ed., *Taxing Capital Income in the European Union: Issues and Options for Reform.* Oxford: Oxford University Press.

Granville, Brigitte. 2003. "Taxation of Financial Intermediaries as a Source of Budget Revenue: Russia in the 1990s" (chapter 8, this volume).

Habermeier, Karl, and Andrei Kirilenko. 2003. "Securities Transaction Taxes and Financial Markets" (chapter 11, this volume).

Honohan, Patrick. 1996. "Does It Matter How Seigniorage Is Measured?" *Applied Financial Economics.* 6 (3): 293–300.

———. 2000. "Financial Policies and Household Saving." In Klaus Schmidt-Hebbel and Luis Servén, eds., *The Economics of Saving and Growth.* Cambridge: Cambridge University Press.

———. 2003. "The Accidental Tax: Inflation and the Financial Sector" (chapter 13, this volume).

Honohan, Patrick, and Joseph E. Stiglitz. 2001. "Robust Financial Restraint." In Gerard Caprio, Patrick Honohan, and Joseph E. Stiglitz, eds., *Financial Liberalization: How Far, How Fast?* New York: Cambridge University Press.

Huizinga, Harry. 2002. "A European VAT on Financial Services." *Economic Policy* 35: 499–534.

Huizinga, Harry, and G. Nicodeme. 2001. "Are International Deposits Tax-Driven?" Economic Paper 156. Economic Commission, Brussels.

Huizinga, Harry, and Soren Bo Nielsen. 2000. "The Taxation of Interest in Europe: A Minimum Withholding Tax?" In Sijbren Cnossen, ed., *Taxing Capital Income in the European Union: Issues and Options for Reform.* Oxford: Oxford University Press.

Jappelli, Tullio, and Luigi Pistaferri. 2003. "Tax Incentives for Household Saving and Borrowing" (chapter 4, this volume). ·

Kirilenko, Andrei, and Victoria Summers. 2003. "Bank Debit Taxes: Yield Versus Disintermediation" (chapter 10, this volume).

Laeven, Luc. 2002. "Pricing Deposit Insurance." Policy Research Working Paper 2871. World Bank, Washington, D.C.

Laurin, Alain, and Giovanni Majnoni, eds. 2003. "Bank Loan Classification and Provisioning Practices in Selected Developed and Emerging Countries." World Bank, Washington, D.C.

Levin, Mattias, and Peer Ritter. 2003. "Taxation of Financial Intermediation in Industrial Countries" (chapter 6, this volume).

Lyons, Richard. 2001. *The Microstructure Approach to Exchange Rates.* Cambridge, Mass.: MIT Press.

OECD. 1994. *Taxation and Household Saving.* Paris: Organisation for Economic Co-operation and Development.

Poddar, Satya. 2003. "Consumption Taxes: The Role of the Value-Added Tax" (chapter 12, this volume).

Stern, Nicholas H., and Robin Burgess. 1993. "Taxation and Development." *Journal of Economic Literature* 31(2): 762–830.

Stiglitz, Joseph E. 1994. "The Role of the State in Financial Markets." In Michael Bruno and Boris Pleskovic, eds., *Proceedings of the World Bank Annual Conference of Development Economics 1993.* Washington, D.C.: World Bank.

Sunley, Emil. 2003. "Corporate Income Tax Treatment of Loan-Loss Reserves" (chapter 9, this volume).

Part I

Theoretical and System-wide Issues

2

Theoretical Perspectives on the Taxation of Capital Income and Financial Services

Robin Boadway and Michael Keen

The financial sector is the proximate source of most capital income, and earns its keep by providing financial services of various kinds. Thus the tax treatment of capital income and financial services shape the environment within which financial intermediation occurs. The level and manner in which capital income is taxed is clearly likely to affect the extent and form of financial intermediation, for instance, and the treatment of financial services will impact directly the provision of such services. The purpose of this chapter, therefore, is to provide a broad background for the wider discussion of financial intermediation in this book by reviewing what is known about—at least some central aspects of—the optimal taxation of capital income and financial services.

While the taxation of capital income and (perhaps to a lesser, but nevertheless increasing, extent) of financial services are recurrent policy concerns in many countries, formal theoretical analyses have often focused more on the positive effects of taxation than on the design of optimal policy. Thus the territory of this chapter is at once dauntingly large and largely unexplored. For both reasons, the treatment is selective and, perhaps, eclectic. If there is a theme running through the selection of topics here, it is that of addressing two strands of thought to be found in the optimal tax literature which, if accepted, would have profound implications for the tax treatment of financial activities. These are the views that capital income should not be taxed, nor should financial services.

The chapter thus starts by reviewing the lessons of theory for the optimal taxation of capital income, the central issue being whether capital income should be taxed at all. This is clearly a pivotal question in thinking about the taxation of financial activities: if it is not optimal to tax (or subsidize) capital income, then the main rationale for taxing the income associated with financial transactions becomes the practical one of bolstering the taxation of labor income (or consumption). The chapter then addresses the issues raised for the optimal design of taxes on capital income—assuming that such taxes are indeed desired—that have been highlighted by financial innovation in recent years. Next, the discussion addresses the more particular, but policy relevant, question of whether, and if so at what rate and (more briefly) how, the services of financial intermediaries should be subject to commodity taxation. The chapter concludes with a discussion of some of the caveats and limitations of the discussion here, some of which are addressed elsewhere in this volume.

The Optimal Taxation of Capital Income

Whatever its underlying source, capital income generally arises as the return on a financial asset—as interest paid on a bank deposit, for example, or as capital gains on share in a company. The tax treatment of capital income—a central feature of any tax system—thus plays a potentially key role in shaping the fiscal environment within which the financial system operates. This section sets out some of the key issues, and continuing controversies, related to the taxation of capital income. The discussion starts by considering the taxation of capital income at household level, and then turns to its taxation at business level.

Two caveats common to all the models discussed should be stressed at the outset. First, all assume that the government can commit to the future path of tax rates and thus ignore the fundamental time inconsistency problem that arises in the taxation of capital income, and so ignore a time consistency problem that is inherent to tax design in the presence of capital accumulation. This point is taken up below.

Second, it is also assumed throughout that the government is unrestricted—other than by its intertemporal budget constraint—in its ability to issue debt. This effectively uncouples the path of capital accumulation from private savings decisions. If the latter would otherwise imply too rapid an addition to the capital stock, the government can soak up the excess by selling debt; if it implies excessively slow accumulation, the government itself can supply funds to finance investment. The central concern in taxing capital income is to bring about the minimum distortion of lifetime consumption and labor supply decisions consistent with the government's intertemporal revenue needs.

The Optimal Taxation of Household Capital Income

There is a large literature on the optimality of taxing capital income—or of not taxing it. Results depend on the type of model being used and the assumptions underlying the instruments and information that are available to the government. The analysis is necessarily dynamic in nature, since capital income is generated from assets that by definition last for more than one period. This in itself not only makes the analysis more complicated, but also raises fundamental issues about how to model dynamic economies. Especially important in this regard is the treatment of bequests. The extreme cases of relevance are the infinite-lived dynastic model, in which bequests are fully operative and agents are perfectly farsighted, and the overlapping-generations (OLG) model, in which there are no bequests. An important distinction between these two cases lies in the ease with which they can accommodate heterogeneous households. In the dynastic model, each cohort is generally and naturally (though not inescapably) formulated as being a single representative agent, so the optimal tax problem adopts the classical Ramsey formulation. The OLG model is better able to handle heterogeneity of the sort that is most relevant for introducing redistributive concerns.

To address these issues, this section begins by considering the proper role of capital income taxation in the three main cases considered in the literature: an economy comprising only one type of individual, who lives for only two periods; the Ramsey growth model of a single infinitely lived individual or dynasty; and an OLG model. A large part of the purpose here is to clarify the links between, and common intuition behind, the results from these different models. The discussion then turns to the case in which agents differ in their earnings capacity (so that capital income taxation may have a redistributional role across income groups), to the effects of restrictions on the instruments and information available to government and, finally, to the time consistency issue.

Homogeneous households The discussion below summarizes the results for the two extreme types of models with homogeneous households—the infinite-lived representative agent model of Ramsey, and the OLG model with a representative agent in each cohort. The discussion draws on the recent review by Erosa and Gervais (2001, 2002).

BENCHMARK TWO-PERIOD CASE It is useful to begin with the simple case of optimal tax design in the context of a single individual (or a number of identical individuals) who lives for only two periods, consuming and supplying labor in each. Though artificial—the government could in this case employ a nondistorting poll tax—this proves useful in understanding the results from (somewhat) more realistic contexts below.

Suppose then that the consumer seeks to maximize lifetime utility $U(C_1,C_2,L_1,L_2)$, and C_t, L_t, denote respectively consumption and labor in period t. Allowing for a full range of tax rates, this optimization is subject to a lifetime budget constraint:

$$(2.1) \quad (1+\tau_{c1})p_1C_1 + \frac{(1+\tau_{c2})p_2C_2}{(1+(1-\tau_r)R)} = (1-\tau_{w1})w_1L_1 + \frac{(1-\tau_{w2})w_2L_2}{(1+(1-\tau_r)R)}$$

where R is the pre-tax interest rate, the p_t and w_t are pre-tax commodity prices and wage rates, and, importantly, both consumption tax rates τ_{ct} and labor tax rates τ_{wt} may vary over time. The government chooses these tax rates to maximize the consumer's utility subject to raising some fixed present value of tax revenue (so that debt policy is implicitly assumed to be unconstrained other than by long-term solvency). A number of observations follow from this simple structure.

First, although equation 2.1 allows for five tax instruments—two on consumption, two on labor, and the capital income tax—there is no loss of generality in restricting attention to any three of these, setting the other to zero. This is because there is no loss of generality in tax models of this kind in taking some good to be untaxed numéraire. Moreover, since the effect of the capital income tax is to distort intertemporal prices, this can be achieved by instead inducing appropriate time variation in the other taxes. Intuitively, with only four commodities, there is no gain in deploying any more than three taxes. Thus there is no loss of generality in supposing, for example, that the government can deploy only the two labor taxes and the capital income tax, so that the consumer's budget constraint is simply:[1]

$$(2.2) \quad p_1 C_1 + \frac{p_2 C_2}{(1 + (1 - \tau_r)R)} = (1 - \tau_{w1})w_1 L_1 + \frac{(1 - \tau_{w2})w_2 L_2}{(1 + (1 - \tau_r)R)}$$

Clearly the distinctive role of the capital income tax is in its effect on prices across periods, having no effect on relative within-period prices.

Second, having chosen instruments in this way, the question of whether or not capital income should be taxed reduces to the question of whether or not a particular pair of commodities should be taxed at the same rate. In equation 2.2, for instance, it can be seen that the key effect of the capital income tax is to distort the relative price of consumption in the two periods. If, therefore, it is optimal to tax consumption in the two periods at the same rate, then it is optimal not to tax capital income. The usefulness of this is that it enables one to invoke established results on the desirability of uniform taxation within subsets of groups. Writing the expenditure function for the consumer's optimization as $E(p_1^*, p_2^*, w_1^*, w_2^*, u)$, where the asterisks indicate tax-inclusive present value prices, it is optimal to tax both consumption goods at the same rate—and hence not to tax capital income—given optimal taxation of labor income in both periods, if the expenditure function takes the implicitly separable form[2] $E(A(p_1^*, p_2^*, u), w_1^*, w_2^*, u)$ for some function $A(.)$.[3] A sufficient condition for this is that the direct utility function take the form $U(\phi(C_1, C_2), L_1, L_2)$, with $\phi(.)$ homogeneous of degree one.

Third, an implication of the preceding observation is that the answer to the question of whether or not it is optimal to tax capital income—or, more generally, the optimal value of t_r—depends on the assumption made as to which other taxes may be levied. If, for instance, one instead allows for taxes on consumption in each period as well as on capital income, the optimal rate of capital income taxation will be zero if it is optimal to tax labor in the two periods at the same rate. For this, it is sufficient—whatever the pattern of pre-tax prices (meaning, in particular, whatever the pre-tax interest rate)—that the expenditure function takes the form $E(p_1^*, p_2^*, B(w_1^*, w_2^*, u), u)$. It may seem surprising that whether or not one wishes to tax capital income turns on what is in effect merely a normalization, since clearly the allocation of resources brought about by the optimal tax system does not depend on what is an essentially arbitrary choice of instruments. The point is, however, that the treatment of capital income required to bring about that allocation depends on the range of instruments deployed. Suppose, for instance, that preferences are such that uniform taxation of consumption in the two periods is optimal, but that the only instruments available are the two taxes on consumption and the capital income tax. If the capital income tax rate is then set to zero, uniform taxation of C_1 and C_2 effectively leaves the relative prices of labor in the two periods undistorted—which is not, in general, optimal.

Fourth, the optimal tax problem has a particularly simple solution if preferences are additively separable over time, so that $U(C_1, C_2, L_1, L_2) = U(C_1, L_1) + \beta U(C_2, L_2)$, (with $\beta > 0$ being a discount factor)—a form of separability quite distinct from the implicit separability of the second observation above. Moreover, the discount factor happens to equal the pre-tax interest rate, so that $\beta = 1/(1 + R)$. In this case it is optimal—whatever the choice of instrument set—not to tax capital income. Both consumption and labor supply are constant over time at the optimum, and those taxes that are deployed (on first and second period consumption, for instance) are optimally time invariant.[4] A converse observation is also useful: if preference is of this intertemporally separable form and the optimum is a steady state in consumption and labor, then that optimal tax system has capital income untaxed and other tax rates time-invariant. (All this is proved in the appendix.) The intuition is simply that, as is well known, these preferences—combined, critically, with an equality between the discount and interest rates—imply that in the absence of tax, the consumer would keep both consumption and labor constant over the life cycle. In effect, consumption and labor are essentially identical commodities in absence of taxation, and there is then no gain, when it comes to designing an inherently distorting tax system, from treating them differently within periods or to distort decisions between them over time. It should be noted that the sufficient conditions just described for it to be optimal not to tax capital are more restrictive than the implicit separability condition above in the sense that it also requires a fortuitous coincidence between pre-tax prices (the interest rate) and preferences (the consumer's discount rate). Nevertheless, this case has a particular importance in this literature: once one moves out of the two-period case into the realm of growth theory, attention naturally focuses on optimal taxation in steady states.

THE RAMSEY GROWTH MODEL   A natural extension of the two-period case just addressed is to that of the infinitely lived individual. In the simplest version of this case, the representative agent's intertemporal utility function is of the additively separable form:

$$(2.3) \qquad \sum_{t=0}^{\infty} \beta^t U(C_t, L_t).$$

Suppose, as in the classic paper by Chamley (1986), that the government uses wage and capital income taxation only. Note that, since there are in effect infinitely many goods, this involves some loss of generality; the usefulness of adding consumption taxation to the policy menu is treated below. The household faces a per period budget constraint:

$$(2.4) \qquad C_t + A_{t+1} = \bar{w}_t L_t + (1 + \bar{r}_t) A_t$$

where $\bar{w}_t$ and $\bar{r}_t$ are the after-tax wage and interest rate, and A_t is the level of household assets. The representative household maximizes equation 2.3 subject to equation 2.4, taking the future path of prices to be given. This yields the stream of household choices $C_t(\bar{w}, \bar{r})$, $L_t(\bar{w}, \bar{r})$, and thus $A_t(\bar{w}, \bar{r})$. Per-period aggregate production is given by a costant returns to scale production function $Y_t = F(K_t, L_t)$, where K_t is the capital stock in period t, which depreciates at rate δ. Denoting the (exogenous) stream of government expenditures by G_t, the economy's resource constraint is:

$$(2.5) \qquad C_t + K_{t+1} - (1 - \delta) K_t + G_t = Y_t.$$

Before-tax factor prices are determined competitively by the relevant marginal productivity conditions: $F_{kt} - \delta = r_t$, $F_{\ell t} = w_t$. Letting B_t be the public debt at time t, the per period government budget constraint is given by:

$$(2.6) \qquad B_{t+1} + \tau_{rt} A_t + \tau_{wt} L_t = (1 + R_t) B_t + G_t$$

where $\tau_{rt} = r_t - \bar{r}_t$ and $\tau_{wt} = w_t - \bar{w}_t$ are the per unit capital and labor income tax rates.[5]

By Walras' Law, either equation 2.3 or 2.4 is redundant. Deleting the former, the planner's problem is then to:

$$(2.7) \qquad \underset{\tau_{wt}, \tau_{rt}, b_t}{Max} \sum_{t=0}^{\infty} \beta^t U[C_t(\bar{w}, \bar{r}), L_t(\bar{w}, \bar{r})] \; s.t.$$

Chamley (1986) shows that the solution to this problem has a striking property, and one that has become extremely influential:[6] if the Ramsey solution converges to the steady state with constant consumption and labor supplies, then the optimal tax on capital income will go to zero. Intuitively, this can be seen as a generalization of the result for the two-period case noted above: if consumption and labor do not change over time, there is no gain from distorting the intertemporal dimension of choice between them.

Even stronger results are obtained by restricting the form of the utility function. If the per period utility function is additively separable with a constant intertemporal elasticity of consumption, so that

$$(2.8) \qquad U(C_t, L_t) = C_t^\sigma - V(L_t), \quad \sigma \in (0,1)$$

then capital income taxation is zero not merely in the limit but from the first period on. In period zero, capital is effectively fixed so is taxed at a confiscatory rate. After that, however, there is no need to tax capital income. The reason why it is not optimal to tax capital income after the first period can again be seen from the two-period case. For these preferences can be shown to imply that the expenditure function (over any finite number of periods) has the implicit separability of the form[7] $E(A(p_1, p_2^*, \ldots), w_1^*, w_2^*, \ldots u)$, so that—given optimal taxation of wage income in each period—there is no gain from taxing capital income.

Though remarkable, it should be stressed that—even apart from the assumption that the government is able to commit to the future path of taxes, and is unconstrained in its debt policy—the general result of capital income taxation being zero in the long run only applies in the steady state. If there are ongoing changes in the structure of the economy that preclude it from converging to a steady state, the result does not apply.

This analysis also assumes that only wage and capital income taxation are used as government policy instruments, which is a real restriction, since there are here more than two consumption goods. As Coleman (2000) has recently pointed out, adding consumption taxation can have fairly dramatic effects in terms of reinforcing the argument for zero capital taxation. Adding more instruments to the government's policy set can only make it less likely that it will be optimal to tax capital income, since there is then less potential need to deploy capital income taxation as a surrogate for missing instruments.[8]

THE OVERLAPPING-GENERATIONS MODEL   Erosa and Gervais (2001, 2002) take the alternative approach of analyzing labor and capital income taxation in an OLG model of identical representative agents, each of whom lives for $J+1$ periods. In obvious notation, the lifetime utility function for a cohort born in period t is now:

$$(2.9) \qquad \sum_{j=0}^{J} \beta^j U(C_{tj}, L_{tj})$$

Labor productivity may vary over the life cycle. Letting z_j be the productivity (measured in units of effective labor supply) at age j, assumed to be the same for all cohorts, the per period budget constraint is now:

$$(2.10) \qquad C_{tj} + A_{tj+1} = \overline{w}_{tj} z_j L_{tj} + (1 + \overline{r}_{tj}) A_{tj}$$

where, note, tax rates are allowed to be both time- and cohort-specific. As before, the representative household of cohort t maximizes equation 2.7 subject to equation 2.8 to determine $C_{tj}(\overline{w}, \overline{r})$, $L_{tj}(\overline{w}, \overline{r})$, and thus $A_{tj}(\overline{w}, \overline{r})$. With a constant population growth rate, the share of households of age j in the population, μ_j, will be constant over time. The per period budget constraint of the government can then be written:

$$(2.11) \qquad B_{t+1} + \sum_{j=0}^{J} \tau_{rtj} \mu_j A_{tj} + \sum_{j=0}^{J} \tau_{\ell tj} \mu_j L_{tj} = (1 + r_t) B_t + G_t$$

The objective function of the government is assumed to be the discounted sum of lifetime utilities, where the discount rate is denoted γ. Denoting by $W_t(\overline{w}, \overline{r})$ the lifetime utility of cohort t, the problem of the government is then to:

$$(2.12) \qquad \underset{\tau_{wt}, \tau_{rt}, b_t}{Max} \sum_{t=0}^{\infty} \gamma^t W_t(\overline{w}, \overline{r}) \ s.t.$$

The solution to this problem is given in Erosa and Gervais (2001, 2002).

In this setting—and in sharp contrast to the Ramsey growth setting of Chamley (1986)—the zero capital income tax result in the long run does *not* apply except in special circumstances. The reason is that now consumption and leisure generally vary over the individual's life cycle even in the steady state.

There are, however, two cases in which the optimal rate of capital income taxation is zero—echoing again the two cases identified in the two-period case above. One is that in which consumption and leisure are constant over the life cycle. This will be the case if the planner's discount rate is the same as the households' ($\gamma = \beta$) and productivity is constant over the life cycle ($z_j = z \forall j$) (This latter feature ensures that not simply hours worked but effective labor supply—a distinction that did not exist in the two-period model—is constant over the life cycle).

The second case is that in which the utility function takes the form of equation 2.8. In this case—as one would now expect—the optimal tax on capital income will again be zero for all periods beyond the first (that is, even if the consumer is not in a steady state).[9]

Note too that these results presume that the government is able to deploy cohort-specific tax rates. If it cannot do so, then some tax on capital income will generally be desirable even in the circumstances just described. (See also Alvarez and others 1992.) More precisely, Erosa and Gervais (2001) are able to show that in this case capital income taxation will be positive if and only if labor supply is decreasing over the life cycle. Of course, if consumption taxation were allowed, no capital income taxes would be required if the optimal consumption tax is constant over time, which is the case under utility functions of the type given in equation 2.6.

Heterogeneous households   Once households differ, the analysis becomes even more complicated. The existing analyses focus on the case in which households differ by income-earning ability, or productivity, and rely on a celebrated result of Atkinson and Stiglitz (1976). Consider an atemporal economy in which all households have identical utility functions defined on labor and a vector of n consumption goods, $U(C_1, \cdots, C_n, L)$. Households differ, however, in their wage rates w_i, where $w_{i+1} > w_i$, reflecting their different abilities or productivities. Following Mirrlees (1971), the government is unable to observe wage rates, but can observe incomes $y_i \equiv w_i L_i$ and so can apply a nonlinear income tax. Also, the government cannot observe individual commodity demands but can observe transactions anonymously, so it can also apply linear (only) excise taxes.

The government is assumed to maximize a quasi-concave objective function, which ensures that redistribution goes from higher to lower wage households. Its problem is to choose a set of tax policies to maximize its objective function subject to a resource constraint, and a set of incentive compatibility ("self-selection") constraints. The constraints ensure that higher-wage households prefer their own incomes (both earned and disposable) to that of lower-wage households; in other words, the constraints state that the greater amount of leisure that the high-ability types could take if they were to earn the same gross income as the low-ability types would be less valuable to them than the consumption they would forego. The Atkinson-Stiglitz theorem says that if the utility function is weakly separable in goods and labor, so that $U(C_1, \cdots, C_n, L) = U(g(C_1, \cdots, C_n), L)$, then differentiated commodity taxes should not be used.

The intuition for this is straightforward.[10] The nonlinear income tax is deployed to achieve the optimal amount of redistribution. At the optimum, incentive constraints will be binding on all but the lowest-wage households; otherwise more redistribution could be accomplished. Differential commodity taxation will thus be useful only to the extent that it weakens the incentive constraints. Under weak separability, the preference ordering over goods is independent of labor supply. Therefore higher-wage "mimickers" would choose the same goods bundle as the lower-wage households they are tempted to mimic. But then differential commodity taxation cannot make it less attractive to them to mimic, and so has no effect other than the adverse one of distorting consumer choice. By the same token, if the Atkinson-Stiglitz separability condition does not apply, the self-selection constraint will be weakened by imposing higher commodity taxes on goods that are more complementary with leisure—which are the ones that will be more heavily demanded by the mimickers.

The Atkinson-Stiglitz result can be applied to the problem of capital income taxation by reinterpreting the distinct goods as consumption at different dates. Differential commodity taxation of the atemporal interpretation then translates into a distortion of intertemporal prices, and so corresponds to the taxation of capital income. Noting this analogy, Stiglitz (1987) shows that if household utilities are weakly separable between goods and labor, then all that is needed is an optimal nonlinear tax within each period, with no tax or subsidy applied to interest income. The reasoning is essentially the same as in the atemporal case: being a differential tax on future consumption, an interest tax would only be used if future consumption were more complementary with leisure than is current period consumption, and an interest subsidy in the case of relative substitutability.[11] If leisure and future consumption are complements, an indirect tax on future consumption weakens the self-selection constraint: higher-wage mimickers will enjoy more leisure, and their consumption bundle will include a higher proportion of future consumption than low-ability persons. A tax on future consumption will make it relatively more difficult for the former to mimic the latter.

Though this analysis is suggestive, there are a number of caveats and restrictions that should be noted. First, if the labor supplies of households of different productivities are not perfect substitutes, interest income taxation or subsidization is called for, depending on the substitutability-complementarity relationships among the different types of labor and capital, as Stiglitz (1987) shows. Second, and more profoundly, the "trick" of reinterpreting commodities as consumption at different dates is more problematic than it may at first appear, and really works only in the two-period case. Once one goes to the more realistic world of multiple periods with labor supplied in several of them, the Atkinson-Stiglitz logic no longer applies. For one thing, as noted in the earlier discussion of taxation with homogeneous households, allowing labor supply to vary for more than one period makes the case for taxing or subsidizing interest income more likely. Even more fundamentally, once households are subject to nonlinear income taxation in successive periods, the nature of their optimization problem and of the government's information constraint becomes much more complicated. For instance, the government may use consumers' first period decisions on earnings to make inferences about underlying ability; and consumers' awareness of this may then affect those earning decisions. To date, there is no fully satisfactory analysis of intertemporal nonlinear income taxation, making it difficult to say anything even vaguely definitive about the case for taxing or subsidizing capital income in a world of heterogeneous households.

Restrictions on tax instruments and information   The above models of optimal taxation assume that the government is both well informed (though not quite fully) and unrestricted in its policy instruments. But the policy environment may be more restrictive than that.

Take, for instance, the Ramsey growth context and suppose that while the government can levy consumption, labor income, and capital income taxes, the labor income tax rate is constrained to be nonnegative. Coleman (2000) demonstrates two remarkable results. First, suppose that at least some of the government revenue raised through taxes is transferred lump sum to the household, whose members then consume it. Since this lump-sum income is spent on taxable consumption goods, a consumption tax is somewhat more general than a labor income tax. If one now constrains labor taxation to be nonnegative as above, labor income should *never* be taxed, while capital income should be *subsidized* in the long run. In effect, the consumption tax is used to raise revenue and cannot be replicated by labor income taxation. On the other hand, if all tax rates must be nonnegative, in the long run it is optimal to tax only consumption, while in the intermediate run, all three tax sources might be used. Second, suppose that all government revenue is used to purchase public goods or services and none is transferred to households as cash. If labor income taxation is precluded from being negative, so a first best cannot be achieved, then a consumption tax is no longer needed beyond the first period: its effects can be replicated by combinations of the other two taxes. One is back in the world of Chamley (1986) discussed above, along with all his results. In particular, capital income taxes converge to zero as the economy converges to a steady state.

Restrictions on instruments may also be important in the context of taxing heterogeneous households. One possibility, for instance, is that the government can use only linear income taxes, perhaps because of restricted administrative capacity. Deaton and Stern (1986) show that in this case differential commodity taxes can be dispensed with if the utility function is not only weakly separable but, moreover, if the sub-utility function of goods is quasi-homothetic so that all Engel curves are linear. In this case—which is clearly more restrictive than that of the Atkinson-Stiglitz result above—commodity taxes do not add anything to the ability of the government to differentiate among households of different income levels. Applying the same intertemporal interpretation as above, the implication is that the circumstances under which capital income taxation can be dispensed with are even more restrictive than those that apply when nonlinear taxes can be used. Again, the results are agnostic with respect to whether taxation or subsidization of capital income is optimal in the event that the required restrictions do not apply

Another line of inquiry, and one that is potentially especially relevant for financial markets, assumes that while the government can observe household labor income (as above), it cannot observe capital income. At best it can tax capital income anonymously and indirectly using a constant tax rate. According to the above analysis, no such capital income tax would be needed if the conditions of the Atkinson-Stiglitz theorem or its extensions were satisfied. Two sets of circumstances have been identified in which capital income might nevertheless be taxed even if the required separability conditions were to hold. The first arises because of the possibility of unobserved bequests. As argued by Boadway, Marchand, and Pestieau (2000) and Cremer, Pestieau, and Rochet (2003), if for some reason the size of bequests is not statistically independent of wage rates, the taxation or subsidization of interest income can be a useful supplement to an optimal nonlinear labor income tax. In particular, a tax (subsidy) should be used if bequests are positively (negatively) correlated with wage rates.   .

Gordon (2001) has identified a second circumstance. He constructs a model in which households choose a portfolio of assets as well as an amount of savings. The portfolio combines a risky asset (equity) and a risk-free asset (debt). He argues that if risk aversion falls with wealth, higher-income households will hold relatively more equity in their portfolios and lower-income households will hold more debt. In these circumstances, distributional consideration means that a subsidy on debt will be optimal.

The time consistency issue   As noted at the outset, all the analyses reviewed above assume that the government can costlessly commit to the future path of tax rates. When it cannot so commit, however, there is an inherent temptation to renege on previously announced plans. The point here is that at any given time, the stock of previously accumulated capital is large relative to the annual flow of new investment. In these circumstances, rational governments will be unable to avoid imposing high taxes on that capital and the income it generates, despite the fact that in the long run these taxes decrease capital accumulation and lead to inefficiencies (Fischer 1980). That is, even though governments would wish to commit, if they cannot do so then they will wish to impose heavier taxes on capital once savings decisions have been made than they intended *ex ante*. This may be one reason why rates of capital income taxation observed in the real world tend to be much higher than optimal tax analysis of the kind above would advocate (though the fact that effective rates of capital income tax are often lower than statutory rates, and sometimes even negative—reflecting the availability of deductions— rather dulls the point.)[12]

This time consistency problem has potentially profound implications for capital income taxation. In politically stable countries, governments may carry sufficient credibility for the problem to be of only limited significance. In others, however—especially, it would seem, many developing countries—the problem may be more profound. Faced with this problem, governments, recognizing that they are unable to avoid excessive taxes on capital income—and that the private sector will also recognize this, and amend its behavior accordingly— can take measures to undo the worst effects of excessive taxation. They may find it desirable, for instance, to allow capital to move to lower tax jurisdictions (Chari, Kehoe, and Prescott 1989) or even to tolerate some degree of evasion of capital income taxes (Boadway and Keen 1998). Other measures to overcome the time consistency problem involve up-front subsidies to investment, such as tax holidays and investment tax credits. Such subsidies may also be based on political economy arguments, such as common agency arguments for political parties providing favors in return for financial support (Marceau and Smart 2003). Designing policies to overcome inefficiencies arising from the political process is, of course, problematic since it is not clear how governments could be persuaded to undertake them.

Optimal Taxation of Corporate Income

There are two main types of arguments for taxing corporate income as part of an optimal tax system. The first—which is the one typically stressed in policy discussion—sees the corporate tax as a withholding device against capital income at source. The second sees the corporate tax as a tax on economic rents earned by corporations. This section considers these in turn.

The withholding role of the corporation tax   Corporations are legal entities, distinct from their owners, in which incomes earned on behalf of shareholders are pooled. If shareholders could be taxed directly on the income they earn through corporate ownership, the withholding role would disappear. Distinct considerations arise, however, in relation to domestic and foreign shareholders.

WITHHOLDING AGAINST THE INCOME OF DOMESTIC SHAREHOLDERS
The case for using the corporate tax as a withholding device against domestic shareholders is based on two presumptions: that it is desirable to tax capital income from all sources at the personal level, and that it is difficult to attribute all income earned through corporations to individual shareholders as it accrues. The key issue here is the difficulty of taxing capital gains on an accruals basis at the personal level (an issue that is discussed later). If, as is almost invariably the case in practice, capital gains are taxed on a realization basis, then income that is retained and reinvested in the corporate sector can be sheltered from personal tax until it is taken out as either sales of shares or future dividends. Taxing corporate income as it is earned is a way of bringing this income into the tax system at the appropriate time.

Designing a corporate tax system for this purpose involves a number of considerations, some of which are difficult to implement perfectly. The base for the corporate tax should be only retained earnings, excluding both interest payments and dividends (since these can readily be taxed at the personal level). All accrued current and capital costs should be deductible, including true depreciation of depreciable assets and the imputed cost of inventory use, natural resources, and intangible assets—and there are well-known difficulties in properly accounting for these.

However, as discussed shortly, there are reasons to include all equity income earned by the corporation to satisfy the other withholding role—that with respect to the income of foreign shareholders, whose dividends escape domestic taxation.

To the extent that the corporate tax is intended to be a withholding device, credit for this withheld tax should be given to shareholders when they eventually take their income out of the corporation. This requires some form of integration applied at the personal level: for example, a tax credit could be given against dividends and capital gains earned in corporations that had paid the corporate tax. This is conceptually straightforward for dividends but problematic for capital gains, since it would require identifying that part of gains that is due to taxed retentions, a daunting task.[13]

Special provisions would need to be applied to deal with some types of ownership. First, corporations might themselves hold shares in others, either subsidiaries or as minority owners. To avoid double taxation of corporate source income, the inter-corporate flows of capital income should be excluded from tax. Thus if the corporate tax applies to corporate retained earnings, capital gains earned by domestic corporations on their shares in other corporations should be tax-exempt.[14] If the tax applies to all corporate equity income, both capital gains and dividends earned by domestic corporations should be exempt. This has obvious implications for financial corporations. Second, careful attention should be paid to the taxation of small corporations. The aim should be to ensure that they are treated on a par with unincorporated businesses so that there are no pure tax incentives for incorporation.

Note that domestic households might still be able to shelter their capital income in foreign corporations, and the domestic corporate tax cannot do anything to mitigate that. If the foreign country has very low corporate tax rates, or if households are able to avoid paying domestic tax by simply failing to report their incomes, households will be able to earn tax sheltered income abroad and there is little the corporate tax system can do to avoid that.

WITHHOLDING AGAINST THE INCOME OF FOREIGN SHAREHOLDERS   Further considerations arise in an open economy. Since the personal income tax is generally levied on a residence basis, and so does not apply to foreign shareholders, the withholding role applies only, in general, to a subset of shareholders.[15] More fundamentally, if investors in a corporation are able to earn some more or less fixed after-tax rate of return on the world market, any tax levied on their capital income will ultimately end up being shifted back to domestic residents through induced capital outflows, and hence a reduced rate of return to immobile domestic factors. In these circumstances, one might not want to tax corporations at all (although time-consistency problems may nonetheless lead to taxation, as mentioned earlier).

But other withholding arguments can be made for taxing foreign-owned corporations. If the country has some power in world capital markets, so that it need not take the after-tax return on world markets as given, then a tax on foreigners will indeed to some extent be borne by them. Most countries, however—and especially developing countries—are not in this position, except perhaps in relation to some natural resources. More important in practice is the observation that, to the extent that foreign-owned corporations can credit tax paid in the host country against corporate income tax in their home country, such a tax will serve mainly to transfer tax revenues from foreign treasuries to the domestic one. This argument seems to have some weight in debtor countries, such as Canada, and is a major consideration in tax-setting in many developing countries. Why creditor countries might allow crediting for taxes paid abroad by their domestic corporations is a matter of continuing research interest.[16] But, given that major investing countries like the United States have such a system, the case for capital-importing countries using a corporate tax is strengthened.

The design of a tax to exploit the tax crediting practices of creditor nations is somewhat different from that whose role is to withhold against domestic shareholders. There is some incentive to mimic the tax structure and rate of the main creditor nations to exploit most effectively the tax revenue transfer. Since tax crediting might be jeopardized by discriminatory treatment of foreign versus domestic corporations, that implies that the tax treatment of corporations of all types will partly be driven by a desire to exploit the transfer of revenues from foreign treasuries.

The need to treat foreign and domestic corporations on a par has a further important implication. Provisions for integrating corporate and personal taxes must be implemented at the personal level rather than the corporate in order to target them to domestic shareholders alone. That is, credit must be made to resident households against corporate taxes paid by domestic corporations in which they have shares rather than, say, credit being paid to corporations that pay out dividends to domestic residents. However, in this case, the rationale for integration is no longer obvious, as Boadway and Bruce (1992) argue. If the marginal investor in a corporation is a nonresident, the degree of integration will affect the domestic resident's incentive to save, while the firm's incentive to invest will be determined by the corporation tax. Thus integrating via the personal tax undoes any tax that might apply at the personal level, rather than undoing the corporate tax; and the corporate tax will effectively be borne by the firms themselves, causing a distortion in investment. Reflecting in part increased awareness of the relative ineffectiveness of integration in open economies, a number of economies have in recent years moved away from integration schemes toward a "classical" form of corporation tax, under which dividends are taxed without allowance for underlying corporation tax paid.[17]

Thus the case for corporate tax itself comes into question in an open economy, except to the extent that it is effective at transferring income from foreign treasuries. Even so, the benefits of that tax-transfer must be offset against resulting investment distortions, which considerably weaken the case for integration.

The corporation tax as a rent collector   The second possible role of
the income tax, and one that has traditionally been stressed in the
academic literature, is that of a tax on economic rents (or "pure"
profits), meaning the excess of revenues over the full opportunity
costs of earning them. The argument is that most economic rents
earned in the economy will be earned in the corporate sector, and so
are conveniently identified and taxed there. An appropriately designed corporate tax—one that is *neutral*, in the sense of not distorting corporate decisions—will divert some of the rents from the
private sector to the public sector. Such a tax will be fully efficient,
and thus economically ideal, in that it does not distort production
decisions by the taxed firm. Whether it is equitable to tax rents at
the level of the firm is another matter. The tax can be viewed as a
confiscatory tax on the current owners of assets that give rise to future rents, which may be regarded as horizontally inequitable to the
extent that other sources of asset wealth are not so taxed.

Rents can come from a variety of sources. One important source
might be the ownership of fixed factors, such as natural resources,
that have no alternative use. Other sources of rent are locational or
informational advantages. Yet another might be the monopoly profits that come with market influence. The economic modeling of neutral corporate taxes has tended to focus on the fixed factor story,
using a dynamic model of the firm (see King 1977; Atkinson and
Stiglitz 1980; Auerbach 1983; Auerbach and Kotlikoff 1987). The
firm is viewed as having a strictly concave production function with
possibly both current and capital inputs. The strict concavity gives
rise to economic rents at the profit maximizing (as well as the social)
optimum. It is straightforward to extend the analysis to take account of other sources of rents, such as monopoly of renewable or
nonrenewable natural resources. As well, the focus of the literature
has tended to be on firms that earn business incomes from the sales
of goods and services rather than those that earn financial income.

International considerations again matter, however. To the extent
that the source of the rents is not specific to a particular location—
access to a particular mineral deposit, for instance, or to a protected
local market—a tax on rents may drive investments to other jurisdictions offering a lower rate of tax.

There are various ways, in principle, to design a corporate tax so
that it is neutral. Two benchmarks are an *economic profits tax* and
a *cash flow tax* (Boadway 1980). An economic profits tax has as its
base the imputed current-period economic profit of the firm. This
requires accounting for all revenues less costs on an accrual basis.
Revenues include those from all sales of goods and services in the

accounting period, all measured on an accrual (rather than cash flow) basis. Costs are more complex. The costs of using current inputs within the accounting period are deducted on an accrual basis. The costs of using capital inputs must be appropriately imputed to each accounting period. For depreciable capital, this involves both true economic depreciation and the full cost of financing the depreciable asset holdings. For depletable assets, it involves the value of resources depleted in the period as well as the financing costs. For inventory, it is the value of goods taken out of inventory plus the cost of financing. For intangible assets, it includes the depreciation of those assets, and so on. Needless to say, there are difficult measurement costs involved in measuring economic profits: appropriate market prices—such as for intangibles—often do not exist. The true values of economic depreciation and depletion of assets are difficult to measure. The costs of financing assets must take account of both debt and equity financing. Costs of depreciation and finance must be adjusted for inflation, and a cost of risk-taking must be imputed to reflect uncertainty about future input and output prices.

These difficulties make the implementation of an economic profits tax virtually unfeasible. It is much easier to apply the cash flow alternative, which takes advantage of the fact that the present value of economic profits is also the present value of cash flows of the firm. A cash flow tax on business income takes as its base the cash flow of revenues from the sale of output less the cash flow cost of inputs as they accrue. There are two main variants of such a tax. Under an "R-base" cash flow tax—in the terminology of the Meade Committee (1978)—net financial inflows related to debt (interest payments and repayments of interest and principal) are excluded from the base. Under an "R+F"-base," they are included; such a tax is equivalent (as a consequence of the identity between the firm's sources and uses of funds) to an "S-based" tax levied directly on net distributions to shareholders (dividends less new equity issues).

Under a cash flow tax, the difficulties of accrual accounting no longer apply. Capital purchases are simply expensed in the accounting year in which they are made, and no allowance need be made for the costs of financing. A cash flow tax avoids the need to measure true depreciation and depletion, the true costs of equity financing, and the costs of risk. Moreover, no inflation accounting is required. This simplicity does come with a cost, at least from the policymaker's perspective. First, neutrality of the cash flow tax requires that the tax rate be constant over time, whereas a pure income tax retains neutrality even if the tax rate changes year by year.[18] Second, it will typically be the case that cash flows are negative for some firms, especially young, growing ones that are engaged in large investments. For the tax to be fully neutral, tax losses must be refundable in the year in which they occur (or be carried forward at an appropriate rate of interest), something that policymakers are notoriously averse to allowing (perhaps reasonably enough, given the potential danger of firms disappearing once they have claimed tax rebates on losses).

This problem can be overcome, and the advantages of cash flow accounting maintained, under a *modified cash flow tax* (Boadway and Bruce 1984). Under this alternative, not all investments are fully expensed in the year in which they occur. Instead any arbitrary amount of them can be added to an account—the undepreciated capital stock for tax purposes. The firm is allowed to draw down the undepreciated capital stock at some rate each year, and a deduction is given to the firm for the financial costs associated with holding that undepreciated capital stock. This scheme retains the virtues of a cash flow tax, especially the use of cash rather than accrual accounting and the avoidance of inflation indexing. It can also avoid the main problem of the cash flow tax, the need for refundability of losses. The ability to draw down the undepreciated capital stock can be restricted to ensure that negative taxable income is not generated. The main difficulty with implementing the tax is to choose an appropriate cost of finance to apply to the undepreciated capital stock.[19]

One form of modified cash flow tax that has attracted particular interest is the "Allowance for Corporate Equity" (ACE) scheme, under which companies are allowed to deduct against tax an amount equal to some notional rate of return on its invested equity (calculated retentions plus new equity issues in the current period). Such a scheme—whose properties are developed in detail by Devereux and Freeman (1991)—was implemented by Croatia in the latter 1990s.[20] Similar schemes—but with the imputed equity taxed at a reduced rate rather than fully exempted—have been adopted in Austria, Brazil, and (until 2001) Italy. These are perhaps the most deliberate attempts that have yet been made to craft the general corporation tax as, in effect, a tax on rents.

The case for a tax on economic rents depends on their quantitative importance. One would expect that some sectors are more likely to generate economic rents than others. Thus rent-type taxes are most often found in relation to the resource extraction.[21] Whether it is useful to apply a rent tax to the entire corporate sector is an open question.

Treatment of financial institutions   It might be argued that there is a possibility of economic profits being a feature of the financial sector, given the usual dominance of a few large firms. In principle, a cash flow-type tax can also be designed to apply to financial income. Two alternatives are possible. One approach would be to treat financial assets accumulated by the firm for the purposes of earning income analogously to the treatment of real capital in the non-financial firm. The costs of holding them would be deductible and the revenues they generate taxable. In a pure cash flow system, the tax base applying to the financial earning of the firm would include financial income less the net acquisition of assets less the real costs associated with intermediation. More formally, denoting by A the income-earning financial assets of the firm, by $\dot{A}$ its rate of change, and by r the interest rate on these assets, the base is $rA - \dot{A} - C$, where C includes all the non-financial costs incurred on a cash flow basis. (Modified cash flow taxation would create an account into which financial assets could be put, similar to the undepreciated stock of capital under the modified cash flow system.)

The other alternative, which is analogous to the S-base described above, would also include net financial transaction with nonshareholders on the liability side. These would include debt transactions as well as liabilities in the form of deposits into the intermediary. For these transactions, the firm would add to its tax base the cash flow transactions arising from the acquisition of these liabilities: net changes in the stock of such liabilities less the payment of interest on them. Denoting the stock of debt by B, the base in this case is $rA - \dot{A} + \dot{B} - \rho B - C.$[22] The case for including these elements of financing arises because of the possibility of the financial institution earning pure profits because of the services it provides and the market power it might have. In the end, the case for imposing a cash flow tax on financial corporations, and the form that tax should take, depend on a judgment as to whether the rents that are earned are significant enough to warrant the administrative costs of imposing the tax.

Summary

The literature on the optimal taxation of capital income is large, disparate, and sometimes difficult. It has focused, to a large degree, on the question of whether capital income should be taxed at all. The answer to this depends on what other instruments are available to the government. If it is unrestricted in its ability to tax consumption and labor income, for instance, then the capital income tax is a redundant instrument, since its effects can be replicated by introducing appropriate time variation in these other taxes. Even when the choice of instruments is such that the capital income tax is not redundant, however, there are important benchmark cases in which it should not be used. This is the case if the optimum happens to have the feature that each individuals' consumption and labor supply remain constant over time—as in the steady state of a Ramsey growth model—or in which intertemporal preferences have the feature that there is no gain from distorting intertemporal prices. Clearly though, these are both restrictive sets of circumstances.

It is a great weakness of the literature—reflecting in part the analytical complexity of the issue—that it gives relatively little firm guidance on the rates at which capital income should be taxed (or even whether the tax should be positive) outside these special cases. All these results are subject, moreover, to the fundamental time consistency problem: even if the government would wish not to tax capital income, it may be forced to do so by the expectation of the private sector that, ex post, some such tax will be optimal. Attention then focuses on the devices that government might use to mitigate this problem, a line of inquiry that is proving fruitful in understanding why it is, for instance, that many developing countries continue to find it attractive to offer tax holidays and other up-front incentives to foreign investors.

Taxing income at the corporate level should be seen as a means to the end of taxing households, and to that extent is ultimately motivated by administrative rather than theoretical concerns. There is potentially an important role for the corporate tax as a means of withholding against personal capital income, and a corporate level tax may be a particularly convenient way of levying a nondistorting tax on rents. In this area at least, theory has provided quite clear guidelines as to proper tax design.

New Financial Instruments and the Capital Gains Problem

The proliferation of new financial instruments over the last two decades or so has raised profound conceptual and practical problems for tax design. These issues—which remain largely unresolved—are not just ones for the most advanced economies to grapple with. They affect emerging market economies with sophisticated financial sectors, and even many relatively low-income countries must address the difficulties they may consequently face from the financial activities of some of their largest (and often foreign-owned) taxpayers. This section briefly reviews the main issues arising from, practice in respect of, and potential policy responses to continuing financial innovation.[23]

Financial Innovation: The Tax Issues

The essence of financial innovation is the creation of new assets by repackaging the cash flows generated by others. This can be done either by disaggregating the cash flows from some asset into a series of constituent parts or by combining the flows associated with a set of distinct assets. Examples of the former would include the stripping of interest and principal payments from debt for sale as separate assets; the use of share options to isolate upside and downside risk in price movements; and the use of notional principal contracts, such as swaps, to create assets with payoff equal to the difference between the payoffs on existing assets. An example of the latter form of repackaging is the convertible debt contract, combining debt obligations with an option to convert the claim into equity at a pre-specified exercise price.

Such repackaging implies, of course, equivalence between the values of the related financial assets (since otherwise costless arbitrage profits could be made by selling some subset and buying another). Holding both a share (with current price S) and a put upon it (current price P) gives the same pattern of payoffs, for example, as holding a zero-coupon bond with principal amount equal to the exercise price of the put (current price B) with principal repayment of S and a call option also with the same exercise price of the put (C).[24] It must therefore be the case that:

$$(2.13) \qquad S + P = B + C.$$

Similarly, holding a forward contract on some asset (being obliged to sell in the future at some specified price) is equivalent to holding a call on the underlying asset and selling a put at the same exercise price, so that $F = C - P$, where F denotes the value of the forward contract. There are other equivalences, of course. A convertible bond, for example, is equivalent to the combination of a standard debt contract and a call option on the company's equity.

The massive financial innovation of recent years has been driven much more by commercial considerations—especially the better management of risk—than by the avoidance of tax. Nevertheless, it clearly holds the potential for facilitating the avoidance in so far as repackaging can bring about a change in the pattern of tax payments. By the same token, differential tax treatment can distort the forms of packaging chosen, and perhaps even prevent the emergence of socially useful financial instruments.

The use of financial transactions to reduce taxation is of course long established. The tax preference for debt over equity, for instance, has long figured centrally in the analysis of corporate financial decisions. Clearly, however, the world has become more complex than that: even the distinction between debt and equity has become less clear-cut with the development of such instruments as the monthly income preferred shares (treated in the United States as debt for tax purposes, but equity for accounting purposes). Perhaps more fundamentally—since the asymmetry between debt and equity is one that could in principle be quite easily removed[25]—financial innovation may increase the scope for exploiting the differential taxation of some items as "income"—in the legalistic sense of being taxable on accrual at normal rates of income tax—and others as "capital," with the latter benefiting from the advantage of taxation on realization rather than accrual and, in many cases, a statutory tax rate below that applied on ordinary income. (Deductions, conversely, are more advantageously taken against ordinary income.) Any difference in statutory rates is, in principle, easily remedied. In this sense the more fundamental issues are those arising from the deferral of tax on capital gains.

Exploiting this feature of most systems has long been a central concern of tax planners. One such device is the use of the "straddle": simultaneously holding and selling short the same asset, then closing the losing side at the end of the tax year (so taking any deduction available for capital losses) and offsetting the position carried forward in a similar way during the next tax year (Stiglitz 1983). Another is the zero-coupon (or "original issue discount") bond: one paying no interest but only a fixed amount on redemption, so yielding all its return in the form of capital gains rather than immediately taxable interest income. The new financial instruments amplify the scope for taking returns as capital rather than income and exploiting the benefits of deferral. Suppose, for instance, that capital gains are tax-exempt if the underlying asset is held for more than five years, but taxable as ordinary income if held for less. Consider the situation of an investor who has held an asset for four years and would like to realize its value but will face a tax charge if she does. Instead of selling the shares now, she might borrow an amount equal to their current value S and simultaneously sell a call and buy a put upon it at exercise price S. The proceeds of the loan can be used to finance consumption of S in year 4; when year 5 comes long, the share itself provides exactly the resources needed to repay the loan and offset the position on the option.[26] At no risk, the investor is thus able to entirely avoid bringing the capital gain into tax. There are other ways of achieving much the same effect. One would be by "bed and breakfasting"—selling the share on the last day of the tax year and repurchasing the next—though in this case risk is not entirely eliminated. The point of the example is rather to illustrate ways in which new instruments can expand the range of avoidance devices available to investors.

This further exposure of the problems posed by the differential treatment of capital and income items is not the only tax issue raised by financial innovation. Commercially advantageous interest rate swaps, for instance, may be rendered unprofitable if withholding taxes are levied on the gross interest payments associated with the swap rather than with the net flows.[27] The proper treatment of stock options given to employees has remained unclear. Should the value of the option at award be treated as employment income, for instance, or should tax be levied only at the time of any realized gain subsequent to the exercise of the option? But it is the issue of deferral that is the most profound.

Current Practice

Many tax systems address the most obvious devices to exploit deferral rules. The United States, for example, seeks to undo straddles by requiring gains on any position offsetting a loss to be treated as realized; and rules are commonly provided for treating accrued gains on zero-coupon bonds as interest. But such rules are ad hoc responses to particular difficulties rather than solutions to the general problem. Straddle rules may pick up investors who simultaneously buy and sell short shares in the same companies, but it may be more difficult to apply them to offsetting positions in different companies, perhaps in different sectors, whose returns are closely correlated. Indeed the adoption of such rules may itself provide an incentive to use more sophisticated financial instruments: the adoption of bed and breakfasting rules, for instance—ignoring the sale of an asset that is repurchased shortly after—may increase the attractions of the option-based device above.

More generally, however—and especially in developing countries—the tax treatment of new instruments is often unclear. Many countries make no explicit provision for such instruments in their tax legislation. Their treatment then becomes a matter of interpretation, precedence, and practice in such matters as the degree to which tax treatment follows accounting rules. Even where explicit rules are in place, they differ significantly. Within the OECD, for instance, some countries treat share options as instruments in their own right (taxing the premium in the hands of the issuer at the time of issue, and the holder on the gain in value at the time of exercise). Others look rather to the transaction in the share (taxing the premium, if at all, only on exercise, and the holder only on subsequent sale of shares acquired at exercise).[28] This variation of treatment is in itself a source of difficulty in an international context,[29] since it creates scope for the exploitation of inconsistencies in, for example, the timing of a taxable event. More fundamentally, it reflects the lack of a coherent intellectual framework for the taxation of financial instruments.

Policy Responses

To a large degree the tax problems posed by financial innovation are not new in themselves. The issue, rather, is that the repackaging that is their essence exposes still more clearly weakness in the pre-existing tax system: most noticeably, the distinction between items taxable as ordinary income and others taxable as capital gain, and most fundamentally, the problems posed by the usual practice of taxing the latter on realization. Financial innovation has thus lent renewed importance to the search for coherence in the taxation of alternative forms of capital income.

Coherence in this context means, in the first instance, neutrality: the principle that taxation should not distort the pattern of financial transactions that investors, both individuals and firms, choose to undertake. Arguments are sometimes made in support of providing tax preference to some kinds of financial income over others. In particular, the preferentially low tax rates on capital gains that many countries offer, often with rates lower the longer an asset is held, are sometimes rationalized as a counter to an inherent short-termism of investors. Most of these arguments, however, have little force. For instance, charging long-term gains at a reduced rate may give further encouragement to holding assets for longer periods—something that the ability to defer taxable gains does in itself, of course. However, it also gives an incentive to realize losses sooner rather than later, in order to take any associated deduction at a higher rate. In any event, the discussion that follows focuses on the question of how to achieve the key benchmark of neutrality.

What is needed, in principle, is some structure that treats identically for tax purposes all conceivable repackaging of any stream of cash flows. Holding a share and selling a call, for instance, should have exactly the same tax consequences, in each state of nature, as borrowing and selling a put. Three main approaches to this problem have been suggested.

One is "bifurcation," meaning the decomposition of an asset into its basic components and taxation by reference to the latter. This is a natural response to some composite assets, such as the convertible bond. More generally, however, it requires the identification of some set of fundamental assets that are the basic objects of the tax rules, together with agreement on a unique decomposition. Nor does this in itself address the difficulties that arise from the taxation of some assets on a realization basis. It is to this problem—"fixing realizations"—that the remaining approaches are centrally addressed.

The second strategy is to "mark-to-market," meaning that tax is charged on the increase in market value of net assets over some reference period (most obviously the start and finish of the tax year). This, in effect, is taxation on accrual. This has the merit of treating all assets uniformly and eliminating any incentive for selective realization. Marking-to-market is indeed the norm for market makers, and there is in principle no difficulty in extending it to the transactions in marketed securities of major companies and wealthy individuals. The method is not easily applied, however, to nonmarketed assets, and indeed one effect of its adoption would be to distort the choice between the two. A further common objection to this approach is that it may also present taxpayers with liquidity problems, requiring them to dispose of some part of the asset in order to pay their tax bill. It is hard to see how this could be a significant problem, however, for most marketed assets to which marking-to-market could plausibly be applied. A more real concern for many governments is that marking-to-market may also increase the volatility of their tax revenues, since gains and losses would all be taxed as they accrue without any smoothing from those who would otherwise choose to defer a gain or hold a loss.

The third approach is to retain taxation on realization but to charge that tax in such a way as to mimic taxation on accrual. Since valuations do not need to be observed continuously, this approach could be applied to a wider set of assets than marking-to-market, and is likely too to imply less volatility of revenues. Three ways of mimicking accrual taxation have been suggested.

One form of mimicry is the method proposed by Vickrey (1939) and the Meade Committee (1978), and it is simply to apportion the realized gain over the holding period and charge tax on realization equal in present value to the tax applicable to the implied series of gains. Consider for instance an asset acquired for price $P(0)$ and sold T periods later for $P(T)$. Denoting the risk-free interest rate by i, the tax charge at realization under this scheme is

$$T_V = \int_0^T \tau g e^{i(1-\tau)(T-s)} P(T) e^{-g(T-s)} ds$$

(2.14)

$$= \frac{\tau g}{g - i(1-\tau)} (1 - e^{[i(1-\tau) - g]T}) P(T)$$

where $g = (1/T)\ln[P(T)/P(0)]$ denotes the average rate at which gains cumulate over the holding period. Any such allocation is essentially arbitrary, however, so that some distortion of holding periods will remain. It remains tax advantageous to defer selling assets holding accrued gains, since, all else equal, those gains will then be allocated over a longer horizon.

An alternative form of mimicry is the suggestion by Auerbach (1991) that taxation at realization be calculated on the assumption that value has accumulated at the risk-free rate of return throughout the holding period, so that liability at realization is

$$(2.15) \quad T_A = \int_0^T \tau i e^{i(1-\tau)(T-s)} P(T) e^{-i(T-s)} ds = \tau(1 - e^{-iT}) P(T)$$

the rationale being that by effectively excluding unexpected gains from tax, this eliminates any tax-induced distortion of realization decisions. One implication of the scheme that may prove hard to sell politically, however, is that investors may have a significant tax liability even on assets on which they have made an ex post loss.

Finally, Bradford (1995) proposes a mimicry system that also has the feature of leaving realization decisions undistorted but, unlike Auerbach's, brings into tax any gain or loss relative to the risk-free return. This works by specifying, when an asset is acquired, a "capital gains tax date" (D) at which any gain is deemed to acquire, the working assumption being that the pre-tax risk-free return is earned at all other times. This gain is brought into tax at a pre-specified tax rate (θ), and tax at the "regular" rate (τ) charged to offset the gain implied by the ability to earn the pre- rather than post-tax return while holding the asset. This implies a total tax charge at realization[30] of:[31]

$$(2.16) \quad T_B = (1 - (1-\theta)e^{-i\tau(T-D)}) P(T) - e^{-i(1-\tau)T} (1 - (1-\theta)e^{i\tau D}) P(0)$$

Though seemingly complex, the intuition behind the scheme is straightforward: by pre-specifying the date at which gains or losses are deemed to arise and taxing away the potential gains from deferring realization relative to that date, the realization decision is left undistorted. And the tax θ, bearing only on unexpected gains or losses, is also nondistorting.

All these schemes are evidently rather complex. They are not impracticable. Italy, for example, has over the last few years used a variant of the Vickrey scheme (as discussed by Alworth, Arachi, and Hamaui 2002). But the recent elimination of the Italian scheme highlights the continuation of unresolved issues in this difficult area of tax policy.

The Optimal Taxation of Financial Services

Financial companies sell financial services. These can take many forms: the service of intermediating between borrowers and lenders, the risk-pooling service of providing insurance, advice on financial arrangements, and so on. To the company, the sale of these services is a source of income to which the general tax principles discussed in the previous section apply. For the purchaser, they are purchases of a commodity fundamentally like any other. The question then arises as to how such purchases should be treated for tax purposes. A complicating feature is that the price paid for financial services may sometimes not be immediately evident. The price paid for insurance, for example, is not the premium itself but the premium less the expected payout. In relation to intermediation, the total price paid by both parties is represented by the difference between borrowing and lending rates. Allocating that price between the two parties is less straightforward, the standard approach being to conceive of these as defined relative to a hypothetical "pure" interest rate. If a borrower pays 15 percent and the lender receives 10 percent, the total price paid by the two of 5 percent might be allocated relative to a pure interest rate of 13 percent, so that the borrower pays 2 percent and the lender 3 percent. Thus the analysis of the preceding section can be thought of as applying to transactions at the pure rate of interest, ignoring the whole question of the associated purchase of financial services. Leaving aside these difficulties, the first fundamental question is conceptually clear: how should the purchase of financial services be incorporated into the wider indirect tax system? The second question is more closely related to the problems of identifying the price paid for financial services: how, in practice, can such services be taxed?

Should Financial Services Be Taxed?

A fundamental guiding principle of tax policy design is that tax should be levied on final consumption, not on intermediate transactions. The intellectual underpinning of this prescription is the production efficiency theorem of Diamond and Mirrlees (1971). If pure profits can be taxed at any rate, and if there are no restrictions on the distorting tax instruments that can be deployed, then a Pareto-efficient tax structure has the feature that intermediate transactions are not distorted. The intuition behind this result—which has proved immensely powerful in addressing a wide range of issues—is straightforward. By definition, a tax reform that eliminates a production inefficiency increases aggregate output, and so must be desirable so long as the government has enough tax instruments at its disposal to ensure that this increased output is shared (in a weak sense) across all consumers.

The question then is how this result is to be applied to financial services. For purchases by businesses, the answer is straightforward: assuming the other conditions of the Diamond-Mirrlees theorem to be satisfied—a point discussed further below—these should be untaxed. The proper treatment of purchases by consumers has proven more contentious.[32]

Purchases by consumers   The proper tax treatment of purchases of financial services by consumers turns out to be a somewhat subtle issue, with the literature pervaded by one fallacy and one half (at best) truth.

The fallacy is the argument that since financial services themselves are obviously not an object of final utility to consumers but merely a form of intermediate transaction to serve more fundamental objects of desire, they should be untaxed. Grubert and Mackie (1999) begin from such a premise, for example, noting that their argument "starts from the view that consumption goods directly yield the consumer utility. They are the arguments of his utility function [whereas] many financial services . . . seem to us unlikely to yield him utility" (p. 25). Chia and Whalley (1999) are also sometimes cited in support of this line, though they are careful not to make quite such an unqualified argument.[33]

The half-truth, however, is the view—most widely found in the strand of the literature most concerned with the practical issues of how one might tax financial services, and the positive effects of doing so—that financial services are a commodity like any other, and so should be taxed like any other.

To see that the first view—financial services should be untaxed because they do not yield utility—is a fallacy, it is enough to pursue its logic still further. For there are many other items that are commonly taxed, or recommended to be so, even though they too are clearly not final objects of utility (except perhaps for a few strange people). Pet food, cutlery, cars, and many other such items are clearly, for most, means to an end—well being of their pets, getting food into their mouths efficiently, transport—rather than ends in themselves. But if these too are intermediate transactions, this argument would imply that they too should be exempt. In the limit, indeed, one could argue—along the lines, for instance, of the notion of capabilities of Sen (1985)—that essentially all commodity purchases are merely inputs to some deeper sense of well being. But it would clearly be nonsense to conclude from this that no commodity purchases by consumers should ever be taxed.

Indeed the view that the final objects of utility cannot in all cases be observed and taxed is the starting point for classical optimal tax theory, which is built upon the problems posed by the unobservability of potential earnings capacity and, hence, of leisure. Optimal tax theory does not generally suppose that the final objects of a household's utility are observed but only its net market trades, and it is the taxation of these trades that is the concern of tax policy design. At risk of belaboring the point, suppose, for example, that a household has utility $u(z)$ defined over some objects z that are unobservable in themselves but produced from observed net market trades x according to some production relation $f(x)$. Then individuals behave as if they maximized a utility function $u^*(x)$, where u^* is the composition $u[f(.)]$, and standard tax theory—including the Diamond-Mirrlees production efficiency theorem—applies with utility so characterized: the key attributes for tax design and reform in this framework, recall, being the patterns of demands for the observable net trades x.[34]

Thus the first question to ask is not whether financial services appear in the utility function—any argument that turns on this is inherently untrustworthy as a guide to optimal tax policy—but how they enter into the pattern of observable net trades.

Consider then the example of a consumer who lives for two periods, with consumption C_1 in the first and C_2 in the second (corresponding prices being P_1 and P_2), with income of Y (only) in the first. Imagine too that the only way to transfer income between the two periods is to obtain a bank account at a fixed cost P_F in order to lend money at the world interest rate R, with the bank also charging for its intermediation services by reducing the return to the lender by charging a spread of P_S. Savings are then

$$(2.17) \qquad S = Y - P_1 C_1 - P_F$$

and second-period consumption is

$$(2.18) \qquad P_2 C_2 = (1 + R - P_s)S$$

Combining the two to eliminate S, the lifetime budget constraint can be written as

$$(2.19) \qquad P_1 C_1 + P_F + \frac{P_2 C_2}{1 + R - P_s} = Y.$$

This has an important implication, stressed by Jack (2000) and Auerbach and Gordon (2002). Imposing a uniform tax at rate τ on consumption in both periods and the fee for opening the account—but, crucially, leaving that "spread" charge P_S untaxed—the budget constraint becomes

$$(2.20) \qquad (1 + \tau)P_1C_1 + (1 + \tau)P_F + \frac{(1 + \tau)P_2C_2}{1 + R - P_s} = Y,$$

which, dividing both sides by $(1 + \tau)$, is equivalent to the budget constraint

$$(2.21) \qquad P_1C_1 + P_F + \frac{P_2C_2}{1 + R - P_s} = (1 - \tau^*)Y$$

where $\tau^* = \tau/(1 + \tau)$. Thus a uniform tax on consumption and the bank fee, but not on the spread charge, is equivalent to a simple tax on income. In particular, focusing for the moment on the simple case in which Y is exogenous, such a tax structure is equivalent to a lump-sum tax, and hence fully nondistorting. Taxing consumption, the bank fee *and* the spread, however, it is easily seen that the tax would not be lump sum.

This provides a simple benchmark for policy. Financial services charged for as a fixed fee should be taxed; those charged for as a spread should not be. (This is one sense in which it is a half-truth to think of financial services as being like any other commodity.) Appealingly enough, this benchmark is not far from current normal practice under the value-added tax (VAT), which is to fully tax fee-type services but exempt (though not zero-rate) implicit charges. The rationale is quite different, however: above it emerges as a matter of principle; in practice it is seen as a matter of administrative practicability.

It should also be stressed, given the remarks above, that these arguments have nothing to do with the structures of the consumer's utility function or preference map. It may be natural to think of the consumer having a standard utility function $U(C_1, C_2)$ defined only on the consumption good. But that is immaterial: the arguments above apply even if the consumer happens to enjoy the act of opening a bank account, or even has preferences defined over the spread they have the misfortune to pay.[35]

These results do, however, need to be interpreted with some care. First, it is natural to think of the result in terms of additivity or otherwise of the budget constraint in items related to financial services, and of leaving the relative prices of consumption items unchanged—the key feature of the mechanics above being that P_F enters the budget constraint (equation 2.19) additively while P_S does not. Notice, however, that one can also combine equations 2.17 and 2.18 to write the lifetime budget constraint as

$$(2.22) \qquad P_1 C_1 + P_F + \frac{P_2 C_2}{1+R} + \frac{P_S S}{1+R} = Y.$$

The budget constraint can thus be written in such a way that an explicit expenditure item $P_S S$ does enter in the "usual" additive way, with the consumer neatly shown to spend their income on four items: the two consumption goods, the bank fee, and services embodied in the spread. With the present value price of P_2 interpreted as defined relative to the "world" interest rate rather than the lending rate $R-P_S$, the same argument as above might now seem to lead to the quite different conclusion that a uniform tax that *included* the spread charge would be lump sum. The reason this is incorrect is because the consumer's optimization problem—whatever their preferences happen to be—must take into account not only the budget constraint (equation 2.22) but also equation 2.17, the "production function" for savings; and in equation 2.17 the imposition of a uniform tax on all four items would not be equivalent to a tax on Y. Thus the issue is not quite whether the budget constraint is additive in expenditure on financial services, or even, arguably, whether it affects the relative price of consumption items. The issue, rather, is whether the budget constraint is additive when full account has been taken of the links between net trades that those services imply. It is in this sense that the nature of financial services as an intermediate good (and, potentially, of many services more generally)—not in terms of their utility relevance—makes them different from other items.

A second and related point is that things might not be as simple as this illustrative example suggests. It may be that neither fees P_S nor the spread P_F are fixed. For example, it could be that the spread falls with the level of savings. In this case large spreads on inframarginal savings have the character of fixed fees and ought to be taxed. By the same token, bank fees P_F may vary with the level of savings, in which case—by the previous arguments—they are like a spread and should be taxed. The implication is that distinguishing between fixed fees and spreads related to saving volumes poses difficult administrative challenges.

The third point to stress is that the results above, from manipulating budget identities, only establish a benchmark of a kind of neutrality—rendering an indirect tax system equivalent to a simple labor income tax; they do not establish any optimality properties. If Y is fixed, and also observable, then a lump-sum tax could be imposed directly. The more interesting case for tax design—the starting point of optimal tax theory—is that in which income is itself a choice variable, reflecting intensity of work effort. As is well known, there is then no presumption that a uniform tax on consumption would be optimal. For that problem of tax design, the desirability of a tax on P_S cannot be ruled out a priori as part of a tax structure that maximizes welfare subject to some government revenue constraint.[36]

The example cited by Chia and Whalley (1999) is instructive in this context. They consider two individuals who acquire identical cars, one purchasing by cash and the other by leasing. Since they each possess the same car, and it is the car that enters their utility functions, Chia and Whalley argue, they should pay the same tax. But their economic situations could be quite different. The individual who purchased in cash may have had to spend a morning collecting the money from the bank, while the individual who is leasing may face binding credit constraints that adversely affect other aspects of their situation, such as the ability to acquire education. These underlying differences between the two, unless dealt with directly by other instruments of public policy, may rationalize treating the two ways of acquiring car services quite differently for tax purposes.

Accepting then that financial services purchased by consumers are in some circumstances a proper subject for taxation, the question then is: At what rate?

The answer is likely to be context-specific, depending not least on the range of other instruments available to government. In a general sense, the appropriate rate will be governed by the same range of considerations that apply to the determination of optimal tax rates more generally: the extent to which the use of financial services serves as a substitute for leisure, and the degree to which taxing financial services eases the self-selection problem by making it less attractive for high-ability types to masquerade as low-ability types.[37] In the example above, for instance, to the extent that payment in cash requires using up time that could otherwise be spent in the market, relatively favorable tax treatment of leasing would be called for. There is, perhaps, a general presumption that insofar as financial intermediation services serve as an alternative to time-consuming activities they should be taxed, if at all, at a relatively low rate.

The issues here are clearly subtle ones, but the broad conclusion seems clear: the fact that financial services are not in themselves an object of utility is in itself of no relevance, and certainly does not imply that their purchase by consumers should not be taxed. While their appropriate treatment is likely to be context-specific, there are reasonable grounds to suppose that the optimal rate of taxation for such services will often be relatively low.

Purchases by business The appropriate treatment, in principle, of business sales and purchases of financial services is less contentious, there being widespread agreement that these—like all other business inputs—should ideally be untaxed. The most compelling rationale for this is again the Diamond-Mirrlees production efficiency theorem.

That theorem does, however, admit exceptions. It fails to apply, in general, if there are restrictions on the government's ability to tax pure profits or if it is in some way constrained in its ability to deploy distorting domestic taxes. In either case, the taxation of intermediate transactions might serve some role as a surrogate for these missing tax instruments. Might either of these considerations have any special force in relation to financial services?

Certainly the financial sector is sometimes popularly supposed to generate excessive profits and/or excessive payments to those working in the sector, and this has been used to garner support for taxes on financial activities. But if it is felt necessary to levy special taxes on these agents, this can often be better done by means of more directly targeted profit or income taxes. The United Kingdom, for instance, levied a windfall profits tax on banks in the early 1980s, while Canada and other countries have annual capital taxes on financial institutions.

There may be cases, however, in which taxing businesses' financial transactions can serve as a partial substitute for missing tax instruments, the most obvious being those in which this can serve as a partial defense against tax evasion. It may be easier to monitor transactions through the banking system than it is to enforce proper payment of taxes on income or wealth, so that some tax on those transactions—perhaps creditable against taxes on income or wealth—may serve as a poor but worthwhile surrogate.

For whatever reason they are imposed, taxes on business use of financial services are liable to generate production inefficiency by distorting input choices away from the use of those services. Firms may take out less insurance, or undertake less investment, than is appropriate in terms of underlying social costs. The consequent distortion of such firm's output prices then cascades through the production system insofar as those outputs become other firms' inputs. Quite how significant these deadweight costs are is a matter for empirical study. Both experience and common sense, however, suggest that businesses are likely to prove adept in ways of restructuring their financial operations to avoid such taxes. With this high responsiveness of the base, the presumption must be that the deadweight cost (per dollar of revenue raised) of taxes on the business use of financial services is likely often to be high.

Can Financial Services Be Taxed?

Accepting then the general principles that financial services purchased by consumers ought to be taxed (albeit perhaps at a low rate) while business purchases should not be, the question arises: How can this be done in practice? In particular, how should financial services be incorporated into the VAT, now the most common form of indirect tax even in developing economies?[38] These issues are discussed in chapter 12, but an overview here may also be helpful.

For financial services provided on a fee-paying basis, such as safekeeping services and financial advice, there is no particular difficulty: VAT (or any other form of sales tax) can be charged in the usual way.

The difficulty arises for services charged for in the margin between the return paid to lenders and that charged to borrowers.[39] The problem is typically not in identifying the aggregate value-added created by intermediation, but in allocating it between consumers (to be taxed) and producers (not to be taxed). This is difficult.

Suppose, for example, that a bank pays its depositors 5 percent and charges its borrowers 15 percent. Clearly the value-added by the bank is $15 - 5 = 10$ percent of deposits (less any material inputs, and assuming too there is no risk of default). This should be taxed. If all loans were to final consumers, this would be the end of the matter. Assume instead that the borrower is a registered firm. How much of the 15 percent should be creditable? The standard conceptual approach on this issue has been to imagine a hypothetical "pure" interest rate at which the lender could have lent (but without enjoying the ancillary services such as clearing offered by the bank) and at which the borrower could have borrowed (had they been able to find suitable lenders without the help of the intermediary). If this pure rate is 12 percent, for instance, then the value-added provided to the borrower is $15 - 12 = 3$ percent of the loan, and the remaining $12 - 5 = 7$ percent is value-added provided to the lender. On a loan of $1,000 and at a VAT rate of 10 percent, the appropriate outcome is thus for the borrower to be charged VAT of $3 and the lender VAT of $7, the total payable thus being 10 percent of the aggregate value-added on 10 percent of $1,000. These VAT payments would be creditable, in the usual way, if lender or borrower is registered.

But this outcome has generally been regarded as impossible to bring about, since it would appear to require, in particular, identifying a "pure" interest rate. This has led most countries using the invoice-credit VAT (which means almost all countries with a VAT) to "exempt" financial intermediation, meaning that tax is not charged on outputs of the financial services sector but nor can tax paid on inputs be reclaimed. Both businesses and consumers thus bear some tax on their purchases of the financial sector, in the indirect form of unrecovered tax paid on the inputs—office equipment, software—used in their production.

Some countries (notably Israel) have instead taxed value-added in financial services by the addition method: that is, by levying tax directly on the sum of wages and profits.[40] A potential alternative is afforded by the subtraction method (as was at one point proposed in Canada), under which tax is simply levied on the excess of a firm's outputs over its inputs. Either method is capable of taxing aggregate value-added in this sector, and indeed either would in principle be perfectly adequate within a wider VAT system based comprehensively on the addition or subtraction method. Neither method, however, sits well with the application of the invoice-credit method in the rest of the VAT system. Neither enables the identification of embodied VAT on a transaction-by-transaction basis, and hence neither allows the systematic crediting of financial services provided to registered traders.

In principle, these difficulties can be circumvented by applying VAT on a "cash flow" basis.[41] Under this system, all inflows of funds, including the receipt of a loan, and all interest receipts, would be treated akin to sales, and be taxable if the recipient is registered. All outflows, including the repayment of loans, or payment of interest, would attract credit if the payer is registered. For example, consider a loan of $1,000 to a registered trader (at 15 percent) financed by a deposit (paid 5 percent) from a consumer. Assume as before that the tax rate is 10 percent. Under the cash flow VAT:

- The bank is liable to pay $100 on the deposit, but this is exactly offset by a credit of $100 on the loan itself. When the loan is repaid, the bank has a net inflow of 10 percent of $1,000 (its spread on the loan) and so owes tax of $10.
- When the loan is made, the business pays tax of $100. When it is repaid, it receives a credit of 10 percent of $1,150 (principal plus interest).

If the government is able to earn the pure rate of interest of 12 percent on its receipt from the business of $100, it is left with net revenue of $112 + 10 − 115 = $7, which is exactly 10 percent of the services of $70 provided to the consumer.

It may be useful to make the general argument algebraically. Denote the amount of the loan by L, the borrowing and lending rates by r_B and r_L respectively, and the tax rate by τ. Also define λ_B and λ_L to take the values 1 and 0 if the borrower (respectively, lender) is registered or not; thus the example above has $\lambda_B = 1$ and $\lambda_L = 0$. In the first period of the loan (assumed for simplicity to last only two periods), the net liability of the bank is zero; that of a borrower is $\lambda_B \tau L$; and the lender receives a credit of $\lambda_L \tau L$. In period 2, the net liability of the bank is $\tau(r_B - r_L)L$; a registered borrower is due a credit of $\tau(1 + r_B)L$, and a registered lender is liable for tax of $\tau(1 + r_L)L$. Assuming that the government obtains a rate of return p on its net receipts in the first period of $\lambda_B \tau L - \lambda_L \tau L$, net revenue in period 2 is:

$$
\begin{aligned}
(2.23) \quad & (1 + p)(\lambda_B - \lambda_L)\tau L + \tau(r_B - r_L)L - \lambda_B \tau(1 + r_B)L + \lambda_L \tau(1 - r_L)L \\
& = \tau L[(1 - \lambda_B)(r_B - p) + (1 - \lambda_L)(p - r_L)]
\end{aligned}
$$

Thus tax is ultimately collected only on that part of the margin (relative to the government's discount rate) that reflects the value-added enjoyed by nonregistered traders.

So long as the interest rate available to the government is identified with the pure interest rate, the cash flow approach achieves the theoretically correct allocation of value-added, and allows a proper crediting of input tax. Intuitively, by crediting inflows and outflows at the same rate, the system ensures that the present value of the revenue raised from registered traders is zero. Revenue is ultimately raised only to the extent of that part of the margin that falls on unregistered traders.

The treatment of pure insurance—insurance with no savings element—is also straightforward under the cash flow VAT. An example is given in box 2.1.

Outside the case of pure insurance, however, the cash flow scheme is cumbersome administratively. Some measures can be taken to alleviate this (for example, by suspending the payment of tax, and refunds, associated with the initial receipt of loans and deposits). But even within the European Union, where the scheme has been closely considered, there are doubts as to its practicability. For developing countries, it seems likely to remain overly complex for some time yet.

It should be emphasized that it is by no means certain that making financial services fully taxable will generate an increase in VAT

Box 2.1 Treatment of Pure Insurance under a Cash Flow VAT

Consider the case in which an insurance company receives premiums of $100 and pays $80 (exclusive of VAT) in claims, so that value added is $20. The tax rate is 20 percent (this being the tax-exclusive rate: that is, the rate charged on values not including tax).

The insurance company is liable to VAT of $20 on its premiums, but allowed a credit of $16 in respect of the claims it pays. Thus the insurer pays net tax of $4, which is 20 percent of the value-added of $20. The credit enables the insurer to send the insured a check for $96 should the insured event occur.

If the insured is a consumer, $96 is just enough to purchase goods to the tax-exclusive value of $80: the credit included in the claim pays the VAT on the replacement goods bought. Total tax collected is thus exactly 20 percent of value-added.

If the insured is registered for VAT, they take a credit of $20 on the premium. When the claim of $96 is received, output tax of $16 is charged, which is exactly offset by an input tax credit of $16 on the replacement property. Total tax collected by the government is zero.

Consistent with the logic of the invoice-credit VAT, the tax thus "sticks" only on final sales to final consumers.

---

revenues. If financial services were fully taxable, revenue would be collected only on sales to final consumers. When they are exempt, in contrast, tax is collected on inputs into the sector.[42] Which will lead to greater revenue is an empirical question. For the EU, Huizinga (2002) sees a substantial potential revenue gain. For many developing countries, however, purchases of financial services by domestic consumers may be quite limited, so that subjecting financial services to VAT is unlikely to be the fiscal panacea for such cash-strapped governments that it may sound.

Concluding Comments

Financial activities are ubiquitous in a market economy, and the policy issues pervasive. This chapter has necessarily focused on some key issues concerning the optimal taxation of capital income generally, and financial services more specifically. The perspective taken in this chapter has been the taxation of financial activities as part of a system of optimal taxation for revenue-raising purposes.

In fact, the tax (and subsidy) system might also be used for corrective purposes—to correct for inefficiencies resulting from market failures. The possibility of market failure is particularly germane in financial markets because of the information asymmetries that are endemic to the sector. Understanding the proper role of tax policy in such circumstances remains under-developed.

Needless to say, this chapter has not been able to cover all aspects of the taxation of financial activities. Some of these issues, notably several distinct policy problems raised by the distinct functions of financial institutions, are at the interface between tax and regulatory policies and are taken up in subsequent chapters; for instance the appropriate tax provision for bad loans in the case of banks, the imposition of reserve requirements, and the provision of deposit insurance (see in particular chapters 5, 7, and 9). Money is itself a key financial asset, so that seigniorage will typically have a role to play in the wider tax system (see, for instance, chapter 13 in this volume, and Poterba and Rotemberg 1990).

Some of the other more important omissions from this coverage—other than the key issue of market failure just mentioned—bear special emphasis:

Financial markets are sometimes seen as being excessively volatile, presumably—the argument is not always well articulated—in the sense that they adjust more rapidly than other markets, creating adjustment problems. This then leads some to advocate taxes on financial transactions as a corrective device. Even in its own terms, however, the argument is not convincing. By thinning the market, such taxes could well increase volatility (Hubbard 1993).

An issue with wider ramifications than finance is the impact of taxation on risk-taking, which has received considerable attention (see for instance Sandmo 1985). The associated issues of optimal policy design, however, have been less studied, and are not addressed here: whenever there is uncertainty in the models developed here and in chapter three, there will be no aggregate uncertainty and all agents will be risk-neutral. In general terms, of course, when risk markets are incomplete there may be scope for welfare-improving interventions. This will depend in large part, however, on whether governments are better able to bear risk than is the private sector, which is far from obviously being the case.

Additionally, the recent literature on corporate governance (surveyed by Becht, Bolton, and Röell 2003) points to inefficiencies (in relation to takeovers, for instance) that tax policy might be used to address. These, however, appear to have received almost no attention.

Many countries, especially it would seem developing ones, adopt tax and other measures intended to nurture the financial sector. Though such policies are often criticized as misplaced, the question of appropriate tax design in the presence of under-developed financial markets seems to have received little attention.

Finally, international considerations raise issues of increasing importance, currently heated aspects including the desirability or otherwise of restricting international tax competition. These issues have generated a large literature, still growing rapidly, that is simply too large to be reviewed here.

These omissions are daunting. Understanding the issues that are addressed here, however, seems fundamental to addressing this wider set of policy problems.

Appendix

Suppose that the government's instruments are taxes on wage income in the two periods and a capital income tax. Maximizing $U(C_1,C_2,L_1,L_2) = U(C_1,L_1) + \beta U(C_2,L_2)$ subject to the budget constraint (equation 2.2), written more compactly as:

$$(A2.1) \qquad C_1 + p_2^* C_2 = w_1^* L_1 + w_2^* L_2$$

(where the price of C has been normalized to unity, and asterisks are used to indicate tax-inclusive prices), the familiar necessary conditions for the consumer's optimization problem are:

$$(A2.2) \qquad U_C^1 = \lambda$$

$$(A2.3) \qquad \beta U_C^2 = \lambda p_2^*$$

$$(A2.4) \qquad U_L^1 = -\lambda w_1^*$$

$$(A2.5) \qquad \beta U_L^2 = -\lambda w_2^*$$

The government's present value revenue constraint is then, in obvious notation,

$$(A2.6) \qquad T_C^2 C_2 + T_w^1 L_1 + T_w^2 L_2 = R$$

where taxes are taken to be defined in specific form: in particular, $T_C^2 = p_2 - p_2^*$, so that capital income taxation is zero iff $T_2^C = 0$.

The optimal tax problem, in primal form,[43] is then addressed by forming the Lagrangean

(A2.7)
$$L = U(C_1,L_1) + \beta U(C_2,L_2) + \alpha(w_1 L_1 + w_2 L_2 - C_1$$
$$- p_2 C_2 - R) + \mu(U_C^1 C_1 + \beta U_C^2 C_2 + U_L^1 L_1 + \beta U_L^2 L_2)$$

where the second term (with multiplier α) captures the government's revenue constraint, obtained from (A2.1) and (A2.3), and the third (with multiplier μ) incorporates the incentive compatibility constraint by combining the consumer's necessary conditions and budget constraint.

The first-order conditions are then

(A2.8) $\qquad U_C^1 - \alpha + \mu(U_C^1 + U_{CC}^1 C_1 + U_{LC}^1 L_1) = 0$

(A2.9) $\qquad \beta U_C^2 - \alpha p_2 + \mu\beta(U_C^2 + U_{CC}^2 C_2 + U_{LC}^2 L_2) = 0$

(A2.10) $\qquad U_L^1 + \alpha w_1 + \mu(U_L^1 + U_{CL}^1 C_1 + U_{LL}^1 L_1) = 0$

(A2.11) $\qquad \beta U_L^2 + \alpha w_2 + \mu(U_L^2 + U_{CL}^2 C_2 + U_{LL}^2 L_2) = 0$

To establish the claims in the text, suppose that $C_1 = C_2$ and $L_1 = L_2$ at an optimum. Then from (A2.8, 9), $U_C^1 = \beta U_C^2/p_2$. Hence from (A2.2, 3), $p_2^* = p_2$, implying $T_2^C = 0$. Moreover, since $U_C^1 = U_C^2$ (by time-invariance of C and L), it must be that $\beta = p_2 = 1/(1 + R)$. Then from (A2.10, 11) $w_1^*/w_1 = w_2^*/w_2$.

Notes

1. This can be seen by noting that equation 2.1 is equivalent to equation 2.2, with τ_r, τ_{w1}, and τ_{w2} in the latter replaced by

$$\tau_r^* = 1 - \frac{1}{r}\left(\frac{(1 + (1 - \tau_r)r)(1 + \tau_{c1})}{1 + \tau_{c2}} - 1\right)\tau$$

$$\tau_{w1}^* = 1 - \frac{1 - \tau_{w1}}{1 + \tau_{c1}}, \text{ and } \tau_{w2}^* = 1 - \frac{1 - \tau_{w2}}{1 + \tau_{c2}}.$$

2. This is essentially a generalization of that of King (1980) and Atkinson and Sandmo (1980) for the special case of a two-period life cycle with labor supply only in the first period. These, in turn, are essentially an application of Corlett and Hague (1953): if leisure is equally substitutable for first and second period consumption, and if the government is free to issue

debt as well as tax labor and capital income, there is no role for capital income taxation.

3. See Deaton (1979). Besley and Jewitt (1995) derive a more general sufficient condition on preferences for uniform taxation to be optimal.

4. More precisely, the first-order conditions characterizing an optimal tax system are satisfied along a growth path of the type just described. The claims in this paragraph are proved in the appendix.

5. There is a slight abuse of notation here, in that these tax rates were specified in ad valorem form above rather than, as here, specific form. The two are equivalent from the perspective of the consumer, so that which one uses is essentially a matter of modeling convenience.

6. See also Atkeson, Chari, and Kehoe (1999); Erosa and Gervais (2001, 2002).

7. This can be seen by noting that lifetime preferences are in this case of the form

$$U(.) = u(\phi(C_1, C_2), L_1, L_2), \text{ where } \phi(.) = \left(\sum_{t=1}^{2} C_t^{\sigma} \right)^{1/\sigma}$$

is homogenous of degree one. This form satisfies the sufficient condition for implicit separability mentioned in the text above.

8. Coleman also notes that if the government is unrestricted in its choice of tax instruments, and assuming that the representative household has positive initial assets, a tax scheme that taxes consumption proportionately and subsidizes labor proportionately at the same tax rate in all periods is effectively a tax on initial wealth, and so is lump-sum. This can be seen by adding a term representing initial assets to the left of equation 2.1. Assuming initial asset wealth is large enough to pay for future tax requirements, a first best is achieved and the optimal tax on capital income would be zero, which would be distortionary. This is essentially the time consistency point in another guise.

9. For the case in which preferences are not separable over time, Erosa and Gervais (2002) show that it will be optimal not to tax capital income from period 1 onward if preferences are of the form $U(G(C_1, C_2), L_1, L_2)$, with G homothetic. This of course is the sufficient condition for implicit separability of the expenditure function mentioned in the third observation of the two-period case.

10. See Edwards, Keen, and Tuomala (1994); Nava, Schroyen, and Marchand (1996).

11. This discussion presumes that interest income is taxed at a constant rate, which would be appropriate if individual capital income could not be observed. If it can be, presumably one might want interest income in the second period to be taxed in a nonlinear fashion.

12. This has long been the case in Sweden, for instance; in the United States, see Gordon and Slemrod (1988).

13. Nevertheless, the task is not hopeless: Norway attempts to do exactly this.

14. This has not been standard practice but, following the German tax reform of 2000, appears to be becoming more common.

15. One could conceive of international cooperation to this effect—each country uses its corporation tax as a withholding device against other's personal income tax system—but this is not observed in practice.

16. Gordon (1992), for instance, argues that a capital exporting country acting as a Stackleberg leader (and as such, taking account of the likely responses of the others) may find it desirable to offer a credit in order to induce a higher tax abroad and thereby stem capital flight.

17. See Fuest and Huber (2000) for an argument that such a system is indeed optimal in an open economy setting.

18. With a falling rate of cash flow taxation, for instance, there is an incentive to bring forward investment in order to take the up-front deduction at a higher rate than the later returns will be taxed. The point is neatly made by Sandmo (1979).

19. Bond and Devereux (1999) argue for the use of the risk-free rate of return.

20. Keen and King (2002) assess the Croatian experience.

21. In fact, in the case of natural resources, there are alternatives to rent taxes as a means of ensuring that some share of resource rents accrue to the public sector, including royalty systems, the sale of leases, and joint public-private ventures (see Boadway and Flatters 1993).

22. In principle, these net liability transactions could also be included in the cash flow tax base of non-financial corporations, as well. As shown by Boadway, Bruce, and Mintz (1983), the neutrality properties of alternative cash flow tax bases varies depending on what one assumes about the determinants of the financial structure of the firm.

23. For more extensive accounts, see Alworth (1998), Edgar (2000), and Warren (1993).

24. A put (call) option is the right, but not obligation, to sell an asset at some pre-specified exercise (or "strike") price. The example assumes European options with expiry date coincident with that on the zero-coupon bond.

25. By, for instance, the adoption of a cash flow or ACE-type corporate tax along the lines discussed above.

26. Denote the price in year 5 by S^*, the net worth of the investor is then $S^* - S + \max[S-S^*,0] - \max[S^*-S,0]$ (this being the value of the share less the obligation on the debt plus the payoff on the put less the cost of the call), which is exactly zero.

27. Under a straight interest rate swap—the exchange of fixed and floating rate obligations—each party makes a net payment equal to the ex-

cess of one interest charge over another. If withholding is levied only on the first component of this net payment, tax payments could exceed the underlying gain associated with the net flows. For an example of this, see appendix II of OECD (1994).

28. OECD (1994).

29. These are discussed in Thuronyi (2001).

30. Auerbach and Bradford (2001) note that this scheme could also be implemented as a generalized cash flow tax, with a deduction for asset acquisitions at a tax rate corresponding to the coefficient on $P(0)$ in equation 2.16 and full taxation of proceeds at the rate corresponding to that on $P(T)$.

31. As explained in Auerbach and Bradford (2001), this is the sum of two charges. The first is that on the "deemed" gain at D, cumulated to time T, given the working assumption that the asset earned the pre-tax risk-free rate at all other dates:

$$g(P(T)e^{-i(T-D)} - P(0)e^{iD})e^{i(1-\tau)(T-D)}$$

The second is the cumulated value of the tax value of accumulating at the pre-tax rather than the post-tax interest rate:

$$P(0)(e^{iD} - e^{i(1-\tau)D})e^{i(1-\tau)(T-D)} + P(T)e^{-i(T-D)}(e^{i(T-D)} - e^{i(1-\tau)(T-D)}).$$

32. For brevity—there being enough issues to deal with—this chapter leaves aside the considerable practical difficulties that arise in distinguishing between purchases of financial services for personal and business use, a much wider problem that affects a whole range of commodities.

33. Chia and Whalley (1999) argue that "No utility per se flows from the use of intermediation services. Since financial services do not enter preferences directly, it may be inappropriate to include them in broadly based indirect taxes such as a VAT" (p. 705). Note, however, the careful and quite correct use of the word 'may,' and the equally careful and correct implicit recognition that it may be optimal to tax financial services at a rate other than prevailing on commodities in general. Indeed they are quite explicit in recognizing that the optimal rate of tax on financial service may not be zero (p. 718).

34. The composition u^* may not have the regularity properties usually required of a utility function. However, one may follow the tradition of optimal tax theory in being somewhat cavalier in the treatment of second-order conditions.

35. Conversely, suppose that one knew for sure that preferences were of the form $U(C_1,C_2)$. Then this example shows that even if one were unrestricted in the ability to tax what appears in the utility function, it may be desirable to tax other items too (the bank fee).

36. It is worth noting that the simulation results reported in Chia and Whalley (1999) do not show the optimal rate of tax on intermediation services to be zero. They merely show that a situation in which consumption in each period and those services are taxed at a uniform rate may be inferior to one in which only consumption is taxed at a uniform rate. As they themselves are at pains to emphasize, this does not imply that the full optimum is characterized by nontaxation of financial services.

37. These are the same considerations as arose above in the context of taxing capital income with heterogeneous individuals.

38. Recall that the basic principle of the usual invoice-credit VAT is that all inputs are taxed but with businesses able to credit this input tax against the tax charged on their outputs. See Ebrill and others (2001) for a recent treatment; this section draws on chapter 7.

39. The discussion here focuses mainly on simple loan transactions. Similar issues apply to insurance contracts with a savings component and to other more complex forms of financial intermediation.

40. Profits for this purpose should in principle be defined on a cash flow basis, with investment immediately expensed.

41. See Poddar and English (1997) and European Commission (undated).

42. This is a simplification: revenue will be less than this to the extent that financial services are exported (hence zero-rated) and greater to the extent that a higher price of financial services leads to higher prices of taxed commodities produced with their help.

43. See, for instance, Atkinson and Stiglitz (1980, pp. 376–80); Deaton (1979).

References

Alvarez, Yvette, John Burbidge, Ted Farrell, and Leigh Palmer. 1992. "Optimal Taxation in a Life Cycle Model." *Canadian Journal of Economics* 25 (1): 111–22.

Alworth, J. S. 1998. "Taxation and Integrated Financial Markets: The Challenges of Derivatives and Other Financial Innovations." *International Tax and Public Finance* 5 (4): 507–34.

Alworth, J. S., G. Arachi, and R. Hamaui. 2002. "Adjusting Capital Gains Taxation: Lessons from the Recent Italian Tax Experience." University of Bocconi. Processed.

Atkeson Andrew, V. V. Chari, and Patrick J. Kehoe. 1999. "Taxing Capital Income: A Bad Idea." Federal Reserve Bank of Minneapolis *Quarterly Review* 23 (1): 3–17.

Atkinson, Anthony B., and Agnar Sandmo. 1980. "Welfare Implications of the Taxation of Savings." *The Economic Journal* 90 (359): 529–49.

Atkinson, Anthony B., and Joseph E. Stiglitz. 1976. "The Design of Tax Structure: Direct vs. Indirect Taxation," *Journal of Public Economics* 6 (1): 55–75.

———. 1980. *Lectures on Public Economics*. New York: McGraw-Hill.

Auerbach, Alan J. 1983. "Taxation, Corporate Financial Policy and the Cost of Capital," *Journal of Economic Literature* 21 (3): 905–40.

———. 1991. "Retrospective Capital Gains Taxation." *American Economic Review* 81 (1): 167–78.

Auerbach, Alan J., and David F. Bradford. 2001. "Generalized Cash Flow Taxation." University of California, Berkeley. Processed.

Auerbach, Alan J., and Roger Gordon. 2002. "Taxation of Financial Services Under a VAT." *American Economic Review*, Papers and Proceedings 92: 411–16.

Auerbach, Alan J., and Laurence J. Kotlikoff. 1987. *Dynamic Fiscal Policy*. Cambridge: Cambridge University Press.

Becht, Marco, Patrick Bolton, and Ailsa Röell. 2003. "Corporate Governance and Control." In George Constantinides, Milton Harris and Rene M. Stulz, eds. *Handbook of the Economics of Finance*. Volume 1A. New York: North Holland.

Besley, Timothy, and Ian Jewitt. 1995. "Uniform Taxation and Consumer Preferences." *Review of Economic Studies* 58 (1): 73–84.

Boadway, Robin. 1980. "Corporate Taxation and Investment: A Synthesis of the Neo-Classical Model." *Canadian Journal of Economics* 13 (2): 250–67.

Boadway, Robin, and Neil Bruce. 1984. "A General Proposition on the Design of a Neutral Business Tax." *Journal of Public Economics* 24 (2): 231–39.

———. 1992. "Problems with Integrating Corporate and Personal Taxes in an Open Economy." *Journal of Public Economics* 48 (1): 39–66.

Boadway, Robin, and Frank Flatters. 1993. "The Taxation of Natural Resources: Principles and Policy Issues." Policy Research Working Paper WPS No. 1210. World Bank, Washington, D.C.

Boadway, Robin, and Michael Keen. 1998. "Evasion and Time Consistency in the Taxation of Capital Income." *International Economic Review* 39 (2): 461–76.

Boadway, Robin, Neil Bruce, and Jack Mintz. 1983. "On the Neutrality of Flow-of-Funds Corporate Taxation." *Economica* 50 (1): 49–61.

Boadway, Robin, Maurice Marchand, and Pierre Pestieau. 2000. "Redistribution with Unobservable Bequests: A Case for Taxing Capital Income." *Scandinavian Journal of Economics* 102 (2): 253–67.

Bond, Stephen R., and Michael P. Devereux. 1999. "Generalised R-Based and S-Based Taxes Under Uncertainty." Working Paper No. 99/9. Institute for Fiscal Studies, London.

Bradford, D. F. 1995. "Fixing Realization Accounting: Symmetry, Consistency and Correctness in the Taxation of Financial Instruments." *Tax Law Review* 50 (4): 731–85.

Brock, Philip L. 2003. "Corrective Taxes and Quasi-Taxes for Financial Institutions and Their Interaction with Deposit Insurance" (chapter 5, this volume).

Caminal, Ramon. 2003. "Taxation of Banks: Modeling the Impact." (chapter 3, this volume).

Chamley, Christophe. 1986. "Optimal Taxation of Capital Income in General Equilibrium with Infinite Lives." *Econometrica* 54 (3): 607–22.

Chari, V. V., Patrick Kehoe, and Edward C. Prescott. 1989. "Time Consistency and Policy." In Robert Barro, ed., *Handbook of Modern Business Cycle Theory.* Cambridge, Mass.: Harvard University Press.

Chia, N. C., and J. Whalley. 1999. "The Tax Treatment of Financial Intermediation." *Journal of Money, Credit and Banking* 31 (4): 704–19.

Coleman, Wilbur John II. 2000. "Welfare and the Optimum Dynamic Taxation of Consumption and Capital Income." *Journal of Public Economics* 76 (1): 1–39.

Corlett, W. J., and D. C. Hague. 1953. "Complementarity and the Excess Burden of Taxation." *Review of Economic Studies* 21 (1): 21–30.

Cremer, Helmuth, Pierre Pestieau, and Jean-Charles Rochet. Forthcoming, 2003. "Capital and Labor Income Taxation in an Overlapping-Generations Growth Model." *Journal of Public Economics.*

Deaton, Angus. 1979. "The Distance Function in Consumer Behavior with Applications to Index Numbers and Optimal Taxation." *Review of Economic Studies* 46 (3): 391–405.

Deaton, Angus, and Nicholas Stern. 1986. "Optimally Uniform Commodity Taxes, Taste Differences and Lump-Sum Grants." *Economics Letters* 20 (3): 263–66.

Devereux, M. P., and H. Freeman. 1991. "A General Neutral Profits Tax." *Fiscal Studies* 12 (1): 1–15.

Diamond, P., and J. A. Mirrlees. 1971. "Optimal Taxation and Public Production, I: Production Efficiency." *American Economic Review* 61 (1): 8–27.

Ebrill, L., M. Keen, J. P. Bodin, and V. Summers. 2001. *The Modern VAT.* Washington: International Monetary Fund.

Edgar, T. 2000. *The Income Tax Treatment of Financial Instruments: Theory and Practice.* Toronto: Canadian Tax Foundation.

Edwards, Jeremy, Michael Keen, and Matti Tuomala. 1994. "Income Tax, Commodity Taxes and Public Good Provision: A Brief Guide." *Finanzarchiv* 51 (4): 472–97.

Erosa, Andrés, and Martin Gervais. 2001. "Optimal Taxation in Infinitely-Lived Agent and Overlapping Generations Models: A Review." Federal Reserve Bank of Richmond *Economic Quarterly* 87 (1): 23–44.

————. 2002. "Optimal Taxation in Life-Cycle Economies." *Journal of Economic Theory* 105 (2): 338–69.

European Commission. Undated. *Value-Added Tax: A Study of the Methods of Taxing Financial Institutions.* Brussels: European Commission.

Fischer, Stanley. 1980. "Dynamic Inconsistency, Cooperation and the Benevolent Dissembling Government." *Journal of Economic Dynamics and Control* 2 (1): 93–107.

Fuest, Clemens, and Bernd Huber. 2000. "The Optimal Taxation of Dividends in a Small Open Economy." Working Paper Series No. 348. Munich: CESifo

Gordon, Roger. 1992. "Can Capital Income Taxes Survive in Open Economies?" *Journal of Finance* 47 (3): 1159–80.

————. 2001. "Taxation of Interest Income in an Open Economy." Paper prepared for the Research Center for Economic Policy (OCFEB) Conference on Tax Policy in the European Union, October 17–19. The Hague: Ministry of Finance http://www.few.eur.nl/few/research/ocfeb/congreseu/.

Gordon, Roger, and Joel Slemrod. 1988. "Do We Collect any Revenue from Taxing Capital Income?" *Tax Policy and the Economy* 2: 89–130.

Grubert, Harry, and James Mackie. 1999. "Must Financial Services be Taxed under a Consumption Tax?" *National Tax Journal* 53 (1): 23–40.

Honohan, Patrick. 2003. "The Accidental Tax: Inflation and the Financial Sector." (chapter 13, this volume).

Hubbard, Glenn R. 1993. "Securities Transactions Taxes: Tax Design, Revenue and Policy Considerations." *Tax Notes* (November 23): 985–1000.

Huizinga, Harry. 2002. "A European VAT on Financial Services." *Economic Policy* 35: 499–534.

Jack, William. 2000. "The Treatment of Financial Services under a Broad-Based Consumption Tax." *National Tax Journal* 53 (4): 841–51.

Keen, Michael, and John King. 2002. "The Croatian Profits Tax: An ACE in Practice." *Fiscal Studies* 23 (3): 401–18.

King, Mervyn A. 1977. *Public Policy and the Corporation.* London: Chapman and Hall.

————. 1980. "Savings and Taxation." In C. A. Hughes and G. M. Heal, eds. *Public Policy and the Tax System.* London: Allen and Unwin.

Marceau, Nicolas, and Michael Smart. 2003. "Corporate Lobbying and Commitment Failure in Capital Taxation." *American Economic Review,* forthcoming.

Meade Committee. 1978. *The Structure and Reform of Direct Taxation.* London: Allen and Unwin.

Mirrlees, James A. 1971. "An Exploration in the Theory of Optimal Income Taxation." *Review of Economic Studies* 38 (2): 175–208.

Nava, Mario, Fred Schroyen, and Maurice Marchand. 1996. "Optimal Fiscal and Public Expenditure Policy in a Two-Class Economy." *Journal of Public Economics* 61 (1): 119–37.

Organisation for Economic Co-operation and Development. 1994. *Taxation of New Financial Instruments*. Paris: OECD.

Poddar, Satya. 2003. "Consumption Taxes: The Role of the Value-Added Tax" (chapter 12, this volume).

Poddar, Satya, and Morley English. 1997. "Taxation of Financial Services under a Value-Added Tax." *National Tax Journal* 50 (1): 89–111.

Poterba, James M., and Julio J. Rotemberg. 1990. "Inflation and Taxation with Optimizing Governments." *Journal of Money, Credit and Banking* 22 (1): 1–18.

Sandmo, Agnar. 1979. "A Note on the Neutrality of the Cash Flow Corporate Tax." *Economic Letters* 4: 173–76.

———. 1985. "The Effects of Taxation on Savings and Risk-Taking." In Alan J. Auerbach and Martin Feldstein, eds. *Handbook of Public Economics*, Vol. 1 Amsterdam: North-Holland.

Sen, Amartya. 1985. *Commodities and Capabilities*. Amsterdam: North-Holland.

Stiglitz, Joseph. E. 1983. "Some Aspects of the Taxation of Capital Gains." *Journal of Public Economics* 21 (2): 257–94.

———. 1987. "Pareto Efficient and Optimal Taxation and the New New Welfare Economics." In Alan J. Auerbach and Martin Feldstein, eds. *Handbook of Public Economics*, Vol. 2. Amsterdam: North-Holland.

Sunley, Emil. 2003. "Corporate Income Tax Treatment of Loan-Loss Reserves" (chapter 9, this volume).

Thuronyi, V. 2001. "Taxation of New Financial Instruments." *Tax Notes International* (October 15): 261–73.

Vickrey, W. 1939. "Averaging Income for Income Tax Purposes." *Journal of Political Economy* 47 (3): 379–97.

Warren, A. C. Jr. 1993. "Financial Contract Innovation and Income Tax Policy." *Harvard Law Review* 107 (2): 460–92.

3

Taxation of Banks:
Modeling the Impact

Ramon Caminal

In most countries banking activity is subject to general taxation (personal and corporate income taxes), but often banking services are treated differently by tax authorities. In some cases, they enjoy favorable treatment. For instance, in the European Union most financial services are exempt from value-added tax (VAT), ostensibly for technical reasons (although the issue is currently under consideration). In other cases, banking services are subject to special taxes, like unremunerated reserve requirements. Unremunerated reserve requirements are an implicit form of bank-specific taxation that work in combination with inflation.

Taxation of banks is of particular interest for various reasons. First, banks are financial intermediaries that perform unique and crucial functions—although in many countries they are subject to increasing competition from investment funds and security markets. Second, banks are heavily regulated and monitored, which reduces the administrative costs of some forms of taxation; at the same time they are subsidized through under-priced deposit insurance and bailouts of insolvent banks. Third, banks often enjoy some monopoly power, especially in the household and small business sectors.

The goal of this chapter is to develop a theoretical framework to analyze the impact of various forms of taxation. The model is based on the modern theory of the banking firm and integrates in a unified framework the most important aspects of banking activity; in particular, monitoring, transaction services, and asset transformation. It is important to understand how each of these functions is affected by taxation. Banks reduce informational asymmetries with their loan applicants[1] by ex ante screening, interim monitoring, and ex post verification of financial returns. Moreover, banks develop long-term, customer-specific relationships that allow them to reuse the information acquired in previous transactions. Bank deposits play an important role in the payment system. They can easily be converted into cash or directly used in transactions through checks, credit, and debit cards. Depositors can also set up automatic payments. Some of these transaction services may be separately priced, but to a large extent they are implicitly paid by accepting a rate of return on bank accounts below those of alternative assets. Finally, banks and other financial intermediaries perform an important asset transformation function. In particular, bank assets are riskier and less liquid than their liabilities. The model presented here abstracts from risk diversification and (as for example with Diamond and Dybvig 1983) focuses exclusively on liquidity insurance.

The model developed in this chapter focuses on how efficiently savings are channeled into various investment opportunities. Thus it takes as given the amount of funds. In this sense it is a partial equilibrium model. The simplest version of the model is presented in the second section and analyzed in the third and fourth sections, and assumes perfect competition in both the deposit and the loan market. A crucial determinant of the incidence of bank taxation is whether the deposit and loan segments are separable: that is, whether deposit and loan interest rates are independently determined. Under conditions of separability, a tax on deposits does not affect lending, and vice versa a tax on bank loans leaves the level of deposits unchanged. The framework developed in this chapter makes heavy use of the separability hypothesis. In particular, it is assumed that banks can invest in a safe asset with an exogenous rate of return. The chapter revisits the separability hypothesis and argues that in the real world the necessary conditions to obtain separability may be violated quite often. However, simultaneous deviations may partially compensate one another, and as a result a model assuming separability may still be a useful benchmark.

Recent improvements in information technology and innovations in financial contracting have increasingly challenged traditional banking activities.[1] The chapter considers explicitly the effects of increasing competition from investment funds and more efficient security markets. Investment funds are characterized as perfect substitutes of banks in the asset transformation function. This is extreme, but it captures the idea that the implications of asset pooling by any large financial intermediary are similar. Another caveat is that some investment funds are already providing a limited amount of transaction services in some countries. If investment funds manage to develop such services, then bank deposits and investment fund holdings will become almost perfect substitutes. In some less developed countries the main source of competition for banks comes from the informal credit sector. Some of the effects may be analogous to those discussed in the chapter, although the normative implications are likely to be very different.

The chapter then turns to imperfect competition. Banks' market power introduces two new effects. First, the distortionary effects of taxes and market power are compounded, and as a result even a small tax rate is likely to have a negative first-order effect on welfare. However, the distortions associated with market power decrease with the ability of banks to price discriminate, which is likely to be significant in the loan market. Second, taxes may at least partially cut into banks' economic profits, and hence reduce the tax burden of investors (which, in a more general model, would reduce the distortion on savings decisions). However, economic profits may prevent banks from taking excessive portfolio risk. The chapter then discusses whether taxes may induce higher risk-taking by altering the rewards to prudent behavior.

Taxation and regulation are shown to interact in various ways. On the one hand, corporate income taxation cannot be exclusively a tax on pure economic profits if capital requirements are binding. On the other hand, if new taxes induce excessive risk-taking behavior, then existing solvency regulation must be strengthened in order to preserve the stability of the banking system. Some of these issues are analyzed in the chapter.

The Benchmark Model

The economy is populated by four types of agents: investors, entrepreneurs, banks, and nonbank financial intermediaries (investment funds). Transactions take place in three consecutive periods, indexed by t, $t = 0, 1, 2$. There is a continuum of ex ante identical investors with mass equal to N, which is assumed to be sufficiently large. Each investor has an endowment of one unit at time $t = 0$. Next, at time $t = 1$ she finds out whether she is impatient—that is, she must consume then and obtain a utility of $u(c_1)$—or she is patient—that is, she must consume at $t = 2$, and obtain utility $u(c_2)$.

Investors' type (whether patient or impatient) is assumed to be the agent's private information. The probability of the two events is, for simplicity, one-half.[2] Ex ante preferences on consumption of real goods are given by expected utility:

$$U = u\,(c_1) + \rho u\,(c_2)$$

where ρ is a positive discount factor and u is a concave (and twice differentiable) function.

Investors have access to the following safe investment technologies:

• Short-term investment: Each unit of investment at $t = 0$ yields one unit at $t = 1$. The same technology can be operated between periods 1 and 2.

• Long-term investment: Each unit of investment at $t = 0$ yields $R > 1$ at $t = 2$. The investment project can be liquidated at $t = 1$, in which case the unit return is Z.

ASSUMPTION 1:

$$R^{-1} < Z < 1$$

In order to simplify the presentation, the time discount factor is fixed:

ASSUMPTION 2:

$$\rho = R^{-1}$$

There is a continuum of heterogeneous entrepreneurs, with mass equal to 1, who have no funds but have access to two types of projects (safe and risky). They can invest one unit in the safe project at $t = 0$ and obtain X at $t = 2$. Alternatively, they can invest one unit at $t = 0$ in the risky project and obtain at $t = 2$ a random financial return

$$\begin{cases} X \text{ with probability } p \\ 0 \text{ with probability } 1 - p \end{cases}$$

plus a non-financial return (private benefit) of $\phi\,(1 - \rho)$.

Entrepreneurs differ only in their probability of success of the risky project, ρ, which is common knowledge. Entrepreneurs are distributed over the interval [0,1] according to the probability density function $h\,(p)$. Let $H\,(p)$ denote the cumulative distribution. Finally, entrepreneurs are assumed to be risk-neutral and wish to consume only at time $t = 2$. In other words, their objective function is the expected net return at time $t = 2$.

ASSUMPTION 3:

$$R + \phi > X > R > \phi$$

As shown below, the first inequality implies that in the absence of monitoring entrepreneurs prefer the inefficient (risky) project. From the second inequality it follows that the safe project has a positive net present value (NPV), which is always higher than the NPV of the risky project (third inequality). However, if p is sufficiently close to one then the risky project also has a positive NPV.

Banks are assumed to perform three functions: monitoring, transaction services, and liquidity transformation. That is, first, they can monitor entrepreneurs, which reduces agency costs in the credit market. Second, they provide transactions services to investors, such as routine payments and check writing. Third, they offer investors liquidity insurance.

More precisely, banks can monitor an entrepreneur, which involves a cost $m > 0$ (measured in time $t = 2$ units) independently of p, and induce the entrepreneur to choose the efficient project (the safe project). Thus bank monitoring sets an upper bound on the size of the agency cost of all entrepreneurs. This is a bit drastic, since in equilibrium all entrepreneurs get credit independently of market conditions. The purpose here is to focus on the choice between bank and nonbank financing rather than on entrepreneurs' credit availability.

Banks' liabilities are also special. As discussed below, banks can provide a better time structure of returns than direct investment. Moreover, by incurring a cost μ per unit of deposit they provide transaction services. These are valued by investors according to the function $v(D)$, where D is the level of bank deposits and v is a concave (and twice differentiable) function, with $v(0) = 0$, $v'(0) = \infty$, and $v'(D) > 0$ if and only if $D < 1$. The utility derived from transaction services enters additively in investors' utility function. Thus investors' ex ante preferences can be written as:[3]

(3.1) $$U = u(c_1) + \rho u(c_2) + v(D)$$

Notice that under such a formulation the supply of deposits will depend not only on the relative return of deposits with respect to alternative assets, but also on investors' income. This is analogous to the interest rate and income effects in the money demand function, which has broad empirical support.

The Walrasian Outcome in the Absence of Taxes and Investment Funds

This section analyzes the equilibrium of a Walrasian system with and without banks.

Direct Investment

First consider the Walrasian equilibrium under direct investment. That is, suppose that there exist perfectly competitive markets to trade the claims on various investment projects, both at $t = 0$ and at $t = 1$. For simplicity, assume that investors pay a cost d at time $t = 1$ (measured in current units) if they sell a claim on one unit delivered at time $t = 2$, but do not incur any transaction cost when purchasing assets at time $t = 0$. This is meant to capture the idea that the cost of acquiring an asset is relatively small but frequent transactions in the secondary market are relatively more costly. One important implication of the above assumption is that at time $t = 0$ investors can perfectly diversify their portfolios and hence act as risk-neutral agents when lending to a particular entrepreneur. Of course, this is extreme. The goal here is to concentrate on the term structure of assets (liquidity insurance) and completely abstract from asset risk. On the other hand, the entrepreneur incurs a nonpecuniary cost (measured in time $t = 2$ units) of f ($< m$), when collecting one unit of funds in the market for securities.

Given the structure of returns and because of limited liability, security design is not an issue in this model. Thus without loss of generality one can assume that entrepreneurs can issue a bond that promises to repay r^b in case of success. If they invest in the risky asset they obtain $p(X - r^b) + (1 - p)\phi$, and if they invest the safe asset they get $X - r^b$. Given Assumption 3 and since investors require $r^b \geq R$, then entrepreneurs of all types prefer to invest in the risky project.

Competition among investors implies that the net benefit from lending to entrepreneurs instead of investing in long-term technology is zero: that is,

$$r^b = \frac{R}{p}$$

Because of limited liability, $r^b \leq X$. As a result, only those entrepreneurs with $p \geq p_o$ can obtain financing in the securities market, where p_o is given by:[4]

$$\frac{R}{p_o} = X$$

Given that entrepreneurs' projects have a two-period maturity, those with $p \leq p_o$ will obtain financing—the market will clear—provided investors wish to invest a sufficient amount in assets with such maturity. Similarly, since the liquidation value of entrepreneurs' projects at time $t = 1$ is zero, it is necessary to check that the secondary market works properly. These issues are discussed in the appendix.

Turn now to investors' decisions. At time $t = 0$ investors must decide how to distribute their unit endowment between short-term assets, $1 - I$, and long-term assets, I. At time $t = 1$ there are potential gains from trade. Patient consumers would like to use the proceeds from short-term assets to buy assets that mature at time $t = 2$, and impatient consumers may be willing to sell their long-term assets. Let q be the price paid by patient consumers at time $t = 1$ for a claim on one unit at time $t = 2$. Hence sellers obtain $q(1 - d)$ per unit. At time $t = 1$ patient consumers are willing to participate in the secondary market provided the implicit return on those assets is not below their alternative investment opportunity (the short-term investment technology). Thus patient consumers are willing to buy the claims sold by impatient consumers provided $q \leq 1$. Similarly, impatient consumers are willing to sell their claims on second period returns only if they find it profitable: that is, if $q(1 - d) R \geq Z$. The following assumption simplifies the analysis considerably.

ASSUMPTION 4:

$$(1 - d)R = Z$$

Under Assumption 4, impatient consumers trade if and only if $q \geq 1$. As a result, the equilibrium price is $q = 1$. At time $t = 0$ investors are able to anticipate the equilibrium price of the secondary market. Hence their consumption profile as a function of their portfolio is given by:

(3.2)
$$c_1 = 1 - I + q(1 - d)RI = 1 - (1 - Z)I$$
$$c_2 = \frac{1 - I}{q} + RI = 1 + (R - 1)I$$

Investors choose I in order to maximize equation 3.1 subject to equation 3.2. The solution is fully characterized by the first-order condition:

$$\frac{u'(c_1)}{u'(c_2)} = \frac{1 - R^{-1}}{1 - Z}$$

Given Assumption 1, $c_1 < c_2$, which implies that $I > 0$.

The assumption about positive transaction costs in the secondary market is not innocuous. In case $d = 0$, then the equilibrium in the secondary market is $q = R^{-1}$ and as a result $c_1 = 1$ and $c_2 = R$. It turns out, as pointed out by Jacklin (1987), that in this case banks cannot improve the market allocation (they cannot provide liquidity insurance). Diamond (1997) and Holmstrom and Tirole (1998) present more sophisticated models of liquidity with implications analogous to the current formulation.

The Role of Banks

Now introduce banks into the picture. They intermediate between investors, on the one hand, and safe investment technologies and entrepreneurs, on the other. Thus when considering lending to entrepreneurs, their opportunity cost of funds is R. The distinctive feature of banks on the asset side is that they can monitor entrepreneurs (at a cost) and induce the efficient project selection. In other words, bank monitoring eliminates any potential inefficiencies originated by entrepreneurs' moral hazard problem. Alternatively, a large literature has focused on a different type of informational failure in the credit market: adverse selection (hidden types), instead of moral hazard (hidden actions). Thus this characterization of the role of banks in reducing informational asymmetries is clearly limited, although it suffices to illustrate how various forms of taxation may reduce banks' contribution to economic efficiency in the credit market (through the disintermediation effect).

Competition among banks implies that a loan contract will require the entrepreneur to choose the safe project and pay back at time $t = 2$ an interest rate:

(3.3) $r^l = R + m$

Clearly, one must assume that monitoring is economically feasible:

ASSUMPTION 5:

$$X > R + m$$

As a result, an entrepreneur with a probability of success on the risky project p, will apply to a bank loan instead of issuing bonds provided the following condition holds:

$$X - r^1 \geq p(X - r^b) + \phi(1 - p) - f$$

The left-hand side is the expected return of borrowing from a bank. In such a case the entrepreneur expects to be forced to choose the safe project. The right-hand side is the expected return of borrowing on the securities market (which is feasible if and only if $p \geq p_o$). Given the equilibrium values of r^1 and r^b such a condition can be written as $p \geq p^*$, where p^* is given by:

$$P^* = 1 - \frac{m - f}{X - \phi}$$

For simplicity, assume that the entrepreneur who is indifferent between the two sources of credit is not constrained in the securities market: that is

ASSUMPTION 6:

$$p^* > p_0$$

Thus entrepreneurs with a low value of p (high agency cost in the securities market) choose to borrow from banks, while entrepreneurs with a value of p close to one (low agency cost) prefer to borrow on the securities market. Notice that banks make credit feasible for entrepreneurs with $p < p_0$ (those who are excluded from the bond market).

Now turn to the liability side of a bank's balance sheet. Bank deposits provide transaction services and on top of this they are able to offer a better time profile of financial returns than direct investment. In particular, a bank deposit could offer investors a return r_1^d if funds are withdrawn at time $t = 1$, and a return r_2^d if they are withdrawn at time $t = 2$. Thus a patient consumer withdrawing at time $t = 1$ can invest the funds withdrawn in the short-term investment technology (or buy claims in the secondary market). Hence, banks must take into account investors' incentive compatibility constraint:

(3.4) $$r_1^d \leq r_2^d$$

Banks do not need to transact in the secondary market because there is no aggregate uncertainty and they can exploit the law of large numbers. Since banks anticipate that half of their depositors will withdraw their funds at time $t = 1$, they need to invest a proportion β, of their deposits in long-term assets, and a proportion $1 - \beta$, in short-term assets, in such a way that:

(3.5)
$$\frac{1}{2}(r_1^d + \mu) = 1 - \beta$$
$$\frac{1}{2}(r_2^d + \mu) = \beta R$$

Eliminating β in the above equations produces the set of all possible combinations of r_1^d and r_2^d that can be offered to investors:

(3.6)
$$r_1^d = \frac{r_2^d}{R} = 2 - \mu \frac{1 + R}{R}$$

If investors decide to deposit in a bank a fraction D of their endowment and to invest directly a fraction $1 - D$, then they can enjoy the following consumption profile:

(3.7)
$$c_1 = r_1^d D + (1 - D)[1 - (1 - Z)I]$$
$$c_2 = r_2^d D + (1 - D)[1 + (R - 1)I]$$

Thus in equilibrium, bank deposit contracts will be part of the solution to the following optimization problem: choose (r_1^d, r_2^d, D, I) in order to maximize equation 3.1 subject to equations 3.4, 3.6, and 3.7 and the feasibility constraint $D \leq 1$.

Notice that the market allocation implies a higher return in the second period than in the first. However, in the absence of the incentive compatibility constraint, banks would offer a structure of returns such that consumption in both periods is the same, which implies that the deposit rate in the first period is higher than in the second.

Clearly, this violates the incentive compatibility constraint (equation 3.4). Hence, in equilibrium:

(3.8)
$$r_1^d = r_2^d \equiv r^M - \mu \equiv \frac{2R}{1 + R} - \mu$$

The first-order condition that characterizes the optimal amount of deposits can be written as:

(3.9)
$$u'(c_1)\frac{R - Z}{R - 1}(r^M - \mu - 1) + v'(D) = 0$$

By pooling assets, banks can in principle offer investors a time profile of financial returns that dominates that of direct investment, since banks do not need to trade in the secondary market or liquidate projects too early. Moreover, deposits provide transaction services. On the negative side, those services are costly, which implies that the overall return on deposits must be lower. Thus one must distinguish two cases depending on the costs of providing transaction services:

• If $r^M - \mu - 1 > 0$, then the optimal amount of deposits is $D = 1$. In this case, deposits dominate direct investment.

• If $r^M - \mu - 1 < 0$, then $D < 1$. In this case, deposits do not dominate direct investment. The cost of providing transaction services is sufficiently large to reduce the level of financial returns, which leaves room for a positive amount of direct investment.

Bank Taxation in the Absence of Investment Funds

This section examines the effects of taxation under perfect competition among banks but in the absence of nonbank financial intermediaries. It looks at five types of taxation: on deposits, loans, value-added, investors' capital income, and banks' corporate income. By focusing on one type of taxes at a time, one can study the effects of "differential" taxation. Since this chapter pays little attention to normative issues, it does not discuss in detail how to achieve tax neutrality with respect to portfolio allocation.

A Tax on Deposits

The structure of the model involves separability between loans and deposits. In particular, loan interest rates or credit availability is not affected by changes in the deposit market. The reason is that banks' opportunity cost of funds in the loan market is the (exogenous) return on the long-term investment technology, and not the deposit rate. Suppose that the government sets a proportional tax on the gross interest rate on deposits, τ^d.[5] Clearly, such a tax will not change the structure of pre-tax deposit rates: $r_1^d = r_2^d = r^M - \mu$. However, investors will take into account such a tax when deciding the amount of deposits, since the after-tax return is now $(1 - \tau^d)r_t^d$, $t = 1, 2$. One must distinguish between two cases:

• If $r^M - \mu - 1 > 0$, then deposits dominate direct investment, and as a result a small τ^d is nondistortionary. If the tax rate is sufficiently large, then the effects are analogous to those of the second case.

• If $r^M - \mu - 1 < 0$, then investors face a trade-off between a higher (composite) return of direct investment and the transaction services provided by bank deposits. In this case, the optimal level of deposits is given by the first-order condition of the representative investor's optimization problem (adaptation of equation 3.9):

$$u'(c_1) = \frac{R-Z}{R-1}\left[(1-\tau^d)(r^M - \mu) - 1\right] + v'(D) = 0$$

Clearly,

$$\frac{dD}{d\tau^d} < 0$$

Taxes affect the supply of deposits through two different channels. A higher tax rate increases the opportunity cost of deposits (the difference between the rates of return of deposits and direct investment). It also reduces investors' disposable income. Both effects reduce the supply of deposits. Notice that the effect of τ^d on deposits depends on the second derivative of functions u (.) and v (.) This allows one to sign such a derivative, but also suggests that it is very difficult a priori to determine how changes in various parameters influence the distortionary effect of taxes. The next proposition summarizes these results.

PROPOSITION 1.   *Under perfect competition in banking and in the absence of investment funds, a tax on deposits has no effect on the loan market. If the costs of providing transaction services are sufficiently small, so that bank deposits dominate direct investment, then a small tax on deposits does not affect the amount of deposits. If the costs of providing transaction services are sufficiently large so that bank deposits do not dominate direct investment, then a tax on deposits reduces the amount of deposits and increases direct investment. Thus two functions of banks are jeopardized: provision of transaction services and liquidity insurance.*

It is immediately clear that even in the second case (deposits do not dominate direct investment), a small tax rate on deposits has only a second-order effect on total welfare, since the market allocation is efficient.

A Tax on Bank Loans

Suppose that the government sets a proportional tax on the gross return on bank loans, τ^l. Let r^l denote the after-tax loan rate. The competitive rate is independent of taxation and hence entrepreneurs must pay $r^l/(1 - \tau^l)$. Therefore, the threshold value of p, p^*, is now given by:

(3.10) $$p^*(\tau) = 1 - \frac{m + \tau^l R - f(1 - \tau^l)}{(1 - \tau^l)(X - \phi)}$$

Thus

$$\frac{dp^*(\tau^l)}{d\tau^l} < 0$$

Under separability, a tax on bank loans does not have any effect on the deposit rate or the provision of transaction services and liquidity insurance. However, it raises the cost of loans, which discourages entrepreneurs away from information-intensive financing and into unmonitored financing.

PROPOSITION 2.   *Under a perfectly competitive banking system and in the absence of investment funds, a proportional tax on bank loans raises loan rates and induces some entrepreneurs to switch from bank to nonbank financing (the level of bank monitoring decreases). It does not have any effect on the deposit interest rate or the level of deposits.*

It has been argued that bank monitoring creates a positive informational externality on the securities market (Besanko and Kanatas 1993).[6] This would not alter the qualitative results, but it would amplify the distortionary effects of taxation.[7]

A Tax on Banks' Value-Added

Consider a tax on banks' value-added under the cash flow approach.[8] Suppose that entrepreneurs are VAT-registered businesses, but depositors are not engaged in commercial activities. At times $t = 0$ and $t = 1$ banks have zero net cash flow and hence they pay no tax. At time $t = 2$ their net cash flow is:

(3.11) $$CF = r^l L + RB - \frac{1}{2}(r^d + \mu)D$$

where L is the amount of loans and B is the amount of investment in the long-run technology (or bonds). Banks' feasibility constraint can be written as:

(3.12) $$L + B = \left[1 - \frac{1}{2}(r^d + \mu)\right]D$$

Using equation 3.12, equation 3.11 can be rewritten:

$$(3.13) \qquad CF = (r^l - R)L + \left[\frac{R+1}{2}(r^M - \mu - r^d) + \mu \right]D$$

In the absence of taxes, r^l and r^d are given by equations 3.3 and 3.8. Substituting these equations into equation 3.13, it can be established that

$$CF = mL + \mu D$$

Notice that such a measure of banks' value-added captures only monitoring and transaction services, but disregards liquidity provision. This is because it has been assumed that asset transformation is costless.

Suppose that the government sets up a tax τ^v on banks' value-added. More specifically, value-added throughout the economy is already taxed at the rate τ^v, and the government lifts the exemption of banking services from general VAT. Under perfect competition after-tax profits in both loans and deposits must be zero. This implies that the equilibrium loan rate is given by:

$$(3.14) \qquad r^l = R + \frac{m}{1 - \tau^v}$$

Similarly, the deposit rate in equilibrium can be written as:

$$r^d = r^M - \mu - \frac{2\tau^v \mu}{(R+1)(1 - \tau^v)}$$

Since the assumption has been made that depositors are outside the VAT system, this implies that lifting the exemption on banking services is equivalent to a tax on deposits. However, since the tax paid on loans reduces the borrowers' tax bill, the effect on the loan market is null. In order to check this last statement, simply notice that under the exemption, those entrepreneurs financed by loans obtain:

$$\pi^E = (X - r^l) - \tau^v X = (1 - \tau^v)X - R - m$$

If the exemption is lifted, then entrepreneurs get:

$$\pi^E = X - r^l - \tau^v(X - r^l + R)$$

The reason is that now entrepreneurs can reduce their tax bill by the amount $\tau(r^l - R)$.[9] Using equation 3.14, one can check that entrepreneurs' profits are identical in both regimes.

PROPOSITION 3. *If borrowers are VAT-registered firms and depositors are not engaged in commercial activities, then lifting the exemption of banking services in the base of the general VAT is equivalent to setting a tax on deposits, with no impact on the loan market.*

A Tax on Gross Interest Income

Consider a proportional tax on investors' gross interest income, τ^Y. The tax base of such a tax includes gross interest from deposits as well as the gross return of direct investment. Clearly, the relative return of deposits and direct investment remains unaffected. However, such a tax reduces the supply of deposits through the income effect. More specifically, if $(r^M - \mu) - 1 < 0$, then the supply of deposits is given by equation 3.9:

$$u'(c_1)\frac{R-L}{R-1}(r^M - \mu - 1) + v'(D) = 0$$

The effect of such a tax comes through c_1. In particular, a higher tax rate reduces disposable income, which implies a reduction in both consumption of real goods and the demand for banks' transaction services (reduces the supply of deposits). Thus we have the following result:

PROPOSITION 4. *Provided that deposits do not dominate direct investment, a tax on interest income reduces the amount of deposits.*

Thus as long as the income effect in the supply of deposits is significant, general taxes like the personal income tax may also have an effect on financial intermediaries.[10]

Banks' Corporate Income Taxes

A complete analysis of the impact of corporate taxation on banking activity requires a satisfactory theory of banks' capital structure. Unfortunately, such a theory is not yet available. The role of banks as intermediaries implies that the bank will tend to have little inside capital. However, if bankers are subject to moral hazard and perfect diversification is not feasible, then equity capital held by insiders provides an incentive for the insiders to do monitoring (Holmstrom and Tirole 1997). In any case, in the real world banks tend to hold relatively low levels of capital[11] and as a result capital requirements are frequently binding.

This model is not able to deal with security design issues, and hence debt and equity are indistinguishable. Nevertheless, it can still provide a preliminary analysis of the effects of corporate income taxation whenever capital requirements are binding. Suppose that banks hold a ratio of capital to loans equal to η, $K = \eta L$.[12] Since aggregate risk or corporate control is not an issue in the present framework, and equity must have the same maturity as loans, potential shareholders will require a rate of return at time $t = 2$ equal to R.[13] Finally, let banks' corporate tax rate be τ^c. Since banks offer depositors a constant interest rate and invest in the short-run technology the exact amount in order to pay impatient depositors, then banks' economic profits can be written as:

$$(3.15) \qquad \pi^B = (r^l - m)L + RB - \frac{r^d + \mu}{2}D - \frac{R}{1 - \tau^c}\eta L$$

Notice that the cost of equity for the bank is $R/(1 - \tau^c)$. Banks' feasibility constraint is:

$$(3.16) \qquad D = \frac{r^d + \mu}{2}D + B + (1 - \eta)L$$

The first term of the right-hand side is the amount invested in the short-run technology. The rest is invested in the long-run technology, B, or in loans, $(1 - \eta)L$ (an amount ηL of loans is financed by equity). Plugging equation 3.16 into equation 3.15 and rearranging:

$$\pi^B = L\left[r^l - m - R\left(1 - \eta + \frac{\eta}{1 - \tau^c}\right)\right] + D\frac{R + 1}{2}(r^M - r^d - \mu)$$

Under perfect competition (and because of separability) banks make zero profits in both deposits and loans. As a result, deposit rates are unaffected by corporate income taxes, $r^d = r^M - \mu$, but loan rates are not:

$$r^l = \left[(1 - \eta) + \frac{\eta}{1 - \tau^c}\right]R + m$$

This leads to the next proposition.

PROPOSITION 5. *If capital requirements are binding, and under perfect competition, a tax on banks' corporate income is equivalent to* *a tax on bank loans. Hence, it raises the loan interest rate (and reduces the amount of loans) but does not affect the deposit rate.*[14]

The result that a corporate income tax is a tax on loans may be more general than it appears. Suppose that capital requirements are not binding but banks' inside capital provides positive incentives to monitor borrowers (as in Holmstrom and Tirole 1997). Then loans and capital are also complementary. Similarly a tax on corporate income would also fall on loans.

Competition from Alternative Financial Arrangements

This section asks to what extent the presence of alternative financial arrangements affects the previous analysis. It focuses on the one hand, on the appearance of other financial intermediaries (mutual and pension funds) that offer investors imperfect substitutes of bank deposits; and, on the other hand, on the impact of more efficient markets for securities, which allow an increasing number of firms to consider issuing bonds as an alternative to bank loans.

Investment Funds

In principle, any large intermediary can supply investors the same asset transformation function offered by banks. Asset pooling allows intermediaries to issue financial contracts with lower risk and higher liquidity. This is the main role of mutual funds and pensions funds. In this dimension, banks are no longer special. Accordingly, in the context of the current model, investment funds are characterized as follows: they can supply the same liquidity services as banks (in particular, they can offer a constant return) but they cannot monitor entrepreneurs or offer investors transaction services. Such a characterization overlooks various observations. First, money market funds in the United States have begun to provide some transaction services.[15] Second, investment funds have been reported in some instances to monitor the management of corporations where they hold stock. Third, various intermediaries seem to specialize in issuing different varieties of financial contracts. Therefore, the proposed characterization must be considered only as a first approximation.

In particular, it is assumed that perfectly competitive investment funds can hold the same portfolio in terms of maturity structure as banks and thus offer investors liquidity insurance. In principle, investment funds (under perfect competition) should offer contracts that allow investors a unit return of r_1^m if they withdraw their funds at time $t = 1$, and r_2^m if they wait until time $t = 2$. The previous analysis of equilibrium deposits leads to the conclusion that perfectly competitive investment funds will offer:

$$r_1^M = r_2^M = r^m \equiv \frac{2R}{1+R}$$

As discussed above, such a structure of returns dominates direct investment. As a result, banks face tighter competition. In the absence of taxes, investors can achieve the following consumption structure as a function of their portfolio:

(3.17)
$$c_1 = r_1^d D + r^M (1 - D)$$
$$c_2 = r_2^d D + r^M (1 - D)$$

Thus the equilibrium deposit contract will be part of the solution to the following optimization problem: choose (r_1^d, r_2^d, D) to maximize equation 3.1 subject to equation 3.17. As expected, deposit interest rates are also constant over time:

$$r_1^d = r_2^d = r^m - \mu = \frac{2R}{I+R} - \mu$$

Thus consumption is the same in both periods, $c_1 = c_2 = c$, and the optimal supply of deposits is given by:

(3.18)
$$-u'(c)\frac{1+R}{R}\mu + v'(D) = 0$$

where

$$c = r^M - \mu D$$

Now the level of deposits can be compared in the absence and in the presence of investment funds (equations 3.9 and 3.18). If $\mu < (R - 1)/(R + 1)$ then bank deposits dominate direct investment, but do not dominate investment fund holdings. Hence competition from investment funds unambiguously reduces the level of deposits. The reason is that without direct investments, investors are at a corner solution $(D = 1)$, but competition from investment funds place investors in an interior solution $(D < 1)$. However, if $\mu > (R - 1)/(R + 1)$, then the effect of investment funds on bank deposits is ambiguous. If the first-order condition equation 3.18 is evaluated at the level of deposits without investment funds, then c_1 is larger, which implies that $u'(c_1)$ is lower. However, the relative price of deposits in terms of consumption is higher. That is,

$$\frac{1+R}{R}\mu > \frac{R-Z}{R-1}(1-r^M+\mu)$$

Hence in this case, the effect of investment funds on deposits is ambiguous. The intuition is straightforward. On the one hand, the presence of investment funds raises the opportunity cost of holding deposits (the price effect). On the other hand, investment funds expand the set of feasible financial returns (income effect). The price effect works against deposits, but the income effect works in the opposite direction.[16] The effect of investment funds on bank deposits is summarized in the following proposition:

PROPOSITION 6. *The presence of investment funds unambiguously reduces the level of bank deposits, if the latter dominates direct investment. The effect on bank deposits is ambiguous, if the latter does not dominate direct investment.*

Having analyzed the effect on the tax base, now turn to the impact of investment funds on the distortionary effects of taxation. Consider again the effect of a tax on deposits. Under competition from investment funds, the amount of deposits will be given by:

$$u'(c_1)\frac{1+R}{R}\left[\tau^d\frac{2R}{1+R}+(1-\tau^d)\mu\right]=v'(D)$$

where

$$c_1=\frac{2R}{1+R}-D\left[\tau^d\frac{2R}{1+R}+(1-\tau^d)\mu\right]$$

Clearly, $dD/d\tau^d < 0$.

Notice that the size of the distortionary effect depends among other things on the degree of convexity of the utility functions—on the sign of $u'''(.)$ and $v'''(.)$. Hence it is rather difficult to make statements based on theoretical arguments about how competition from investment funds influences the effect of taxes.

Because of separability, competition from investment funds does not affect the impact of a tax on loans.

PROPOSITION 7.   In the presence of investment funds, a tax on deposits unambiguously reduces the level of deposits. Provided that
bank deposits do not dominate direct investment, the effect of a deposit tax may be higher or lower than in the case where bank deposits only compete with direct investment. Bank-specific taxes can
reduce only monitoring and provision of transaction services, since
liquidity insurance is also provided by banks' competitors.

More Efficient Security Markets

On the asset side, banks in some industrial countries are increasingly facing tighter competition from security markets (development
of commercial paper market). This could translate into a decrease
in the transaction costs incurred by entrepreneurs when they borrow on security markets (a reduction in f).

In order to study the effect of a change in f on the credit market
equilibrium, refer again to equation 3.10:

$$p^*(\tau^l) = 1 - \frac{m + \tau^l R - f(1 - \tau^l)}{(1 - \tau^l)(X - \phi)}$$

Thus the effect of a reduction in transaction costs on the entrepreneurs' choice of the source of funds is simply:

$$\frac{dp^*(\tau^l)}{df} = \frac{1}{X - \phi} > 0$$

Unsurprisingly, a reduction in transaction costs will reduce the number of entrepreneurs who choose to apply for a bank loan instead
of issuing securities. What is less obvious is the effect of f on the impact of taxes. Notice that:

$$\frac{d^2 p^*}{d\tau^l df} = 0$$

That is, the level of f does not affect the impact of taxes on the
threshold level p^*. Hence the impact of f on the size of the distortion caused by taxes depends exclusively on the distribution of entrepreneurs: that is, on the shape of $h\,(p)$.

It could be reasonable to expect that, in the relevant range,
$h'(p^*) < 0$. That is, if the securities market is inefficient (f large), then
p^* is close to 1, and hence the number of firms borrowing on the
securities market is small. Moreover, a small tax would reduce the

threshold but would induce only a few additional entrepreneurs to switch from bank lending to unmonitored lending. However, if transaction costs are very low, then the threshold level p^* could fall in a region where the density of entrepreneurs is substantially higher. As a result, a tax would have a larger impact on bank lending. Although reasonable, this was only a conjecture on the shape of the distribution of entrepreneurs on the relevant dimension. To summarize:

PROPOSITION 8. *As security markets become more efficient, the level of bank loans falls as more firms choose to obtain their funds in the security markets. The distortionary effect of taxes may increase or decrease, although the former appears more likely.*

Taxing Imperfectly Competitive Banks

Banks seem to enjoy some degree of market power, at least in the household and small business sectors.[17] Monopoly power creates distortions in the allocation of resources, provided banks can neither perfectly price discriminate across customers nor offer nonlinear prices. Price discrimination seems particularly likely in the loan market, since rates are individually tailored. This section examines how market power and taxes interact. It considers two polar cases. The first assumes that banks enjoy market power in the deposit market but cannot offer nonlinear prices (depositors are identical). The second assumes that banks enjoy market power in the loan market and can perfectly price discriminate (the loan size is exogenous).

Monopoly Power in the Deposit Market

This subsection extends the model above to allow for monopoly power in the deposit market. Thus banks compete not only with one another but with a perfectly competitive investment fund industry. Suppose there are two banks, A and B (given the static nature of the game, it can easily be generalized to n banks). Preferences of the representative investor are given by:

$$U = u(c_1) + \rho u(c_2) + v(D_A, D_B)$$

where D_i is the amount of deposits in bank i, $i = A, B$. For simplicity, following Matutes and Vives (2000), the examination restricts itself to a quadratic function:

$$v(D_A, D_B) = \alpha(D_A + D_B) - \frac{1}{2}(D_A^2 + 2\lambda D_A D_B + D_B^2)$$

where λ represents the degree of substitutability between deposits at the two banks, $0 < \lambda < 1$. As $\lambda \to 0$ then the two goods become independent and banks become monopolists. In the opposite extreme, as $\lambda \to 1$ then the two goods become perfect substitutes and (under interest rate competition) the market for deposits becomes perfectly competitive.

The timing of the game is as follows. First, banks simultaneously set their deposit interest rates; next investors choose how much to deposit into each bank and in investment funds. It is easy to show (see appendix) that if bank owners face the same liquidity shocks as investors, then in equilibrium they offer deposit contracts with constant interest rates, $r_{i1}^d = r_{i2}^d = r_i^d$. Mutual funds also offer a constant interest rate: $r^M = 2R/(1 + R)$. As a result, investors' consumption profile is also constant over time: $c_1 = c_2 = c$. Thus given (r_A^d, r_B^d), investors choose (D_A, D_B) in order to maximize

$$U = \frac{1+R}{R}u(c) + v(D_A, D_B)$$

subject to

(3.19) $c = r^M - (r^M - i_A^d)D_A - (r^M - i_B^d)D_B$

where i^d denotes the after-tax deposit rate: that is, $i_i^d = (1 - r^d)r_i^d$. The supply of deposits is obtained by inverting the first-order conditions. For $i, j = A, B, i \neq j$.

$$D_i = a - b\Omega(r^M - i_i^d) + k\Omega(r^M - i_j^d)$$

$$a \equiv \frac{\alpha}{1+\lambda}$$

(3.20) $$b \equiv \frac{1}{1-\lambda^2}$$

$$k \equiv \frac{\lambda}{1-\lambda^2}$$

$$\Omega \equiv \frac{1+R}{R}u'(c)$$

For convenience it is assumed that banks are relatively large to be able to affect interest rates, but sufficiently small so as not to affect investors' consumption.[18] Thus the supply of deposits to bank i increases with the deposit rate set by bank i and decreases with the deposit rate set by the rival bank. In case of identical deposit rates, the

aggregate supply of deposits decreases with the difference between
the return on investment funds, r^M, and the return on deposits, i^d.
Such a margin depends on three factors: intermediation costs, μ,
taxes, and monopoly power. If the margin is zero, then investors put
all their funds in bank deposits. As the margin increases, the aggregate supply of deposits decreases. It is assumed that banks need to
set a positive deposit rate in order to attract a positive amount of
deposits: that is,[19]

ASSUMPTION 7:

$$a - (b - k)r^M \Omega < 0$$

If one plugs equation 3.20 into equation 3.19, then one gets consumption as a function of the deposit rates. In case of equal deposit
rates, $i_A^d = i_B^d \equiv i^d$,

$$c = r^M - 2(r^M - i^d)[a - (b - k)\Omega(r^M - i^d)]$$

Notice that a higher deposit rate may increase or decrease consumption. A higher deposit rate, on the one hand, reduces the opportunity cost of deposits and induces investors to demand more
transaction services at the cost of lower consumption (substitution
effect). On the other hand, it expands the feasible set that tends to
increase both the demand for transaction services and the demand
for real consumption (income effect).

The appendix also shows that if bank owners are subject to the
same liquidity shocks as investors (and have the same preferences
on financial returns), then the banks' expected return from deposits
is equal to $r^M = 2R/(1 + R)$. Thus given the interest rate set by other
banks, r_j^d, and the tax rate on deposits, τ^d, bank i chooses r_i^d in
order to maximize:

$$\pi_i = [r^M - \mu - r_i^d]D_i \, (r_i^d, r_j^d)$$

where $D_i \, (r_i^d, r_j^d)$ is given by equation 3.20.
Evaluating the first-order condition at the symmetric equilibrium:

$$(3.21) \qquad r^d = \frac{b(r^M - \mu)(1 - \tau^d) + (b - k)r^M - \frac{a}{\Omega}}{(2b - k)(1 - \tau^d)}$$

Notice that Ω depends on c, and hence on r^d. Therefore, the effect
of τ^d on r^d and i^d is complex. The direct effect of τ^d on i^d is clearly

negative. However, if a higher tax implies lower consumption, and hence higher Ω, the indirect effect has a positive sign. Nevertheless, the appendix shows that the direct effect always dominates the indirect effect and hence:

$$\frac{di^d}{d\tau^d} < 0$$

A direct implication of this result is that a tax on deposits reduces the level of deposits:

$$\frac{dD}{d\tau^d} < 0$$

Similarly, because of Assumption 7, the direct effect of τ on r^d is positive, but if a higher tax implies higher consumption the indirect effect is negative. In this case, the appendix shows, that for some parameter values the indirect effect dominates. In general, the direct effect dominates, provided the difference between the return on investment funds, r^M and the return on deposits, i^d, is not too large. In other words, it is more likely that $dr^d/d\tau^d > 0$ if intermediation costs and the tax rate are not too large, and banks do not have too much monopoly power.[20]

Deposit taxes unambiguously reduce investors' utility, since they reduce the after-tax deposit rate and hence investors' feasible set shrinks. The effect of taxes on banks' profits is less straightforward. In the case that $dr^d/d\tau^d > 0$, clearly taxes reduce bank profits since the supply of deposits faced by each bank shifts downward. In the case $dr^d/d\tau^d < 0$, there is the possibility that softer rate competition more than compensates the decrease in the aggregate supply of deposits, and as a result bank profits increase rather than decrease with taxes. However, this is highly unlikely, since taxes reduce deposit rates only if banks have sufficient monopoly power, so that the strategic complementarity effect (the reduction in rate competition) is not an important determinant of bank profits. In other words, for most parameter values a tax on deposits falls on both investors and banks.

PROPOSITION 9. *A tax on deposits unambiguously decreases the net interest rate received by investors and hence it reduces the amount of deposits. If the interest margin is not too large (which occurs as a combination of low intermediation cost, low tax rate, and low monopoly power) then it increases the deposit rate paid by banks. As a result, the burden of the tax is shared by investors and bank owners.*

Notice that in this case a small tax has a first-order effect on welfare since in the absence of taxation, the level of deposits is too low because of banks' monopoly power. However, the model may be abstracting from other important distortions. For instance, Whitesell (1992) argues that since one of the alternatives to bank deposits, cash, is typically taxed by inflation, in the absence of bank-specific taxes, the level of deposits may actually be too high.

Now turn to corporate income taxation. The analysis is similar to the case of perfect competition. In particular, monopoly rents after taxes are given by:

$$\pi^B = (1 - \tau^c)L\left[r^l - m - R\left(1 - \eta + \frac{\eta}{1 - \tau^c}\right)\right] + D\frac{R+1}{2}(r^M - r^d - \mu)$$

Therefore the incentives to set deposit rates are unchanged. Hence the corporate income tax is a tax on pure economic profits. At the same time, as discussed earlier, corporate income taxation distorts loan rates. In other words:

PROPOSITION 10. *If capital requirements are binding, a tax on banks' corporate income is equivalent to a tax on both economic profits and loans. Thus it raises the loan rate and reduces bank profits.*

Similarly, a value-added tax under the same conditions described above is a tax on deposits and hence it distorts the deposit rate. The burden of the tax tends to be shared by bank owners and investors.

Monopoly Power in the Loan Market

Suppose that all entrepreneurs have access to the securities market but the loan market is segmented in such a way that each entrepreneur can borrow only from a particular bank.[21] Thus banks do not interact with one another and the only limit to their market power comes from the securities market. As discussed, provided $p \geq p_0$ entrepreneurs can get credit in the securities market at the rate R/p and will select the risky project. Hence monopolistic banks will find it optimal to set an interest rate r^l that leaves the entrepreneur (with $p \geq p_0$) indifferent between borrowing from the bank or from the securities market:

$$(3.22) \qquad X - \frac{r^l}{1 - \tau} = p\left(X - \frac{R}{p}\right) + \phi(1 - p) - f$$

That is,

$$\frac{r^l}{1-\tau} = (1-p)(X-\phi) + R + f$$

provided such loan rate is above the average cost, $r^l \geq R + m$.[22] In other words, a bank lends to entrepreneurs at the rate given by equation 3.22, if and only if $p_0 \leq p \leq p^*$, where p^* is given by

$$p^* = 1 - \frac{\tau R + m - (1-\tau)f}{(1-\tau)(X-\phi)}$$

(3.23)

Notice that equations 3.10 and 3.23 are equivalent. Since banks can price discriminate (to the same extent that markets do) then monopoly power does not involve any additional distortion and affects only the distribution of surplus between banks and entrepreneurs. Taxes have the same distortionary effects analyzed for the case of perfect competition above. Also, notice from equation 3.22 that the loan rate by entrepreneurs, $r^l/(1-\tau)$, is independent of the tax rate. Hence only the marginal entrepreneurs are affected by taxation (they are induced to switch to market financing) but the bulk of the tax falls on bank owners. Consequently, the following result is obtained:

PROPOSITION 11. *The effect of loan taxation on entrepreneurs' choice of credit is the same under perfect competition and monopoly. Thus a small tax rate has a second-order effect on welfare and, moreover, the burden of the tax falls exclusively on bank owners.*

The above proposition may have important implications for the design of optimal taxes.[23] Under perfect competition and constant returns to scale, taxing intermediaries is dominated by other forms of taxation (Diamond and Mirrlees 1971). However, if banks are local monopolists and able to price discriminate, then a tax on bank loans may be part of the optimal tax system, since it is a tax on pure economic profits and a small rate has only second-order effects on welfare (Caminal 1997).

The relationship between monopoly power and the allocation of monitoring effort could be affected by a double moral hazard problem (Holmstrom and Tirole 1997; Besanko and Kanatas 1993). If banks cannot commit ex ante to monitor borrowers, then they need to be given incentives to exert efficient levels of monitoring effort. Inside capital is one possible source of incentives. Monopoly power is another one (Caminal and Matutes 1997). In the latter case if taxation falls on bank owners, then incentives to monitor may be jeopardized.

Bank Solvency

It is commonly agreed that banks' moral hazard is one of the relevant factors behind banking failures. Because of limited liability and amplified by risk-insensitive deposit insurance, bank owners wish to take excessive risk. Direct supervision is not sufficient, and solvency requirements force banks to take on more capital, which involves a higher cost. It has been suggested that an efficient complementary measure is to protect banks' profits either by relaxing competition policy in banking (Perotti and Suarez 2001) or by setting deposit interest rate ceilings (Hellmann, Murdock, and Stiglitz 2000). The relationship between market structure and risk-taking has been well documented empirically.[24] When banks' moral hazard problem is binding, then taxation is likely to affect incentives to prudent behavior. However, different types of taxes may have different effects on risk-taking attitudes.

To illustrate this point, consider what happens when certain changes are introduced to the monopoly power version of the model. First, deposit interest rates are set by the authorities. Second, banks can invest in two types of long-run assets. A safe asset yields a rate of return equal to R with probability one at time $t = 2$. Instead, a risky asset yields at time $t = 2$ a rate of return equal to γ with probability θ, and 0 with probability $1 - \theta$.

ASSUMPTION 8:

$$\gamma > R > \theta_\gamma$$

Thus the risky asset yields a higher return in case of success—although from an ex ante point of view it is dominated by the safe asset (lower expected return and higher risk). Investors are not concerned about banks' investment policies because deposits are assumed to be protected by a flat-fee deposit insurance system. For simplicity (and this is the third departure from the basic monopoly model above), bank owners are risk-neutral and care only about consumption at $t = 2$. Suppose that the government sets a binding deposit rate ceiling, which is constant over time, $r^d < r^M - \mu$. If at time $t = 1$, banks do not pay back r^d to impatient consumers, then the bank is intervened and owners obtain zero. Hence it is a dominant strategy for banks to invest in short-term assets such that they can meet their payment obligations at time $t = 1$.

$$1 - \beta = \frac{1}{2}(\overline{r^d} + \mu)$$

Banks can still choose whether to allocate the rest of the funds to the safe or to the risky asset. In case of prudent behavior, the amount of profits per unit of deposits is given by:

$$\pi^P = R\beta - \frac{\overline{r^d} + \mu}{2} = R - \frac{R+1}{2}(\overline{r^d} + \mu)$$

If a bank chooses to invest in the risky asset, then expected profits per unit of deposits is:

$$\pi^R = \theta\left[\gamma\beta - \frac{\overline{r^d} + \mu}{2}\right] = \theta\left[\gamma - \frac{\gamma+1}{2}(\overline{r^d} + \mu)\right]$$

Hence banks choose prudent behavior if and only if $\pi^P \geq \pi^R$: that is,

$$\overline{r^d} \leq \frac{2(R - \theta\gamma)}{R - \theta\gamma + 1 - \theta} - \mu \equiv \overline{r} - \mu < r^M - \mu$$

Thus if the interest rate ceiling is below the threshold level, $\overline{r} - \mu$, then the bank chooses to invest in the safe asset. Otherwise they take excessive risk. Since the threshold level is strictly below the competitive return on deposits, this implies that the regulator faces a tradeoff: either to grant banks a certain level of profits at the cost of lowering deposit rates and transaction services, or to induce banks to take excessive risk.

Now consider the effect of a tax on deposits. Taxes and rate ceilings can be combined in two different ways. First, the ceiling can be set on the rate that banks pay: r^d, in our notation. In this case, clearly a tax falls entirely on investors and it does not affect banks' risk-taking incentives. Second, the ceiling can be set on the rate that investors receive, $\overline{i^d} = (1 - \tau^d)r^d$. In this case, the tax falls entirely on banks and if the following condition holds:

$$\frac{\overline{i^d}}{1 - \tau^d} > \overline{r} - \mu \geq \overline{i^d}$$

then taxes induce risk-taking.

In the case that deposit rates are freely determined, a tax on deposits would tend to fall on both investors and bank owners. As in Hellman, Murdock, and Stiglitz (2000), the reduction in profits induces banks to take excessive risk,[25] although the analysis becomes more tedious because of the income effect in the supply of deposits.

Now consider a tax on banks' corporate income. In the absence of capital requirements banks will choose to hold zero capital[26] and the returns from prudent and risky behavior will be respectively:

$$\pi^P = (1-\tau^c)\left[R - \frac{R+1}{2}(\overline{r^d}+\mu)\right]$$

$$\pi^R = (1-\tau^c)\theta\left[\gamma - \frac{\gamma+1}{2}(\overline{r^d}+\mu)\right]$$

Clearly, risk behavior is unaffected by taxation of banks' corporate income.[27] The next proposition summarizes the main message of this section.

PROPOSITION 12. *Whenever bank solvency requires positive economic profits, taxation may induce excessive risk-taking. For instance, a tax on deposits that increases banks' costs of funds will make riskier portfolios relatively more attractive. However, a proportional tax on pure economic profits is neutral with respect to risk.*

Thus if the main priority of the government is to preserve bank solvency, a tax on deposits must be accompanied by a change in regulation. There are two main options: higher capital requirements and additional market power. Capital requirements may not be efficient and sometimes may even induce higher risk-taking.[28] Alternatively, the government can grant banks more monopoly power (through additional entry and branching restrictions, softer competition policy, rate regulation, and so on). In other words, if the social costs of banking failures are sufficiently large, then it may be optimal to allow banks to make a certain amount of profits, which implies that a tax on deposits must go along with additional regulatory changes. As a result, the burden of taxation falls exclusively on banks' customers.

Some Reflections on the Assumptions and Wider Implications

This section considers the extent to which relying on the assumption of separability weakens the empirical relevance of the model, and also discusses empirical evidence and macroeconomic implications.

Separability between Loans and Deposits Revisited

The incidence of bank taxation depends on whether there is separability between loans and deposits: that is, whether conditions in one of the markets affect equilibrium prices in the other. The model developed in this chapter makes heavy use of the separability hypothesis. In particular, in the model banks have access to safe investment technology, which represents simultaneously the expected return of the funds collected through deposit contracts, and the opportunity cost of the loans to entrepreneurs. This is a convenient artifact that requires further discussion.

The literature tends to identify separability with the following set of conditions:[29]

• Banks are able to borrow and lend in a perfect bond market at an exogenous interest rate. This is the case, for instance, if there is an organized interbank lending market, whose interest rate is fixed either by monetary authorities or by arbitrage with international capital markets.
• The costs of granting loans and capturing deposits are additively separable. In other words, the marginal cost of loans is independent of the level of deposits, and vice versa.
• The supply of deposits and the demand for loans are independent.
• The probability of failure for banks is zero.

Clearly, these conditions are quite restrictive. If the banking industry is an oligopoly and the economy is closed (or capital mobility is imperfect) then the first may not hold. Also, there may be economies of scope and the second may fail. Finally, as Dermine (1986) shows, if the bank's probability of failure is positive, there is deposit insurance, and banks enjoy limited liability, then the (monopolistic) bank's optimization problem ceases to be separable. A higher deposit rate increases the probability of default, which reduces the cost of lending one additional unit.[30]

The above discussion suggests that many real world situations are likely to deviate in various dimensions from separability. Nevertheless, a model assuming separability may be more useful than it might appear at first sight. The reason is that simultaneous deviations may compensate each other to some extent.

Consider the interaction between loans and deposits through costs. In particular, assume that monitoring costs are reduced with the level of deposits: that is, m is a function of D, with $m'(D) < 0$. This may be explained by the fact that banks use information from deposits in their loan-granting decisions (Fama 1985).[31] In this case, the effects of a tax on deposits would clearly spill over into the loan market. In particular, an increase in the deposit tax rate would depress deposits (unless investment funds are absent and bank deposits dominate direct investment), which would increase monitoring costs.

As a result, loan rates would increase and some entrepreneurs would turn to the securities market to get their funding.

Now consider the case of bankruptcy risk. Because of limited liability banks perceive a lower cost of funds as the probability of bankruptcy increases. As a result, banks become more aggressive in the credit market, pricing their loans at lower rates. In this context a tax on deposits falls partially on bank profits (the ex ante deposit rate increases) and hence the probability of bankruptcy increases, which pushes loan rates downward.

Thus if both channels operate at the same time, it is unlikely that a tax on deposits leaves loan rates unaffected, but the size of the effect may be small and, more importantly, of ambiguous sign.[32]

Empirical Evidence on the Effect of Taxation

The empirical evidence on the effects of bank taxation is rather fragmented. One important cross-country study is Demirgüç-Kunt and Huizinga (1999). Unfortunately, their information on the shape of the implicit and explicit tax schedules is rather imprecise, particularly in the former case. They find that reserves reduce interest margins and profits, especially in less developed countries, which may reflect the fact that the opportunity cost of reserves (the implicit tax) is higher in less developed countries. They also present evidence favorable to a complete pass-through of corporate income tax to bank customers. In fact, their regression analysis shows that both interest margin and profitability increase with the tax on corporate income.

There are some earlier empirical studies on the incidence of reserve requirements. Bartunek and Madura (1996) study the effects of two unique reserve requirement adjustments in the early 1990s. The results indicate that not all of the benefit from the reduction in the implicit tax resulting from the lowering of reserve requirements was passed on to depositors and borrowers. The larger banks tended to experience strong favorable valuation effects.[33]

The existing evidence on the incidence of reserve requirements (Bartunek and Madura 1996) seems compatible with the results above. Provided size is positively related to market power, shareholders of large banks are expected to capture a larger share of the benefits from the reduction in reserve requirements. Depositors are also expected to benefit from such a reduction.

However, the evidence on banks' corporate income taxes (Demirgüç-Kunt and Huizinga 1999) does not fit well into the picture. First, the positive effect of taxation on profitability is difficult to reconcile with any sensible economic model. Second, the complete pass-through result suggests that banking is a perfectly competitive industry (otherwise such a tax would fall on economic profits), which is at odds with most of the evidence.

Macroeconomic Implications

The fact that reserve requirements are an implicit form of taxation has long been recognized.[34] Such a requirement induces banks to hold a higher fraction of their deposits in the form of non-interest-bearing reserves, which reduces the average return of banks' portfolios and increases their demand for monetary base. Thus the reserve requirement operates as a tax by increasing seigniorage revenue (by expanding the base of the inflation tax). More specifically, under certain assumptions, a reserve requirement is equivalent to a proportional tax on deposits plus an open market sale of government bonds of an amount equivalent to the volume of resources kept captive by the requirement (Romer 1985; Bacchetta and Caminal 1994).

Thus the non-monetary model was unable to accommodate a precise description of reserve requirements and hence the interaction between banking activity, inflation, and the government budget constraint was missing. This is an important limitation for at least two reasons. First, in practice inflation is only imperfectly controlled by monetary authorities. As a result, the implicit tax is likely to have an arbitrary (random) component. Second, the inflation tax affects not only bank deposits but also one of their imperfect substitutes: cash. Thus a complete analysis of the effect of reserve requirements on the level of deposits should consider how inflation and reserve ratios affect the choice between cash and deposits; otherwise the welfare implications may be misleading (Whitesell 1992). In particular, if reserve requirements are interpreted as a tax on deposits, then the model here is likely to overstate their distortionary effects.

A related issue is the modeling of transaction services. This is bound to be important for a normative analysis but not so much for the positive analysis conducted in this chapter. This study treated transaction services provided by banks as an additional consumption good by including them as an argument of investors' utility function. Alternatively, it could have been assumed that deposits reduce transaction costs. Results on optimal taxation may strongly depend on such a choice.[35]

The model analyzed in this chapter has focused on the role of banks in the allocation of savings and abstracted from the substitutability between capital and labor and from the determination of the level of savings. In dynamic general equilibrium models, capital

·taxation creates a gap between the rate of return on savings and the marginal product of capital. The optimality of capital income taxation depends on various circumstances. In infinitely lived representative consumer models, it is well known that capital income taxes cannot be part of the optimal tax system in steady state (Chamley 1986).[36] Bank taxes are also capital income taxes and on top of that they affect the efficiency of the allocation of funds to various investment opportunities. Thus if our model is incorporated in a standard general equilibrium framework, then one would expect to obtain the same results as under standard capital income taxes, augmented by the additional distortionary effects that the study has identified.[37]

There is another body of literature, both empirical and theoretical, that relates financial intermediation and long-run growth. Some of these models characterize banks as institutions that either provide liquidity services or alleviate informational asymmetries.[38] In some cases, the engine of growth is a capital externality, following Romer; in others, it is innovation effort. Once again, the role of banks can be described as reducing the gap between the return on savings and the marginal return on investment. Externalities in research and development or in capital accumulation transform level effects into growth effects. The empirical evidence is compatible with a positive relationship between financial development and economic growth, although it is more difficult to establish the direction of causality.[39] Overall, this literature suggests that bank taxation could have negative implications for long-run growth.[40]

Concluding Remarks

This chapter has developed a theoretical framework to analyze the impact of various forms of taxation. Banks have been characterized as intermediaries able to perform three main functions: asset transformation, provision of transaction services, and monitoring. Investors can directly access security markets, but the resulting portfolios are relatively illiquid. In addition, they may or may not have access to investment funds, which also perform an asset transformation function. On the other side of market, some entrepreneurs may have access to security markets (unmonitored credit), but those entrepreneurs with high-risk projects prefer information-intensive credit (bank loans) over uninformed credit (commercial paper). The total amount of funds is exogenous, and hence the model focuses on the allocation of those funds among alternative financial arrangements. The main results can be stated as follows:

• Under certain conditions, the loan and deposit markets are separable, and hence a tax on deposits does not affect either loan rates or monitoring activity. Similarly, a tax on loans does not affect either deposit rates or the provision of transaction services and liquidity insurance. The benchmark case where all these conditions are met may be more useful than it appears at first sight since multiple deviations from the benchmark may partially compensate one another. Some of the results listed below presume that separability holds.

• If borrowers are VAT-registered firms and investors are not, then a value-added tax is equivalent to a tax on deposits. If loans and bank capital are complementary (which occurs, for instance, when capital requirements are binding) then a tax on banks' corporate income is equivalent to a tax on both economic profits and loans.

• A tax on deposits tends to reduce the level of deposits and increase direct investment and/or investment fund holdings. As a result the level of transaction services is reduced and, if investment funds do not exist, investors enjoy a lower level of liquidity insurance. In the absence of investment funds, it may be the case that deposits dominate direct investment and a small tax rate does not create any distortion. Imperfect competition in the deposit market has two effects. First, it distorts the laissez-faire equilibrium and hence even a small tax rate has a first-order effect on total welfare. Second, taxes fall partially on economic profits, which alleviates the tax burden of investors (and potentially reduces the distortion on savings decisions).

• A tax on bank loans reduces the amount of lending and monitoring effort and induces more firms to borrow on the securities market. The size of the distortion is likely to increase with the efficiency of the securities market. The effect of banks' market power in the loan market is similar to that in the deposit market, except that banks' ability to price-discriminate is higher in this market. In the extreme case that individual banks compete exclusively with capital markets, then a tax on bank loans may fall exclusively on bank owners.

• A general tax on capital income reduces the level of deposits, since investors' willingness to pay for banks' transaction services increases with their disposable income.

• A tax on deposits may induce banks to invest in riskier portfolios. If bank solvency is the top priority, then such a tax must be introduced only if at the same time banks are given more monopoly power. In this case the tax would fall entirely on banks' customers.

Summarizing, bank taxation increases the gap between the marginal return on investment and the marginal return on savings (like general capital income taxation). On top of that, it tends to reduce the efficiency of the transformation of savings into investment by reducing banks' contributions. However, if banks' market power is excessive (that is, beyond the level required by the goal of preserving the stability of the banking system) then the overall distortion associated with bank taxation may substantially shrink.

One important limitation of the current discussion is that it has overlooked tax enforcement problems. In particular, if foreign financial intermediaries are available, then evasion could be relatively easy and the impact of taxing domestic financial intermediaries may be substantially altered. On the other hand, taxes on financial intermediaries may induce more cash transactions, reduce financial records within intermediaries, and make monitoring firm income more costly for tax authorities. This may undermine the collectibility of other taxes. These issues are beyond the scope of this chapter.

Other extensions of the current framework appear to be fruitful. First, a complete welfare analysis of the disintermediation effects of taxation requires an explicit consideration of alternative means of payment (cash) and potential informational spillovers from bank monitoring to security markets. Second, it would be nice to transform the current model into a building block of a standard dynamic general equilibrium model in order to develop a more complete picture of the aggregate effects of taxation.

Appendix
Market Clearing under Direct Investment

At time $t = 0$ an amount of funds $I N$ are invested in long-term assets. All entrepreneurs with $p \leq p_0$ obtain financing if the following condition on the probability distribution H holds:

$$1 - H(p_0) = L < I N$$

There is no need to worry about market clearing in the secondary market since both buyers and sellers are indifferent between trading in the secondary market and in alternative assets. However, it is important that claims on entrepreneurs' projects are not liquidated. In particular, the following condition must hold:

$$\frac{1}{2} R[1 - H(p_0)] < \frac{1}{2} N(1 - I)$$

The left-hand side is the amount of claims on entrepreneurs' projects that must be sold in the secondary market and the right-hand side is the total demand for claims. In the text it has been shown that $I > 0$. Also, if consumer's degree of risk aversion is not too small, then $I < 1$. In other words, investors always have a diversified portfolio (they hold both short-term and long-term assets). Therefore, provided N is large enough the above two conditions will be satisfied.

The Objective Function of Oligopolistic Banks

Suppose that bank shareholders are subject to the same liquidity shocks as investors: that is, half the shareholders will turn out to be impatient and the other half will turn out to be patient. To accommodate such liquidity shocks, it can be arranged that patient shareholders buy the shares of those who claim to be impatient at time $t = 1$ at a prespecified price. Let π_1 denote the payment received by impatient shareholders per unit of deposits. Thus each impatient shareholder of bank i receives $2\pi_1 Di$. Similarly, let π_2 denote the payment received by patient shareholders per unit of deposits at time $t = 2$; that is, each patient shareholder receives $2\pi_2 Di$. If bank i commits to pay depositors (r_{i1}^d, r_{i2}^d), then it must invest a fraction $1 - \beta$, on short-term assets:

(A3.1)
$$1 - \beta = \frac{1}{2}(r_{i1}^d + \mu) + \pi_1$$

Also, the budget constraint at time $t = 2$ determines residual profits:

(A3.2)
$$\pi_2 \equiv \beta R - \frac{1}{2}(r_{i2}^d + \mu)$$

Solving equation A3.1 for β and plugging it into equation A3.2, yields the shareholders' intertemporal budget constraint:

(A3.3)
$$\pi_2 = R\left(1 - \frac{r_{i1}^d}{2} - \frac{r_{i2}^d}{2R} - \pi_1\right) - \frac{R+1}{2}\mu$$

Under the assumption that banks cannot affect investors' consumption (see note 16) and if other banks and investment funds set constant interest rates, then the supply of funds to bank i is given by:

(A3.4)
$$D_i = a - bu'(c^d)\left(\Delta_{i1} + \frac{1}{R}\Delta_{i2}\right) + k\frac{R+1}{R}u'(c^d)\Delta j$$

where c^d is the constant level of consumption by investors, $i \neq j$, and

$$\Delta_{it} = r^M - (1 - \tau)r_{it}^d$$

Finally, if $\Delta_{i1} = \Delta_{i2}$ then such a constant level is denoted by Δ_i. Thus given the constant interest rate set by the rival bank, r_j^d, bank i's shareholders choose r_{i1}^d, r_{i2}^d, π_1 and π_2 in order to maximize:

$$U = u(c_1^s) + \frac{1}{R}u(c_2^s)$$

where

$$c_1^s = 2\pi_1 D_i$$

$$c_2^s = 2\pi_2 D_i$$

and subject to the budget constraint of equation A3.3 and D_i given by equation A3.4. From the first-order conditions it follows that:

$$r_{i1}^d = r_{i2}^d = r_i^d$$

$$\pi_1 = \pi_2$$

As a result, bank i's shareholders also enjoy a constant level of consumption, given by:

$$c^s = (r^M - \mu - r_i^d)D_i$$

This expression is the starting point of the analysis in the text. Notice that the above time structure of shareholder returns makes the plan incentive compatible, since patient shareholders have no incentive to pretend to be impatient.

Taxation and the Oligopolistic Deposit Rate

It has been assumed that individual banks cannot affect aggregate consumption, but clearly taxes do affect consumption. Thus the effect of taxes on the deposit rate cannot be computed by simply taking the partial derivative in equation A3.4.

Let $v_i(D_A, D_B)$ denote the partial derivative with respect to D_i. Then:

$$v_i(D_A, D_B) = \alpha - D_i - \lambda D_j$$

where $i \neq j$. The previous assumption can be adapted on the saturation point by assuming that in a symmetric allocation the marginal utility of investing all the funds in deposits is zero:

$$v_i\left(\frac{1}{2}, \frac{1}{2}\right) = \alpha - (1 + \lambda)\frac{1}{2} = 0$$

Hence $\alpha = 1/2$.

The equilibrium level of consumption in a symmetric equilibrium can be written as:

(A3.5) $c = r^M - 2(r^M - i^d)D$

where D is the level of deposits at each bank: that is

(A3.6) $D = a - (b - k)\dfrac{1 + R}{R} u'(c)(r^M - i^d)$

Totally differentiating equations A3.5 and A3.6 and solving yields:

(A3.7) $\dfrac{dc}{di^d} = \dfrac{2\left[a - 2(b - k)\dfrac{1 + R}{R} u'(c)(r^M - i^d)\right]}{1 - 2(b - k)\dfrac{1 + R}{R} u''(c)(r^M - i^d)^2}$

The denominator is positive but the sign of the numerator is ambiguous. A change in the after-tax interest rate makes the relative price of deposits cheaper (substitution effect), which induces less consumption, but also expands the feasible set (income effect), which induces higher consumption.

From equation 3.21 in the text, it follows that

(A3.8) $i^d = \dfrac{b(r^M - \mu)(1 - \tau^d) + (b - k)r^M - \dfrac{a}{\Omega}}{(2b - k)}$

Applying the implicit function theorem to this equation, one can compute the effect of taxation on the after-tax interest rate:

$$\frac{di^d}{d\tau^d} = \frac{-b(r^M - \mu)}{(2b - k) - \dfrac{au''(c)}{\Omega}\dfrac{dc}{di^d}}$$

Using equation A3.7, one can show that the denominator has a positive sign:

$$(2b-k)\left[1-2(b-k)\frac{1+R}{R}u''(c)(r^M-i^d)^2\right]-$$
$$\frac{2au''(c)}{\Omega}\left[a-2(b-k)\Omega(r^M-i^d)\right]>0$$

The first three terms are positive and the fourth is negative. However, the sign of the last three terms is equal to the sign of:

$$\Gamma \equiv \frac{a^2}{\Omega}+(b-k)(2b-k)\frac{1+R}{R}(r^M-i^d)^2-2a(b-k)(r^M-i^d)$$

Since

$$u'(c)<1+\lambda<\frac{2-\lambda}{1-\lambda}\equiv\frac{2b-k}{b-k}$$

it follows that:

$$\Gamma>\left(a\sqrt{\frac{R}{1+R}}-(r^M-i^d)\sqrt{(b-k)(2b-k)\frac{1+R}{R}u'(c)}\right)^2>0$$

Therefore it has been shown than a higher tax rate implies a lower after-tax deposit rate.

Turn now to the effect of taxation on the pre-tax deposit rate, r^d. Totally differentiating equation 3.21 with respect to r^d, c, and τ yields:

$$dr^d=\frac{(b-k)r^M-\dfrac{a}{\Omega}}{(2b-k)(1-\tau^d)^2}d\tau+\frac{\dfrac{a}{\Omega}\dfrac{u''(c)}{u'(c)}}{(2b-k)(1-\tau^d)}dc$$

From the definition of i^d, it follows that

$$dc=\frac{dc}{di^d}\left[(1-\tau^d)dr^d-r^d d\tau^d\right]$$

where dc/di^d is given by equation A3.7. Hence

$$\frac{dr^d}{d\tau^d}=\frac{M_0}{M_1}$$

where

$$M_0 \equiv \frac{(b-k)r^M - \dfrac{a}{\Omega}}{1-\tau^d} - \frac{a}{\Omega}\frac{u''(c)}{u'(c)}r^d\frac{dc}{di^d}$$

$$M_1 \equiv (2b-k)(1-\tau^d) - \frac{a}{\Omega}\frac{u''(c)}{u'(c)}(1-\tau^d)\frac{dc}{di^d}$$

Notice that if $dc/di^d > 0$, then $dr^d/d\tau^d > 0$. However, in principle the sign of dc/di^d is ambiguous. In fact, such ambiguity is easily translated into the sign of $dr^d/d\tau$. In general, from equation A3.8, it follows that:

(A3.9) $$r^M - i^d = \frac{b[\tau r^M + (1-\tau)\mu] + \dfrac{a}{\Omega}}{2b-k}$$

Now look at two extreme cases. First, suppose $\mu = \tau = 0$. If one were to plug equation A3.9 into equation A3.7, evaluated at $\mu = \tau = 0$, it can be checked that $dc/di^d > 0$, and hence $dr^d/d\tau^d > 0$.

By continuity, provided μ and τ are not too large, then a proportional tax on deposits raises the before-tax deposit rate.

Second, suppose that banks are monopolists: that is, $\lambda = 0$. Consider the case $\tau^d = 0$. This implies that $b = 1$ and $k = 0$. As a result,

$$\frac{dc}{di^d} = \frac{-2\Omega\mu}{1 - \dfrac{1+R}{2R}u''(c)\left(\mu + \dfrac{1}{2\Omega}\right)^2} < 0$$

The numerator of $dr^d/d\tau$ can be written as follows:

$$M_0 = r^M\left[1 - \frac{1}{4u'(c)}\right] + \frac{u''(c)}{u'(c)}\frac{\mu r^d}{1 - \dfrac{1+R}{2R}u''(c)\left(\mu + \dfrac{1}{2\Omega}\right)^2}$$

For any value of $\mu > 0$, there exists a utility function such that $4u'(c)$ is higher but arbitrarily close to one. As a result, the first term is positive but arbitrarily small, while the second term is negative. In fact, as $4u'(c)$ goes to one, the first term goes to zero, while the second goes to a strictly negative number.

Finally, the denominator of $dr^d/d\tau$ can be written as follows:

$$M_1 = 2 - \frac{u''(c)}{u'(c)}\frac{\mu}{1 - \dfrac{1+R}{2R}u''(c)\left(\mu + \dfrac{1}{2\Omega}\right)^2}$$

Therefore, provided $4u'(c)$ is close enough to one and I is positive but not too large, then M_1 is positive and M_0 is negative. In this case, a higher tax rate induces a lower pre-tax deposit rate.

Notes

1. Recent changes in the size and composition of bank activities are discussed, for instance, in Mishkin (1996) and Allen and Santomero (2001).

2. Thus as in Diamond and Dybvig (1983), investors' preferences are extreme: the utility of consumption is positive either at $t = 1$ or at $t = 2$.

3. It makes sense to assume that transaction services are enjoyed the same period that consumption takes place (impatient consumers at time $t = 1$, and patient consumers at time $t = 2$). Banks pay the costs of providing those services accordingly. Finally, the function v represents the expected value of deposits.

4. It is easy to check that, provided f is not too large, entrepreneurs' participation constraint is not binding. In other words, all entrepreneurs that can get financing are willing to accept it.

5. A reserve requirement is equivalent to a proportional tax on deposits, except for the timing of revenues. If banks can price transaction services separately, then it is easy to show that a proportional tax on deposits is equivalent to a proportional tax on transaction services. That is, if both taxes are required to raise the same amount of revenue, then they must cause the same distortion on the level of deposits.

6. Empirical support is provided by James (1987).

7. In the absence of the externality, a small τ^I has only a second-order effect on welfare. However, if banks create a positive externality to the securities market, even a small tax would have a first-order effect on welfare.

8. See Poddar and English (1997).

9. Under the cash flow method, borrowers should pay τ^v on their capital inflow at time $t = 0$, and then get a credit of $\tau^v r^I$ on their capital outflow at time $t = 2$. This discussion assumes that the tax payment associated with a cash inflow of a capital nature can be carried forward to the period during which the capital transaction is reversed, although the deferral is subject to interest charges at the market rate, R. This is the cash flow method with Tax Calculation Account (Poddar and English 1997).

10. One may wonder about the effect of a general tax on firms' profits. In the present model, the demand for credit is inelastic and hence such a tax would create no distortion. However, in a richer model, the amount of entrepreneurial projects may also depend on their net return. In that case, profit taxes are likely to reduce bank loans.

11. One reason why banks find equity financing expensive (sometimes prohibitively expensive) is adverse selection (Stein 1998). Boyd and Gertler

(1993) observe that for the U.S. banking industry, the equity to assets ratio has been steadily declining since 1980.

12. Solvency ratios usually take the form of a minimum ratio of capital to a risk-weighted measure of assets. The present formulation gives a positive weight only to loans to entrepreneurs.

13. Investors will be willing to buy banks' equity at an implicit rate of return R only if deposits do not dominate direct investment: that is $r^M - \mu - 1 < 0$. This subsection deals only with this case.

14. In case capital requirements are computed in such a way that all bank assets get a positive weight, and provided deposits and equity are the only source of funds for banks, then it can readily be shown that separability breaks down and corporate taxes also affect deposit rates.

15. However, Whitesell (1992) argues that money market funds may provide efficient services for very large transactions, but that cash and checks are more efficient for small and medium-size transactions, respectively.

16. The empirical evidence seems to indicate that the emergence of pension and mutual funds has mostly affected directly held assets, but not so much bank assets. See the discussion in Allen and Santomero (2001).

17. Market power may be partly created by regulation (entry and branching restrictions, interest rate ceilings, and so on). It has been shown that deregulation and liberalization have increased competition and reduced bank profits. See Keeley (1990) and Demirgüç-Kunt and Detragiache (1999). Other traditional factors may be crucial to explain banks' market power in the household and small business sector, including geographic differentiation, specialization, and customer-specific investments.

18. The representative investor can be thought of as a coalition of multiple agents, each one in charge of a small fraction of total savings and instructed to maximize the coalition's objective function, anticipating that all returns are pooled before consumption takes place. This is somewhat analogous to the celebrated assumption in Lucas (1990).

19. This is actually an assumption on the marginal utility of consumption, since this is equivalent to $4u'(c) > 1 - \lambda$.

20. In the limit as λ goes to one (Bertrand competition), the deposit rate converges $r^M - \mu$ (the perfectly competitive deposit rate). Hence $dr^d/d\tau^d = 0$ and taxes fall entirely on investors.

21. One possible justification could be that banks and entrepreneurs have been engaged in a long-run relationship and at a point in time the incumbent bank has an advantage in monitoring previous customers, which is sufficiently large to imply complete segmentation of the loan market.

22. For those borrowers with $p < p_o$ the monopolist will set a loan rate $r^l = (1 - \tau)X$.

23. As in the case of perfect competition, in this context a tax on banks' corporate income, provided capital requirements are binding, is equivalent to a tax on bank loans. Also, a tax on banks' value-added, under the same conditions, is exclusively a tax on deposits.

24. Keeley (1990) blames the decline of charter values due to liberalization and deregulation for the increase in failures in the U.S. banking industry since the 1980s. Demirgüç-Kunt and Detragiache (1998) also point at liberalization as one of the factors that explain banking crises in a large set of countries. Inappropriate regulation accompanying liberalization seems to aggravate crises.

25. However, there is a countervailing effect. Lower bank rents may discourage bank monitoring and increase credit rationing. As a result, banks' portfolios may be less exposed to aggregate risk. See Caminal and Matutes (2002). The relation between market structure, regulation and financial fragility is also studied in Matutes and Vives (1996 and 2000).

26. The argument below is robust to the introduction of capital requirements. More specifically, capital requirements are likely to reduce risk-taking, but their presence does not alter the neutrality of a tax on profits.

27. In general the treatment of loss offsets may affect banks' risk-taking behavior. However, in this particular model, if the tax law allows a rebate in case of default, nothing changes since bank owners cannot appropriate the rebate.

28. See Hellmann, Murdock, and Stiglitz (2000) and references quoted there.

29. See Freixas and Rochet (1997) for a more detailed discussion.

30. If banks offer "tied-up contracts" (consumers can obtain credit from a bank only if they deposit their cash in the same bank, or they get a lower loan rate if they do so) then the third condition fails. Chiappori, Pérez-Castrillo, and Verdier (1995) show in the context of the Salop model that in an unregulated banking sector this type of contract would never emerge, but it does if deposits are subject to interest rate ceilings (in this case banks are willing to subsidize credit).

31. See also Mester, Nakamura, and Renault (1998) for empirical evidence.

32. If the interest rate on the safe asset is determined by domestic supply and demand conditions, and in the absence of government intervention, then a tax on deposits will tend to increase the loan rate. The size of this effect depends on the elasticity of savings with respect to their average return and on the weight of deposits in total savings.

33. For similar evidence, see Osborne and Zaher (1992). The earlier studies on the incidence of reserve requirement are discussed in Demirgüç-Kunt and Huizinga (1999).

34. See, for instance, Fama (1980).

35. See Kimbrough (1989) and Chia and Whalley (1999).

36. Results are different if agents have finite horizons (Erosa and Gervais 2002).

37. Some of the literature on banking in general equilibrium has focused on the role of banks on the propagation of shocks and on the transmission of monetary policy. See, for instance, Smith (1998) and Fuerst

(1994). From an international perspective, the ability to tax the banking industry may be drastically reduced after the liberalization of the domestic financial system. See Bacchetta and Caminal (1992).

38. An example of the first type is Bencivenga and Smith (1991). Greenwood and Jovanovic (1990) and De la Fuente and Martin (1996) belong to the second group.

39. Levine (1997) provides an excellent survey of the main theoretical arguments as well as of the empirical evidence.

40. See Roubini and Sala-i-Martin (1995) for a model with this type of result.

References

Allen, Franklin, and Anthony Santomero. 2001. "What Do Financial Intermediaries Do? *Journal of Banking and Finance* 25 (2): 271–94.

Bacchetta, Philippe, and Ramon Caminal. 1992. "Optimal Seigniorage and Financial Liberalization." *Journal of International Money and Finance* 11 (6): 518–38.

———. 1994. "A Note on Reserve Requirements and Public Finance." *International Review of Economics and Finance* 3 (1): 107–18.

Bartunek, Ken, and Jeff Madura. 1996. "Wealth Effects of Reserve Requirement Reductions in the 1990s on Depository Institutions." *Review of Financial Economics* 5 (2): 191–204.

Bencivenga, Valerie, and Bruce Smith. 1991. "Financial Intermediation and Endogenous Growth." *Review of Economic Studies* 58 (2): 195–209.

Besanko, David, and George Kanatas. 1993. "Credit Market Equilibrium with Bank Monitoring and Moral Hazard." *Review of Financial Studies* 6 (1): 213–32.

Boyd, John, and Mark Gertler. 1993. "US Commercial Banking: Trends, Cycles and Policy." In Olivier Blanchard and Stanley Fischer, eds., *NBER Macroeconomics Annual*. Cambridge Mass.: MIT Press.

Caminal, Ramon. 1997. "Financial Intermediation and the Optimal Tax System." *Journal of Public Economics* 63 (3): 351–82.

Caminal, Ramon, and Carmen Matutes. 1997. "Can Competition in the Credit Market Be Excessive?" CEPR Working Paper 1725. London: Centre for Economic Policy Research.

———. 2002. Market Power and Banking Failures. *International Journal of Industrial Organization* 20 (9): 1341–61.

Chamley, Christophe. 1986. "Optimal Taxation of Capital in a General Equilibrium with Infinite Lives." *Econometrica* 54 (3): 607–22.

Chia, Ngee-Choon, and John Whalley. 1999. "The Tax Treatment of Financial Intermediation." *Journal of Money, Credit, and Banking* 31 (4): 704–19.

Chiappori, Pierre-André, David Pérez-Castrillo, and Thierry Verdier. 1995. "Spatial Competition in the Banking System, Localization, Cross-subsidies and the Regulation of Interest Rates." *European Economic Review* 39 (5): 889–919.

De la Fuente, Angel, and Jose Marín, 1996. "Innovation, Bank Monitoring, and Endogenous Financial Development." *Journal of Monetary Economics* 38 (2): 269–301.

Demirgüç-Kunt, Aslı, and Enrica Detragiache. 1999. "Financial Liberalization and Financial Fragility." In Boris Pleskovic and Joseph E. Stiglitz, eds., *Proceedings of the 1998 World Bank Conference on Development Economics.* Washington, D.C.: World Bank.

Demirgüç-Kunt, Aslı, and Harry Huizinga. 1999. "Determinants of Commercial Bank Interest Margins and Profitability: Some International Evidence." *World Bank Economic Review* 13 (2): 379–408.

Dermine, Jean. 1986. "Deposit Rates, Credit Rates and Bank Capital: The Monti-Klein Model Revisited. *Journal of Banking and Finance* 10 (1): 99–114.

Diamond, Douglas. 1997. "Liquidity, Banks, and Markets." *Journal of Political Economy* 105 (5): 928–56.

Diamond, Douglas, and Philip Dybvig. 1983. "Bank Runs, Deposit Insurance, and Liquidity." *Journal of Political Economy* 91 (3): 401–19.

Diamond, Peter, and James Mirrlees. 1971. "Optimal Taxation and Public Production, Part I: Production Efficiency, Part II: Tax Rules. *American Economic Review* 61 (1): 8–27 and 61 (2): 261–78.

Erosa, Andrés, and Martin Gervais. 2002. "Optimal Taxation in Life-Cycle Economies." *Journal of Economic Theory* 105 (2): 338–69.

Fama, Eugene. 1985. "What's Different about Banks? *Journal of Monetary Economics* 15 (1): 29–40.

Freixas, Xavier, and Jean-Charles Rochet. 1997. *Microeconomics of Banking.* Cambridge, Mass.: MIT Press.

Fuerst, Timothy. 1994. "Monetary Policy and Financial Intermediation." *Journal of Money, Credit, and Banking* 26 (3): 362–76.

Greenwood, Jeremy, and Boyan Jovanovic. 1990. "Financial Development, Growth, and the Distribution of Income." *Journal of Political Economy* 98 (5): 1076–1107.

Hellmann, Thomas, Kevin Murdock, and Joseph E. Stiglitz. 2000. "Liberalization, Moral Hazard in Banking, and Prudential Regulation: Are Capital Requirements Enough?" *American Economic Review* 90 (1): 147–65.

Holmstrom, Bengt, and Jean Tirole. 1997. "Financial Intermediation, Loanable Funds, and the Real Sector." *Quarterly Journal of Economics* 112 (3): 663–91.

———. 1998. "Private and Public Supply of Liquidity." *Journal of Political Economy* 106 (1): 1–40.

Jacklin, Charles. 1987. "Demand Deposits, Trading Restrictions, and Risk Sharing." In E. Prescott and N. Wallace, eds., *Contractual Arrangements for Intertemporal Trade*. Minneapolis: University of Minnesota Press.

James, Christopher. 1987. "Some Evidence on the Uniqueness of Bank Loans." *Journal of Financial Economics* 19 (2): 217–35.

Keeley, Michael. 1990. "Deposit Insurance, Risk, and Market Power in Banking." *American Economic Review* 80 (5): 1183–1200.

Kimbrough, Kent. 1989. "Optimal Taxation in a Monetary Economy with Financial Intermediaries." *Journal of Macroeconomics* 11: 493–511.

Levine, Ross. 1997. "Financial Development and Economic Growth: Views and Agenda." *Journal of Economic Literature* 35 (2): 688–726.

Lucas, Robert. 1990. "Liquidity and Interest Rates." *Journal of Economic Theory* 50 (2): 237–64.

Matutes, Carmen, and Xavier Vives. 1996. "Competition for Deposits, Fragility, and Insurance." *Journal of Financial Intermediation* 5 (2): 184–216.

———. 2000. "Imperfect Competition, Risk-taking, and Regulation in Banking." *European Economic Review* 44 (1): 1–34.

Mester, Loretta, Leonard Nakamura, and Micheline Renault. 1998. "Checking Accounts and Bank Monitoring." Working Paper 98/25. Federal Reserve Bank of Philadelphia.

Mishkin, Frederic. 1996. "Bank Consolidation: A Central Banker's Perspective." NBER Working Paper 5849. Cambridge, Mass.

Osborne, Dale K., and Tarek S. Zaher. 1992. "Reserve Requirements, Bank Share Prices and the Uniqueness of Bank Loans." *Journal of Banking and Finance* 16 (4): 799–812.

Perotti, Enrico, and Javier Suarez. 2001. "Last Bank Standing: What Do I Gain If You Fail?" University of Amsterdam. Processed.

Poddar, Satya, and Morley English. 1997. "Taxation of Financial Services under a Value-Added Tax: Applying the Cash-Flow Approach." *National Tax Journal* 50 (1): 89–112.

Romer, David. 1985. "Financial Intermediation, Reserve Requirements, and Inside Money: A General Equilibrium Analysis." *Journal of Monetary Economics* 16 (1): 175–94.

Roubini, Nouriel, and Xavier Sala-i-Martin. 1995. "A Growth Model of Inflation, Tax Evasion, and Financial Repression." *Journal of Monetary Economics* 35 (2): 275–301.

Smith, R. Todd. 1998. "Banking Competition and Macroeconomic Performance." *Journal of Money, Credit, and Banking* 30 (4): 793–815.

Stein, Jeremy. 1998. "An Adverse-Selection Model of Bank Asset and Liability Management with Implications for the Transmission of Monetary Policy." *Rand Journal of Economics* 29 (4): 466–86.

Whitesell, William. 1992. "Deposit Banks and the Market for Payment Media." *Journal of Money, Credit, and Banking* 24 (4): 483–98.

4

Tax Incentives for Household Saving and Borrowing

Tullio Jappelli and Luigi Pistaferri

Modern theories of intertemporal consumption choice emphasize that individuals may save for a variety of motives: to smooth life-cycle fluctuations in income (the retirement, or life-cycle motive), to face emergencies arising from income or health risks (the precautionary motive), to purchase durable goods and housing, and to accumulate resources for one's heir (the bequest motive) (Browning and Lusardi 1996).

Individual choice may be affected by the government policies that, in virtually all countries, target private saving. Government targeting is selective, and tends to affect not only the overall level of saving but also the allocation of saving among its many different forms.

Raising the overall level of saving is often viewed as an effective way to raise investment and growth. Many forms of government intervention thus aim at simply increasing the volume of saving, but leave the ultimate decision about the allocation of saving to the individual. In other cases government intervention mandates individuals to save in specific forms or for specific purposes. For instance, in almost all countries governments promote retirement saving, because having insufficient resources during retirement entails a high burden not only for the elderly lacking these resources, but also for society as a whole. Promoting saving for housing and other goods to which policymakers assign high priority (education, health, or life protection) is also a popular goal. This chapter reviews the literature on these tax incentives, with special focus on long-term saving, housing, and household liabilities.

In very poor countries households rely on informal markets for credit transactions, so government intervention has a limited role in shaping household saving and portfolio allocations. The chapter therefore places special emphasis on the importance of tax incentives and saving instruments available in middle-income countries with relatively developed financial markets (as in several Latin American and East Asian countries). It is precisely in middle-income countries that mandatory saving instruments are more widespread, and often the only effective way of raising the overall level of saving and shaping household portfolios. In this area, the most developed countries have accumulated a wide experience in designing and implementing various tax incentives schemes. This experience can be used to evaluate the effectiveness of tax incentives and to draw lessons for middle-income countries.

A careful review of the international tax codes reveals that in most middle-income countries the tax system targets long-term, retirement saving instruments. This is hardly surprising given the role of retirement saving as the most important and widely available household financial asset. The tax features of pension funds are of special interest, given the recent wave of reforms of the social security system in Latin America and East Asia. Almost invariably, mandated contributions to pension funds are tax exempt, and very often voluntary contributions to long-term saving instruments are also heavily favored by the tax code. This chapter therefore concentrates mainly on mandated contributions to pension funds, although it also devotes some space to the tax treatment of other, more "sophisticated" assets available in industrialized countries. The second area of widespread government intervention in middle-income countries is incentives to save for housing accumulation plans. These programs are absent in industrialized countries, but quite common in several middle-income countries.

The chapter is divided into five parts, each addressing a particular saving instrument and area of policy intervention. The first section begins by reviewing the interest rate effect on personal saving. The specific question addressed is whether public policies affecting the real rate of interest impact the overall level of saving. The second section examines the effect of tax incentives on long-term mandatory saving programs. In the absence of tax incentives, mandated assets are a substitute for private accumulation and should not affect national savings. However, the tax deductibility of mandated contributions present in almost all countries can be an effective way of influencing not only the composition of wealth, but also the overall level of saving. On this front, the chapter presents international evidence based on regression analysis showing a positive association between the national saving rate and the stock of mandated assets in household portfolios.

The third section examines government programs that target saving for home purchase. Direct subsidies to home mortgages, deductibility of mortgage interest payments, and reduced loan rates are just a few examples of government intervention in this area. But the most striking instruments are mandatory contributions to provident funds designed to accumulate resources for a down payment against home purchase. The interplay between saving for retirement and saving for housing accumulation is also of special interest in this area. The fourth section explores government programs that target saving for health and education, while the fifth section analyzes the effect of tax incentives to borrow, rather than to save.

For each of these five important issues, the chapter examines empirical evidence on the main characteristics of government programs, with a special focus on middle-income countries. It also addresses a number of issues that should be of interest to policymakers. First, on which grounds should government policy target some assets rather than others? Second, do tax-sheltered assets and liabilities lead to substitution away from more heavily taxed savings instruments or do they affect the overall level of saving? And finally, is there any lesson that can be drawn from the experience of developed countries for the design of saving and borrowing incentives in middle-income countries? Three simple models in the appendix summarize the effect on saving of the interest rate, mandated pension contributions, and tax incentives to borrow.

Incentives for Voluntary Retirement Saving

The interest rate effect on personal saving has attracted a long tradition of research, both theoretically and empirically. The specific question that this literature addresses is whether public policies affecting the real rate of interest affect the overall level of saving. Although taxing the return to saving can have a strong effect on household asset selection and allocation, theoretical models, such as the standard two-period model of intertemporal choice presented in the first part of the appendix, are ambivalent regarding the effect on the overall level of saving, even when one considers models with uncertainty and precautionary saving (Bernheim 2002).[1] Nor has the empirical literature been able to pin down this effect.

The empirical literature on saving and taxation has grown tremendously in recent years. Bernheim (2002), Besley and Meghir (2001), Honohan (2000), and Poterba (2000) provide surveys of the

most recent developments, and interested readers are encouraged
to refer to these excellent contributions. This chapter confines itself
to summarizing the main empirical strategies that have been used to
test the interest rate effect on saving. They can be broadly divided
into three groups: estimation of saving function with time-series or
cross-country data, Euler equation estimates of the intertemporal
elasticity of substitution, and analysis of specific tax reforms.

The earliest approach consists of specifying a saving function and
estimating the interest rate elasticity controlling for other determinants of saving. Many such studies have been performed with time-
series data from individual countries, and with cross-country or
panel data from both the industrialized and developing countries.
Honohan (2000) reviews several studies based on individual country
time-series or cross-country data and concludes that "more studies
have found a positive interest rate elasticity than a negative one, but
the coefficients have generally been small and often insignificant" (p.
83). Possible reasons why this approach has been inconclusive stem
from aggregation problems (some investors might have a positive
elasticity of saving, others a negative one) and endogeneity of interest rates and other variables introduced in saving regressions.

The Euler equation for consumption states that consumption
growth depends on the difference between the real rate of interest
and the intertemporal rate of time preference. The sensitivity of consumption growth with respect to the real interest rate is the elasticity of intertemporal substitution in consumption. Since Hall's (1978)
seminal contribution, the possibility of estimating structural preference parameters with the Euler equation has attracted enormous interest among applied economists. More recently, the approach has
shifted attention from studies using aggregate data to analyses based
on household panel data, which allow rigorous treatment of aggregation issues. After more than two decades of empirical studies,
however, the approach has also been largely inconclusive, at least as
far as pinning down the interest rate elasticity is concerned.

First of all, it is now clear that estimation of Euler equations
poses extremely difficult econometric problems, particularly in the
presence of short panel data, omitted variables due to precautionary
saving and liquidity constraints, and non-separabilities between consumption and leisure (Browning and Lusardi 1996). Second, the sensitivity of consumption growth to the real interest rate is hard to estimate with panel data on households, because at any given point in
time households face the same real rate of interest. Researchers must
therefore rely on the variability of marginal tax rates affecting the
after-tax return to saving. Third, most empirical studies find that the
elasticity of substitution is positive and generally less than one, but

estimates vary considerably over this range (Bernheim 2002). Finally, even high values of the elasticity do not necessarily imply a positive interest rate elasticity of saving. Even though a high value of the elasticity makes it more likely that the substitution effect dominates the income effect, the Euler equation delivers information about the shape of the consumption profile, not about the level of consumption and saving.

A third generation of studies has approached the issue at hand studying the portfolio and saving effect of specific tax reforms. Table 4.1, drawn from Poterba (2001), reports information on saving incentives for major industrial nations' voluntary retirement plans. With the exception of France and Japan, these programs are widely available in industrialized countries. The specific tax provision and generosity of saving incentives vary considerably, but the basic features are common. Households can contribute up to a specific limit to retirement saving accounts (such as Individual Retirement Accounts (IRAs) and 401(k) plans in the United States, Individual Saving Accounts in the United Kingdom, and life insurance plans in Italy), using pre-tax dollars. These plans have provided the ground for empirical research trying to assess to what extent contributions to tax deferred saving accounts represent "new saving," or merely a substitution between tax-favored and other assets. The advantage of this approach is that it is based on clear experiments, and on rigorous econometric methods.

At the theoretical level, however, it is not clear whether tax-deferred saving accounts should increase the overall level of saving. This may be the case even in situations in which the interest effect on saving is positive (that is, the substitution effect dominates the income and wealth effects).[2]

This point is made most clearly by Besley and Meghir (2001). Following their example, assume that individuals can invest in only two assets, both of which have a gross rate of return r and one of which is tax-free up to a certain level of investment L. An individual can invest up to L in the tax-favored asset, yielding r. Any savings above L yield a net of tax return $r(1-\theta)$.

In the absence of uncertainty, the effect of the tax incentive on the allocation of wealth is clear: investors put as much wealth as they can in the tax-favored asset, up to the limit L. The effect on the level of saving, however, is ambiguous. If desired saving is less than L, all wealth is allocated in the tax-favored asset and, under the assumptions of the appendix, an increase in r increases saving. If instead desired saving is higher than L, individuals would have saved more than L even in the absence of incentives. In such a situation, the effect is reversed. Besley and Meghir show that the effect of the tax

Table 4.1. Saving Incentives in Voluntary Retirement Funds in Major Industrial Nations

Country	Retirement saving accounts?	Contribution limit	Contributions deductible?	Special notes
Canada	Yes	$9,400 ($15,500 Canadian), indexed	Yes	Limits on foreign stock; carry forward unused contributions
France	No	—	—	—
Germany	Yes	*Vermogensbildungsgesetz*, limit $2,200	Yes	Investment in "long term funds"; other programs to accumulate housing down payments
Italy	Yes	2% of wages or $1,414	Yes	—
Japan	No	—	—	Universal *maruyu* postal saving accounts were phased out in 1986
Netherlands	Yes	1,700 Guilders, or approximately $850 per year for employee saving scheme	Yes	"Employee saving scheme" and "premium saving scheme"; four year vesting period before withdrawal
United Kingdom	Yes	Personal pensions, contributions of 17.5–40 percent of earnings; individual Saving Accounts (ISAs), limit of £5000/year contribution starting in 2000	Yes	ISAs face restrictions on investment choices; total contribution limits were higher in years before 2000
United States	Yes	$2,000 for Individual Retirement Accounts, $10,500 for 401(k) plans	Yes	Other variants include Roth IRAs and 403(b) plans

Source: Poterba (2001).

incentive depends on the relation between investors' wealth and the limit L, and on the intertemporal elasticity of substitution. In practice, then, the same incentive can generate a wide range of heterogeneity of individual responses.

Engen, Gale, and Scholz (1996) point out another feature of tax-deferred saving accounts: that is, that they are less liquid than conventional saving. The saving incentive might reduce savings of those who do not behave according to the intertemporal choice model, but have a fixed saving target. For these individuals, the incentive and the higher return on saving will make it easier to reach the target, because they must give up fewer resources for the same target. A further criticism of the approach based on the analysis of tax reform is that none of the studies is able to estimate the interest rate elasticity of saving and thus provide information valuable to policymakers. Finally, tax incentives reduce tax revenues and therefore public saving. In order to conclude that tax incentives increase capital accumulation, one must therefore consider not only the effect of tax incentives on private saving, but also the revenue loss associated with the incentives. Most of the studies in this area, however, adopt a partial equilibrium framework.

As mentioned, the main question addressed by the literature is whether tax-deferred saving accounts such as 401(k)s and IRAs—introduced in the United States in 1978 and 1986, respectively—represent "new saving" or a substitution between tax-favored and conventional assets. Despite these "clean" tax experiments, a consensus has yet to emerge. On the one hand, Poterba, Venti, and Wise (1996) argue that IRAs and 401(k)s increase saving.[3] Engen, Gale, and Scholz (1996) conclude instead that they produce mainly a reallocation effect of household portfolios, and little effect on intertemporal choice.

If a scheme does have a total saving effect, then one would expect the saving of the participants to be higher than that of non-participants, as indeed it is on average. But participants are also on average wealthier and nearer to retirement than non-contributors. So perhaps the preferences of participants are different as well: for instance, that the wealthy contribute to IRAs because they have a higher taste for saving than non-contributors. In short, cross-sectional studies suffer from an identification problem caused by unobserved heterogeneity and self-selection issues. Panel data, tracking the behavior of investors over time, can help the researcher to control, at least to some extent, for fixed individual heterogeneity. In principle, one can establish if investors have chosen to save more or less after the introduction of a tax-advantaged scheme. But even in this case it is difficult to attribute the decision to increase saving to the introduction of the scheme. An investor might choose to save more for reasons that are totally unrelated to the existence of the scheme (for instance, because the investor is reaching retirement age, or because he would like to purchase a home).

To summarize, of the many studies that have analyzed the interest rate effect on saving, none has found convincing evidence of a systematic relation between the two variables, so that the emerging consensus is that rate-of-return effects on saving are at best small. Time-series data suffer from aggregation problems. After the initial enthusiasm, researchers have realized how difficult it is to tackle the econometric and identification issues in structural Euler equations for consumption. The analysis of tax reform, and particularly of the incentives provided by IRAs and 401(k)s in the United States, has delivered conflicting and inconclusive evidence, despite the great number of high-quality empirical investigations spurred by two major U.S. tax reforms. On a balanced reading of this literature, as summarized by Poterba, Venti, and Wise (1996); Engen, Gale, and Scholz (1996); Bernheim (2002); and Besley and Meghir (2001), there is broad consensus (at least in the United States) that tax-deferred saving accounts have induced massive portfolio shifts toward tax-favored assets, but much less consensus on whether saving incentives have actually increased saving.

Promoting Mandatory Saving

Besides creating a fiscal wedge between pre-tax and after-tax returns, governments affect household saving and borrowing in a variety of ways. The most important programs in middle-income countries promote saving through mandated contributions to pension funds and housing saving accounts. These contributions are mandatory, and crowd out almost automatically conventional saving. However, contributions are generally granted preferential treatment by the tax code, and might therefore be a far more effective way of promoting the overall level of saving than tax-deferred saving accounts based on voluntary contributions.

There are several reasons for setting up mandatory saving programs. First, policymakers often target domestic saving, on the assumption that increasing domestic saving promotes investment, job creation, and growth. Another reason is that mandatory saving programs might be the only effective way of providing the elderly with adequate resources to be spent during retirement, particularly when people are myopic or do not have enough information to plan for relatively long horizons. Moreover, if saving for retirement were left only to the discretion of the individual, free-riding behavior might impose a high burden to society as a whole. After all, the wide implementation of these programs and the fact that a considerable portion of household wealth is locked in mandatory saving programs indicates the social approval of schemes designed to ensure people with adequate reserves to be spent during retirement.

Apart from the effect on domestic saving and capital stock, a further motivation for promoting pension funds and other institutional investors is the desire to encourage so-called popular capitalism through mandatory or voluntary contributions to saving accounts earmarked for retirement. The development of the contractual saving industry is widely thought to have a favorable impact on the deepening and diversification of the financial system. Moreover, individuals might have greater incentives to perform on the job when they have a direct stake in the performance of the economy through the holding of risky assets.[4]

This section describes the characteristics of these programs, particularly in Latin American and East Asian countries. The second part of the appendix shows, in the context of a simple model of the impact of mandated contributions on private and national saving, that the existence of tax concessions on mandatory savings can result in higher overall savings. Empirical evidence based on cross-country data is presented showing that reserves of mandatory pension systems and private pension fund assets do indeed increase national saving, as predicted by the model. The focus is mainly on pension funds, although several remarks apply to unfunded plans as well.

Portfolio Effects of Mandatory Contributions

In the simple model outlined in the second part of the appendix, mandatory contributions displace private accumulation one-for-one. In more realistic cases, this need not be the case. A first important issue is how to measure mandatory saving and pension wealth. Then one needs to distinguish between the portfolio effect of mandatory assets and their effect on national saving. The first two issues are analyzed in this section, while the next section provides empirical evidence on the impact of mandatory retirement saving on national saving.

In general, individual pension assets are defined as the difference between the present discounted value of future pensions and the present discounted value of contributions. Clearly, these depend on legislation (the contribution rate and the pension award formula), expected inflation, expected retirement age, expected rates of return, and mortality. Computation of pension wealth is therefore difficult, for both defined benefits and defined contribution plans.

Individual expectations are usually hard to measure. In the case of social security wealth, the problem is exacerbated by the fact that expectations depend on long-run phenomena (for instance, income growth and rates of return many years from now) and on the possibility of pension reforms changing individual retirement options and pension award formulae. For this reason pension wealth can be estimated only with a high degree of approximation.

Since Feldstein's (1976) seminal contribution, the empirical literature has tried to pin down the *wealth replacement effect* by regressing private assets on pension wealth. With individual-level data, a widely adopted specification is:

$$a = f(t) + \alpha y^p + \beta X + \sigma PW + \varepsilon$$

where a is private wealth, $f(t)$ an age polynomial, y^p permanent income, X a set of demographics, and PW the present discounted value of pension benefits. Permanent income can be estimated using the method proposed by King and Dicks-Mireaux (1982). The parameter σ measures the wealth replacement effect, which should equal -1 in case of complete crowding out.

Most empirical studies find some, but less than full offset of pension wealth on private wealth or saving: that is, negative values of σ but higher than -1. This suggests a degree of substitution between the two sources of wealth that is substantially lower than predicted by the theory (Mackenzie, Gerson, and Cuevas 1997). There are many potential explanations for this finding. Since there is no space to discuss all of them in detail, this discussion limits itself to a broad summary.

Gale (1998) shows that the parameter σ might be a downwardly biased estimate of the displacement effect. The bias is induced by the use of a measure of disposable income that is net of pension contributions, rather than the appropriate measure, which instead treats contributions as mandatory savings. Gale also shows that the bias is likely to be higher for the young. Once the correction is implemented, his estimate of σ (based on U.S. Survey of Consumer Finances data) ranges from -0.52 to -0.77.

There are other theoretical reasons that can explain a low estimate of σ. Pension wealth is illiquid, and cannot be used as a collateral. If the consumer is liquidity constrained, an increase in pension wealth is not necessarily followed by an increase in current consumption.

Precautionary saving can have similar effects. An increase in private wealth offset by a decline in pension wealth can reduce uncertainty and thus increase current consumption. Also in this case, the offset is less than complete. A related issue is that consumers are uncertain about the overall solvency of the social security system and the prospect of future pension reforms. If this is the case, they may revise their social security wealth expectations downward and save more in the current period.

Another factor that may have a bearing on the wealth replacement effect is the extent of financial education of the household. Many households have short-run horizons, either because of liquidity constraints or myopia. They will therefore prefer one dollar of financial wealth rather than one dollar of pension wealth. Indeed, Gale shows that the displacement effect is stronger for individuals who contribute to IRAs and for college graduates.

This discussion has so far neglected the possibility that consumers respond to an increase in pension wealth by retiring earlier (a fact that cannot be captured in the simple two-period model of the appendix). But according to the life-cycle hypothesis, saving and wealth increase with the length of retirement. Feldstein (1976) shows that this *induced retirement effect* can potentially invert the sign of the relationship between private and pension wealth (the estimate of σ could be smaller in absolute value or even turn positive).[5]

The Effect of Mandatory Saving on National Saving

Tax incentives for pension funds exist in virtually all countries. Most tax codes allow contributions to pension funds to be made out of pre-tax income, or to attract a tax rebate. Investment income of pension funds is often allowed to accumulate free of tax. Many countries even allow some part of the benefits to be paid out tax-free or at a concessionary tax rate.

A regime in which contributions and returns are exempt is a classical example of an expenditure tax, treating saving as any other form of consumption. On the other hand, a regime in which contributions are taxed and benefits are exempt corresponds to a regime in which accruals to both earnings and saving are taxed. In practice, the various tax regimes can have different effects, depending on the marginal tax rate during the working span and the marginal tax rate at retirement.

Whitehouse (2000) provides a description of the tax treatment of pensions in the OECD countries. With the exception of Australia, France, Iceland, and Japan, pension contributions are made out of pre-tax income or attract a tax rebate. There is always a limit on deductibility of contributions. In the majority of OECD countries income accruing in the pension fund accumulates tax free, but there are exceptions. Australia, Denmark, and Sweden tax, partially or totally, the real return of the fund. On the other hand, all countries except New Zealand tax withdrawals, although at different degrees. For instance, some countries allow withdrawal of a tax-free lump sum, while others apply tax penalties to early withdrawals.

Outside the OECD, the tax treatment of pension funds follows similar principles: contributions and returns are usually exempt, while benefits are taxed. Table 4.2 describes the main features of the tax treatment of mandatory contributions to pension funds for a selected group of Latin American and East Asian countries that have recently reformed their pension systems. In Argentina, Chile, Colombia, Costa Rica, Mexico, and Uruguay contributions and investment income are exempt, while benefits are taxed. In Latin America the exception is Peru, where contributions and benefits are taxed but investment income is exempt.

The situation is more heterogeneous in East Asia, where all but one of the countries listed in table 4.2 (the Philippines) feature exempt contributions. In all but one also (Indonesia) pension benefits are also tax-free, while investment income is taxed in the Philippines and Thailand, and partly in Indonesia. Malaysia and Singapore operate a national, publicly managed, provident fund system, while Indonesia has a private management structure.

Figure 4.1 plots histograms of the GDP share of the sum of reserves of mandatory pension systems and private pension fund assets in selected countries of Latin America, Asia, and Africa. Chile, Malaysia, Singapore, and South Africa stand out, with a GDP share of 50 percent or higher. Pension fund assets are positively associated with the ratio of national saving to GDP, as shown in figure 4.2. One possible interpretation of the positive correlation is that the tax provisions attached to mandatory saving programs are associated with higher national saving, as discussed.

Since the positive relation between pension fund assets and national saving might be driven by other variables, the discussion now turns to regression analysis. The following reduced form for national saving is estimated:

$$\frac{S}{Y} = \alpha_o + \alpha_1 \rho + \alpha_2 \frac{S_g}{Y} + \alpha_3 DEP + \alpha_4 \frac{PFA}{Y} + \varepsilon$$

where Y denotes GDP, S national saving, ρ the growth rate of GDP, S_g government saving, DEP the dependency ratio (defined as the ratio of those aged less than 15 or more than 65 and total population), and PFA the sum of reserves of mandatory pension systems and private pension fund assets as a ratio to GDP.[6] All variables are

Table 4.2. Tax Treatment of Mandatory Retirement Funds in Latin America and East Asia

Latin America	Year implemented	Contributions	Investment income	Benefits
Argentina	1994	Exempt	Exempt	Taxed
Bolivia	1997	n.a.	n.a.	n.a.
Chile	1981	Exempt	Exempt	Taxed
Colombia	1994	Exempt	Exempt	Exempt up to a ceiling
Costa Rica	1998	Exempt	Exempt	Taxed
El Salvador	1997	n.a.	n.a.	n.a.
Mexico	1997	Exempt	Exempt	Taxed
Peru	1993	Taxed	Exempt	Taxed
Uruguay	1996	Up to 20% of earnings are exempt	Exempt	Taxed
East Asia				
Brunei		Exempt	Exempt	Exempt
Indonesia	1997	Exempt	Funds bank deposits and returns on listed local securities are exempt. Returns on open-ended mutual funds, unlisted securities and property are taxed.	Taxed
Malaysia	1991	Exempt	Exempt	Exempt
Philippines	1998	Employees' contributions are taxed. Employers' contributions are exempt for qualified occupational plans.	Taxed	Exempt
Singapore		Exempt	Exempt	Exempt
Thailand	1998	Exempt	Exempt	Exempt

Sources: Whitehouse (2000); Holzmann, MacArthur, and Sin (2000).

Figure 4.1. Pension Fund Assets in Developing Countries
(percent of GDP)

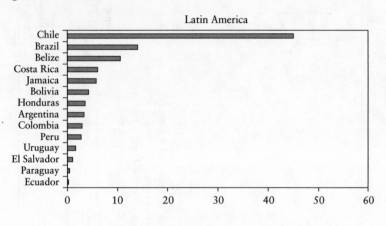

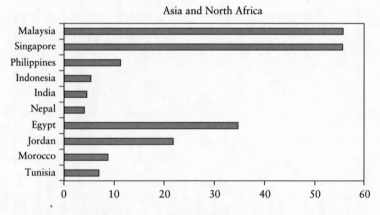

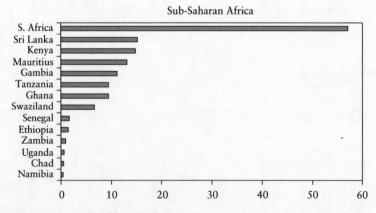

Source: See note to table 4.3.

Figure 4.2. National Saving and Pension Fund Assets in
Developing Countries (percent of GDP)

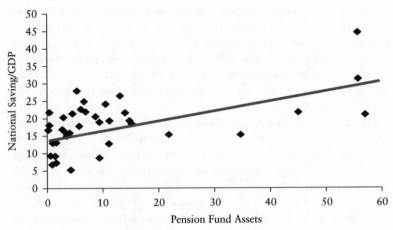

Source: See note to table 4.3.

averaged over the 1985–95 period. Data sources and variables definition are reported in the data appendix.

The purpose of the regression is to summarize the main determinants of national saving and, in particular, the correlation between tax-favored pension fund assets and national saving, once other variables affecting national saving are controlled for.[7]

The reason for using national saving as the dependent variable is that national saving is measured as national income less total (private plus public) consumption, a measure that does not rely on the definition of mandatory saving. On the other hand, private saving definitions are largely arbitrary depending, among other things, on the way mandatory contributions and pension withdrawals are treated. Furthermore, national saving is independent from inflation, while conventional definitions of private saving require a measure of private sector income, which is affected by the loss incurred from the depreciation of nominal assets due to inflation.

Several studies have estimated versions of this equation with time series data on individual countries, international cross-sections, or panels of countries (Modigliani 1993; Masson, Bayoumi, and Samiei 1998). According to the life-cycle model, saving should be positively related to the growth rate of income, and negatively affected by the dependency ratio ($\alpha_1 > 0$ and $\alpha_3 < 0$). Models with finite horizons also suggest that national saving increases with government saving ($\alpha_2 > 0$). However, according to the Ricardian equivalence proposition, public and private saving are perfect substitutes, so that an increase in government saving should not affect national savings ($\alpha_2 = 0$).

The proposed specification can be used to assess the impact of mandatory and contractual saving on the national saving rate. The discussion above highlights that in the absence of tax incentives, pension fund assets are a substitute for private accumulation and should not affect national saving ($\alpha_4 = 0$). If instead contributions are favored by the tax code, there should be a positive effect on national saving ($\alpha_4 > 0$).

Table 4.3 reports the regression results. The first regression relies on a cross-section of 60 countries for which complete records were available. The GDP growth rate and the government saving rate are associated with higher national saving, while an increase in the dependency ratio reduces national saving. All coefficients are statistically different from zero at the 1 percent level. These findings are in agreement with previous studies and provide strong evidence for the life-cycle model. The effect of pension fund assets is positive and statically different from zero in the less developed countries (LDC).[8]

To check the robustness of these results, a sensitivity analysis was performed allowing for changes in the estimation method, the definition of government saving, the sample used, and the omission of other variables potentially affecting national saving. The second specification re-estimates using a robust method to control for the impact of influential values.[9] The third and fourth regressions rely on a definition of inflation-adjusted government saving, which is available for a subset of the countries in our sample.

The last two regressions report OLS and robust estimates based on the 38 LDC countries in the sample. In no case is the general pattern of results affected. In particular, the coefficient of pension fund assets ranges from 0.14 to 0.18 percent, and is statistically different from zero at the 1 percent level in all specifications, providing support for the proposition that tax-favored pension contributions raise national saving, at least in LDC countries. In the sample of LDC countries, the first quartile of the distribution of pension fund assets is 1.6 percent, and in the third quartile is 11.2 percent. The estimates indicate that the thought experiment of increasing pension fund assets from the first to the third quartile is associated with an increase in national saving of 1.3 to 1.7 percentage points of GDP.

The baseline specifications also include a number of additional variables that could potentially affect the national saving rate: the real interest rate (measured as the difference between the nominal interest rate on government bills and the actual inflation rate), per capita income, the Gini coefficient of income inequality, the GDP ratio of social security expenditures (taken from Palacios and Pallarès-Miralles

Table 4.3. National Saving Regressions

Variable	Total sample		Total sample, inflation-adjusted government saving		LDC sample	
	OLS	Robust regression	OLS	Robust regression	OLS	Robust regression
GDP growth	1.389 (2.44)	1.470 (2.66)	2.232 (4.61)	2.298 (5.07)	1.478 (2.05)	1.562 (2.26)
Dependency ratio	−0.520 (−2.92)	−0.497 (−2.87)	−0.566 (−3.00)	−0.669 (−3.79)	−0.493 (−2.29)	−0.502 (−2.43)
Government saving / GDP	0.453 (2.06)	0.582 (2.73)	0.239 (1.66)	0.249 (1.85)	0.195 (0.65)	0.339 (1.18)
Pension fund assets / GDP	−0.005 (−0.16)	−0.026 (−0.80)	−0.041 (−1.16)	−0.049 (−1.51)	—	—
(Pension fund assets / GDP) × LDC	0.167 (2.54)	0.179 (2.79)	0.143 (2.31)	0.173 (3.00)	0.168 (2.67)	0.156 (2.58)
LDC dummy	−4.333 (−1.47)	−4.724 (−1.65)	−3.852 (−1.40)	−2.625 (−1.02)	—	—
Constant term	36.666 (5.33)	36.231 (5.42)	35.733 (4.98)	38.878 (5.79)	31.443 (2.91)	31.976 (3.08)
Number of countries	60	60	48	48	38	38

Note: The table reports national saving regressions using a sample of 22 OECD countries and 38 developing countries. The third and fourth regressions use the inflation-adjusted definition of government saving. The last two regressions are based on a sample of 38 developing countries. *T* statistics are reported in parenthesis.

Source: See data appendix.

2000), and a dummy variable for each continent. The coefficients of these variables are not statistically different from zero.

Fostering Accumulation of Housing

When governments extend incentives for retirement saving, they change household portfolio allocations, but not necessarily the intertemporal allocation of consumption. If instead the tax code targets specific goods, such as housing, education, or health, it changes not only the margins of intertemporal choice, but also consumption allocations between different goods. This section reviews government intervention in the promotion of saving targeted to housing. The next section examines tax incentives to save for education, health, and other "merit" goods.

Programs whose aim is to foster the accumulation of housing take various forms, ranging from direct government investment, subsidies, and contributions to households or firms, to indirect support for housing accumulation through tax incentives. One rationale for government intervention in this area is the notion that housing is an investment good, hence tax-deductible capital costs are in principle offset by imputed rental values. In practice the offset is modest, as the market value on which imputed rents are computed is underestimated (Duebel 2000). So the main reason is to shift the portfolio allocation of wealth toward goods to which society assigns an important weight in alleviating poverty and in raising living conditions, much like targeting retirement saving is a remedy to household myopia and potential free-riding problems.

This chapter aims at a broad description of tax incentives to save and to borrow, so it does not discuss direct government intervention in the housing market. Instead, it focuses on instruments designed to raise household saving for housing finance: mandatory contributions to specially designed housing funds, contractual saving for housing, subsidies to financial intermediaries providing housing funds and, in the fifth section, mortgage interest rate relief schemes.

In some industrialized countries (notably Austria, France, and Germany), housing finance has traditionally relied on contractual saving (Impavido, Musalem, and Tressel 2002). According to these contracts, households save an agreed amount over an extended period at pre-specified terms. At the end of this period, households are eligible for a loan to purchase or renovate an owner-occupied house. The saving schemes are characterized by fixed, below-market rates on savings and subsequent loans. The advantages of contract saving for housing are threefold. First, they provide adequate information to potential borrowers. Second, they make funds available for down payments. Finally, they offer protection against volatile financial markets (Lea and Renaud 1995). The government has a relevant role in these programs, by providing saving premiums and tax benefits.

The rationale for these programs is that they allow poor households to access mortgage loans for home purchase that would be otherwise unavailable. This might be even more important in less developed countries, where many households lack the income to qualify for a loan and/or financial institutions tend to screen out these households because mortgages require regular payments over the long run, as well as income stability—conditions that are unlikely to be met by poor households. Limited competition among financial institutions amplifies these market failures.

In the German Bauspar scheme, the principle is one of reciprocity. Contractual deposits are mobilized by specialized institutions and are available only to make loans to participants. Savers fulfilling the terms of the contract receive a government interest premium proportional to the amount saved (up to a maximum).

The French system is traditionally more integrated with capital markets and contractual saving for housing works like an account with subsidized return. In contrast to the German model, savers can keep their savings in the housing fund without obtaining the loan if they find the deposit yield attractive. Deposit institutions can use the deposits to finance housing loans or purchase bonds in the secondary mortgage market. As in Germany, French savers enjoy a government interest premium on contractual saving over the banks' deposit rate. Lea and Renaud (1995) provide a thorough discussion of the pros and cons of contractual saving schemes for housing, and conclude that the success of these programs critically depends on financial and price stability, two conditions that are seldom met in LDC countries.

Housing banks enjoy a wide range of subsidies, including direct tax-based funding; direct deposits with tax-preferred or regulation-preferred status or government guarantees; and exemption from income taxation, stamp duties, and lien registration costs. They play a prominent role in several developing countries, such as Argentina, Brazil, India, Indonesia, Jordan, Korea, Thailand, and Venezuela (Duebel 2000).

But the most striking programs to foster the accumulation of housing are mandatory contributions to housing funds, widespread in several Latin American and East Asian countries. Table 4.4 reports the main features of these programs. They differ quite widely in the amount of contributions, eligibility, and loan characteristics. Contributions to housing funds are usually based on payroll tax, with one

Table 4.4. Mandatory Housing Funds

Country	Program	Main features
Argentina	FONAVI	Prior to 1991 mandatory contributions were 5 percent of the wage tax. Since 1991, mandatory contributions have been 40 percent of the fuel consumption tax. To qualify for a loan, household monthly income must range between $500 and $1,000. The household then assigns 25 percent of income to monthly repayment installments. Terms are up to 25 years.
Bolivia	FONVIS (phased out in 1998)	The program featured deductions from public sector salaries earmarked for social housing improvement and construction. The current system is based on tax incentives for long-term saving.
Brazil	FGTS	The fund is made up of mandatory monthly deposits by employers into accounts held in the names of their employees at the Federal Savings Bank. The contribution rate is 8 percent. Loans with FGTS funds are targeted to low-income families with monthly income of up to 12 minimum wages (approximately US$933). Average loans amount to approximately R$20,000 (US$11,500).
Colombia	CAV	Mandatory contributions amount to one month of wages. Withdrawal is allowed for home purchase, as well as for workers who go back to school, if they quit or are dismissed.
Jamaica	National Housing Trust	Established in 1976. It is funded by statutory deductions from employers, employees, and self-employed individuals. Contributors must earn more than the minimum wage. The contribution rate is 5 percent (2 percent from employees, 3 percent from employers). The self-employed contribute 3 percent. Funds are available for first home purchasing after a minimum of 3.5 years of contributions, for a maximum amount of JA$800,000 (per contributor).

Table 4.4. Mandatory Housing Funds *(continued)*

Country	Program	Main features
Mexico	INFONAVIT	Mexican employers contribute 5 percent of their payroll to the fund, up to a maximum of 10 times the statutory minimum wage. The contributions accumulate in the national housing fund, used by INFONAVIT to award 30-year mortgage loans, with an average interest rate of 6 percent plus an adjustment for the annual increase in the minimum wage.
Peru	FONAVI (phased out in 2000)	Peruvian employers contributed 5 percent of total wages (salary plus bonuses) to the housing fund. The scheme (converted to an "emergency solidarity tax") was phased out in January 2000.
Philippines	PAG-IBIG Home Development Mutual Fund	Mandatory contributions are 1 percent for employees earning not more than 1.5 million pesos per month; 2 percent for those earning more than 1.5 million. All employers contribute 2 percent of the monthly compensation for all employees covered by the social security system and the Government Service Insurance System.
Venezuela	Ahorro Habitaçional	Mandatory contributions for public and private employees are 1 percent of wages for employees and 2 percent for employers. The self-employed can participate in the program on a voluntary basis with a contribution rate of 3 percent. Homeowners and individuals over 60 are exempt from the contribution.

Source: Duebel (2000).

notable exception: in Argentina, contributions are no longer from the income payroll tax but from the fuel consumption tax.

Many of these programs were not originally earmarked for housing, but have evolved to allow contributors to withdraw funds for home purchase. For instance, in Brazil the FGTS (*Fundo de Garantia de Tempo de Serviço*) was established in 1967 as a severance pay fund in the case of termination without just cause. It requires employers to deposit a (tax-deductible) 8.3 percent of the worker's pay in a restricted saving account in this fund, managed by the National

Housing Bank, in the names of their employees. The account earns interest of 3 percent a year, in addition to a monthly adjustment to compensate for inflation.[10] Employees may withdraw the balances in these bank accounts if they have been dismissed without just cause, if the firm is liquidated, at retirement, or to purchase a personal residence under a government-approved housing financing scheme. In case of dismissal without just cause, the employer is obliged to pay the employee an additional amount equivalent to 40 percent of the accumulated balance in the employee's FGTS bank account.[11]

Mandatory saving is sometimes targeted to both retirement and housing. Table 4.5 lists some selected examples around the world. In Malaysia, for instance, accumulated Employees Provident Funds can be used to serve retirement purposes (60 percent), home purchase (30 percent), and even medical expenses (10 percent). Similar provisions, subject to limits, exist in Colombia and some Asian countries.

The stated targets of most mandatory savings programs for housing are low-income households. However, experts have lamented that most of the social/public housing projects have in practice favored middle-income rather than poor households. In Venezuela only 8 percent of households contributing to the *Ahorro Habitaçional* fund have actually received a housing unit (under the *Ley of Politica Habitaçional*). In Mexico, INFONAVIT has assisted little more than 11 percent of households contributing to the fund. In Peru, the FONAVI fund has been in effect no more than an additional payroll tax imposed on employers.[12] Experts have also noted that mandatory contributions to housing funds tend to distort credit markets and inhibit their development.

Targeting Merit Goods: Education, Health, and Life Protection

Virtually all industrialized countries provide some form of tax incentives for saving toward education, and tax deductibility of educational expenses, health and life insurance premiums, and out-of-pocket medical expenses. Education, health, and life protection can be regarded as merit goods and, in the case of education and health, long-term growth enhancing factors. These programs are absent or of negligible importance in less developed countries. Table 4.6 describes the features of some of these programs and tax provisions for selected countries.

A striking addition to the wide range of tax concessions and other government interventions already influencing the college tu-

Table 4.5. The Interaction between Mandatory Pension
Funds and Housing Finance

Country	Program	Main features
Colombia	CAV	Mandatory contributions equal to one-month wages are made to the CAV. If the pension fund exceeds 110 percent of minimum wages, it can be used for home purchase.
Malaysia	Employees Provident Fund (EPF)	Contributions to the EPF are apportioned into three accounts: 60 percent is for retirement, 30 percent is for housing or pre-retirement plans (to be eligible for pre-retirement withdrawal the account holder must be over 50 years old), and 10 percent is for medical expenses. The withdrawal can be used to buy or build a house, or to pay off a housing loan. A member is eligible to apply for withdrawal if he has not made any previous withdrawals to buy or build a house and has not attained the age of 55 at the time of application.
Philippines	Reserve funds of the social security system	Borrowing for housing against a share of the accumulated pension fund is possible.
Singapore	Central Provident Fund (CPF)	Borrowing for housing against a share of the accumulated pension fund in CPF is possible. In fact, over half of withdrawals in recent years have been for housing purposes.
Sri Lanka	Employees Provident Fund (EPF)	The EPF is the largest mandatory saving program in Sri Lanka. The contribution rate is 12 percent for employers and 8 percent for employees. Contributions are taxed (that is, they are paid out of after-tax income), but income from accumulated funds and benefits are exempt. It is possible to withdraw funds from retirement accounts to purchase a home.

Sources: Whitehouse (2000); Holzmann, MacArthur, and Sin (2000).

ition motive for saving in the United States (see Feldstein 1995; Souleles 2000) is the Education IRA, introduced by the Taxpayer Relief Act of 1997. Under this scheme an annual, non-deductible contribution of up to $500 per year per child (tapering off for high-income households) may be invested until the child reaches age 18. Withdrawals to pay for college expenses for the child are tax-free.

Table 4.6. Tax Incentives for Education, Health, and
Life Protection

	Main features
Education	
United States	Education IRA, introduced in 1997. An annual, non-deductible contribution of up to $500 per year, per child may be invested until the child reaches age 18. Withdrawals to pay for college expenses for the child are tax-free. Single taxpayers earning an adjusted gross income above $95,000 ($150,000 on a joint return) are not eligible.
United States	Tax deductibility of up to $2,500 on qualified student loans; tax credits of up to $1,500 of undergraduate education and up to $1,000 for any post-high school education.
Germany	Tax deductibility of 30 percent of tuition fees of government-approved private schools.
Health	
United States	Major out-of-pocket health expenses deductible (excluding private health insurance premiums).
Italy	Major out-of-pocket health expenses deductible (including private health insurance premiums).
Argentina	Private long-term health insurance tax-deductible, subject to limits.
Taiwan	Private long-term health insurance tax-deductible.
Germany	Private long-term health insurance tax-deductible, subject to limits.
India	Private long-term health insurance tax-deductible up to a cap.
Japan	Private long-term health insurance tax-deductible up to a cap.
Life protection	
United States	Investment income is not taxed but withdrawals and contributions are. Employer-provided group term policies up to $50,000 are not taxed.
Canada	Investment income and withdrawals are tax-free if they provide only an insurance, rather than an investment, element.
United Kingdom	Withdrawals are tax-free, but returns are taxed. Tax relief on premiums phased out in 1984.

Table 4.6. Tax Incentives for Education, Health, and Life Protection *(continued)*

	Main features
Life protection, *continued*	
Germany	Contributions are tax-deductible subject to a cap; returns are not subject to tax.
Italy	Contributions are tax-deductible subject to a cap and a time limit for life insurance products specifically designed to supplement social security pensions; withdrawals are taxed.
Japan	Contributions are tax-deductible subject to a cap and a time limit; withdrawals are partially tax-exempt.
France	Contributions are tax-deductible subject to a cap and a time limit; withdrawals are taxed.
Argentina	Contributions are tax-deductible subject to a cap; returns are tax-free.
India	Contributions are tax-deductible; returns are taxed.
Singapore	Contributions are tax-deductible subject to a cap; returns are taxed.
Taiwan	Contributions are tax-deductible subject to a cap; returns are taxed.

Sources: Whitehouse (2000); Holzmann, MacArthur, and Sin (2000).

In most European countries schools are public and higher education is funded by general taxation with limited tuition fee expenses, and accordingly a lower need to save to meet this capital outlay. Nevertheless, in some countries private education expenses receive some limited tax advantage (as in Germany and Italy).

The tax code also influences the demand for health insurance. Major health expenses are tax deductible in a handful of countries, particularly where the government-provided healthcare system is absent or deemed to be of poor quality. In the United States, out-of-pocket medical expenditures above a threshold (currently 7.5 percent of adjusted gross income) can be deducted from adjusted gross income. This excludes health insurance premiums paid by employees. In Italy both private health insurance premiums and a limited amount of out-of-pocket medical expenses are tax deductible. Among developing countries, Argentina, India, and Taiwan offer tax deductibility of private long-term health insurance subject to some limits.

Finally, several countries' tax systems contain incentives to encourage life insurance contributions.[13] Many life insurance contracts are structured to embody a significant element of saving with only a modest insurance component. Typically, the tax advantages are granted only if the investors commit to long-term contracts, which can be seen as a substitute for retirement saving.[14] Tax deductibility tends to be operative on the financial component of the contract, rather than on the pure insurance component—although Canada provides an exception in this respect.

In the United States accumulated reserves in life insurance contracts are relatively unimportant because administrative costs lower the net returns offered below the pre-tax return on the assets that back the policies. In Italy, life insurance premiums were partly tax-deductible between 1987 and 2000, but the tax system did not discriminate between the saving and the insurance component. The 2000 tax reform maintains incentives only for the financial component.[15] In developing countries (such as Argentina, India, Singapore, and Taiwan) tax systems feature partial tax deductibility of contributions to life insurance policies.[16]

From a public policy perspective, it would be interesting to know how the schemes discussed above compare with non-financial based incentives that achieve the same broad goals; for instance, comparing the effectiveness of tax incentives for education with direct subsidies, or tax deductibility of health-related expenses with deductibility of health insurance premiums. Which types of scheme are most effective in enhancing education or improving health standards; which are prone to abuse; and what are the redistributive impacts and macroeconomic consequences of the different incentive regimes? So far the evidence is scant, particularly in developing countries, preventing clear-cut policy advice in this area.

Incentives to Borrow

In many developed countries tax incentives to save coexist with tax incentives to borrow in the form of tax deductibility of interest payments. Such allowances may have important implications for the structure of household portfolios and for the overall level of saving. For instance, in almost all EU countries and in the United States a portion of mortgage interest rate payments is tax-deductible (Maclennan, Muellbauer, and Stephens 1998). On the other hand, few countries offer tax incentives for consumer credit and educational loans (see the discussion above for details on education).

Table 4.7, drawn from Poterba (2001), summarizes the type of borrowing incentives for house purchase and consumer credit that exist in nine major OECD countries. Because of the low level of de-

Table 4.7. Tax Treatment of Borrowing, Selected OECD Countries

Country	Is mortgage interest deductible?	Tax treatment of consumer borrowing
Canada	No	Not deductible
France	Yes	Not deductible
Germany	No	Not deductible
Italy	Only for first-time homebuyers	Not deductible
Japan	No, but new homebuyers enjoy a tax credit for up to six years	Not deductible
Netherlands	Yes	Deductible subject to a cap
Sweden	Yes	Fully deductible until 1991. Not deductible afterward.
United Kingdom	No (effective April 2000)	Not deductible
United States	Yes, subject to a rarely binding limit	Not deductible. Home equity loans up to $100,000 are tax-deductible.

Source: Poterba (2001).

velopment of credit markets, such programs are seldom present in less developed countries.

Only one of the nine nations, the Netherlands, currently allows tax deduction for consumer credit, subject to a limit (in Sweden, tax deductibility of consumer credit was phased out in 1991). Households can deduct mortgage interest payments in five out of nine nations. In the United Kingdom the tax deduction was phased out in April 2000 (see below). In Japan taxpayers are not allowed to deduct mortgage interest payments, but enjoy a special tax credit for first-time home purchase, subject to a time limit. Three countries—France, the Netherlands, and the United States—allow relatively unrestricted deductions for mortgage interest. A fourth, Italy, allows mortgage interest deductions only for first-time homeowners. In the United States, households cannot deduct interest on more than $1 million of mortgage debt; in practice, this constraint rarely binds. In light of this cross-sectional heterogeneity in tax rules, one should expect households to allocate a greater share of their portfolios to housing assets in France, the Netherlands, and the United States, and to rely more on mortgage debt in these countries, than in other nations.

Tax deductibility of loan payments reduces the after-tax interest rate paid on the loan. Theoretically, for net borrowers the effect and substitution effects discussed in the first part of the appendix go in the same direction: an increase in the interest rate increases interest payments (the income effect), as well as the relative price of current consumption with respect to future consumption (the substitution effect). For both reasons, borrowing and current consumption decline. Thus on theoretical grounds the removal of tax incentives to borrow should be accompanied by a decline in debt (that is, an increase in saving). Yet tax incentives for borrowing have been the subject of much less investigation than incentives to save. Ideally, such investigation should be carried out at the microeconomic level, exploiting the variability induced by tax reforms that change the incentives of different household groups to borrow.

A good example in this respect is the U.K. MIRAS (Mortgage Interest Relief at Source) experiment. Before MIRAS, there were two sources of potential cross-sectional variability. Mortgagers received tax relief on the interest on the first £30,000 of a mortgage; the tax relief increased with the marginal tax rate. Moreover, until 1988 the £30,000 limit applied on single mortgagers rather than the property: that is, unmarried people could each receive relief on loans up to £30,000, including more than one on the same property. In 1988 the government eliminated such distortion. According to Hills (1990) this tax change, advertised five months in advance, was a contributory factor to the overheating of the U.K. housing market in 1988.

The model in the last section of the appendix shows that quantity constraints on borrowing generally distort the intertemporal consumption profile. In practice, policymakers might still want to discourage household borrowing, because they might target saving and investment at the expense of consumption. The experience of several developed countries is consistent with this argument. For instance, in South Korea and Taiwan, selective credit ceilings have been placed on mortgage loans with the explicit aim of fostering industrial investment.[17]

Conclusion

This survey began with the consideration that there are good reasons for encouraging household saving. First of all, there is considerable evidence that even in closed economies or economies with imperfect capital mobility, higher saving leads to more productive investment and ultimately wider economic development. A second compelling argument for promoting pension funds and the life insurance industry is that the contractual savings industry can have a favorable impact on the diversity and efficiency of the financial system. Proponents argue that they can contribute to the establishment of so-called popular capitalism, enhancing the incentives to perform of individuals with a direct stake in the holding of risky financial assets.

While the arguments in favor of promoting saving are widely accepted and theoretically compelling, there is less consensus on the ways to achieve this goal and on the interpretation of the empirical evidence. A first issue is whether governments should rely on tax incentives to encourage voluntary retirement saving—but leave the ultimate decision to save up to the individual consumer—or should governments rely on mandatory retirement programs.

Tax incentives to save can be justified on the ground that they do not distort the intertemporal choice between consumption and saving: a regime in which contributions and returns are tax-exempt treats saving as any other form of consumption. However, in practice this is not the case, as shown in the second section above, because in most countries the tax code does not achieve neutrality. And there is considerable empirical debate as to the effectiveness of tax incentives in promoting saving: most studies conclude that tax incentives affect the allocation of household portfolios, but the effect on the amount saved is less clear-cut. Tax incentives also raise serious distributional issues, particularly in developing countries, as only individuals in the upper tail of the income distribution have the resources and the financial information required to take advantage of the incentives. Finally, tax incentives have a cost in terms of revenue losses. To the extent that losses are shared more equally than gains, tax incentives to save might adversely affect the distribution of resources in the economy. For these reasons, promoting voluntary saving might not be the right instrument for achieving the goals outlined above.

However, mandatory saving programs avoid the free-riding problems that would arise if individuals were free to choose the amount of saving; they force even myopic individuals to set aside resources to be spent during retirement. If the policy goal is to increase investment and growth and promote popular capitalism, mandatory saving programs are more likely to succeed than voluntary saving schemes, even at the cost of distorting the intertemporal allocation of resources that households would choose otherwise.

Besides retirement saving, there is a wide range of instruments that governments apply to promote saving for specific goods (housing, education, and health). The widest area of intervention is housing, where the most striking instruments are mandatory contributions to provident funds designed to accumulate resources for a down payment against home purchase. Several countries also encourage saving for education and medical expenditures, while still others encourage (or discourage) borrowing. At the moment, the interplay between these different saving instruments, their distortionary impact on household portfolios and, ultimately, their effectiveness in achieving sectoral and macroeconomic goals have been subject to many fewer empirical studies. A priori, one can expect considerable portfolio effects from these programs, but in the absence of detailed studies it is difficult to evaluate their overall effectiveness. For instance, mandatory saving programs for housing clearly raise the share of wealth allocated to housing. However, the effectiveness in raising the overall homeownership and saving rates can be undermined by displacement effects on other forms of wealth, bureaucratic costs in managing the provident funds, government revenue costs, and the associated distributional impacts.

There is ample ground for detailed studies on these and related issues, but at the moment the evidence is scant, particularly in developing countries, preventing clear-cut policy advice in this area. The studies would require microeconomic surveys to sort out individuals affected and not affected by the tax incentives, and detailed data on the composition of household portfolios to track the response of the individual wealth components to the presence of incentives to housing, health, education, and borrowing.

While the discussion above applies to developed and developing countries alike, this study concludes by singling out two issues that are likely to be of particular importance in developing countries. The evidence for developing countries indicates that pension coverage is far from complete. Extending pension coverage, and the associated tax benefits, might be far more important than introducing sophisticated saving incentives. Besides affecting national saving, pension coverage can have a number of other effects, such as in raising the attachment of workers to firms and labor productivity. Needless to say, financial transaction costs are high in many developing countries.[18] These costs are compounded by judicial and bureaucratic costs, which in many countries represent a hidden tax on business and financial transactions (Djankov and others 2002). This implies that the return and incentive to save can be increased by making the environment more competitive and efficient without resorting to explicit tax instruments.

Appendix. Analytical Framework for Assessing the Impact of Tax Incentives on Saving

This appendix sets out a simple model of saving and examines the impact of tax incentives.

A Two-period Model of Saving

To provide a background to some of the issues analyzed in the second section, it is useful to consider the effect of changes in the after-tax return to saving in the simplest intertemporal choice model. Consider the standard two-period consumption model, where the individual maximizes utility

$$\max u(c_1, c_2)$$

subject to an intertemporal budget constraint:

$$c_1 + \frac{c_{21}}{1+r(1-\theta)} = a_1 + y_1 + \frac{y_2}{1+r(1-\theta)} = a_1 + h_1$$

where c_1 and c_2 denote, respectively, first and second period consumption, a_1 indicates beginning-of-period wealth, and h_1 represents human capital: that is, the present discounted value of current and future (after-tax) income. The individual receives $r(1-\theta)$ on resources carried on from the first period to the second, where r is the real rate of interest and θ is the tax rate on asset income.

The standard assumption is that the utility function is concave, and that the marginal utility of consumption is positive and decreasing: that is, $\partial u(.)/\partial c_j > 0$, $\partial^2 u(.)/\partial c_j^2 < 0$, for $j=1, 2$. The first-order condition of the maximization problem is:

$$\frac{\partial u(.)/\partial c_1}{\partial u(.)/\partial c_2} = 1 + r(1-\theta)$$

If first period consumption is reduced by one unit, second period consumption increases by $1+r(1-\theta)$. Thus $1+r(1-\theta)$ represents the price of first period consumption in terms of second period consumption. Using the intertemporal budget constraint, the optimization problem delivers two demand functions:

$$c_1^* = f[r(1-\theta), a_0 + h_0]$$
$$c_2^* = g[r(1-\theta), a_0 + h_0]$$

Given the assumptions about the utility function, an increase in total wealth raises both c_1^* and c_2^*. The after-tax real interest rate has three effects on first period consumption. If $c_1^* < a_1 + y_1$—that is, if the individual is a net saver in the first period—an increase in the after-tax return increases asset income received in the second period, raising both c_1^* and c_2^* (the income effect). The same increase in $r(1-\theta)$ raises the price of first period consumption, increasing c_2^* at the expense of c_1^* (the substitution effect). Finally, an increase in $r(1-\theta)$ reduces human capital and consumption in both periods (the wealth effect). While the substitution effect and the wealth effect reduce c_1^*, the income effect tends to raise it. The overall impact of the interest rate on first period consumption and saving is therefore ambiguous.

On the other hand, if $c_1^* > a_1 + y_1$—that is, the individual is a net borrower in the first period—the income effect also tends to reduce c_1^* because the borrower would have to pay higher interest in the second period. Thus an increase in the interest rate for a net borrower always reduces first period consumption (increases saving). The effect of a change in the return to saving therefore depends on the distribution of the endowments over the life cycle. Even when the effect can be signed, the strength of the effect depends on the concavity of the utility function: that is, on the intertemporal elasticity of substitution. As indicated in the second section above, the effect is ambiguous not only theoretically, but also empirically.

The Tax Treatment of Mandatory Contributions

This appendix studies the effect of the deductibility of mandated contributions on the composition of household wealth and on the overall level of saving. Consider a standard overlapping generations model, where households maximize utility and are subject to a general income tax rate τ and to a mandatory contribution to a fully funded pension fund μ. In the first period, income taxes and mandated contributions are a fixed proportion of wages. In the second period, capital income and pension benefits are taxed at the same general income tax rate τ. Further consider two cases. In a first scenario, pension contributions are levied on first period income and are not tax-deductible. In the second scenario, contributions are fully tax-deductible.[19] Assume that the contribution rate does not exceed the propensity to save that would prevail in the absence of pensions.

The effect of mandated pension contributions on national saving arises from the tax treatment of contributions, and does not require that saving responds positively to changes in interest rates. Consider the log-utility case, in which income and substitution effects cancel each other out. Since second period income is zero by assumption, there is no wealth effect. Consumers solve the problem:

$$max \ \ln c_{t,\,t} + \beta \ln c_{t,\,t+1}$$

In the first scenario, with a mandated pension fund yielding the same return as private savings, the budget constraints in the two periods are:

$$c_t^y + s_t^p = w_t(1 - \tau - \mu)$$

$$c_{t+1}^o = [(1 + r_{t+1})s_t^p + (1 + r_{t+1})w_t\mu](1 - \tau) = (1 + r_{t+1})(1 - \tau)[s_t^p + w_t\mu]$$

The intertemporal budget constraint is:

$$c_t^y + \frac{c_{t+1}^o}{(1+r_{t+1})(1-\tau)} = w_t(1-\tau)$$

In the absence of population and income growth, national saving is the sum of mandated and private (or discretionary) saving, s_t^m and s_t^p respectively:

$$s_t(nd) = s_t^p + s_t^m = \frac{\beta}{1+\beta}w_t(1-\tau)$$

Mandated savings $s_t^m = \mu w_t$ and private savings is $s_t^p = \left[\frac{\beta(1-\tau)}{1+\beta} - \mu\right]w$.

The first point to note in the expression for national saving is the negative effect of τ on after-tax wages and therefore saving. The interest rate channel is not operative here, because log utility has been assumed, and because it has also been assumed that second period income equals zero.

The second point to note is that a change in μ does not affect $s_t(nd)$. National saving would be the same even in the absence of forced saving. However, an increase in mandatory savings (s_t^m) will reduce private savings (s_t^p) one-for-one (a wealth replacement effect). This poses important definitional issues when measuring and comparing saving across countries that differ in the extent of mandatory programs. In particular, mandatory contributions to pension funds, paid either by employees or employers, should be counted as part of income and therefore household saving. On the other hand, the pension paid in the second period, $[(1 + r_{t+1})w_t\mu](1 - \tau)$, should not be considered as part of income because it is matched by an equal reduction in pension wealth. Thus first period saving is $s_t(nd)$ and second period dissaving is just $-c_{t+1}^o$.

In this simple closed-economy framework, national saving translates into investment, thereby increasing the capital stock. In fact, appending a capital market equilibrium condition and assuming that the production function is Cobb-Douglas, $y = Ak^\alpha$, one obtains a closed form solution for the steady-state capital stock:

$$k(nd) = \left[\frac{\beta(1-\tau)(1-\alpha)A}{1+\beta}\right]^{\frac{1}{1-\alpha}}$$

As with the national saving, the steady-state capital stock is decreasing in τ and unaffected by the contribution rate μ.

Consider now a situation in which contributions to mandatory pension funds are tax-exempt, so that the income tax is computed on income net of the contribution. As discussed in the chapter, this is the standard case in most industrialized and developing countries. The budget constraints in the two periods are:

$$c_t^y + s_t^p = (w_t - \mu w_t)(1 - \tau) = w_t(1 - \tau)(1 - \mu)$$

$$c_{t+1}^o = (1 + r_{t+1})(1 - \tau)(s_t^p + w_t\mu)$$

and the resulting intertemporal budget constraint is:

$$c_t + \frac{c_{t+1}^o}{(1 + r_{t+1})(1 - \tau)} = w_t\left[(1 - \tau) + \tau\mu\right]$$

National saving is then:

$$s_t(d) = \frac{\beta}{1 + \beta} w_t\left[(1 - \tau) + \tau\mu\right]$$

By comparing the two expressions for national saving, one sees that saving is higher in the economy where contributions are tax-deductible:

$$s_t(d) - s_t(nd) = \frac{\beta}{1 + \beta}\mu\tau w_t$$

The difference in national saving depends on the contribution rate and on the tax rate. For reasonable values of μ and τ, saving can be substantially higher in an economy with tax-deductible contributions. By appending a capital market equilibrium condition, one can also derive the steady state capital stock

$$k(d) = \left[\frac{\beta\left[(1 - \tau) + \tau\mu\right](1 - \alpha)A}{1 + \beta}\right]^{\frac{1}{1-\alpha}}$$

that is clearly higher in the economy with tax-deductible contributions.

Often only a fraction of the workforce contributes to pension funds. Denoting this fraction by λ, national saving is a weighted average of the saving of contributors and non-contributors. While the fraction does not affect national saving in the economy with no deductions, when contributions are tax-deductible national saving increases with pension fund coverage:

$$s_t = \frac{\beta}{1+\beta}\left\{w_t(1-\tau)(1-\lambda)+w_t\left[(1-\tau)+\tau\mu\right]\lambda\right\}$$

One can extend this simple framework in several directions. In endogenous growth models (for instance, models where output is a linear function of the capital stock), the growth rate of the capital stock and of national income, rather than the levels of the two variables, increases with pension coverage and with the mandatory contribution rate.

It has implicitly been assumed here that the tax rate finances government consumption that is simply wasted. But in more realistic setups, government expenditure might impact the productivity of the private sector. If the government budget is balanced, one can show that in an economy with tax-deductible contributions the required tax rate is lower than in an economy without deductions. Equivalently, for given tax rate, the capital stock is higher in the economy with deductions. However, during the transition to a tax-favored regime, even though the tax treatment of mandatory contributions promotes pension saving, it might defer government revenues. Finally, only dynamic efficient economies have been considered here. In dynamically inefficient situations eliminating tax deductions is one way to approach the golden rule of capital accumulation.

The Effect on National Saving of Tax Incentives for Borrowing

To see the implications on national saving of changes in incentives to borrow, consider a simple overlapping generations model with two types of individuals: a fraction λ with endowments in the first period and nothing in the second (net savers), and a fraction $(1 - \lambda)$ with endowments only in the second period (net borrowers). Assume for simplicity that the proportion of the two types in the population is exogenous. Net borrowers borrow from net savers in the first period, and repay their debt in the second period. This framework requires only minimal change in assumptions and notation with respect to the model in the previous section of this appendix.

Net borrowers face an interest rate on borrowing given by $(1 + r_b) = (1 + r)(1 + \phi - \theta)$, where ϕ is the cost of financial intermediation (assumed exogenous) and θ is the tax incentives (say, deductibility of consumer credit or mortgage interest). For simplicity, it is assumed that ϕ is wasted during the intermediation process. Net savers face an interest rate on lending equal to r. Assume also that $r_b > r$ (that is, $\phi > \theta$). First period saving of the "net savers" is:

$$s_t^l = \frac{\beta}{1+\beta}w_t$$

First period saving of "net borrowers" is negative:

$$s_t^b = -\frac{1}{1+\beta}\frac{w_{t+1}}{(1+r)(1+\phi-\theta)}$$

Clearly, raising the incentive θ will reduce the interest rate on borrowing, increase debt, and therefore reduce saving. Note that $u_1 = \beta(1 + r_i)u_2$ where for a net borrower r_i is the borrowing rate and for a net saver it is the lending rate. Thus the Euler equation implies that individual consumption growth is higher for net borrowers than for net savers.

Aggregate wealth in period t is the sum of the saving of the savers and the dissaving of the borrowers:

$$\lambda N_t s_t^l + (1-\lambda)N_t s_t^b = \frac{\beta}{1+\beta}w_t\lambda N_t - \frac{1}{1+\beta}\frac{w_{t+1}(1-\lambda)N_t}{(1+r)(1+\phi-\tau)}$$

An increase in θ increases borrowing and first period consumption of net borrowers and therefore lowers aggregate saving. Thus aggregate wealth falls with θ. Note also that reducing the cost of financial intermediation ϕ will increase first period borrowing and reduce saving.

The capital market equilibrium condition is $K_{t+1} = \lambda N_t s_t^l + (1 - \lambda)N_t s_t^b$. Suppose that population is stationary. With a Cobb-Douglas production function, the marginal product of labor is $w = w = A(1 - \alpha)k^\alpha$ and the marginal product of capital is $(1 + r) = \alpha Ak^{\alpha-1}$. The steady state capital stock is:

$$k = \left[\frac{\lambda\gamma(1-\alpha)A}{1+\dfrac{(1-\lambda)\gamma(1-\alpha)}{\alpha(1+\phi-\theta)}}\right]^{\frac{1}{1-\alpha}}$$

where $\gamma = [\beta/(1 + \beta)]$. The capital stock also falls with θ.

While this model shows that incentives to borrow generally depress saving, the growth effect of tax incentives to borrow is less clear-cut, particularly in models with endogenous growth. The model takes for granted that there are two types of individuals in the economy. But suppose that individuals with no endowment in the first period would like to borrow to finance human capital investment. In turn, this might prompt a higher wage rate in the second period. Then, introducing tax incentives to borrow will tend to foster human capital accumulation and, in models in which human capital is an engine for growth, the steady-state growth rate (De Gregorio 1996).

Data Appendix. Data Used in the Estimation

Data used in the regressions for national saving can be downloaded from ftp://monarch/worldbank.org/pub/prddr/outbox. National saving is defined inclusive of all external transfers. Public sector data refer to central government. The definition of the public sector is that of consolidated central government: that is, budgetary central government plus extra-budgetary central government plus social security agencies. This definition thus excludes local and regional governments. A detailed description of the data set can be found in Schmidt-Hebbel and Servén (1999). The original database includes 150 countries and spans the years 1960 to 1995. For each country, this chapter takes the 1985–95 average. Each series consists of an Excel file; the files used are given in the table below. Data for pension fund assets and public expenditure on pensions are drawn from Palacios and Pallarès-Miralles (2000).

Variable	File
Gross national saving as a share of GDP	FORMU333.XLS
Government saving as a share of GDP	FORMU342.XLS
GDP at current prices	FORMU16.XLS
GDP at 1987 prices	FORMU17.XLS
Total population	CONST263.XLS
Population younger than 15	CONST264.XLS
Population older than 65	CONST265.XLS
Dependency ratio	(CONST264.XLS+ CONST265.XLS)/ CONST263.XLS
Pension fund assets as a share of GDP	Sum of reserves of mandatory pension systems and private pension fund assets as a share of GDP. *Source*: Palacios and Pallarès-Miralles (2000).
Public expenditure on pensions as a share of GDP	Includes all government expenditures on cash transfers to the elderly, the disabled, and survivors, and the administrative costs of these programs.

Source: Palacios and Pallarès-Miralles (2000).

Countries Used in Estimation for National Saving

Argentina, Australia, Austria, Belgium, Belize, Bolivia, Brazil, Canada, Chad, Chile, Colombia, Costa Rica, Denmark, Ecuador, Egypt, El Salvador,

Ethiopia, Finland, France, The Gambia, Germany, Ghana, Greece, Honduras, India, Indonesia, Ireland, Italy, Jamaica, Japan, Jordan, Kenya, Luxembourg, Malaysia, Mauritius, Mexico, Morocco, Namibia, Nepal, Netherlands, Norway, Paraguay, Peru, Philippines, Portugal, Senegal, Singapore, South Africa, Spain, Sri Lanka, Swaziland, Sweden, Switzerland, Tanzania, Tunisia, Uganda, United Kingdom, United States, Uruguay, and Zambia.

Notes

1. The aggregate tax elasticity of saving depends not only on preference parameters, but also on the distribution of wealth. Cagetti (2001) shows that life-cycle models of wealth accumulation in which the precautionary motive is quantitatively relevant also imply extremely low intertemporal elasticities, in contrast to models without uncertainty (Summers 1981). Such models thus imply small effects for tax-favored saving instruments on the saving of the median household. But if the richest 5 percent of the population behaves differently (for example, being less risk-averse, or being more affected, as entrepreneurs, by capital income taxation), aggregate wealth may still exhibit a large interest rate elasticity. Thus the distribution of wealth is a crucial parameter to evaluate the impact of tax incentives. This is particularly relevant in developing countries where wealth inequality tends to be higher than in most industrialized nations.

2. Behavioral theories suggest that people do not optimize in the neoclassical sense and fail to provide adequately for their retirement because of lack of self-control (Thaler and Shefrin 1981; Thaler 1990). Targeted saving instruments may therefore serve as a focal point for inconstant people to actually accomplish their savings goals. For recent evidence on this point, see Madrian and Shea (2001).

3. They estimate that about half the contributions to IRAs represent new saving, 30 percent is financed by the tax saving allowed by the same IRAs, and the remaining 20 percent is a pure portfolio effect.

4. For instance, Moscowitz and Vissing-Jorgensen (2002) find that in the United States, households with private equity ownership invest on average almost two-thirds of their private holdings in a single company in which they have an active management interest.

5. Feldstein notices that such effect tends to be particularly relevant just after the introduction of a pay-as-you-go system, when contributions bear little relation to annuities and workers revise their expectations concerning the age of retirement.

6. Using the stock of pension fund assets in a flow (saving) regression might be criticized on the grounds that the stock reflects not only the generosity of the mandatory scheme but also its maturity. Nevertheless, introducing stock variables in aggregate saving or consumption regressions is a well-established practice in applied economics. For instance, in tests of the

life-cycle hypothesis it is quite common to regress saving on wealth, and many tests of the Ricardian equivalence proposition rely on regressions of private consumption on the stock of public debt.

7. The purpose of the regressions is descriptive, so this study does not attempt to account for the possible bias induced by the endogeneity of some of the right-hand side variables (such as GDP growth), the role of omitted variables (such as corporate savings), and time aggregation issues. See Loayza, Servén, and Schmidt-Hebbel (2000) for a discussion of these and related issues.

8. Bailliu and Reisen (1997) also find that mandatory funded pensions promote national saving in developing economies. Their findings are consistent with a model based on mandatory contributions and credit constraints faced by low-income workers.

9. The robust estimation method performs an initial OLS regression, calculates the Cook's distance, eliminates the gross outliers for which the Cook's distance exceeds 1, and then performs iterations based on Huber weights followed by iterations based on a biweight function (a routine programmed in the STATA econometric software).

10. In the early 1970s the Brazilian government also introduced a housing saving account that was exempt from income tax and indexed to inflation.

11. At the time of writing, the Brazilian Parliament is discussing reducing the contribution rate to FGTS from the current level of 8.3 percent to a 2 percent level. Moreover, in case of lay-offs the employer will not have to give severance pay or pay the 40 percent penalty to the FGTS.

12. In the late 1990s the Fujimori government transformed the housing fund into an "Emergency Solidarity Tax" and, after January 2000, the new government phased out the mandatory contribution scheme because of its unpopularity.

13. See Poterba (1994) for an overview of saving through insurance contracts in G7 countries.

14. For instance, in France, Italy, and Japan, tax deductibility of premiums is available only for contracts 5 years or longer.

15. Jappelli and Pistaferri (2002) find that there is little responsiveness of contributors' decision to invest to changes in the return of the policy induced by changes in the tax deductibility of the premiums.

16. Many countries tax bequests. Among developing countries, Brazil, Chile, and Singapore do; India, Indonesia and Mexico do not; and Argentina levies a transfer fee on the beneficiary. Critics of the estate tax claim that it has an adverse effect on investment and saving, as it raises the cost of capital and it makes it harder for family businesses to survive the deaths of their founders.

17. This is witnessed by country studies. Park (1991, p. 41) argues, "One advantage of the repressive financial system in Korea, and to a lesser degree in Taiwan, may have been its ability to supply long-term finance. . . .

Without government intervention the profit-oriented behavior of the commercial banks would have resulted in the dearth of long-term finance."

18. One example are migrants' remittances, an important source of saving for developing countries. The Multilateral Investment Fund (2001) presents evidence that a typical Latin American migrant in the United States remits 15 percent of her wages; however, transfer costs (which include transfer fees, exchange rate commissions, check cashing fees, and other charges at the point of receipt) absorb about 15 percent of any sum transferred.

19. A situation in which contributions are not tax-deductible but benefits are tax-exempt is not examined because it is rarely observed in practice.

References

Bailliu, Jeanine, and Helmut Reisen. 1997. "Do Funded Pensions Contribute to Higher Savings? A Cross-country Analysis." Development Center Technical Papers 130, Paris: OECD. Processed.

Bernheim, Douglas B. 2002. "Taxation and Saving." In Alan J. Auerbach and Martin Feldstein, eds., *Handbook of Public Economics*. Amsterdam: Elsevier Science Publisher.

Besley, Timothy, and Costas Meghir. 2001. "Tax Based Saving Incentives." London School of Economics, Department of Economics. Processed.

Browning, Martin, and Annamaria Lusardi. 1996. "Household Saving: Micro Theories and Micro Facts." *Journal of Economic Literature* 34 (4): 1797–1855.

Cagetti, Marco. 2001. "Interest Elasticity in a Life-Cycle Model with Precautionary Saving." *American Economic Review Papers and Proceedings* 91 (2): 418–21.

De Gregorio, José. 1996. "Borrowing Constraints, Human Capital Accumulation and Growth." *Journal of Monetary Economics* 32 (1): 79–104.

Djankov, Simeon, Rafael La Porta, Florencio Lopez-de-Silanes, and Andrei Schleifer. 2002. "Courts: The Lex Mundi Project." NBER Working Paper 8890. Cambridge, Mass. Processed.

Duebel, Achim. 2000. "Separating Homeownership Subsidies from Finance." Land and Real Estate Research Paper 14. World Bank, Washington, D.C. Processed.

Engen, Eric M., William G. Gale, and John Karl Scholz. 1996. "The Illusory Effects of Saving Incentives on Saving." *Journal of Economic Perspectives* 10 (Fall): 113–38.

Feldstein, Martin S. 1976. "Personal Taxation and Portfolio Composition: An Econometric Analysis." *Econometrica* 44 (4): 631–49.

———. 1995. "College Scholarship Rules and Private Saving." *American Economic Review* 85 (3): 552–66.

Gale, William G. 1998. "The Effects of Pensions on Household Wealth: A Reevaluation of Theory and Evidence." *The Journal of Political Economy* 106 (4): 706–23.

Hall, Robert E. 1978. "Stochastic Implications of the Life Cycle-Permanent Income Hypothesis: Theory and Evidence." *The Journal of Political Economy* 86 (6): 971–87.

Hills, John. 1990. *Unraveling Housing Finance.* Oxford: Clarendon Press.

Holzmann, Robert, Ian W. MacArthur, and Yvonne Sin. 2000. "Pension Systems in East Asia and the Pacific: Challenges and Opportunities." Social Protection Discussion Paper 14. World Bank, Washington, D.C. Processed.

Honohan, Patrick. 2000. "Financial Policies and Household Saving." In Klaus Schmidt-Hebbel and Luis Servén, eds., *The Economics of Saving and Growth.* Cambridge: Cambridge University Press.

Impavido, Gregorio, Alberto R. Musalem, and Thierry Tressel. 2002. "Contractual Savings, Capital Markets and Firms' Financing Choices." In Shanayanan Devarajan and F. Halsey Rogers, eds., *World Bank Economists' Forum* Volume 2. Washington, D.C.: World Bank.

Multilateral Investment Fund. 2002. "Remittances to Latin America and the Caribbean." Inter-American Development Bank, Washington, D.C. Processed.

Jappelli, Tullio, and Luigi Pistaferri. 2002. "Tax Incentives and the Demand for Life Insurance: Evidence from Italy." *Journal of Public Economics.* Forthcoming.

King, Mervyn A., and Louis Dicks-Mireaux. 1982. "Asset Holdings and the Life-Cycle." *Economic Journal* 92 (2): 247–67.

Lea, Michael J. and Bertrand Renaud. 1995. "Contractual Savings for Housing: How Suitable Are They for Transitional Economies?" World Bank Policy Research Working Paper 1516. Washington, D.C.

Loayza, Norman, Luis Servén, and Klaus Schmidt-Hebbel. 2000. "What Drives Private Saving Across the World?" *The Review of Economics and Statistics* 82 (2): 165–81.

Mackenzie, George A., Philip Gerson, and Alfred Cuevas. 1997. "Pension Regimes and Saving." Occasional Paper 153. International Monetary Fund, Washington, D.C. Processed.

Maclennan D., John Muellbauer, and M. Stephens. 1999. *Asymmetries in Housing and Financial Market Institutions and EMU.* Discussion Paper 2062. CEPR, London. Processed.

Madrian, Brigitte, and Dennis F. Shea. 2001. "The Power of Suggestion: Inertia in 401(k) Participation and Savings Behavior." *Quarterly Journal of Economics* 116 (4): 1149–87.

Masson, Paul, R. Tamim Bayoumi, and Hossein Samiei. 1998. "International Evidence on the Determinants of Saving." *World Bank Economic Review* 12 (3): 483–501.

Modigliani, Franco. 1993. "Recent Declines in the Savings Rate: A Life Cycle Perspective." In Mario Baldassarri, ed., *World Saving, Prosperity and Growth*. New York: St. Martin's Press.

Moscowitz, Tobias J., and Annette Vissing-Jorgensen. 2002. "The Returns to Entrepreneurial Investment: A Private Equity Premium Puzzle?" *American Economic Review*. Forthcoming.

Multilateral Investment Fund. 2001. Remittances to Latin America and the Caribbean. Washington, D.C.: Inter-American Development Bank.

Palacios, Robert, and Montserrat Pallarès-Miralles. 2000. "International Patterns of Pension Provision." World Bank, Washington, D.C. Processed.

Park, Yung Chul. 1991. "The Role of Finance in Economic Development in South Korea and Taiwan." Paper presented to the CEPR Conference on Finance and Development in Europe, Santiago de Compostela, December.

Poterba, James M. 1994. *Public Policies and Household Saving*. Chicago: University of Chicago Press.

———. 2000. "Taxation, Risk-Taking, and Household Portfolio Behavior." In Alan J. Auerbach and Martin Feldstein, eds., *Handbook of Public Economics*. Amsterdam: Elsevier Science Publisher.

———. 2001. "Taxation and Portfolio Structure: Issues and Implications." In Luigi Guiso, Michalis Haliassos, and Tullio Jappelli, eds., *Household Portfolios*. Cambridge, Mass.: MIT Press.

Poterba, James M., Steven F. Venti, and David A. Wise. 1996. "How Retirement Saving Programs Increase Saving." *Journal of Economic Perspectives* 10 (Fall): 91–112.

Schmidt-Hebbel, Klaus, and Luis Servén. 1999. "Aggregate Saving and Income Distribution." In Klaus Schmidt-Hebbel and Luis Servén, eds., *The Economics of Saving and Growth*. Cambridge: Cambridge University Press.

Souleles, Nicholas. 2000. "College Tuition and Household Savings and Consumption." *Journal of Public Economics* 77 (2): 185–207.

Summers, Lawrence H. 1981. "Capital Taxation and Accumulation in a Life Cycle Growth Model." *American Economic Review* 71 (4): 533–44.

Thaler, Richard H. 1990. "Saving, Fungibility and Mental Accounts." *Journal of Economic Perspectives* 4 (1): 193–205.

Thaler, Richard H., and H. M. Shefrin. 1981. "An Economic Theory of Self-control." *Journal of Political Economy* 89 (2): 392–406.

Whitehouse, Edward. 2000. "The Tax Treatment of Funded Pensions." London: Axia Economics. Processed.

5

Corrective Taxes and Quasi-Taxes for Financial Institutions and Their Interaction with Deposit Insurance

Philip L. Brock

Prudential and monetary policy instruments act as potentially corrective quasi-taxes on financial intermediaries and they interact with other taxes. Among the most important of these instruments are deposit insurance programs, which have become increasingly widely used in the past two decades.[1] Concern about prudential regulations to accompany deposit insurance has grown with the realization that deposit insurance may create a potentially large contingent liability for the government when banks become insolvent. In response to this concern, there has been an outpouring of books and articles on prudential bank regulation and on the design of a financial safety net.[2]

Informational asymmetries between borrower and lender underpin the existence of financial intermediaries. The informational disparities lead to problems with moral hazard and adverse selection that may limit the scope of direct lending or cause it to dry up. Banks and other financial intermediaries can reduce the problems of moral hazard and adverse selection by holding a diversified loan portfolio that permits them to reduce the per borrower cost of monitoring. That is, they reduce the costs of lending by serving as delegated monitors for many depositors.

While banks can frequently improve upon direct lending between lenders and borrowers, informational asymmetries also face depositors in their dealings with banks. These asymmetries have historically been an important element in bank runs. Governments have often cited the instability of banks as a reason for intervening in the regulation of the financial system. Governments attempt to stabilize and improve the efficiency of financial intermediaries by the creation of deposit insurance and central bank lender-of-last resort powers. The implicit and explicit guarantees associated with the government's policies require accompanying corrective taxes and quasi-taxes to minimize regulatory moral hazard. Corrective taxation frequently falls short of the mark, with the result that government deposit guarantees may encourage risk-taking and the misallocation of society's resources.

This chapter examines the interaction between deposit insurance, taxation, and prudential regulation (viewed as a form of quasi-taxation). The analysis of deposit insurance, capital requirements, interest rate controls, and credit ceilings that follows is done from the perspective of corrective taxation in the presence of a deposit guarantee. The analysis of an indirect tax highlights the impact of the tax on the size of the government's contingent liability associated with deposit insurance. The analysis of a reserve requirement on capital inflows demonstrates the offsetting prudential and risk-inducing incentives created by reserve requirements.[3]

Why Have Deposit Insurance?

In economies characterized by incomplete information and incomplete markets, competitive market equilibria will generally not be Pareto-efficient. Greenwald and Stiglitz (1986) have shown that tax interventions and subsidies can often be designed that are potentially Pareto-improving when information is incomplete. Finance is especially prone to incomplete markets stemming from incomplete information. In financial transactions, asymmetric information generally leads to the need for costly verification of a borrower's reported returns.

Townsend (1979) and Gale and Hellwig (1985) have shown that debt contracts economize on verification costs since verification is required only when default takes place. Debt contracts, like other insurance contracts, encounter problems related to moral hazard and adverse selection.[4] These problems are essentially tied to the convexity of returns associated with a debt contract. At the point of de-

Figure 5.1. Debt Contracts with Alternative Liability Rules

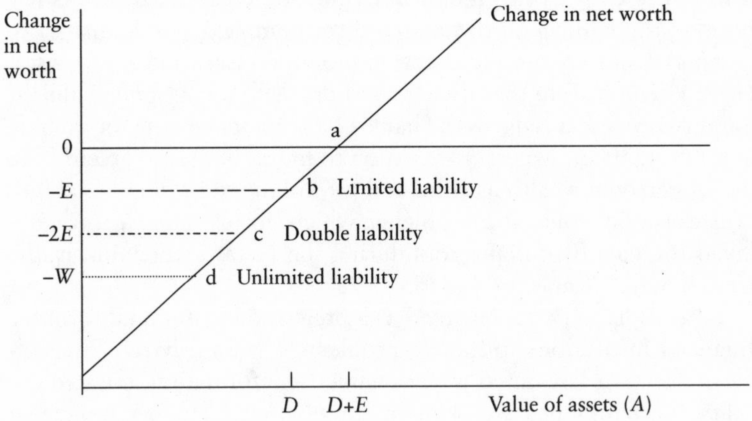

fault, a borrower has an incentive to add risk to the project. If the additional risk pays off, the borrower can avoid default. If not, the borrower is no worse off in default than before.

Figure 5.1 illustrates how the convexity in returns for a bank varies under different liability arrangements. Bank owners contribute an amount (E) of equity. At point (a), where deposits plus equity equal the value of the bank's assets (A = D + E), the net worth of bank owners is their paid-in capital E. Under limited liability, the face value amount of equity E represents the maximum bank owners can lose if the bank goes bankrupt. In figure 5.1, the kink in the profit line for bank owners occurs at point (b) because bank owners cannot lose more than E. It is this convexity in the profit line associated with the kink at point b that accentuates moral hazard and adverse selection in banking.

Alternative liability arrangements shift the point at which the profit line has a kink, but do not eliminate the convexity of returns associated with the use of debt contracts. Double liability was the norm in U.S. banking prior to the Great Depression. Under double liability bankers were personally liable for bank losses up to an amount equal to their equity stake in the bank. Such an arrangement produces a kink in returns at point (c). Unlimited liability places a banker's pledgeable wealth at stake, so that the kink takes place at point (d).

Both unlimited and double liability have drawbacks that have restricted (or eliminated) their current use in banking legislation. As Carr and Mathewson (1988) emphasize, unlimited liability creates a moral hazard among bank owners who must monitor one another's personal wealth, since all owners are responsible for bank losses. The costs of this monitoring may limit the size of banks (by limiting the number of owners) and the complexity of loans (more complex loans are more difficult to monitor). Carr and Mathewson (1988) demonstrate that owners and depositors may prefer limited liability because it reduces the bank's costs of controlling moral hazard among bank owners. In addition to moral hazard problems, the use of personal wealth as collateral for unlimited or double liability creates special collection problems, which, for example, greatly delayed the payoff of depositors during the Great Depression in the United States (Kane and Wilson 1998).

Limited liability has emerged as a preferred institutional form for financial institutions to handle problems of moral hazard and adverse selection associated with asymmetric information. Limited liability for banks has well-known drawbacks, including nontrivial monitoring costs by depositors and free riding in monitoring that can lead to bank runs and the inefficient liquidation of banks. There thus arises the question of whether the Greenwald and Stiglitz (1986) hypothesis of Pareto-improving taxes and subsidies can be applied to limited liability financial institutions. Along these lines, Banerjee and Besley (1990) and John, John, and Senbet (1991) have shown that a profit tax and creditor subsidy can reduce the convexity in payoffs to bank owners associated with limited liability. The variance of after-tax profits is smaller than before-tax profits, so such a tax mitigates moral hazard. If the tax proceeds are used to subsidize the cost of deposits, then the combination of tax and subsidy can reduce moral hazard. In both papers, the combination of taxes and subsidies creates a Pareto-improving insurance mechanism (relative to limited liability) that lowers the cost of credit.[5]

As a practical matter, direct government subsidies to deposits are rarely seen. An alternative approach to the question of potentially Pareto-improving government interventions is to examine observed subsidies and determine whether there are taxes that would result in Pareto improvements relative to laissez faire (that is, limited liability). One of the most important subsidies to banks—or more precisely, a tax-and-subsidy scheme—is government deposit insurance. Deposit insurance lowers the cost of deposits to banks (as potential depositors no longer require as high a default-risk premium), but it may also accentuate moral hazard and adverse selection by reducing or eliminating the incentive of depositors to incur monitoring costs.[6] Whether or not deposit insurance is Pareto-improving depends on the monitoring and corrective tax policies that are implemented in conjunction with the insurance.

This view of deposit insurance as one element of a potentially Pareto-improving tax and subsidy package is the starting point for this chapter's model of corrective taxation of deposit insurance. In the model, deposit insurance lowers the cost of credit to banks but also transfers the control of moral hazard from depositors to the regulatory authority. The model details regulatory and tax interventions that attempt to control moral hazard in the presence of deposit insurance.

The model has two periods.[7] The first period is the investment period and the second period is the consumption period. There is a countable infinity of risk-neutral agents in the economy. Bankers are able to undertake risky indivisible projects but have insufficient funds to undertake the projects on their own. Depositors cannot undertake projects. A representative investment project requires one unit of funds and has a state contingent payoff in period 2 of $a_i(s)$. The state of the world is assumed to have a uniform distribution over the interval $[0, \bar{s}]$. The cost of funds is the risk-free gross return (r^*) given by world capital markets, so that bankers are willing to undertake projects whose expected returns equal or exceed r^*:

$$(5.1) \qquad \int_0^{\bar{s}} a_1(s) f(s) ds \geq r^*.$$

Lenders, however, can only verify the returns by incurring a monitoring cost (γ). As in Townsend (1979) and Diamond (1984, 1996), monitoring in the case of default will provide the banker with the incentive to tell the truth about the project's outcome. Deposit contracts for any individual deposit $d_i < 1$ will take the following form, where r is the contracted (gross) interest rate, $(1 - \gamma) a_1(s) d_i$ is the payment (net of monitoring costs) when the banker defaults, and $r^* d_i$ is depositors' required rate of return:[8]

$$(5.2) \qquad \int_0^{\bar{s}} \min[rd_i, (1 - \gamma) a_1(s) d_i] f(s) ds = r^* d_i.$$

In equation 5.2 depositors bear the downside risk of the banker's project in exchange for a high promised return $(r > r^*)$ when the project turns out well. High costs of monitoring by depositors will preclude the financing of some projects that meet the criterion of equation 5.1.

A deposit guarantee transfers the cost of monitoring from depositors to the government by placing the default risk with the government. In this model, having the government monitor on behalf of the lenders eliminates the duplication of monitoring costs.[9] A guarantee to depositors also requires the government to undertake the monitoring by placing the default risk with the government. With deposit insurance in place, depositors contract with the bank at the international rate r^*, as shown in equation 5.3:

$$(5.3) \qquad \int_0^{\bar{s}} \min[r^* a_1(s) + v_1(s)]f(s)ds = r^*$$

where

$$(5.4) \qquad v_1(s) \equiv \max[0, r^* - a_1(s)].$$

Equation 5.3 states that depositors receive the contracted payment on deposits (r^*) in nondefault states. In default states, depositors receive the cash flow from the risky project ($a_i(s)$) plus the amount of the deposit guarantee, $v_1(s)$. Equation 5.4 states that resources from the government's guarantee fund will always meet the bank's payment shortfall $[r^* - a_1(s)]$.

As Merton (1977, 1978) first demonstrated, government deposit insurance, which is a third-party guarantee to depositors made by the government, can be analyzed equivalently as a put option on the value of a bank's assets. The government's deposit insurance eliminates default risk for depositors and creates rents for bankers by lowering the interest rate that they must pay to attract deposits. Equally important, it eliminates duplication in monitoring by depositors, thereby reducing the resource costs associated with financial intermediation. The lower costs of intermediation, in turn, permit an expansion in the number of projects that are profitable to undertake.

The Fiscal Cost of Deposit Insurance

To the extent that deposit insurance protects the payments system by preventing bank runs, the existence of an insurance program may not involve actual outlays of funds. This is the message of the well-known Diamond-Dybvig (1983) model of bank intermediation, where government-provided deposit insurance eliminates bank runs at no cost to the government. In practice, deposit insurance is often expensive to the government. Government payouts associated with deposit insurance have often been very large, as documented by Lindgren, Garcia, and Saal (1996) and Caprio and Klingebiel (2002). Honohan and Klingebiel (2003) analyze a sample of 40 countries in which governments spent an average of 12.8 percent of GDP in connection with explicit and implicit deposit insurance commitments. In a number of countries, including Indonesia, Chile, Thailand, and Uruguay, the fiscal costs of banking system intervention during the last 20 years exceeded 30 percent of GDP.

A large part of the fiscal cost is a transfer from taxpayers to bank borrowers, owners, and lenders that will involve a transfer of wealth but not necessarily the misallocation of resources (Boyd, Chang, and Smith 1998). However, a deposit guarantee also subsidizes risktaking. Returning to this chapter's model, with deposit guarantees the banker may undertake projects whose expected return is less than r^*. Privately profitable projects may not be socially profitable projects in the presence of deposit guarantees, since the presence of the guarantees lowers the privately required rate of return to below r^* (by the amount of the expected value of the guarantees):

$$(5.5) \qquad \int_0^{\bar{s}} a_1(s)f(s)ds \geq r^* - \int_0^{\bar{s}} v_1(s)f(s)ds.$$

Equation 5.5 shows that whenever there is an expected payment to depositors associated with deposit insurance, $\int_0^{\bar{s}} v_1(s)f(s)ds > 0$, the expected transfer may result in the incentive to invest in socially unprofitable projects.

Controlling the Fiscal Costs of Deposit Insurance

Controlling the fiscal costs (more accurately, the contingent fiscal liability) associated with deposit insurance is a way of preventing banks from investing in socially unproductive projects. Honohan and Klingebiel (2003) provide empirical evidence that failure to implement prudential controls of various types has a significant impact on the escalation of fiscal costs.

The most direct way to limit the fiscal cost is to charge a deposit insurance premium that taxes away the expected value of the government's deposit guarantee. In the model this would amount to setting the insurance premium equal to v_1 for project $a_1(s)$. However, there is a growing literature that questions the ability of governments to set actuarially fair-priced deposit insurance in the presence of adverse selection.[10] Kaufman and Wallison (2001) note that even though the U.S. Federal Deposit Insurance Corporation (FDIC) now has the authority to set risk-based insurance premiums, it has not implemented a truly risk-based system. In any case, governments have chosen to charge deposit insurance premiums that do not tax away the expected value of the guarantee (see Laeven 2002).

In order to limit the fiscal cost associated with deposit insurance, governments have more actively engaged in the use of bank capital requirements. In the model it will be convenient to express the capital requirement as a ratio of bank capital to liabilities (e). Given the capital requirement, $d = 1/(1 + e)$ of deposits are required to finance a project $a_1(s)$. Equation 5.6 indicates that the capital requirement will reduce the government's payment when the bank defaults, although it will not eliminate the payment for low enough realizations of the project.

$$(5.6) \qquad v_1(s) \equiv \max\left[0, \frac{r^*}{1+e} - a_1(s)\right]$$

The capital requirement works as an instrument of prudential regulation in the presence of a deposit guarantee. But as Black, Miller, and Posner (1978, p. 387) note, the government and banks will be in a natural conflict over the amount of capital in the presence of the deposit guarantee. This conflict tends to weaken the regulatory impact of the capital requirement, since banks will take measures to overstate regulatory capital. Equally important, banks can choose to expand their loan portfolios in a way that adds risk rather than diversifies away risk. Banks will do this even in the presence of a capital requirement, as the following example demonstrates. Suppose that the representative bank is now assumed to have a new investment opportunity (which may or may not be socially profitable) that requires one unit of resources and generates a state-contingent return $a_2(s)$:

$$(5.7) \qquad \int_0^{\bar{s}} a_2(s)f(s)ds \gtrless r^*.$$

Whether the banker finds the new project privately profitable depends on whether the new project raises the expected cash flows going to the bank. The banker remains subject to the equity requirement e as a fraction of new deposits, so that financing a new project will result in the following deposit payoff structure:

$$(5.8) \qquad \int_0^{\bar{s}} \min\left[2\frac{r^*}{1+e}, a_1(s) + a_2(s) + v_2(s)\right] f(s)ds = 2\frac{r^*}{1+e}$$

where

$$(5.9) \qquad v_2(s) \equiv \max\left[0, 2\frac{r^*}{1+e} - a_1(s) - a_2(s)\right].$$

As before, the deposit guarantee eliminates risk to the depositors by creating a contingent liability of the government. There are two factors that determine the profitability of undertaking the second project. The first is the expected return on the second project relative to the cost of financing the project (equation 5.7). The second factor is the impact of the second project on the expected value of the government's deposit guarantee. Pooling of risk across the two projects will reduce the expected size of the government's contingent liability. On the other hand, bankers may find it privately profitable to increase portfolio risk by choosing new projects whose returns are positively correlated with those of the first project. More precisely, the banker will invest in the second project if the following condition holds:

$$(5.10) \qquad \int_0^{\bar{s}} a_2(s)f(s)ds > r^* - \int_0^{\bar{s}} [v_2(s) - v_1(s)]f(s)ds.$$

Equation 5.10 indicates that bankers may have the incentive to undertake new socially unprofitable projects (where the expected return is less than r^*) whenever the new projects raise the overall riskiness of the bank's portfolio and, hence, the expected value of the government's deposit guarantee. A high capital requirement on the bank will not prevent the bank from choosing a new project that increases the value of the government's guarantee $\left(\int_0^{\bar{s}} [v_2(s) - v_1(s)]\right.$

$f(s)ds > 0\Big)$. In fact, to the extent that new projects have a low expected return $\left(\int_0^{\bar{s}} a_2(s)f(s)ds \approx r^*\right)$, projects that are chosen by the banker will be those that increase the riskiness of the portfolio. This result is known as asset-substitution moral hazard. Gennotte and Pyle (1991), Besanko and Kanatas (1996), and Calem and Rob (1999) find that raising capital requirements may also increase risk-taking by banks due to managerial moral hazard.

Peltzman (1970) notes that although bank regulators can either require problem banks to reduce portfolio risk or to increase capital, they rarely intervene directly in banks' portfolio decisions, since they lack the private information that bankers use when making loans. As a result, most efforts are spent on capital regulation. By 1988 these efforts resulted in the Basel Accord's risk-weighted capital requirements. A number of economists have noted that since the risk-weighted capital requirements do not address the overall riskiness of bank portfolios, they will not generally solve the problem of socially unproductive investments by banks in the presence of deposit guarantees. Risk-weighted capital requirements under the Basle Accords have given rise to what Jones (2000) and Mingo (2000) call "regulatory capital arbitrage" that has lowered the effective risk-based capital requirements of many banks to well below the 8 percent standard set by the Accords.

Apart from the difficulties associated with capital requirements (whether risk-weighted or not) in richer countries, there are operational difficulties in transferring these requirements to the banking environments of many developing countries. Kane (1994) concludes that the transfer of the standards of the Basle Accords to these countries was "economically inappropriate and politically infeasible" due to insufficient information-gathering capacity, deficiencies in the legal systems, and lack of arms-length regulatory enforcement. Caprio and Honohan (1999) also note that in many developing countries bank capital is impaired by failure to declare loans non-performing and by relying on financially related firms to buy a bank's stock, thereby lowering the true capital of the bank.

Given the difficulties associated with the use of risk-based deposit insurance premiums or risk-based capital requirements, a number of economists have called for the use of more "blunt instruments" to lower the size of the contingent liability associated with deposit insurance, especially for developing countries. One of these instruments is deposit rate ceilings. A number of recent studies all present findings that indicate the potential drawbacks of deregulated interest rates for bank risk.[11] Hellman, Murdock, and Stiglitz (2000) have recently argued that (possibly nonbinding) interest rate ceilings in combination with capital requirements can eliminate excessive risk-taking by banks that is connected to deposit insurance.

An alternative view of deposit rate ceilings comes from economists who stress the role of market discipline (allowing depositors potentially to incur capital losses) as an alternative to bank regulation. In this view, placing depositors at risk not only lowers the government's contingent deposit liability, but it disciplines banks by requiring them to pay a risk premium based on their asset portfolio (Demirgüç-Kunt and Huizinga 2000). Martinez Peria and Schmukler (2001) show that depositors did in fact exert market discipline (resulting in higher interest rates and withdrawal of deposits) during financial crises in Argentina, Chile, and Mexico during the 1980s and 1990s. These empirical results correspond to periods of generalized financial distress in which the ability of the government to make good on its deposit guarantees was in question. On the other hand, Billett, Garfinkel, and O'Neal (1998) and Jordan (2000) question the usefulness of depositor discipline on an individual bank basis. They note that when bank risk increases, banks find it easy to substitute insured deposits for departing uninsured funds. The empirical evidence for the United States is that by offering small premiums over the market rate on insured deposits, banks at risk have been able successfully to neutralize market discipline.

In essence, the problem with deposit rate ceilings to promote stability (as in Hellman, Murdock, and Stiglitz 2000) or with freely determined deposit rates to promote market discipline is that deposit insurance tends to create a highly elastic supply of deposits to individual banks. In terms of this chapter's analytical model, depositor discipline at the bank level requires that depositors expend resources on monitoring banks, as in equation 5.2. Deposit insurance weakens the incentive to expend these resources when the deposit insurance system is well capitalized.

Depositor discipline will occur at a system-wide level if there is an upper limit $(\bar{v})$ on government insurance payments that would result in depositor losses in some states of the world. In this chapter's model, the supply of deposits to an individual bank is perfectly elastic, so that deposit rate ceilings will never be binding and depositor discipline will never apply to a single bank. If the government has a ceiling $(\bar{v})$ on its deposit guarantee funding, the guarantee will be a risky one for depositors. Equation 5.12 states that the government will pay out no more than $(\bar{v})$ even if the shortfall in the promised payment to depositors $[r/(1 + e) - a_1(s)]$ exceeds $(\bar{v})$. Higher deposit rates will reflect the possible government default on its deposit guarantees. Equations 5.11 and 5.12 with guarantor risk are the counterparts to equations 5.3 and 5.4 without guarantor risk. As a result of the cap $(\bar{v})$ on payments to depositors in equation 5.12, the guarantee is less valuable ($\hat{v}_1 < v_1$), so that depositors respond by demanding a higher contractual interest rate ($r > r^*$).

$$(5.11) \qquad \int_0^{\bar{s}} \min\left[\frac{r}{1+e}, a_1(s) + \hat{v}_1(s)\right] f(s) ds = \frac{r^*}{1+e}$$

where

$$(5.12) \qquad \hat{v}_1(s) \equiv \max\left[0, \min\left(\frac{r}{1+e} - a_1(s), \bar{v}\right)\right].$$

If the aggregate investment of banks in new projects increases the government's expected liability associated with the deposit guarantee, then the deposit rate will exceed the riskless rate. Depositor discipline will respond to the potential insolvency of the government's deposit insurance fund rather than to the portfolio choices of any single bank.

Another "blunt" instrument is quantitative restrictions on the expansion of credit by banks. These restrictions have often taken the form of credit ceilings, which are effectively 100 percent marginal reserve requirements on new deposits (so new deposits cannot be used for loans). Another form of quantitative restrictions is capital controls that limit the amount of borrowing a bank can undertake (thereby limiting the expansion of loans). A major problem with capital controls is that they eliminate the funding of both good loans and bad loans, by good banks and bad banks. Quantitative restrictions give rise to lobbying pressures by bankers on those bureaucrats who are in charge of the quantitative controls. Black, Miller, and Posner (1978) note that this kind of regulation suppresses competition beyond the level needed for regulatory purposes and also tends to expand its reach into other areas (such as controls over which sectors of the economy can be financed). Barth, Caprio, and Levine (2003) have expanded upon this critique of government regulatory failure with what they call the "grabbing hand" approach to government banking regulation (as opposed to the "helping hand" view of a benign government that corrects market failures and limits the negative side effects of deposit insurance).

Becker (1983) and others have shown that efficiency-enhancing actions on the part of the government are more apt to be undertaken than those actions that are purely redistributive. In their model, deposit insurance is efficiency-improving because it economizes on total monitoring costs of banks. Along with the gain in efficiency is an added opportunity for "rent seeking" by interest groups. Guo (1999) provides convincing evidence of rent seeking in the political, bureaucratic, and legal delays surrounding the Federal Savings and Loan Insurance Corporation's resolution of failed savings and loan institutions in the United States in the 1980s. Kroszner and Strahan (2001) discuss legislative strategies to implement efficiency-enhancing bank regulatory reforms while simultaneously blunting rent seeking by the private sector and "grabbing hand" behavior by the government.

Taxation of Banks for Non-Prudential Reasons

There is virtually no literature on the interaction of the taxation of banks with the government's deposit guarantee. The single exception appears to be Santomero and Trester's (1994) analysis of the interaction between different national taxation practices and a common deposit insurance fund in a unified Europe. Since there is little literature to cite, this section examines the implications of taxation within the model developed in this chapter.

In this model, the incidence of taxation will fall either on bank owners or on the government as provider of deposit insurance.[12] Suppose that the government taxes the gross return on banks' projects at the rate (t). The banker's expected profits (π) are the following:

$$(5.13) \qquad \pi \equiv \int_0^{\bar{s}} \max\left[(1-t)a_1(s) - \frac{r^*}{1+e}, 0\right] f(s)ds.$$

In states where the banker pays off depositors, the tax lowers banker's income and expected profits. In states where the banker defaults, equation 5.14 indicates that the tax raises the size of the government's contingent liability:

$$(5.14) \qquad v_t(s) \equiv \max\left[0, \frac{r^*}{1+e} - (1-t)a_1(s)\right].$$

In one limiting case (where banks never default), the tax just reduces bank profits. In the other limiting case (where banks always default), the tax results in a one-for-one increase in the government's deposit insurance liability. When the bank defaults in some (but not all) states of the world, the tax reduces bank profits and simultaneously increases the government's expected deposit insurance liability. This result is similar to Caminal's (2003) result that greater taxation of deposits raises the probability of bank failure, although Caminal does not explicitly consider the impact of deposit taxation on the government's deposit insurance liability.

Demirgüç-Kunt and Huizinga (2001) analyze the ability of foreign banks to engage in profit shifting as a way of minimizing the impact of taxation. Banks engage in a different type of profit shifting when the incidence of bank taxes is ultimately borne by the deposit insurance fund and taxpayers who finance the fund. To the extent that the shifting is intertemporal, the resources that the government gets from taxing banks will ultimately be paid for partially by future taxpayers. In that sense, what appears to be tax revenue from banks may approximate state-contingent government debt (since the size of the deposit guarantee payout will generally be state-contingent).

The tax also alters the banker's incentive to invest in projects. Equation 5.14 indicates the conditions under which a bank will find it privately profitable to undertake a project in the presence of a project tax and a deposit guarantee:

$$(5.15) \qquad \int_0^{\bar{s}} (1-t)a_1(s)f(s)ds \geq r^* - \int_0^{\bar{s}} v_t(s)f(s)ds.$$

The direct effect of the tax on projects' returns may reduce the expected after-tax return to less than the world interest rate, thereby decreasing the attractiveness of investment. But the incidence of the tax on the deposit insurance fund also raises the value of the deposit guarantee, thereby increasing the attractiveness of marginal projects with high default probabilities. The direct and indirect effects work in opposing directions.

Reserve Requirement Interactions with Deposit Insurance

Reserve requirements are a form of bank taxation when they are nonremunerated or remunerated at less than market interest rates. Yet at the same time reserve requirements affect the portfolio composition of a bank, reducing the amount of loans for a given equity ratio. Reserve requirements are therefore a hybrid between an indirect tax on banks and an additional equity instrument. As such, they have an ambiguous impact on the size of the contingent liability associated with deposit insurance.

One use of reserve requirements is to control capital inflows. A number of authors have analyzed the welfare impact of reserve requirements as capital controls.[13] Chile and Colombia each raised reserve requirements in response to increased capital inflows at various periods during the 1980s and 1990s. These higher reserve requirements were therefore marginal requirements that affected only new sources of external funding for banks. The following analysis assumes a similar use of reserve requirements as they affect the marginal investment decisions by banks. Unlike other previous analyses, the model highlights the interaction between the corrective and distorting aspects of reserve requirements on new investment decisions in the presence of deposit guarantees.

Suppose that the bank has invested in a project $a_1(s)$ and now wishes to invest in a project $a_2(s)$. The government wishes to curtail excessive investment in new projects and decides to subject all new deposits to a reserve requirement (k). The government pays a return $(\hat{r})$ on required reserves, where $0 \leq \hat{r} \leq r^*$. In order to finance the second project the bank must now set aside required reserves (kd) as well as add equity (ed) to bank capital. Solving the balance sheet equation $1 + kd = d + ed$ shows that the bank will require $d = 1/(1 + e - k)$ of new deposits to finance the new project.

The reserve requirement will alter the expected value of the government's deposit guarantee in two ways. First, to the extent that the government remunerates required reserves at a rate less than the deposit rate, the reserve requirement will be a tax on banks. Second, the reserve requirement acts as a higher marginal equity requirement on the bank. The equity requirement ed involves $e/(1 + e - k)$ of new bank capital, which is greater than the equity requirement $e/(1 + e)$ on the old project. The greater equity stake of the banker reduces the banker's incentives to undertake a risky project.

The offsetting tax-like and equity-enhancing effects of the reserve requirement are tied to the term (θ) capturing the bank's promised payment to depositors associated with the second project $r^*/(1 + e - k)$ net of any remuneration on required reserves $\hat{r}k/(1 + e - k)$:

$$(5.16) \qquad \theta \equiv \frac{r^* - \hat{r}k}{1 + e - k}.$$

The expression θ in equation 5.16 is the net cost to the bank of debt financing of the second project (that is, the cost of deposits r^* minus whatever the government pays on required reserves $\hat{r}k$). To the extent that required reserves pay less than the international interest rate $(\hat{r} < r^*)$, the government's policy acts like a tax to raise the cost of debt financing above the riskless rate.

The reserve requirement will affect the expected value of the government's deposit guarantee. In comparison with the guarantee $v_2(s)$

without reserve requirements (equation 5.9), the guarantee will now take the following form:

$$(5.17) \qquad \hat{v}_2(s) \equiv \max\left[0, \frac{r^*}{1+e} + \theta - a_1(s) - a_2(s)\right].$$

Increasing the reserve requirement will have an ambiguous effect on the size of the guarantee.[14] On one hand, if reserves are remunerated at the international interest rate, the value of the guarantee is *decreasing* in the size of the reserve requirement:

$$(5.18) \qquad \frac{\partial \theta}{\partial k_{|\hat{r}=r^*}} = \frac{-er^*}{(1+e-k)^2} < 0 \quad \Rightarrow \quad \frac{\partial}{\partial k_{|\hat{r}=r^*}} \int_0^{\bar{s}} \hat{v}_2(s)f(s)ds < 0.$$

On the other hand, if required reserves are not remunerated ($\hat{r}=0$), then the government's guarantee is *increasing* in the size of the reserve requirement:

$$(5.19) \qquad \frac{\partial \theta}{\partial k_{|\hat{r}=0}} = \frac{r^*}{(1+e-k)^2} > 0 \quad \Rightarrow \quad \frac{\partial}{\partial k_{|\hat{r}=0}} \int_0^{\bar{s}} \hat{v}_2(s)f(s)ds > 0.$$

Non–interest-bearing reserve requirements will only lower the government's deposit guarantee if they tax the project enough to keep the bank from financing it. The tax effect is captured in equation 5.20 by the term $(r^* - \hat{r})k/(1 + e - k) \geq 0$, which is the opportunity cost to the bank of holding required reserves. The bank will undertake the new project if the following condition holds:

$$(5.20) \qquad \int_0^{\bar{s}} a_2(s)f(s)ds > r^* + \frac{(r^* - \hat{r})k}{1+e-k} - \int_0^{\bar{s}}\left[\hat{v}_2(s) - v_1(s)\right]f(s)ds,$$

where $v_1(s) \equiv \max[0, r^*/(1 + e) - a_1(s)]$ is the government's contingent liability associated with the original project.

If required reserves are paid the international rate, the tax term disappears and the reserve requirement then acts to offset the marginal risk-taking incentives associated with the deposit guarantee that are shown in equation 5.10. With the payment of interest on reserves at the international rate, equation 5.20 differs from equation 5.10 only by the higher marginal equity requirement. If required reserves are not remunerated, then there are two offsetting factors affecting investment in the second project. As in equation 5.15, the tax term discourages investment in all new projects, but the increase in the expected size of the guarantee associated with the tax encourages risky project selection for those investments that are undertaken.

Other Topics

There are several other issues related to the corrective taxation of banks due to government deposit guarantees. The first is charter value. One way to mitigate the moral hazard associated with deposit insurance is to give banks something valuable that they will lose if they become insolvent. Marcus and Shaked (1984) showed at a theoretical level the importance of charter value in lowering the incentive of banks to gamble for resurrection when their underlying loan portfolio is weak. Keeley (1990) provided strong evidence that increased competition in the U.S. banking industry in the 1980s caused an erosion of charter values that caused banks to raise the riskiness of the loan portfolios and to reduce their capital. Other more recent papers, such as Matutes and Vives (2000), also find links between the degree of competition in the banking industry and the level of risk-taking. Limiting competition to reduce moral hazard from deposit insurance is a form of taxation on borrowers and depositors. The use of regulation to restrict competition in banking is often counter-productive, partly because sheltered banks may become "too big to fail" as well as politically powerful enough to "capture" their regulators.

The second issue is liquidity requirements. In the presence of deposit guarantees or a lender of last resort, banks will have dampened incentives to hold liquid assets to meet liquidity shocks. Liquidity requirements then become a corrective quasi-tax on banks. Since emergency liquidity provision is traditionally the role of the central bank, liquidity requirements on banks involve the combined functions of deposit insurance and lender of last resort. Recent papers by Williamson (1998), Repullo (2000), and Sleet and Smith (2000) have addressed liquidity provision by a lender of last resort in the presence of deposit insurance. In addition to liquidity requirements as a corrective quasi-tax, penalty rates on discount windows function as a corrective tax to deter overly illiquid asset portfolios. In these papers coordination between the deposit insurance agency and the central bank is an important aspect of the corrective measures.

A final issue is state-contingent taxation of banks. Dewatripont and Tirole (1994), Nagarajan and Sealey (1998), and Marshall and

Prescott (2001) suggest that taxation of banks contingent on the macroeconomic environment provides a way of separating idiosyncratic risk of bank failure (for which banks should be held accountable) from macroeconomic risk (which may be beyond the control of banks). If banks are subject to ex post state-contingent penalties, then these penalties can be an effective deterrent to overly risk-taking behavior. A drawback is that with limited liability the state-contingent penalties will have a dampened impact on banks' behavior. Kaufman and Wallison (2001) have pointed out that the current U.S. deposit insurance system is essentially one with state-contingent deposit insurance premiums on the banking industry as a whole.

Conclusion

This chapter has developed a conceptually straightforward model to pull together the large literature on corrective taxation of financial intermediaries in the presence of government deposit insurance. Although deposit guarantees can improve economic efficiency by protecting the payments system and by reducing duplication of monitoring costs by the private sector, they can also create regulatory moral hazard by increasing banks' incentives to invest in socially unproductive projects and to add risk to asset portfolios. These unwanted byproducts of deposit insurance can be mitigated by the use of deposit insurance premiums, bank capital requirements, interest rate ceilings, credit ceilings, and reserve requirements. Each of these corrective instruments has limitations and unfavorable side effects, so that there is no "one size fits all" set of prudential regulations to correct the moral hazard associated with the government's provision of deposit insurance. Perhaps the most surprising finding of the chapter is the scarce attention that has been paid to the impact of noncorrective bank taxes on the contingent liability associated with deposit guarantees. To the extent that the incidence of bank taxes is shifted onto a deposit insurance fund, tax revenue may in certain instances (especially when banks are close to insolvency) be essentially equivalent or isomorphic to the proceeds from the sale of state-contingent government debt.

Notes

1. Countries adopting these programs have included Bahrain, Chile, Colombia, Congo, Denmark, Ecuador, El Salvador, Greece, Ireland, Italy, Jamaica, Kenya, Korea, Mexico, Nigeria, Peru, Portugal, Sri Lanka, Swe-

den, Switzerland, Tanzania, Turkey, the United Kingdom, and Venezuela (Demirgüç-Kunt and Detragiache 2000).

2. Among the books are Benston and others (1986); Brock (1992); Dewatripont and Tirole (1994); Lindgren, Garcia, and Saal (1996); Calomiris (1997); Eichengreen (1999); and World Bank (2001). Some recent articles include Bhattacharya, Boot, and Thakor (1998); Brock (2000); Kane (2000); Barth, Caprio, and Levine (2001); Claessens and Klingebiel (2001); Freixas and Santomero (2001); Stiglitz (2001); and Kuritzkes, Schuermann, and Weiner (2002).

3. Although the use of corrective taxes and quasi-taxes to offset the impact of deposit insurance forms the vast bulk of the literature (especially the recent literature) on bank regulation, there are other potential areas for corrective taxes. These may include, with the usual caveats, market concentration, macroeconomic instability, and income distribution. This chapter is concerned solely with corrective taxation as it applies to deposit guarantees and the associated problems of informational asymmetries.

4. Debt contracts are a type of insurance contract, with a borrower's collateral serving as a deductible and the loan cost acting as the premium for the policy. Lenders are like insurers who receive interest and fees for the loan, but who also bear the risk of loss if the borrower defaults.

5. In related work, de Meza and Webb (1999) show that a balanced budget tax-and-subsidy scheme may be Pareto-improving in the presence of adverse selection in credit markets. In earlier work, de Meza and Webb (1987) showed that taxation in the presence of adverse selection in financial markets may enhance efficiency but did not address the issue of Pareto-improving tax/subsidy schemes.

6. Calomiris (1989) provides convincing evidence that prior to 1933 state deposit insurance systems in the United States had a similar purpose "to insulate the economy's payments system from the risk of bank failures." Deposit insurance can also protect small savers. Bradley (2000) documents that insured U.S. postal savings bank accounts for small savers both preceded and partially motivated federal deposit insurance coverage in 1933. As Rochet (1999) has pointed out, banks are different from other firms because their creditors are also their customers. The creditors of other firms are larger, more sophisticated, and better able to assess firm risk than small depositors of banks. For banks, the government acts as the representative of small depositors in collecting information and establishing norms of prudential regulation. Dewatripont and Tirole (1994) have made this representation hypothesis the core concept in their theory of prudential regulation of banks. Benston (2000) also stresses that "government-provided deposit insurance can achieve economies of information for consumers, who need not incur the costs of investigating and monitoring banks or the deposit insurance contracts that they offer."

7. The model is patterned loosely after James's (1988) analysis of "off-balance-sheet" banking. Deposit guarantees are a type of off-balance-sheet activity.

8. Assume for the moment that the project is entirely debt financed.

9. Assume that these monitoring costs on a per depositor basis are negligible, so that $\gamma / n \to 0$ as the number of depositors (n) per project becomes large.

10. Chan, Greenbaum, and Thakor (1992); Giammarino, Lewis, and Sappington (1993); Nagarajan and Sealey (1998); and Freixas and Rochet (1998).

11. Bhattacharya (1982); Smith (1984); Aharony, Saunders, and Swary (1988); Bundt, Cosimano, and Halloran (1992); and Honohan (2001).

12. This is because depositors must be paid an expected gross return of r^* and banks own their projects (so that there are no borrowers).

13. These include Chinn and Dooley (1997); Aizenman and Turnovsky (1999); De Gregorio, Edwards, and Valdés (2000); and Herrera and Valdés (2001).

14. The algebraic expression for the ambiguous effect is: $\partial\theta/\partial k = r^* - (1 + e)\hat{r}/[1 + e - k]^2$.

References

Aharony, Joseph, Anthony Saunders, and Itzhak Swary. 1988. "The Effects of DIDMCA on Bank Stockholders' Returns and Risk." *Journal of Banking and Finance* 12 (3): 317–31.

Aizenman, Joshua, and Stephen Turnovsky. 1999. "Reserve Requirements on Sovereign Debt in the Presence of Moral Hazard—on Debtors or Creditors?" NBER Working Paper 7004. Cambridge, Mass.

Banerjee, Abhijit, and Tim Besley. 1990. "Moral Hazard, Limited Liability and Taxation: A Principal-Agent Model." *Oxford Economic Papers* 42 (1): 46–60.

Barth, James, Gerard Caprio, Jr., and Ross Levine. 2001. "Banking Systems around the Globe: Do Regulation and Ownership Affect Performance and Stability? In Frederic S. Mishin, ed., *Prudential Regulation and Supervision: Why It Is Important and What Are the Issues.* Cambridge, Mass.: National Bureau of Economic Research.

———. 2003. "Bank Regulation and Supervision: What Works Best?" *Journal of Financial Intermediation.* Forthcoming.

Becker, Gary. 1983. "A Theory of Competition Among Pressure Groups for Political Influence." *The Quarterly Journal of Economics* 98 (3): 371–400.

Benston, George. 2000. "Is Government Regulation of Banks Necessary?" *Journal of Financial Services Research* 18 (2–3): 185–202.

Benston, George, Robert Eisenbeis, Paul Horvitz, Edward Kane, and George Kaufman. 1986. *Perspectives on Safe and Sound Banking.* Cambridge, Mass.: MIT Press.

Besanko, David, and George Kanatas. 1996. "The Regulation of Bank Capital: Do Capital Standards Promote Bank Safety?" *Journal of Financial Intermediation* 5 (1): 160–83.

Bhattacharya, Sudipto. 1982. "Aspects of Monetary and Banking Theory and Moral Hazard." *Journal of Finance* 37 (2): 371–84.

Bhattacharya, Sudipto, Arnoud Boot, and Anjan Thakor. 1998. "The Economics of Bank Regulation." *Journal of Money, Credit, and Banking* 30 (4): 745–70.

Billett, Matthew, Jon Garfinkel, and Edward O'Neal. 1998. "The Cost of Market versus Regulatory Discipline in Banking." *Journal of Financial Economics* 48: 333–58.

Black, Fisher, Merton Miller, and Richard Posner. 1978. "An Approach to the Regulation of Bank Holding Companies." *Journal of Business* 51 (3): 379–412.

Boyd, John, Chun Chang, and Bruce Smith. 1998. "Deposit Insurance: A Reconsideration." Working Paper 593. Federal Reserve Bank of Minneapolis.

Bradley, Christine. 2000. "A Historical Perspective on Deposit Insurance Coverage." *FDIC Banking Review* 13 (1): 1–25.

Brock, Philip. 1992. *If Texas were Chile: A Primer on Banking Reform.* San Francisco: ICS Press.

———. 2000. "Financial Safety Nets: Lessons from Chile." *The World Bank Research Observer* 15 (1): 69–84.

Bundt, Thomas P., Thomas F. Cosimano, and John A. Halloran. 1992. "DIDMCA and Bank Market Risk: Theory and Evidence." *Journal of Banking and Finance* 16 (6): 1179–93.

Calem, Paul, and Rafael Rob. 1999. "The Impact of Capital-Based Regulation on Bank Risk-Taking." *Journal of Financial Intermediation* 8 (4): 317–52.

Calomiris, Charles. 1989. "Deposit Insurance: Lessons from the Record." Federal Reserve Bank of Chicago *Economic Perspectives,* 13 (May/June):10–30.

———. 1997. *The Postmodern Bank Safety Net: Lessons from Developed and Developing Economies.* Washington, D.C.: The AEI Press.

Caminal, Ramon. 2003. "Taxation of Banks: Modeling the Impact" (chapter 3, this volume).

Caprio, Gerard, and Patrick Honohan. 1999. "Restoring Banking Stability: Beyond Supervised Capital Requirements." *Journal of Economic Perspectives* 13 (1): 43–64.

Caprio, Gerard, and Daniela Klingebiel. 1997. "Bank Insolvency: Bad Luck, Bad Policy, or Bad Banking?" In Michael Bruno and Bruno

Pleskovic, eds., *Annual World Bank Conference on Development Economics 1996*. Washington, D.C.: World Bank.

———. 2002. "Episodes of Systemic and Borderline Financial Crises." In Daniela Klingebiel and Luc Laeven, eds., *Managing the Real and Fiscal Effects of Banking Crises*. World Bank Discussion Paper No. 428. Washington D.C.

Carr, Jack L., and G. Frank Mathewson. 1988. "Unlimited Liability as a Barrier to Entry." *Journal of Political Economy* 96 (4): 766–84.

Chan, Yuk-Shee, Stuart I. Greenbaum, and Anjan Thakor. 1992. "Is Fairly Priced Deposit Insurance Possible?" *The Journal of Finance* 47 (1): 227–45.

Chinn, Menzie, and Michael P. Dooley. 1997. "Financial Repression and Capital Mobility: Why Capital Flows and Covered Interest Rate Differentials Fail to Measure Capital Market Integration." *Monetary and Economic Studies* 15 (4): 81–103.

Claessens, Stijn, and Daniela Klingebiel. 2001. "Competition and Scope of Activities in Financial Services." *World Bank Research Observer* 16 (1): 19–40.

De Gregorio, José, Sebastian Edwards, and Rodrigo Valdés. 2000. "Controls on Capital Inflows: Do They Work?" *Journal of Development Economics* 63 (1): 59–83.

de Meza, David, and David Webb. 1987. "Too Much Investment: A Problem of Asymmetric Information." *Quarterly Journal of Economics* 102 (2): 281–92.

———. 1999. "Wealth, Enterprise, and Credit Policy." *Economic Journal* 109 (1): 153–63.

Demirgüç-Kunt, Aslı, and Enrica Detragiache. 2000. "Does Deposit Insurance Increase Banking System Stability? An Empirical Investigation." World Bank, Development Research Group, Washington, D.C. Processed (April).

Demirgüç-Kunt, Aslı, and Harry Huizinga. 2000. "Market Discipline and Financial Safety Net Design." World Bank, Development Research Group, Washington, D.C. Processed (April).

———. 2001. "The Taxation of Domestic and Foreign Banking." *Journal of Public Economics* 79 (3): 429–53.

Demirgüç-Kunt, Aslı, and Edward J. Kane, 2002. "Deposit Insurance Around the Globe: Where Does It Work?" *Journal of Economic Perspectives* 16 (2): 175–95.

Dewatripont, Mattias, and Jean Tirole. 1994. *The Prudential Regulation of Banks*. Cambridge Mass.: MIT Press.

Diamond, Douglas. 1984. "Financial Intermediation and Delegated Monitoring." *Review of Economic Studies* 51 (3): 393–414.

———. 1996. "Financial Intermediation as Delegated Monitoring: A Simple Example." Federal Reserve Bank of Richmond *Economic Quarterly* 82/3: 51–66.

Diamond, Douglas, and Philip Dybvig. 1983. "Bank Runs, Deposit Insurance and Liquidity." *Journal of Political Economy* 91 (3): 401–19.

Eichengreen, Barry 1999. *Toward a New International Financial Architecture: A Practical Post-Asia Agenda.* Washington, D.C.: Institute for International Economics.

Freixas, Xavier, and Jean-Charles Rochet. 1998. "Fair Pricing of Deposit Insurance. Is it Possible? Yes. Is it Desirable? No." *Research in Economics* 52 (3): 217–32.

Freixas, Xavier, and Anthony Santomero. 2001. "An Overall Perspective on Banking Regulation." University of Pennsylvania. Processed.

Gale, Douglas, and Martin Hellwig. 1985. "Incentive-Compatible Debt Contracts: The One-period Problem." *Review of Economic Studies* 52 (4): 647–63.

Gennotte, Gerard, and David Pyle. 1991. "Capital Controls and Bank Risk." *Journal of Banking and Finance* 15 (4–5): 805–24.

Giammarino, Ronald, Tracy Lewis, and David Sappington. 1993. "An Incentive Approach to Banking Regulation." *The Journal of Finance* 48 (4): 1523–42.

Greenwald, Bruce C., and Joseph E. Stiglitz. 1986. "Externalities in Economies with Imperfect Information and Incomplete Markets." *Quarterly Journal of Economics* 101 (2): 229–64.

Guo, Lin. 1999. "When and Why Did FSLIC Resolve Insolvent Thrifts?" *Journal of Banking and Finance* 23 (6): 955–90.

Hellmann, Thomas, Kevin Murdock, and Joseph E. Stiglitz. 2000. "Liberalization, Moral Hazard in Banking, and Prudential Regulation: Are Capital Requirements Enough?" *American Economic Review* 90 (1): 147–65.

Herrera, Luis O., and Rodrigo Valdés. 2001. "The Effect of Capital Controls on Interest Rate Differentials." *Journal of International Economics* 53 (2): 385–98.

Honohan, Patrick. 2001. "How Interest Rates Changed Under Financial Liberalization: A Cross-Country Review." In Gerard Caprio, Patrick Honohan, and Joseph E. Stiglitz, eds., *Financial Liberalization: How Far, How Fast?* New York: Cambridge University Press.

Honohan, Patrick, and Daniela Klingebiel. 2003. "The Fiscal Cost Implications of an Accommodating Approach to Banking Crises." *Journal of Banking and Finance.* Forthcoming.

James, Christopher. 1988. "The Use of Loan Sales and Standby Letters of Credit by Commercial Banks." *Journal of Monetary Economics* 22 (3): 395–422.

John, Kose, Teresa A. John, and Lemma W. Senbet. 1991. "Risk-shifting Incentives of Depository Institutions: A New Perspective on Federal Deposit Insurance Reform." *Journal of Banking and Finance* 15 (4-5): 895–915.

Jones, David 2000. "Emerging Problems with the Basel Capital Accord: Regulatory Capital Arbitrage and Related Issues." *Journal of Banking and Finance* 24 (1): 35–58.

Jordan, John S. 2000. "Depositor Discipline at Failing Banks." *New England Economic Review* March/April: 15–28.

Kane, Edward. 1994. "Difficulties of Transferring Risk-Based Capital Requirements." Policy Research Working Paper 1244, World Bank, Washington, D.C.

———. 2000. "Designing Financial Safety Nets to Fit Country Circumstances." Boston College. Processed (May).

Kane, Edward, and Berry Wilson. 1998. "A Contracting-Theory Interpretation of the Origins of Federal Deposit Insurance." *Journal of Money, Credit, and Banking* 30 (3): 573–95.

Kaufman, George, and Peter Wallison. 2001. "The New Safety Net." *Regulation* 24 (2): 28–35.

Keeley, Michael. 1990. "Deposit Insurance, Risk, and Market Power in Banking." *American Economic Review* 80 (5): 1183–1200.

Kroszner, Randall S., and Philip E. Strahan. 2001. "Obstacles to Optimal Policy: The Interplay of Politics and Economics in Shaping Bank Supervision and Regulation Reforms." In Frederic S. Mishkin, ed., *Prudential Supervision: What Works and What Doesn't*. Chicago: University of Chicago Press and NBER.

Kuritzkes, Andrew, Til Schuermann, and Scott Weiner. 2002. "Deposit Insurance and Risk Management of the U.S. Banking System: How Much? How Safe? Who Pays?" Financial Institutions Center Working Paper 02-02, University of Pennsylvania, Wharton School, Philadelphia.

Laeven, Luc. 2002. "The Pricing of Deposit Insurance." Policy Research Working Paper 2871. World Bank, Washington, D.C.

Lindgren, Carl-Johan, Gillian Garcia, and Matthew Saal. 1996. *Bank Soundness and Macroeconomic Policy*. Washington, D.C.: International Monetary Fund.

Marcus, Alan, and Israel Shaked. 1984. "The Valuation of FDIC Deposit Insurance Using Option-Pricing Estimates." *Journal of Money, Credit, and Banking* 16 (4): 446–60.

Marshall, D., and E. S. Prescott. 2001. "Bank Capital Regulation with and without State-Contingent Penalties." *Carnegie-Rochester Conference Series on Public Policy* 54 (1): 139–84.

Martinez Peria, Maria Soledad, and Sergio Schmukler. 2001. "Do Depositors Punish Banks for Bad Behavior? Market Discipline, Deposit Insurance, and Banking Crises." *The Journal of Finance* 56 (3): 1029–51.

Matutes, Carmen, and Xavier Vives. 2000. "Imperfect Competition, Risk Taking, and Regulation in Banking." *European Economic Review* 44 (1): 1–34.

Merton, Robert C. 1977. "An Analytic Derivation of the Cost of Deposit Insurance and Loan Guarantees: An Application of Modern Option Pricing Theory." *Journal of Banking and Finance* 1 (1): 3–11.

———. 1978. "On the Cost of Deposit Insurance When There are Surveillance Costs." *Journal of Business* 51 (3): 439–52.

Mingo, John. 2000. "Policy Implications of the Federal Reserve Study of Credit Risk Models at Major US Banking Institutions." *Journal of Banking and Finance* 24 (1): 15–33.

Nagarajan, S., and C. Sealey. 1998. "State-Contingent Regulatory Mechanisms and Fairly Priced Deposit Insurance." *Journal of Banking and Finance* 22 (9): 1139–56.

Peltzman, Sam. 1970. "Capital Investment in Commercial Banking and Its Relationship to Portfolio Regulation." *Journal of Political Economy* 78 (1): 1–26.

Repullo, Rafael. 2000. "Who Should Act as Lender of Last Resort? An Incomplete Contracts Model." *Journal of Money, Credit, and Banking* 32 (3): 580–605.

Rochet, Jean-Charles. 1999. "Solvency Regulations and the Management of Banking Risks." *European Economic Review* 43 (4–6): 981–90.

Santomero, Anthony, and Jeffrey Trester. 1994. "Structuring Deposit Insurance for a United Europe." Financial Institutions Center Working Paper 94-22. University of Pennsylvania, Wharton School, Philadelphia.

Sleet, Christopher, and Bruce D. Smith. 2000. "Deposit Insurance and Lender-of-Last-Resort Functions." *Journal of Money, Credit, and Banking* 32 (3): 518–75.

Smith, Bruce D. 1984. "Private Information, Deposit Interest Rates, and the 'Stability' of the Banking System." *Journal of Monetary Economics* 14 (3): 293–317.

Stiglitz, Joseph E 2001. "Principles of Financial Regulation: A Dynamic Portfolio Approach." *World Bank Research Observer* 16 (1): 1–18.

Townsend, Robert. 1979. "Optimal Contracts and Competitive Markets with Costly State Verification." *Journal of Economic Theory* 21 (2): 265–93.

Williamson, Stephen. 1998. "Discount Window Lending and Deposit Insurance." *Review of Economic Dynamics* 1 (1): 246–75.

World Bank. 2001. *Finance for Growth: Policy Choices in a Volatile World.* New York: Oxford University Press.

Part II

Practical
Experience

6

Taxation of Financial Intermediation in Industrial Countries

Mattias Levin and Peer Ritter

This chapter presents a broad overview of the recent changes that have occurred in the industrial countries in taxation of income from capital and other aspects of tax affecting financial intermediation, together with an interpretation of the reform thinking underlying these changes. The chapter first focuses on the overall question of how to tax capital income. It notes how this has become a central issue as rates have declined and tax bases have broadened, and highlights the emergence of dual tax systems as an increasingly popular way forward. The chapter then examines the practical issues in the taxation of different financial instruments, noting in particular the problems that arise by retaining for tax purposes a distinction between debt-type and equity-type instruments. It further considers the treatment of new instruments that can blur this distinction, as well as that between income and capital gains, and points out the importance of timing issues in this context. The chapter follows with a brief review of some of the special issues surrounding the taxation of intermediaries, documenting the diversity of special taxes, implicit and explicit, to which they can be subject, despite a trend towards elimination.

Two general but often conflicting tax criteria have been central in shaping the voluminous body of law on the taxation of financial intermediation in industrial countries. The ability-to-pay principle represents a normative judgment about the equitable distribution of the tax burden across individuals. The economic efficiency principle aims to keep the allocative distortions from taxation at a minimum.

In aiming at the goals of equity, efficiency, and simplicity, tax systems must also adapt to changing economic circumstances. These changes include the increase in the elasticity of capital flows with respect to price, and hence to taxation, following liberalization of capital flows. However, tax systems are difficult to reform. This is partly because of the political consequences of changing the distribution of the tax burden, partly because of dogmatism regarding principal features in the tax law, and partly because of the complex interrelationships between the various taxes raised—just to mention a few reasons.

Overall, the same principles apply to the taxation of financial institutions as for other companies. However, some issues become much more important, including the timing of realized gains, short-term versus long-term investments, and the valuation of income streams.

The treatment of capital income differs sharply across countries. Some countries tax capital income as part of total income, often at progressive rates. Other countries have particular tax rates for capital income, often on a proportional basis. Still other countries do not tax capital gains.

Most countries do not tax all dividends equally. Exceptions are often made for shares traded on or off exchanges. Furthermore, interest income is often taxed differently depending on the instrument (public bonds are often tax-exempt) or institution (bank deposits are often exempt).[1]

Numerous special regimes and deductions apply to financial investments, as encouraging these investments often is regarded as an important policy objective: to encourage risk capital or to stimulate pension savings, for example.

This chapter describes how industrial countries have grappled with these challenges in reforming their taxation of financial intermediation. Despite the inherent difficulties of tax reform, most countries have undergone significant reforms since the 1980s. The main drivers for tax reform since the 1980s have been an eagerness to reduce the distorting effect of high marginal tax rates (rate cutting) while preserving financing commitments (base broadening). But taxation of financial intermediation has been affected by a number of additional concerns:[2]

• Location of financial activity (competition between financial centers)

- Disintermediation (a growing array of financial institutions)
- Demographics (the need to stimulate private savings to fund pensions)
- Financial innovation (new instruments shaped to circumvent traditional taxes)

Sometimes these reforms have been forward-looking responses to the general challenges outlined above. In most cases, however, reform has been more reactive and provisional, at a minimum leading to a decrease in rates and refinement of systems dealing with globalization (including imputation systems, transfer pricing, anti-avoidance measures, and information exchange).

Thus overall, the tax systems in place still bear the same contours as before reform started in the 1980s. But it is increasingly doubtful whether that kind of reactive response is sufficient in the face of current challenges. An alternative systematic response to the challenges faced by industrial countries are dual income tax systems, which tax all returns from capital at a lower, proportional rate compared to ordinary income, which remains taxed at progressive and higher rates. A more fundamental approach would be to opt for a consumption-based tax system to ensure neutrality toward financing and intertemporal allocation.

Taxation of Capital and Other Income

A central issue in the taxation of financial intermediation is the treatment of capital income for tax purposes (see also chapter 2). Before looking at the major reform trends in this regard, it will be convenient to review the relevant concepts of income.

Definition of Income

As a measure of the ability-to-pay, the Haig-Simons (H-S) concept of income—broadly, the sum of current consumption and changes in net worth—has remained at center stage in taxation in the industrial countries.[3] In principle this concept is meant to be independent of the source (labor or capital). As regards changes in net worth, they can be taxed as they accrue or when they are realized.

The debate around this concept of income is centered on three issues that are relevant to financial instruments. The economic sense of the H-S concept has been called into question: for example, by stressing that it may lead to an intertemporal misallocation of resources through the taxation of changes in wealth. Even if one accepts the H-S concept and thus taxation of changes in wealth, the choice between taxation on the accrual or realization basis remains.

First, should changes in net wealth be taxed? Proponents defend the H-S concept by claiming that it corresponds to the principle of "ability to pay." A change in wealth would constitute a change in the amount that could possibly be spent on consumption and should thus be taxed. Critics argue that this view is static; it ignores that wealth is deferred consumption and hence the savings that build up wealth are out of current income that is already taxed. These critics have instead suggested tax systems built on current consumption or on cash flows, exempting the opportunity cost of capital from tax.

Second, should capital income and other income be taxed at the same rate? Many countries distinguish between income from capital assets and other income by applying different rates. This distinction also relates to the differential treatment of debt and equity in most tax systems. At the root of this distinction is the belief that ownership should be taxed differently from other sorts of income (including the lending of capital). Financial instruments can be designed to avoid such a distinction. In contracts, dual income tax systems separate labor from other income with the allocative argument that in order to minimize tax distortions, factors with the lower elasticity of supply should be taxed higher. The schedular approach of the dual income tax departs systematically from the H-S approach.

Third, should the taxation of the net change in wealth be on accrual or on realization? The H-S dictum that changes in net wealth are to be taxed is still prevailing in industrial countries, although in practice capital gains are often not taxed. Many suggestions for reform of financial instruments taxation focus on the measurement of changes in net wealth. The traditional way, taxation on realization, has been defended mostly on practical considerations; in particular that valuation is often difficult. These considerations may be valid for traditional assets like land or paintings by old masters. Financial instruments however can be used to defer realization and also often do not even encompass an asset but only payment flows. Hence financial instruments may require a reconsideration of the traditional approach to measure capital gains.

Tax Reform in the 1980s: Reducing Distortions

A steady increase in tax rates (to help finance growing welfare commitments) and deteriorating economic performance in the 1970s helped trigger a more critical assessment of the distorting effects of

Table 6.1. Cutting Tax Rates

	Personal income tax Top marginal rate (no. of brackets)			Corporate income tax Top marginal rate		
	1970s	1989	2001	1970s	1980s	2002
US	70 (14)	28 (2)	38.6 (5)	46	34	40
DE	56 (4)	54.5 (4)	48.5 (4)	56	50	38.4
UK	83 (11)	40 (3)	40 (3)	52	35	30
FR	64.7 (13)	56.8 (13)	53.3 (6)	50	34	34.3
IT	72 (32)	50 (6)	45 (5)	25	36	40.3
NL	72 (9)	72 (3)	52 (3)	46	35	34.5

Sources: Knoester 1993; European Commission 2001; IBFD, 2001; Van den Noord and Heady, 2001.

taxation in many countries during the 1980s (Messere 1999, 2000; Duisenberg 1993; Knoester 1993; Steinmo 1995). Existing systems were seen as deficient in each of the major dimensions.

- Efficiency: Statutory marginal rates were high—for example, marginal personal income tax rates were over 80 percent in Sweden, and 70 percent in the United States and the United Kingdom— which led to substantial tax avoidance.
- Equity: Tax systems were not as redistributive as expected, considering the high marginal rates. The reason was that the rates were effectively lowered by numerous exemptions and the regressive characteristics of social security contributions.
- Simplicity: Decades of using the tax system as a means to achieve objectives of a nonfiscal nature had resulted in complex systems with numerous exemptions, allowances, regimes, and so on. As a result, compliance costs and administration costs had soared (Duisenberg 1993).

In the reforms of the early 1980s, countries generally tried to render their tax systems more efficient by cutting marginal income tax rates. Countries also made systems simpler by cutting the number of tax brackets (table 6.1).

With little reduction in expenditure commitments, the tax changes had to be revenue neutral: that is, not affect the overall tax revenue. Countries therefore broadened the tax base, partly by eliminating exemptions, special regimes, and so on, and partly by taxing more forms of income. This is of particular importance for the focus of this chapter, as countries have turned to taxing capital income and capital gains to a larger extent than before in order to compensate for the decrease in tax rates (table 6.2). Some countries

Table 6.2. Examples of Base-Broadening Measures
in the 1980s

Country	Personal	Corporate
US	• Abolition of favorable treatment of capital gains • Repeal of tax-sheltered investments • Elimination of special business reductions	• Abolition of Investment Tax Credit • Reduction in the deductibility of R&D expenditure
UK	• Increase in taxation of earnings (for example, benefits in kind such as cars) • Reduction of tax subsidy on owner-occupied housing • Capital gains brought in under income tax	• Abolition of 100% first-year allowance for investments in plant and machinery • Depreciation allowances for investment brought into line with true economic depreciation
FR	—	• Elimination of investment tax credits • Elimination of favorable depreciation allowances (actual life)
NL	• Taxable compensation allowance • No deduction for social security taxes • Lower personal exemptions	—

Source: Knoester 1993.

also *changed the composition* of their tax base, for example by relying more on indirect taxes, primarily VAT (Messere 2000).

Reform Since the 1990s: Contours of an Ideal System?

Reform since the 1990s has aimed at simplifying the tax system by continuing to rein in exemptions, thus broadening the tax base, while at the same time decreasing the tax rates. Reforms have also tried to deal with increasing capital mobility, attempting to find ways of taxing capital without provoking capital flight (see, for example, OECD 1998).

The motives for reforming personal capital income taxes are largely the same as for overall tax reform:

• *Efficiency*: Faced with decreasing levels of gross savings in general and household savings in particular, and as a high level of private savings has become increasingly desirable from a public point of view (to provide risk capital, or to cater to individual pension needs), countries have increasingly tried to stimulate financial savings by tax cuts (see Bosworth and Burtless 1992, Feldstein 1995). In some countries this has taken the form of general tax cuts. In others, however, it has taken the form of an increase in special regimes (Gordon 2000). Few countries have, however, radically changed their tax systems in order to stimulate savings.

• *Equity*: Traditionally, some countries have tried to use taxes to redistribute capital wealth (for example, wealth taxes, inheritance taxes) for the sake of vertical equity. In order to achieve horizontal equity, taxes on dividends have in many cases been reduced or abolished in order to bring them in line with taxes on interest income (Messere 1999).[4]

• *Simplicity*: While the number of income categories and brackets has often been reduced, in those countries that have started to tax capital gains the complexity of the tax system has increased rather than decreased.

Three general approaches have been employed in the treatment of capital income.

Including capital income in personal income taxes   Some countries have brought in capital income under the ordinary personal income tax, thus widening the tax base. Under such a system, capital income flows are taxed progressively under the personal income tax. This would be in accordance with the logic of the Haig-Simons approach. On that front, personal income tax rates in the EU remain higher than in other industrial countries. However, tax rates have decreased substantially since the 1980s, with the average top rate falling from about 56 percent in 1983 to 47 percent in 2001.[5] Some countries have moved faster and further than others. Belgium and the United Kingdom have cut more than France and Germany, for example. However, in other countries, such as Denmark and Luxembourg, top rates have actually increased.[6]

While some countries continue to tax capital gains separately, most countries have either incorporated capital gains under income taxation or, as will be further detailed next, started to tax all capital income (gains, dividends, and wealth) at a separate proportional rate.

Taxing capital income separately: dual income tax systems   The reforms outlined above, no matter how voluminous, have remained piecemeal rather than comprehensive. Therefore in most cases so far, reform has not offered a coherent response to the challenges posed by globalization. Faced with the increasing mobility of capital, some

Table 6.3. Dual Income Tax Systems

	Denmark	Finland	Norway	Sweden
Year introduced	1987	1993	1992	1991
Capital income tax rates (percent)				
• Corporate	32	28	28	28
• Other	39.7–59	28	28	30
Personal income tax rates	39.7–59	22.5–54.5	28–41.5	31–56
Elimination of double taxation of corporate profits				
• Distributions	Yes	Yes	Yes	No
• Retentions	No	No	Yes	No
Withholding taxes on nonresidents				
• Dividends	Yes	Yes	Yes	Yes
• Interests	No	No	No	No
• Royalties	Yes	Yes	No	No

Sources: Cnossen 2000; IBFD 2001.

countries have chosen an alternative path by imposing dual, if not multiple, income taxes. The aim has been to tax capital income at a lower rate in order to prevent tax evasion (Huizinga and Nicodème 2001). In the late 1980s to early 1990s, the Nordic countries (Denmark, Finland, Norway, and Sweden) adopted such dual income tax (DIT) systems. Under dual income tax systems all income is scheduled into two types:

• *Capital income*: This includes business profits (return on equity), dividends, capital gains, interest, rents, and rental values. Capital income is taxed at a proportional rate.

• *Personal income*: This includes wages and salaries, fringe benefits, pension income, and social security benefits. Personal income is taxed at progressive rates.

This led to significant cuts in capital income tax rates and often a decrease in the progressiveness of the personal income tax rate (table 6.3). Why did the traditionally social-democratic Scandinavian countries decided to launch such a reform?

The reasons were a willingness to reduce the distortionary effect of progressive income taxes, to strengthen incentives for private savings, and to eliminate the numerous possibilities for tax arbitrage and tax avoidance deriving from the vast array of exemptions and deductions available on capital income (Nielsen and Sørensen 1997).

An associated benefit was that reform would lead to higher tax revenues as a result of the widening of the base.

The Nordic countries have not levied withholding taxes on non-residents' interest income, or in some cases on royalty income, however (Cnossen 2000). This may give rise to tax avoidance. One reason may be that due to the collective dynamics in the EU, such taxes could contribute to capital flight.

The attractiveness of dual income systems lies in their relative pragmatism and simplicity. A low and flat rate on capital income has been heralded as a pragmatic way of dealing with the greater elasticity of supply of capital, the difficulties of verifying capital income, and maintaining international competitiveness. It is in that respect not surprising that dual income systems have become popular in the Nordic countries, which are small and open economies faced with the significant risk of capital outflow if their capital income taxation is too high. Moreover, by applying the same rate to all sources of private capital income, the tax system also becomes simpler.

The main criticism regards equity. Dual tax rates may give rise to tax shifting, which negatively affects horizontal equity. As capital income holders are often wealthier, it also affects vertical equity compared to the Haig-Simons concept in place.[7] This was indeed the main political problem in implementing these reforms. For example, at the time of the reform, the trade union leader in Sweden complained to the social democratic government that he would never be able to defend the reform in front of his members, as it made him (a relatively high-income earner) much better off than under the old tax system. Nevertheless, as the broadening of the tax base and the elimination of numerous exemptions from capital income tax led to calls for continued tax relief for special interest groups, the governments were able to defend the reforms in the name of general interest.

In 2001 the Netherlands introduced a tax system similar to DIT. Instead of a capital income tax, a wealth tax was established.[8] In the beginning of 2003 Germany was debating to move to a system similar to a DIT.

The main attraction of DIT is that while it reduces distortions and takes into account the different elasticities of supply, by keeping progressive taxes on personal income and removing numerous exemptions on capital income, policymakers continue to hold instruments to maintain the tax system as reasonably progressive.

Allowance for corporate equity   The tax system known as the allowance for corporate equity (ACE) has its origin in the cash flow approach to taxation. For a cash flow corporation tax, the idea is to take the difference between sales revenue and expenses as the tax base. Expenses would include purchases of capital goods (gross investment). Neither distributed earnings nor interest would be deductible. The main advantage is neutrality with respect to financing of investment.

In the ACE system, the tax base equals the accounting profit in a given period (net of depreciation and interest payments) minus the allowance for corporate equity (shareholder equity times the "protective rate of interest"—the market rate of interest) at the beginning of the period. Deducting the market rate of interest from the corporate equity makes investment choices neutral to whether they are financed by retained earnings, debt, or equity. Positive corporate equity would be equivalent to a deferred payout of investment income from the perspective of the cash flow tax, and this return is taxed (net of the market rate of interest) each period. The accounting profit thus consists of this change in corporate equity plus the dividends paid (as the distribution of generated earnings) minus new equity. The ACE implies that only pure profits are taxed. A major advantage in implementation of the ACE over the cash flow tax is that the ACE would retain usual accounting practices.

The ACE system has been implemented in Croatia.[9] At the personal level, wage income and the gains from the disposal of real estate and other property titles are taxed. There are no capital gains or savings taxes; the taxation of distributed profits and interest (exceeding the return over the market rate of interest) at the company level is final. Since the market rate of interest is tax-free, the system is nondistortive toward the intertemporal allocation of consumption.

Leaving capital gains untaxed at the personal level may look like a violation of vertical equity compared to the Haig-Simons concept in place in most countries. However, from an intertemporal perspective, the ACE system taxes *all* consumption fully. Those who save more will be taxed when they consume their savings, but will be credited for the opportunity cost of saving. Since individuals are the owners of companies after all, the ACE taxes pure profits only once at the corporate level.

As will become clear shortly, the two features of the ACE system, namely intertemporal neutrality and neutrality toward the choice of financing, play an important role in the taxation of new financial instruments. By and large it is the violation of one or both of these characteristics that makes the taxation of financial instruments so complex.

To sum up, in general the tax reforms of the 1980s and 1990s lowered statutory rates and broadened the base. As a result, the effective marginal tax rate at the corporate level has remained stable over this period (Devereux, Griffith, and Klemm 2002).

Taxation of Financial Instruments

A tax system is neutral against financing choices when a given present discounted pre-tax flow of profits yields the same discounted after-tax income, irrespective of the means of finance. Furthermore, taxation affects the opportunity cost of investment and hence its level by affecting the intertemporal allocation of expenditure.

The Traditional Approach

In almost all tax systems one or more of the three sources of finance for investment (retained earnings, debt, and equity issuance) experiences different tax treatment from the others. As discussed in detail below, the tax treatment of interest often gives an incentive to debt financing, while the distribution of earnings to shareholders is often discouraged by the tax system via the corporate tax rate. This not only favors a deferral of dividend distribution but also opens room for tax arbitrage via new financial instruments that can replicate any given payment pattern, thereby undoing the traditional distinction between debt and equity. To uphold the categorization, such tax arbitrage is often countered with anti-avoidance legislation.

Most tax systems make a distinction between the returns payable to a financial instrument (that is, between interest and dividend income). Moreover, these returns are often taxed at rates different from those applicable to capital gains. However, new financial instruments can be used to blur the distinction between each of these categories and hence be used to transfer returns from one category to another. Here too, the resulting tax avoidance is often countered by the authorities with anti-avoidance rules and classification of new financial instruments into either the debt or equity category. Even when these distortions are removed and all means of financing carry the same statutory tax rate, a further distortion can arise. This is the timing: the point in time at which a capital gain is considered taxable. In particular, when capital gains are taxed upon realization (that is, either the sale or the payment at the terminal date of a particular instrument) there may be an incentive to defer the realization of gains (see chapter 2).

One reason for this distinction between interest and dividends may be a "proprietary view of the corporation": interest is paid to outsiders, dividends to owners.[10] According to this line of reasoning, dividends are seen as a non-deductible distribution of profits to those who hold control. This has been the rationale for a preferential treatment of debt. If the Modigliani and Miller (1958) suggestion that debt and equity are equivalent from a financing point of view were valid, a differential treatment of debt and equity might have consequences on tax revenue but little on efficiency. However, recent corporate governance literature stresses the difference in control rights of the two instruments in determining the corporate financial structure ("financial contracting") and derives conditions for an optimal debt-equity ratio. Even when financial structure through embedded control rights matters for an efficient allocation of funds, it is not clear whether the government should try to influence the allocation of funds with differential taxation, since this would again necessitate a tenable distinction between debt and equity taxation. Another argument for government intervention in the financing decisions could be financial market failures (see chapter 2).

Taxation of Interest Income

Granting household loans favorable deductions Most industrial countries have traditionally granted households deductions from tax where the underlying loan is for business purposes. However, industrial countries have increasingly granted favorable tax treatment for other investment purposes as well. Some examples can be found in table 6.4.

Corporate funding: the beneficial tax treatment of debt As for corporate funding decisions, most tax systems in industrial countries favor debt financing. Accordingly, the interest expenses to service the loan is deductible from taxable income (trading profits).[11] In contrast, income already included in corporate income taxes is taxed a second time when distributed as dividend income and when the instrument is sold. As a result, tax wedges on debt are much lower than the wedges on new equity or retained earnings (table 6.5). As illustrated below, some studies have found that tax wedges for companies' funding decisions in the manufacturing sector may be higher for equity than for either retained earnings or debt.

Meanwhile, the taxation of interest income has decreased. One reason, apart from an eagerness to stimulate (a particular form of) savings, is the deregulation of capital flows in general and in Europe in particular. The liberalization of capital flows in the EU in the 1980s led countries to decrease taxation on interest income, as can be observed in the figure 6.1, which shows a decline from over 50 percent on average to just 30 percent (Huizinga and Nicodème 2001). For example, following the removal of the last exchange control measures in 1990, France decreased the tax on long-term bond interest income from 27 to 18.1 percent and later to 15 percent (Maillard 1993). Following reforms in 1997–98, Italy's capital in-

Table 6.4. Tax Exemption of Interest Expenses Depending on the Purpose of the Loan

Country	Business purposes	Nonbusiness investment	Principal residence	Secondary residence	Other
BE	√	√	√	—	—
DK	√	P	P	P	P
DE	√	√	—	—	—
ES	√ (if not taxable under objective exemption, then no exemption)	P (up to gross income arising from renting immovable property)	P (deductible up to certain sum and other conditions)	—	—
FR	√	N (excluding rental real property)	P	—	—
IE	√	√	P	—	—
IT	P	—	—	—	—
LU	√	√	P	P	P
NL	√	√ (only if interest is attributable to taxable income)	√	√	—
AT	√	—	P (only construction)	P (only construction)	—
UK	√	—	P (limits on rate of relief and ceiling on amount of loan)	—	—
US	√	√	P (home acquisition debt)	P (home acquisition debt)	—
JP	√	N	N	N	N

Notes: √ = Full exemption granted. P = Partial exemption granted. N = Not deductible. AT Austria; BE Belgium; DE Germany; DK Denmark; ES Spain; FR France; IE Ireland; IT Italy; JP Japan; LU Luxembourg; NL Netherlands; UK United Kingdom; US United States.
Source: Lee 2002.

come taxation is among the lowest of industrial countries, perhaps reflecting Italian authorities' attempt to lure capital back onshore (OECD 2001). Cnossen (1996) argues that "in reality, most interest is not taxed at all due to the symbiosis between interest deductibility at company (and personal) level and the existence of capital-rich tax-exempt investors, such as pension funds, life insurance companies and social security funds."

Table 6.5. Marginal Effective Tax Wedges in
Manufacturing, 1999

Country	Retained earnings	Sources of financing New equity	Debt	Standard deviation[a]
BE	1.36	2.54	−0.60	1.29
DK	1.89	2.43	2.49	0.27
DE	0.89	2.53	1.28	0.70
ES	3.20	2.23	1.65	0.64
FR	3.58	7.72	0.67	2.89
IE	1.52	4.12	0.69	1.46
IT	1.27	1.27	0.39	0.41
LU	3.57	2.37	1.62	0.80
NL	0.46	5.33	2.46	2.00
AT	0.74	2.65	0.06	1.10
UK	2.88	2.40	1.55	0.55
US	1.66	4.79	1.42	1.54
JP	3.30	5.50	−0.09	2.30
OECD[b]	2.02	4.03	1.09	1.23
EU[b]	1.95	3.24	1.01	0.91

Notes: The entries in the table show the "degree to which personal and corporate tax systems scale up the real pre-tax rate of return that must be earned on an investment, given that the household can earn a 4 percent real rate of return on a demand deposit" (OECD methodology based on the method in Fullerton and King 1984). Calculations are based on top marginal tax rates and a 2 percent inflation rate. Weighted average of different types of investment: machinery 50 percent, buildings 28 percent, inventories 22 percent. See table 6.4 for country names.
[a]The standard deviation of the entries in the other three columns.
[b]Weighted average across available countries (based on 1995 GDP and PPPs).
Source: Van den Noord and Heady 2001.

Figure 6.1. Average Taxes on Interest Income on Residents
in the EU, 1983–2000

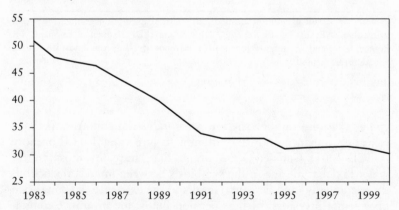

Source: Huizinga and Nicodème 2001.

Despite an overall fall in rates, significant divergences remain (table 6.6). Some countries have high rates (exceeding 30 percent in Germany and Switzerland), some have low rates (15 percent in Belgium and France), while some countries impose no taxation at all (Denmark, Luxemburg, and the Netherlands). However, these rates must be seen in conjunction with the whole tax system. For example the German tax rate is basically a withholding tax, which becomes relevant in personal income taxation only after high exemptions. For the majority of savers, this tax would be effectively zero. In the beginning of 2003 Germany was discussing a move to taxing capital income at source at a uniform rate, thus abandoning capital gains taxation under the personal income tax rates.

Taxation of Equity Dividends

Countries have also tried to bolster portfolio investments in general and the use of equity in particular. This has the associated benefit that it increases the amount of risk capital available to companies. The United Kingdom was a European precursor in this area, with the introduction in 1983 of a Business Expansion Scheme aimed at stimulating investments in new firms and the establishment of Personal Equity Plans in 1986 (Leape 1993). Other countries have since followed suit.

Reforms aimed at stimulating equity financing   Industrial countries have increasingly come to regard the unfavorable tax treatment of equity as problematic. This is especially the case in the EU, where following the launch of the euro, the European Commission, the European Parliament, and member states are actively trying to achieve full integration of capital markets in order to extend financing sources to companies and decrease their cost of capital. Tax rules that punish equity financing are thus increasingly anachronistic.

Often the tax system distorts the decision whether to pay out the returns on equity to shareholders or to retain earnings. The distribution of corporate returns by dividends is often discouraged by taxing capital gains at a personal level at a lower rate than dividends (the case in Austria, Belgium, Germany, Greece, the Netherlands, Spain, and Switzerland; see table 6.7).

Reducing double taxation   There are three main alternative approaches to dealing with double taxation of equity (see table 6.8):

• *Classical system*: Countries with this system do not allow the shareholder any credit for corporate income tax paid when dividends are being taxed. Thus there is an element of double taxation. Most such

Table 6.6. Taxation of Interest Income in Some
Industrial Countries

Country	Interest received Gross	Interest received Net	Interest withholding tax Resident	Interest withholding tax Nonresident[a]	Top tax rate on interest income from government bonds Resident	Top tax rate on interest income from government bonds Nonresident
BE	—	√[b]	15	0–15	15	0
DK	√	—	0	0	60.5[c]	0
DE	√	—	31.65[d]	0	53.8[c]	0
HE	—	—	15–20	10–45	15	7.5
ES	√[e]	—	18[e]	0	48[c]	0
FR	—	√[b]	15	0–15	15	0
IE	—	√	24[f]	0–15	24[g]	0
IT	—	√	27	0–15	12.5	0
LU	√	—	0	0	47.15[c]	0
NL	√	—	0	0	60[c]	0
AT	—	√[b]	25	0	25	0
PT	—	√[b]	20	10–20	20	20
FI	—	√	29	0	29	0
SE	—	√	30	0	30	0
UK	√	—	20[h]	0	20[i]	0
US	√[j]	—	0	0	n.a.	n.a.
CH	√	—	35	0–35	n.a.	n.a.
JP	—	√	20	20	n.a.	n.a.

—Gross or net interest income not taxed.
n.a. Not available.
Note: See table 6.4 for additional country names: HE Greece; PT Portugal; FI Finland; SE Sweden; and CH Switzerland.
[a]Rate depends on double tax treaty.
[b]Interest received net of withholding tax, which is either final or creditable against income tax liability depending on choice of taxpayer.
[c]Capital income included in personal income tax. Reported rate thus top marginal income tax rate.
[d]30% federal withholding tax plus 5.5% solidarity surcharge.
[e]Interest income normally part of ordinary income taxation. If interest generated for longer than two years, only 70% of income subject to income tax.
[f]A reduced rate applies for Special Saving Accounts. Tax refunded in special circumstances (such as charitable organizations).
[g]Tax creditable against income tax liability.
[h]Interest from bank and building societies paid net of tax (20%), but may be paid gross for nontaxpayers who register. Some National Saving products exempt, but interest on others received gross automatically. Withholding tax on interest creditable against income tax liability.
[i]Interest on some government securities paid net of tax (20%) but may be received gross in certain circumstances. Withholding tax on interest creditable against income tax liability.
[j]Interest from federal securities exempt from state and local taxation; state and local securities exempt from federal tax.
Sources: Haufler 2001; Joumard 2001; Lee 2002.

Table 6.7. Tax Treatment of Dividends and Capital Gains on Shares, 1998, Resident Taxpayers

		Taxation of dividends		*Taxation of capital gains*
Country	*Rate (%)*	*Rules*	*Rate (%)[a]*	*Rules*
BE	15	Withholding tax that can be final (taxpayer's option)	0	Capital gains by individuals not engaged in business activity not taxable.
DK	25	Final withholding tax	40	Rate applies to a taxable base arising from the disposal of shares exceeding DKr 35,000.
DE	48.47	Taxed as ordinary gross income or as ordinary income with creditable withholding tax. (Under review at the time of printing.)	0	Capital gains realized through private transactions of resident individuals generally not subject to income tax.
HE	—	—	0	Gains derived from sale of movable property (other than nonlisted companies with limited shares and limited liability companies) are not taxed.
ES	28.57	Several possibilities: treated as ordinary income, exempt, creditable withholding tax.	56	Treated like ordinary income. For holding periods longer than 2 years, net gain is reduced by 25% for each additional year.
FR	33.33	Taxed as ordinary income with withholding tax, always creditable against ordinary income tax.	26	Capital gains on securities are taxed at this flat rate (comprising basic rate of 16% plus social surcharges).
IE	—	Treated as ordinary income, 21% dividend imputation credit which is always creditable against ordinary income tax.	40	For gains on the disposal of shares in nonquoted trading companies held for at least 3 years, 26%.
IT	10–12.5	Withholding tax, fully creditable against ordinary income tax.	12.5	Net capital gains on shares and other securities are subject to a substitute tax that replaces individual income tax.
LU	25	Treated as ordinary income. Creditable withholding tax.	46.6	No separate capital gains taxed in Luxembourg.
NL	25	Treated as ordinary income, creditable withholding tax.	0	In general capital gains are not included in taxable base.
AT	25	Withholding tax that can be final at taxpayers' option.	0	In general capital gains are not included in taxable base.

(Table continues on next page.)

Table 6.7. Tax Treatment of Dividends and Capital Gains
on Shares, 1998, Resident Taxpayers (*continued*)

	Taxation of dividends		Taxation of capital gains	
Country	Rate (%)	Rules	Rate (%)[a]	Rules
PT	25	Withholding tax that can be final at taxpayers' option.	10	Net annual gains from the disposal of shares are in principle subject to a tax at a final rate of 10% unless the transferor opts for its inclusion in his taxable income.
FI	28	Taxed as ordinary income with creditable withholding tax.	28	Income from capital is subject only to a national income tax.
SE	30	Taxed as capital income.	30	In general, all capital gains realized by an individual are included in the category income from capital. Income from capital is taxed separately nationally (no municipal taxes apply).
UK	—	Taxed as ordinary gross income, 20% dividend imputation credit which is creditable against ordinary income tax liability.	40	Capital gains of an individual are aggregated with his income and are taxed at income tax rates.
US	—	Taxed as ordinary gross income. (Under review at the time of printing.)	25	Assets must be held for more than one year, otherwise gains are taxed as ordinary income.
CH	35	Treated as ordinary income. Creditable withholding tax.	0	Capital gains are exempt.
JP	20–35	Depending on amount of dividend paid by a single company: ordinary income with 20% creditable withholding tax, 35% final withholding tax, or 20% optional withholding tax.	21.2	For listed companies, a central rate augmented by a local rate. If sale of asset is trusted to securities company, separate withholding tax.

—Dividends not taxed.
Note: See tables 6.4 and 6.6 for country names.
[a]Top personal tax rate.
Source: Van den Noord and Heady 2001.

countries levy a withholding tax at source (company) when dividends
are being paid. The majority of the EU's member states, the United
States, Switzerland, and Japan operate under this system. (In January
2003 the U.S. administration proposed the exemption of dividends).

Table 6.8. Ways of Dealing with Double Taxation

Country	Classical system	Imputation system	Other systems
BE	√ Shareholder has option of paying withholding tax as final tax on dividend income.	—	—
DK	√ Withholding tax final and replaces personal income tax.	—	—
DE	—	—	√ New system from 2002: earlier imputation system replaced with half-rate system under which half the dividends received from German corporations taxed under personal income tax (applies to foreign shares as well).
HE	—	—	√ Exempt: dividends exempt from personal income tax.
ES	—	√ Full imputation system, but coupled with withholding tax, which is creditable against personal income tax.	—
FR	—	√ Full imputation system.	—
IE	√ Since April 1999 a classical system. Prior to that, partial imputation (dividend treated as normal income, but 21% imputation, creditable against ordinary income tax).	—	—
IT	—	—	√ Choice between imputation credit and a reduced flat tax rate on dividends.
LU	√ Withholding tax credited against personal income tax liability.	—	—

(Table continues on next page.)

Table 6.8. Ways of Dealing with Double Taxation *(continued)*

Country	Classical system	Imputation system	Other systems
NL	√ Withholding tax credited against personal income tax liability.	—	—
AT	√ Shareholder has option of paying withholding tax as final tax on dividend income.	—	—
PT	—	—	√ Shareholder is entitled to a tax credit, coupled with a withholding tax on dividends. Both set off against personal income tax liability.
FI	—	√ Full imputation system, but coupled with withholding tax, which is creditable against personal income tax.	—
SE	√ Withholding tax final and replaces personal income tax.	—	—
UK	—	√ Partial imputation system with non-withholding tax on dividends.	—
US	√ Under recently tabled proposals (January 2003), the United States would move to an exemption system, as equity dividends would be entirely exempt from tax.	—	—
CH	√ Withholding tax credited against personal income tax liability.	—	—
JP	√ Withholding tax credited against personal income tax liability.	—	—

√ Classical system.
— No imputation or other system.
Note: See tables 6.4 and 6.6 for country names.
Sources: Lee 2002; Van den Noord and Heady 2001.

- *Imputation system*: This system also typically imposes a withholding tax, but imputes full or partial adjustment to the shareholder's taxable income based on the tax rate already applied at company level. Six of the EU's member states operate such a system. France is currently debating the scope of the dividend imputation, more particularly whether to confine "dividends" only to regular dividends (as agreed by the general shareholder meeting) or also to exceptional distributions of revenues. It has been claimed, however, that imputation systems cannot easily take into account cross-border shareholdings. For this reason, Germany abolished its full imputation system in 2001. The corporate tax rate was decreased and cannot be imputed anymore at the personal level. The resulting double taxation of dividends is mitigated by the provision that the personal income tax rate applicable to dividends will be halved. Preferential treatment of retained earnings was an explicit goal of this reform. In Italy there are also proposals to move from the imputation system to the classical system. One argument is to avoid granting the imputation credit in financial operations between taxable and tax-exempt companies.

- *Exemptions*: Finally, a few countries (the United States if recent proposals are adopted, and Greece) operate a system under which no credit is given for corporate tax but dividends themselves are entirely exempt from taxation.

Several suggestions have been made for reform.[12] On the one hand, the advantageous treatment of debt through interest deductibility could be removed, so that neither interest nor dividends would be eligible for relief at the corporate level. One proposal in this direction is the comprehensive business income tax (CBIT), discussed in the United States. On the other hand, both interest and dividends could be granted the same relief at the corporate level and then taxed at the personal level. This is usually known as dual (or full) imputation. However, even a full imputation system can favor retained earnings against outside finance, if the corporate tax rate is below the (personal) income tax rate of dividends and interest income.

The proposal known as ACE, described above, is intended to remove this effect. This would grant a tax relief at the level of the nominal rate of interest for the company's total equity capital. Only profits in excess of the normal return on investment ("pure profits") would be taxed. The taxation at the level of the company is final; dividends or interest are not taxed again at the personal level. The ACE would be a move toward an expenditure-based system of taxation.

Capital Gains Taxes

Capital gains are the taxable gains (and losses) that are realized on the disposition of a (financial) asset. The tax rate often depends on the time the asset was held. This reflects a distinction between asset trading (which is seen as an ordinary income-generating activity) and investing. Since the intention of the asset holder is not always obvious to tax authorities (unless the asset holder is specifically licensed as an asset trader), legal distinctions often rely on ad hoc demarcations, such as the time during which an asset was held or a set of criteria concerning the asset holder. Such date rules are arbitrary, however, as illustrated by a recent tax reform in Germany where the period was increased from six to twelve months (and abolished altogether for final taxation at the corporate level).

Capital gains are often more lightly taxed than interest and dividend income. For example, in Belgium while interest and dividend income are taxed at 15 percent, capital gains from shares are untaxed. Similar favorable treatments of capital gains apply in many other industrial countries, including Italy and Switzerland. Between 1965 and 1982 the relative importance of capital gains taxes declined in most OECD countries except France and Japan. Capital gains taxes generate little revenue: less than 1 percent of total tax revenues in the great majority of countries. If capital gains are subject to a lower tax than dividends, there is an incentive for a company to retain earnings and defer dividend payments or to engage in so-called dividend stripping: that is, for an investor to sell shares before profits are paid out and subsequently buy them again.

Countries apply different methods in determining the taxable capital gain. The most common principle of timing is taxation on realization. This is the point in time when a party to a transaction has the unconditional legal right or obligation to an amount. Hence under realization valuation, changes in value become tax relevant when amounts are due under a contract (payable or receivable). Even if capital and income are taxed at the same rate, taxation on realization provides an incentive to an early realization of losses and a deferral of gains.

For the two other methods unrealized gains and losses also become tax-relevant. One model of capital gains taxation is the so-called "accretion taxation." This model is also referred to as mark-to-market. Financial instruments are taxed according to their market value. All changes in value are taken into account. If they were taxed at the same rate as other forms of income (such as labor), this would correspond to the Haig-Simons ideal of comprehensive income taxation, according to which all net changes in wealth should be taxed.[13] A variant is to tax only those returns that are expected ex ante. This is "accrual taxation," where the change in value at the end of the fiscal year is calculated using either the risk-free interest rate or methods of accounting to calculate the expected growth in value of the instrument (such as yield-to-maturity) at the time of purchase. Actual changes in value that occur after the resolution of uncertainty following the issue (that is, the difference to their expected value) thus remain untaxed.[14] This can lead to a tax benefit if such losses can be deducted against other forms of income. A further variant is to tax only the change in value of the asset while exempting the market rate of interest. This last form would be a step to expenditure taxation, where only pure profits are taxed. The ACE described above is an example. Since the market rate of interest is exempt from taxation, any unrealized expected gains do not lead to tax distortions. Chapter 2 describes some ways to accomplish formulary accrual taxation.

The taxation of unrealized gains has been criticized on two grounds. First, the tax valuation of assets may be quite costly for firms and also for tax authorities when monitoring compliance. In order to reduce compliance costs, it has been suggested (Alworth 1998) that financial accounting rules, using market valuations of assets, should be applied for tax purposes, at least for large firms. Such marking-to-market may also imply low monitoring costs on the side of the tax authority. If unrealized capital gains are very high, the asset holder may be forced to sell the asset in order to pay the tax. In response to the first criticism, it has been suggested that accretion taxation be applied only to liquid instruments. Furthermore, financial accounting may require the company to discount its debt obligations using its credit rating. If a borrower got into financial difficulties and revised its outlook on future profits downward, the resulting increase in the discount rate of the liabilities could lead to a taxable gain.[15] Recent developments in the United States indicate that some financial accounting systems may also leave too much judgmental leeway to the individual accountant.

Second, the marking-to-market taxation is criticized as leading to liquidity problems. This can probably be solved, however. Even if an asset is taxed only at the time of its disposal, there are ways to include the implicit tax credit of unrealized gains into the final tax payment ex post.[16]

Taxation of Personal Financial Wealth

Net wealth taxes are raised once a year on the stock of certain assets subtracting associated debts. One of the aims of wealth taxes is vertical equity: taxing the wealthy and redistributing income. However, wealth taxes are at odds with the Haig-Simons concept. A number of OECD countries apply them (Finland, France, Iceland, Luxembourg, the Netherlands, Norway, Spain, Sweden, and Switzerland) (Van den Noord and Heady 2001).

Figure 6.2. Average Tax on Financial Wealth in the EU, 1983–2000

Source: Huizinga and Nicodème 2001.

Most of the countries imposing wealth taxes have levied them for a long time (the Netherlands started in 1892, for example) although some countries have imposed them more recently (for example, Spain in 1978; France in 1982, subsequently withdrawn and later reimposed in 1989). Over time, taxing wealth has become rather complex and today involves significant administrative work to discover and valuate wealth. In addition, the tax incidence is undermined by tax planning (for example, by inflating liabilities or investing in under-assessed assets). In some cases, the administrative burden has become disproportionate to the yield. Germany, for example, therefore decided to abandon them. In the EU, many countries have eliminated wealth taxes following the liberalization of capital flows in the 1980s (Austria in 1994; Denmark and Germany in 1997) (Huizinga and Nicodème 2001) (figure 6.2).

Moreover, in 2001 the Netherlands abolished their capital gains taxation and replaced the existing net wealth tax. Net wealth at the personal level is now taxed presumptively. Changes in wealth—which incorporates savings deposits, bonds, and stocks and some real estate but excludes pension wealth—are presumed to rise in value by 4 percent a year, irrespective of their actual return. A 30 percent tax rate is applied on this presumptive amount, leading to a net wealth tax of 1.2 percent (Bovenberg and Cnossen 2001).

New Financial Instruments

The taxation of new financial instruments has three basic features around which the legislation has evolved.[17] First, most countries retain a distinction between interest and dividends. Second, they distinguish between income and capital amounts. Third, the taxation depends on the method of accounting for the payments from the instrument.

Hybrid instruments combine features of both equity and debt. Taxation of hybrids often depends on the distinction between debt and equity through debt relief at the corporate level but also on different treatment at the personal level (except for a full imputation system). The traditional approach to these instruments is to allocate each instrument into either the debt or equity category according to sets of criteria. These vary between countries. For example, in Germany, in order to classify as debt, instruments may carry cash flow rights, but must avoid rights in liquidation. Preferred shares, for example, fall under equity. In France, the tax authorities have not taken a definite position as to the classification of many of such instruments (including preferred shares) in order not "to be bound by a position it would have taken" (David 1996, p. 56). In the United Kingdom, the list of derivatives taxed equivalently to debt instruments was broadly extended in 2002, excluding equity-linked instruments held for nontrading purposes. In the United States, the bifurcation technique is applied to many of these instruments, whereby hybrid instruments are decomposed into debt and equity components, which are taxed accordingly. The drawback is that there are multiple ways to decompose hybrids, also necessitating a set of classification rules.

The distinction between changes in capital values and income[18] carries over to most financial instruments. In the United States, for example, the tax treatment of options depends on whether the underlying property is a capital asset. Hedging in the United States does not depend on any underlying asset, allowing transferring gains and losses between categories. The United Kingdom has long distinguished between income and capital amounts, but since 1994 debt and some derivatives (the list was extended in 2002) are attributed to income. In Germany an option is treated as two separate transactions. The premium is taxed as income to the option writer on the sale of the option; the purchase as expenditure. The second transaction depends on the contingency the option specifies. If the option is exercised, the gain or loss on both sides is taken as a capital gain. If the option is not exercised, then the capital account transaction does not become tax relevant. If the option was not worth exercising but the holder sold it at a price just above zero, the holder's loss would become tax-relevant. Still, for a private individual, as long as the capital gain from exercising an option falls outside the period in which capital gains are taxable, there is no tax. Rules are different for businesses. Although Germany taxes capital gains (within the time limit) at the same rates as income, there are limits as to set off gains and losses between capital and other income.

The above-mentioned timing rules for the tax recognition of gains and losses are significant for the use of new financial instruments. Taxation upon realization implies that increases in value do not become relevant as long as no amounts are due. This is equivalent to granting the taxpayer an interest-free loan over the unrealized increase in value (or denying him a loss relief). For some well-known cases (such as zero coupon debt obligations), anti-deferral measures are used, which amount to some form of accrual taxation. As explained above, taxation on accrual still leads to ex post incentives (after the resolution of uncertainty) to selectively realize losses and defer gains, in particular if gains and losses are not treated symmetrically. So-called "straddle" transactions can be used to exploit this. The solutions available are marking-to-market or the accrual taxation with limitation on deductibility of losses. [19]

Most countries apply different timing rules to different instruments, under different criteria. The rules may vary according to the category of taxpayer; for example, financial intermediaries are more often subject to mark-to-market valuation. France applies marking-to-market to financial instruments that are traded on an organized exchange. Some countries, primarily in continental Europe, treat gains and losses asymmetrically as a consequence of their financial accounting principles, with recognition of unrealized losses, while gains are only recognized upon realization. In the United Kingdom, almost all instruments except for equity are now taxed as they are reflected in the accounts: that is, either on an accruals basis or marking-to-market. Derivatives are mostly taxed marking-to-market. As explained above, accrual taxation does not tax changes in value beyond those expected at the time of purchase.

Some derivatives are for risk management only; they are pure bets with an expected value of zero ex ante. Examples include futures and swaps. In Germany, such instruments are valued marking-to-market, but only if delivery or close-out are within the capital gains taxation limit of one year. Hence unrealized gains or losses after one year remain untaxed.[20] In New Zealand risk-management instruments are taxed on realization.

The United States determines timing mostly on the basis of capital-income distinction, using the bifurcation approach already mentioned (fixed element taxed as accrual, residual unpredictable element taxed on realization) to approximate the accrual approach (Warren 2001). The major practical difficulty here is choosing among the multiple ways of decomposing the financial instrument: continuing financial innovation precludes a conclusive categorization. The United States also permits marking-to-market taxation for some instruments, such as futures and currency contracts and securities held by traders.

To summarize, at the root of most timing issues are the debt-equity and the capital-income distinctions. New financial instruments can be used to replicate a given pattern of payments transcending the borders between such tax rate distinctions. Most tax systems respond to this by lists of classifications of instruments, while trying to maintain the class (and hence tax rate) distinctions. Other countries apply uniform tax rates across all returns that are not labor income, along dual income tax lines. New Zealand (see below) tries to approximate accrual taxation for all types of what it calls "financial arrangements."

In other words, if a tax system were designed to respect neutrality toward the means of financing an investment as well as neutrality toward the intertemporal allocation of expenditure, the complexity surrounding the taxation of (new) financial instruments would be radically reduced.

Hedging

The use of financial instruments to eliminate the risk of an underlying asset is called hedging. Although most countries apply "separate transactions valuation" if financial instruments are used for hedging purposes, such instruments often receive a special tax treatment. In many countries they are "integrated" to be taxed as a unit, so that offsetting positions are taken into account; usually the tax treatment is matched to that of the underlying asset. The rationale is that under a regime taxing financial positions when they are realized, the "separate transactions principle" could lead to asymmetries in the timing of the taxation of gains and losses across instruments.

Tax authorities face the problem of determining what constitutes a hedge. In the United States the taxpayer must identify a hedge in his financial and tax books on the day it is concluded. With the separate taxation of capital and income amounts, hedge accounting can serve to transfer the losses of the hedge to the income account if not tied to the underlying asset (Edgar 2000). In France, the declaration is at the end of the year. Hedges are subject to three conditions: the transaction must be for the forthcoming year, the underlying position must be "on a different market," and the variations of all positions should be correlated, leaving open the question how large the covariance should be (David 1996).

Under an ideal accrual regime, the integration of instruments to a hedge for tax purposes might be unnecessary, since the whole portfolio would be taxed and offsetting positions essentially matched

(Edgar 2000). However, even in that case, if the underlying position were nontraded debt or shares or non-financial assets, hedge accounting may be justified. France uses a mark-to-market approach to risk-managing instruments if they are traded on an organized market. However, when they are tied to a transaction that is not traded on an organized market, then the instruments can constitute a hedge and their taxation is tied to the realization of the underlying transaction. New Zealand, with its accrual legislation, in general does not allow for the integration of hedging positions, nor does the United Kingdom.

Recent Policy Developments

The tax policy response to new financial instruments has often been to sort new products into existing categories of debt or equity; income or capital amounts; and realization or marking-to-market timing. Since financial instruments can be used to transcend the boundaries between these categories for a given payment pattern, such tax legislation is often accompanied by classification plus anti-avoidance rules. More substantial reforms attempt to tackle these categorizations. These reforms also depend on the assumed perspective about the ideal concept of income. The respective view determines the rate of capital gains taxation, the tax accounting rule of capital gains, and the interest (and equity) deductibility.

In 1987, *New Zealand* implemented a system that uses accrual rules to come close to the Haig-Simons ideal of taxation. A wide definition of "financial arrangements" covers instruments that are debt or have debt components and involve contingent payments. This category seems to encompass instruments where an advance of funds gives the right to receive a return, be it fixed or contingent. Shares are excluded. For such financial arrangements accrual taxation is attempted, as well as for those instruments for which marking-to-market is not possible. The accrual takes a company's financial account as a basis, though the law tries to limit deferral allowed by accounting practices. Where possible, tax per financial instrument is calculated using yield-to-maturity accounting. For new financial instruments that involve only risk management—and thus for which internal rate of return methods are not possible—a "base price adjustment" is made, which amounts to taxation at the time the asset is realized. Accretion taxation is limited to traded futures and forward contracts for foreign exchange. However, the historical distinction between interest and dividends was retained. *Australia* is discussing a similar system, with a much broader approach to accretion taxation.

Since 2002 the *United Kingdom* has broadly acknowledged marking-to-market taxation while the returns are largely attributed away from capital income in some cases to revenue income in almost all, thus removing a possible distortion. Such accretion taxation is approximated by the U.S. practice of bifurcation, where financial instruments are disaggregated into a fixed-income and a contingent component, which are taxed on accrual and on realization, respectively, albeit at different rates.

The *dual income tax (DIT) countries* of the Nordic area adopted a schedular approach. This eliminated the distortions between interest and dividends, as well as the distinction between income and capital amounts. The timing issue from realization-based recognition of capital gains is partially solved through a mix between accrual and realization systems (Edgar 2000).

The tax system of *Italy* was overhauled in 1998. Business income is now calculated in a value-added fashion, the tax base being the annual change in the business accounts (sales revenue minus cost of intermediate goods), which are taxed at a flat rate. Neither labor costs nor interest payments are deductible. This removes the tax distortions relating to the debt-equity distinction (including tax avoidance strategies). In addition, an allowance for new total equity (issues and retained earnings starting from 1996) was introduced. Since ACE taxation narrows the corporate tax base and would in principle lead to higher statutory tax rates (Bond 2000), normal profits were not fully exempt from the Italian tax. Thus the Italian system has been characterized as a mixture between DIT and ACE (Bordignon, Giannini, and Panteghini 2001). The valuation of capital gains at a personal level was designed to counter the incentives to deferral (Alworth, Arachi, and Hamaui 2002). The applied valuation method depends on the way financial instruments are held. If they are held in a "managed portfolio" through an authorized intermediary, taxation is on an accrual basis, and taxes are paid through the intermediary. Private individuals can alternatively list their holdings in their tax declaration ("tax return method") or have taxes deducted on a transactional basis through an intermediary ("administered portfolio method"). For the latter two methods, taxation was on realization, where an "equalizer" was applied to make it correspond to accrual taxation. The "equalizer" was calculated by retrospective taxation methods.[21] This avoided the aforementioned liquidity problem with accrual taxation of unrealized gains. Traded securities with observable prices were taxed on realization while capitalizing accrued gains with the risk-free interest rate. Securities not traded on exchanges were capitalized ex post with the risk-free interest rate using the average price increase over the holding period. Foreign mutual funds were capitalized with their internal rate of return. There were limits as to offsetting gains and losses between several categories of capital income. The "equalizer" was introduced in 2001 and repealed because of interest group pressure and a change in government in the same year, so it never came into effect. While the Italian reforms taxed capital gains at a lower rate than other income (including dividends and interest), at the personal level the approach resembles Haig-Simons more at the personal level than at the corporate level.

Croatia adopted the allowance for corporate equity system in 1994 (Rose and Wiswesser 1998; Wenger 1999). Business profits were calculated as the difference in total equity over the financial year to which a standardized rate of interest (to approximate a nominal market return) was credited. Hence only pure profits were taxed. Unrealized revaluations of assets would increase the company's total equity. The imputation of the nominal risk-free interest rate to corporate equity implies that the company is fully compensated for an early realization of gains. A creditor is taxed on the interest received, whereas the debtor can deduct the interest paid. Since the market rate of interest is deducted from the company accounts, the investor would be indifferent between the choices of financing and any interest in excess of the market rate would be taxed only once. At the personal level, capital gains tax was zero and neither interest nor dividends were taxed as income. Thus business profit taxation was final at the company level. Distortions between debt, equity, and retained earnings as well as incentives to selective realization of gains and losses were avoided. Following a change in government, Croatia abandoned the allowance for the market rate of interest in 2001. However, similar tax reform is now under preparation in *Bosnia*.

Taxation of Intermediaries

Banks and other financial institutions generate significant value-added, both in terms of profits and high revenue employees. Financial intermediaries also have a pivotal role in the economy, as they contribute to the smooth functioning of credit flows and thus economic growth. Just as the taxation of financial instruments may distort saving and investment decisions, getting taxes wrong on the intermediary level may affect the smooth functioning of financial intermediation.

Problems of Defining the Tax Base

In principle, the taxable income of financial intermediaries is determined in the same way as the income of other companies (Fitzgibbon and Walton 1990). However, a number of issues (such as interest income, trading income, and risk management income) make it more difficult to determine what constitutes taxable income for financial companies than for other industries. These difficulties arise for many reasons:

- *Difficulties of valuation*: While the sophistication of financial markets means that market prices exist for many services and products of financial institutions, valuation for tax purposes is nevertheless not straightforward. For example, what is the outstanding value of assets and liabilities for tax purposes of loans? How should the value of new financial instruments be assessed? To what extent should financial accounting practices be used for tax purposes?

- *VAT*: Unlike other goods and services, it is difficult to attach an explicit price to many financial services. As a result, financial services are exempt from VAT in most countries.[22] This is not without problems, however. It gives rise to conflicts between tax authorities and financial intermediaries over what line to draw between a financial intermediary's financial activities—which are VAT-exempt—and non-financial activities—for which VAT is due. Moreover, as financial intermediaries do not receive any credits on the VAT-exempt services they sell, they have to pay more VAT on their inputs. It also gives rise to complex apportionment systems whereby intermediaries are supposed to apportion input credits between taxable (input-creditable) or exempt (non-creditable) activities (Wurts and Fenton 2002). Even within the EU the apportionment methods vary widely between member states. Overall, there is no easy way to deal with financial services and VAT. Exemption is a second-best solution, but currently there are no workable alternatives. Recent research suggests that advances in information technology and the changed relationship between banks and their clients may overcome some of these obstacles (Huizinga 2002).

- *Cross-border groups*: The problems of determining taxable income are magnified in the case of groups with permanent establishments abroad. The most acute problem in this respect is the allocation of income between the permanent establishments and the home office. This problem is more pronounced for permanent establishments in the field of finance than for other industries. First, financial permanent establishments are increasingly offering services from the full value chain, such as front-office and back-office trading services. Second, it is more difficult to divide the tax base in financial services, as a financial transaction involves no physical movement of goods, rather just accounting entries (IFA 1996).

- *Tax evasion*: Given the problems of correctly valuing the assets and liabilities of financial intermediaries and given banks' extensive

international networks of branches and subsidiaries, it is not surprising that banks are well-placed to make good use of the current
practices of dealing with the taxation of international groups (such as
manipulating transfer pricing) (Demirgüç-Kunt and Huizinga 2001).

None of these issues is unique for financial intermediaries, but
the associated problems are more pronounced.

Taxation of Funds

While investment in funds is often induced by tax systems at the investor and fund level, most tax administrations regard the company
managing a fund as a taxable entity and thus subject to corporate
income tax.

In order to capture the overall tax burden, it is necessary to look
at tax at the management company level, fund level, and investor
level. Generally, the tax treatment of fund management companies
in industrial countries takes one of the following forms:

• *Not subject to tax*: Funds are not considered a "taxable person," and thus are not taxed (Belgium), or are exempt from taxes
(Finland).

• *Subject to tax, but exempt*: In some countries, a fund normally
subject to tax may be exempt if it fulfills certain conditions (for example, on basis of activity, as in Luxembourg).

• *Eligible for a special tax base*: In some countries, funds are
subject to tax but the taxable income (base) is much lower than
for other companies (investment companies in Belgium) or reduced
(paid distributions to investors subtracted from taxable income in
Sweden and the United Kingdom).

• *Subject to a special tax rate*: In some countries, funds are subject to tax but at special (low) rates (such as in the Netherlands,
where the rate can sometimes reach 0 percent).

• *Fully subject to tax but compensation is made available at the
investor level*: In some countries, the fund is fully subject to tax, but
investors are normally compensated for the tax paid at fund level
via reduction or exemption of tax at investor level (the imputation
system in the United Kingdom, for example) (IFA 1997).

Moreover, the overall tax level differs between different kinds of
funds. Generally, pension and insurance funds receive more favorable tax treatment than investment funds, with mutual funds falling
in between. The reason for this more favorable treatment is the
gains to society from citizens catering to their own pension needs
and risk exposure. One example of taxation in the field of funds is
provided below: namely insurance companies (table 6.9). As can be

Table 6.9. Taxation of General Insurance Companies

Country	Income tax (%)	VAT	Premium taxes (%)	Other taxes
BE	39	Exempt	3–9.25 (Compensatory funds: 0.25–10)	• 0.17% on value of goods held by nonprofit pension funds • 9.25% tax on profits on policies • 4.5% on 190% of payroll
DK	30	Exempt	1–50	• 0.6–4% on deeds
DE	25	Exempt	2–15	• 1% tax on capital formation
ES	35	Exempt	6	• 1% financial institution overhead tax
FR	33.33	Exempt	7–30 (Compensatory funds 1.9–8.5)	• 4.25–13.6% social contribution tax • 0.1% turnover tax on value of shares, stocks, real estate, etc. • Stamp duties • Profit sharing plan • Professional tax
IE	10	Exempt	2	• 1% on share capital
IT	36	Exempt	2.5–21.25 (Compensatory funds	• Special tax on securities
LU	30	Exempt	1–6.5) 4–6	• Municipal business tax (varies, 10% Luxembourg) • 0.5% wealth tax • 0.2% net wealth tax on capital • 1% capital investment tax
NL	35	Exempt	7	• 1% of share capital
AT	34	Exempt	1–10	• 1% of capital contributions • 0.04–0.15% stock turnover tax (bonds, shares)
PT	32	Yes, but recovered on pro rata basis.	0.45–12	• License fees
FI	29	Exempt	22	—
SE	28	Exempt	15	—
UK	30	Exempt	5	—
US	35	Exempt	3–4	• States' capital and franchise taxes
CH	35	Exempt	2.5–5	• 0.5% on shareholder equity

Note: AT Austria; BE Belgium; CH Switzerland; DE Germany; DK Denmark; ES Estonia; FI Finland; FR France; IE Ireland; IT Italy; LU Luxembourg; NL Netherlands; PT Portugal; SE Sweden; UK United Kingdom; US United States.
Sources: OECD 1999; Lee 2002.

seen, insurance companies are subject to corporate income tax in all industrial countries but pay no VAT (except Portugal). Moreover, insurance companies must pay taxes on the premiums they distribute. There are also wide divergences between industrial countries regarding other taxes an insurance company may be subject to (such as payroll taxes, transaction taxes, and wealth taxes).

An additional problem is that defining the precise taxable base becomes difficult when the fund management service is bundled with other financial services. This is the case when, for example, an insurance company holds a fund's assets and claims on its own books instead of just managing them. Reduced tax rates for funds open the opportunity for tax avoidance through accelerated losses for non–tax-exempt entities, as a tax-exempt fund can hold an offsetting position with accelerated gains on a financial instrument without (or with fewer) tax consequences.

The tax picture of funds would not be complete without looking at the taxation of the fund holder. Individuals are often encouraged to save via tax incentives. Such incentives are particularly common in the field of pension savings. Favorable tax treatment of pension savings is one of the most important expenditures in many OECD countries. The tax treatment has taken many forms. The most common is to grant tax allowances for private pension contributions and exempt returns on fund assets while benefits remain taxed (the so-called EET approach). But even within the EU, three member states operate an ETT-system (Exempt contributions, Taxed investment income and capital gains of the pension institution, and Taxed benefits) and two member states operate a TEE-system (Taxed contributions, Exempt income, Exempt benefits).

Taxes on Raising and Transferring Capital

There are other forms of taxation on equity capital that burden the use of equity relative to debt. The trend here is one of reduction of such taxes, and in certain cases, elimination. Nevertheless, six EU member states impose a stamp duty of 1 percent on capital issues, and eight levy a stamp duty on transactions in shares or bonds (table 6.10). The transactions duties were abolished in Germany in 1991, but were reintroduced in the United Kingdom in 1997 at 0.5 percent on stock exchange transactions.[23]

Implicit Taxes: Reserve Requirements

The original motivation for requiring credit institutions to hold reserves was to ensure that they had sufficient liquidity to meet de-

Table 6.10. Stamp Duties, 2001

Country	Stamp duty on issues Rate (%)	Stamp duty on issues Comments	Stamp duty on transactions Rate (%)	Stamp duty on transactions Comments
BE	0.5	—	0.2	—
DK	0	—	0.5	Shares only
DE	0	—	0	—
HE	1	—	0.5	Bonds
			0.3	Shares
ES	1	—	0	—
FR	0	—	0.15–0.3	Shares only: 0.3% up to a turnover of €153,000. More than €153,000: 0.15%.
IE	1	Joint stock companies	1	Bond and public loans not taxed
IT	1	0% on bonds	0.14	Shares traded outside recognized stock exchange
			0.009	Government bonds
LU	1	0.5% on family companies	0	—
NL	0.55		0	—
AT	1	0% on bonds	0	—
PT	0	—	0.002–0.015	—
FI	0	—	0	—
SE	0	—	0	—
UK	0	—	0.5	—
CH	1	0.06–0.12% on bonds	0.15	Domestic securities
			0.3	Foreign securities

Note: See table 6.9 for additional country names. HE Greece; AT Austria.
Source: Swiss Federal Tax Administration.

mands for withdrawal of deposits. A more recent motivation has been the contribution of reserves in smoothing short-term money market interest rates and the long-term money creation process by its effect on bank's lending, credit creation, and other activities.

A reserve requirement means that banks must hold a specific level of reserves at the central bank. Most countries that impose reserves allow averaging: that is, banks have to hold the specified level of reserves on average over a specific time (table 6.11). There are, however, drawbacks with reserve requirements:

• First, the requirement to hold reserves diminishes the amount of capital available for relending, thus reducing banks' ability to create deposits and thus the overall money creation process.

• In addition, if the reserves are remunerated at below-market rates, the effect of compulsory reserves can be compared to the effects of a tax.

• As reserve requirements impose an additional cost on banks, they may cause arbitrage incentives if reserve requirements are not equally imposed in all countries. That has indeed been the case (in the EU, for example) and has been one of the reasons why reserve rates have been decreased or have become remunerated in recent years, as further described below.

• In many countries, requirements are imposed only on certain credit institutions. This creates distortions. Those distortions have been another reason why requirements recently have been brought down.

In light of these drawbacks, most industrial countries have reduced the reserve requirement ratio since the 1990s. France lowered requirements between 1990 and 1992, the United States lowered theirs in 1992, and Germany followed suit in 1994 and 1995 (Davies 1998). Nevertheless, most industrial countries, with a few notable exceptions (such as the United Kingdom and Canada) continue to impose reserve requirements.

Considering the negative effects of reserve requirements and a few notable examples of countries that operate a monetary policy without such requirements, it may perhaps be surprising that the countries participating in the European Monetary System decided

Table 6.11. Reserve Requirements in Selected Industrial Countries

	US	EURO	UK	SE	DK	JP	CA
Reserve requirement (% of liabilities)	3–10[a]	2[b]	0	0	0	0.05–1.3	0
Averaging	Yes	Yes	—	—	—	Yes	Yes
Length of period	2 weeks	1 month	—	—	—	1 month	4–5 weeks
Penalties	Discount rate +2%	—	—	—	—	Discount rate +3.75%	Bank rate n.a.
Remuneration	No	Rate of refinancing operations	—	—	—	—	—

[a]Interest-bearing and non–interest-bearing checking accounts.

[b]Overnight deposits; deposits with agreed maturity up to two years; deposits redeemable at notice up to two years; debt securities issued with agreed maturity up to two years; and money market paper. Zero percent reserves required for deposits with agreed maturity or period of notice over two years, repos, debt securities issued with maturity over two years.

Source: Davies 1998; European Central Bank.

to maintain the practice at the launch of the euro. However, one reason might have been that most of the euro-members had reserve requirements in place before joining, including France, Germany, and Italy. In a 1998 press release, the European Central Bank (ECB) stated that "without the use of a minimum reserve system, the ESCB [European System of Central Banks] would be faced with a relatively high volatility of money market interest rates, which would require the frequent use of open market operations for fine-tuning purposes."

The required rate of reserves in the euro-system is 2 percent of liabilities, calculated as an average over a month. The reserve base is composed of overnight deposits, deposits with agreed maturity up to two years, deposits redeemable at notice up to two years, debt securities issued with agreed maturity up to two years, and money market paper. In addition, the euro-system provides two standing facilities, enabling credit institutions to deposit excess liquidity or access additional liquidity if they so wish. As a result, the ECB is able to intervene less frequently in the market (currently once a week).

The ECB introduced two features aimed at reducing the competitive disadvantage of those credit institutions that are based in the euro-area and thus falling under the reserve obligation. First, credit institutions are allowed to deduct a lump sum of €100,000 from their reserve liability base. As a result, credit institutions with a small reserve base do not have to hold reserves. Second, the reserve holdings are remunerated. The applicable rate is the rate of ECB refinancing operations.

Some countries, however, do not have reserve requirements, such as the *United Kingdom*. The Bank of England instead requires its settlement banks, on a daily basis, not to let their accounts go into overdraft. In order to prevent volatile money market interest rates, the Bank of England tries to forecast the demand for reserves, resorting to frequent open market operations (normally twice a day). However, such forecasting is difficult and as a result, the volatility of UK overnight interest rates is high by international standards (Davies 1998).

In the *United States*, all deposit institutions (commercial banks, saving banks, savings and loan associations, and credit unions) must maintain reserves on certain types of deposits (transaction deposits—that is, interest-bearing and non–interest-bearing checking accounts). The Monetary Control Act allows the Federal Reserve to impose rates of between 8 and 14 percent. The reserve requirements are imposed at a sliding upward scale. For the first $7.1 million of a bank's transactions, a rate of 0 percent is imposed. For the next $41.3 million of a bank's transaction accounts, a 3 percent reserve rate applies. Beyond that, a rate of 10 percent applies. These rates are adjusted annually according to different formulas. No reserves are imposed on personal time deposits and euro-currency liabilities. The average reserve requirement is imposed over a two-week period. Despite persistent lobbying, no remuneration is paid on compulsory reserves. Such a change would have to be approved by Congress, which so far has been reluctant because of the revenue loss it would entail.

Overall, there is thus a trend to decrease reserve requirements, as alternative means to achieve the end (operational efficiency of monetary policy, solvency of financial institutions) exist. In addition, in light of increasing awareness of the tax-like features of the reserves system, some countries (including those in the euro-system) have decided to remunerate compulsory reserves.

Conclusion

Since the 1980s industrial countries have engaged in numerous tax reforms. The aim has been to make tax systems more efficient, fair, and simple. Reform has generally operated within given structures by cutting rates and broadening tax bases. These general trends are mirrored in the taxation of financial intermediation. Countries have tried to improve efficiency by cutting rates and have broadened the bases by reducing certain exemptions, while creating new tax favored savings policies.

Globalization and the increasing elasticity of supply of capital increase the difficulties of taxing capital income. It is therefore surprising that countries continue to tax capital income to such a large extent. Political considerations and bureaucratic and legal inertia go some way toward explaining why industrial countries have not moved further toward reducing the taxation of capital income. But perhaps the reason is simpler: Tax competition is not as strong as is usually thought.

Reforms have in general been reactive to the development of financial instruments. The distinction between interest and dividends has been maintained in many countries, while the rules to sort particular financial instruments into these categories have been refined. The distinction between income and capital amounts has been given up in some countries. The tax accounting of gains and losses often follows financial accounting principles. Since financial accounting currently differs across countries, tax treatment of the timing of gains and losses does too. It remains to be seen whether the change in financial accounting practices (perhaps their harmonization) will affect the taxation of financial instruments.

As regards the taxation of financial instruments, the two areas of concern are efficiency and tax evasion. While in industrial countries financial instruments are used to minimize tax liability, taxpayers in developing countries may follow less sophisticated routes. General compliance is probably more of an issue in developing countries. This should not be neglected in discussing ways to tax capital gains. Accrual taxation may require some sophistication on the part of tax accountants; marking-to-market also requires sophisticated capital markets. With underdeveloped capital markets and the need to favor investment, developing countries may gear their tax policy to focus more on efficiency. This could imply avoiding following the historical peculiarities of developed tax systems. Rather, tax legislation on financial intermediation might be embedded in a broader perspective on taxation.

Developing countries, with less complex tax systems in place, may therefore perhaps be bolder. There is no need for developing countries to fall into the same traps of tax system design. Indeed, the example of Croatia illustrates that it is practically possible to introduce and operate a consumption-based system. However, as illustrated by the fate of the Italian tax reform, there are limits to political acceptance of bold reform initiatives.

Notes

1. Generally, nonresidents are treated differently from residents. Often what constitutes taxable income differs. Countries have generally tried to reduce the complexity of taxing nonresidents by imposing withholding taxes at source. In most cases, these taxes are set at a rate aimed at equalling the tax conditions that residents experience. In some cases, however, nonresidents receive more beneficial tax treatment than residents. Moreover, withholding rates mirror the underlying complexity of taxing residents. As a result, withholding rates often differ between types of income (dividends vs. interest) and types of instrument (for example, equity vs. bonds, public vs. private).

2. As well as those mentioned, within the European Union the need to avoid discrimination against residents of other EU member states has been an important driver of change in recent years. Important as this has been, it is rather specific to the case of an economic union and thus is not discussed here.

3. This section draws on Van den Noord and Heady (2001); see also Devereux (2000).

4. Many academic papers stress the particularly distorting effects and efficiency losses of this understanding of "equity." Not taxing the accumu-

lation of capital (at its opportunity cost) would not violate interpersonal equity, because capital accumulation reflects the intertemporal allocation of consumption. As long as in this dynamic sense expenditure is taxed, interpersonal equity would be safeguarded.

5. This may be compared with a reduction in the average rate of corporate income tax in the EU from 44 to 34 percent.

6. This and other factual material in the chapter has been drawn from IBFD (2001).

7. Van den Noord and Heady (2001). For a discussion on the efficiency/equity aspects of dual income taxation, see Nielsen and Sørensen (1997), who defend DIT on efficiency grounds. Lower taxation of wealth, in fact, means a lower taxation of foregone consumption.

8. Bovenberg and Cnossen (2001).

9. Rose and Wiswesser (1998) and Keen and King (2002) give a favorable assessment of the implementation that began in 1994. The system was abandoned in 2001 for political reasons.

10. Edgar (2000). The study summarizes how financial instruments in their analytical form can be separated into three building blocks. Credit-extension instruments give the right to a principal in return for the lending of funds, the classical case being debt. Price-fixing instruments give rise to the purchase or sale of an asset at a specified price, such as futures, forwards, and swaps. Price-insurance instruments give the holder the right, but not the obligation, to buy or sell an asset. Among the latter are classical common shares, which can be seen as a call option on the assets of the firm.

11. See Michielse (1996), Valkonen (2001), and Joumard (2001), for example.

12. For a survey, see Cnossen (1996).

13. Although in a dual income system the income from capital and from labor are taxed at a different rate, this in principle leaves open the question whether capital gains are taxed on accrual or on realization.

14. Known as "unanticipated deferral" in the tax literature (Edgar 2000, pp. 80–83 and 218–39). Since their expected value is zero (if losses and gains are treated symmetrically), their taxation would affect risk-taking. If the financial instrument is capitalized with the risk-free interest rate, the diversifiable and undiversifiable risk will remain tax-free.

15. Muray (2001).

16. See chapter 2, this volume, and Alworth, Arachi, and Hamaui (2002).

17. The examples in the text are intended to illustrate the diversity of national legislation. For a comprehensive survey, see Plambeck, Rosenbloom, and Ring (1995). For a summary of the issues, see Alworth (1998); Thuronyi (2001).

18. In dual income tax system countries, the distinction between capital and income is different. Income basically means labor income, while capital means the return on assets other than human capital.

19. Such risk arbitrage is explained in Edgar (2000, pp. 89 and 219).

20. Until 1999 this was the case only if a taxable yield could be derived from the provision of an underlying capital asset for a fixed period, so that price-fixing instruments—like index-linked options and futures—were not taxable.

21. See chapter 2 for an analytical description.

22. In the EU, for example, the 6th VAT directive (77/388/EEC) excludes VAT for financial services.

23. For further discussion of securities transactions taxes, see chapter 11.

References

Alworth, Julian. 1998. "Taxation and Integrated Financial Markets: The Challenges of Derivatives and other Financial Innovations." *International Tax and Public Finance* 5 (4): 507–34.

Alworth, Julian, Giampaolo Arachi, and Roni Hamaui. 2002. "Adjusting Capital Income Taxation: Lessons from the Recent Italian Tax Experience." Bocconi University, Milan. Processed.

Boadway, Robin, and Michael Keen. 2003. "Theoretical Perspectives on the Taxation of Capital Income and Financial Services" (chapter 2, this volume).

Bond, Stephen. 2000. "Levelling Up or Levelling Down? Some Reflections on the ACE and CBIT Proposals, and the Future of the Corporate Tax Base." In Sijbren Cnossen, ed., *Taxing Capital Income in the European Union: Issues and Options for Reform*. Oxford: Oxford University Press.

Bordignon, Massimo, Silvia Giannini, and Paolo Panteghini. 2001. "Reforming Business Taxation: Lessons from Italy?" *International Tax and Public Finance* 8 (2): 191–210.

Bosworth, Barry, and Gary Burtless. 1992. "Effects of Tax Reform on Labour Supply, Investment and Saving." In *Journal of Economic Perspectives* 6 (1): 3–25.

Bovenberg, Lans, and Sijbren Cnossen. 2001. "Fundamental Tax Reform in the Netherlands." *International Tax and Public Finance* 8 (4): 467–80.

Cnossen, Sijbren, 1996. "Company Taxes in the European Union: Criteria and Options for Reform." *Fiscal Studies* 17 (4): 67–97.

————. 2000. *Taxing Capital Income in the European Union: Issues and Options for Reform*. Oxford: Oxford University Press.

David, Cyrille. 1996. "General Introduction." In Geerten Michielse, ed., *Tax Treatment of Financial Instruments*. The Hague: Kluwer Law International.

Davies, Haydn. 1998. "Averaging in a Framework of Zero Reserve Requirements: Implications for the Operation of Monetary Policy." Bank of England Working Paper No. 84. London.

Demirgüç-Kunt, Aslı, and Harry Huizinga, 2001. "The Taxation of Domestic and Foreign Banking." *Journal of Public Economics* 79 (3): 429–53.

Devereux, Michael P. 2000. "Issues in the Taxation of Income from Foreign Portfolio and Direct Investment" In Sijbren Cnossen, ed., *Taxing Capital Income in the European Union: Issues and Options for Reform*. Oxford: Oxford University Press.

Devereux, Michael P., Rachel Griffith, and Alexander Klemm. 2002. "Corporate Income Tax Reforms and International Tax Competition." *Economic Policy* 35: 451–95.

Duisenberg, Willem F. 1993. "Tax Reform in Perspective." In Anthonie Knoester, ed., *Taxation in the United States and Europe: Theory and Practice*. New York: St. Martin's Press.

Edgar, Tim. 2000. "The Income Tax Treatment of Financial Instruments: Theory and Practice." Canadian Tax Paper 105, Canadian Tax Foundation, Toronto.

European Commission. 2001. "Company Taxation in the Internal Market." European Commission Staff Working Paper 1681. Brussels.

Feldstein, Martin. 1995. "Fiscal Policies, Capital Formation, and Capitalism." *European Economic Review* 39 (3–4): 399-420.

Fitzgibbon, Christopher P. J., and Miles Walton. 1990. *Taxation and Banking*. London: Sweet & Maxwell.

Fullerton, Don, and Mervyn A. King. 1984. *The Taxation of Income from Capital: A Comparative Study of the United States, the United Kingdom, Sweden and West Germany*. Chicago: The University Press of Chicago.

Gordon, Roger H. 2000. "Taxation of Capital Income vs. Labour Income: An Overview." In Sijbren Cnossen, ed., *Taxing Capital Income in the European Union: Issues and Options for Reform*. Oxford: Oxford University Press.

Haufler, Andreas. 2001. *Taxation in a Global Economy*. Cambridge: Cambridge University Press.

Huizinga, Harry. 2002. "A European VAT on Financial Services." *Economic Policy* 35: 499–534.

Huizinga, Harry, and Gaëtan Nicodème. 2001. "Are International Deposits Tax Driven?" DG ECFIN Economic Paper, No. 152. Brussels: European Commission.

IBFD (International Bureau of Fiscal Documentation). 2001. *The Taxation of Private Investment Income*. Amsterdam.

IFA (International Fiscal Association). 1996. *Principles for the Determination of the Income and Capital of Permanent Establishments and Their Applications to Banks, Insurance Companies and Other Financial Institutions* (Cahiers de Droit Fiscal International Vol. 81a). The Hague: Kluwer Law International.

————. 1997. *The Taxation of Investment Funds* (Cahiers de Droit Fiscal International Vol. 82b). The Hague: Kluwer Law International.

Joumard, Isabelle. 2001. "Tax Systems in European Union Countries." Economics Department Working Paper 301, OECD, Paris.

Keen, Michael, and John King. 2002. "The Croatian Profit Tax: An ACE in Practice." *Fiscal Studies* 23 (3): 401–18.

Knoester, Anthonie, ed. 1993. *Taxation in the United States and Europe: Theory and Practice*. New York: St. Martin's Press.

Leape, Jonathan I. 1993. "Tax Policies: The United Kingdom." In Anthonie Knoester, ed., *Taxation in the United States and Europe: Theory and Practice*. New York: St. Martin's Press.

Lee, Kyung Geun. 2002. "Taxation of Financial Intermediation." Background note for Workshop on Taxation of Domestic Financial Intermediation, April 8. World Bank, Washington, D.C. Processed.

Lodin, Sven-Olof. 2001. "International Taxes in a Rapidly Changing World." *International Bureau of Fiscal Documentation Bulletin* 55 (1): 1–7.

Maillard, Didier. 1993. "Tax Policies: France." In Anthonie Knoester, ed., *Taxation in the United States and Europe: Theory and Practice*. New York: St. Martin's Press.

McLure, Charles E. Jr. 2001. "Globalization, Tax Rules and National Sovereignty." *International Bureau of Fiscal Documentation Bulletin* 55 (8): 328–41.

Messere, K. C. 1993. *Tax Policy in OECD Countries: Choices and Conflicts*. Amsterdam: IBFD Publications BV.

————. 1999. "Half a Century of Changes in Taxation." *International Bureau of Fiscal Documentation Bulletin* 53 (8–9): 340–65.

————. 2000. "20th Century Taxes and Their Future." *International Bureau of Fiscal Documentation Bulletin* 54 (1): 2–29.

Michielse, Geerten, ed. 1996. *Tax Treatment of Financial Instruments*. The Hague: Kluwer Law International.

Modigliani, F. and M. H. Miller. 1958. "The Cost of Capital, Corporation Finance and the Theory of Investment." *American Economic Review* 48 (3): 261–97.

Muray, R. 2001. "Changes to the Taxation of Financial Instruments." *International Tax Review* (April) (www.internationaltaxreview.com).

Nielsen, Søren Bo, and Peter Birch Sørensen. 1997. "On the Optimality of the Nordic System of Dual Income Taxation." *Journal of Public Economics* 63 (3): 311–29.

OECD (Organisation for Economic Co-operation and Development). 1998. *Harmful Tax Competition—An Emerging Global Issue.* Paris: OECD.

———. 1999. "Taxing Insurance Companies." *OECD Tax Policy Studies* No. 4. Paris.

———. 2001. *Economic Survey—Italy 2001.* Paris.

Plambeck, Charles, David Rosenbloom, and Diane Ring. 1995. "Tax Aspects of Derivative Financial Instruments: General Report." In International Fiscal Association, ed., *The Taxation of Financial Derivative Instruments* (Cahiers de Droit Fiscal International Vol. 80b). The Hague: Kluwer Law International.

Rose, Manfred, and Rolf Wiswesser. 1998. "Tax Reform in Transition Economies: Experiences from the Croatian Tax Reform Process of the 1990s." In Peter Birch Sorensen, ed., *Public Finance in a Changing World.* Cambridge: Cambridge University Press.

Steinmo, Sven. 1995. "The Politics of Tax Reform." In Cedric Sandford, ed., *More Key Issues in Tax Reform.* Bath, England: Fiscal Publications.

Thuronyi, Victor. 2001. "Taxation of New Financial Instruments." *Tax Notes International* 24 (3): 261–73.

Valkonen, Tarmo. 2001. "The Finnish Corporate Income Tax Reform and the Financial Strategy of Firms: A General Equilibrium Approach." *Empirica* 28 (2): 219–39.

Van den Noord, Paul, and Christopher Heady. 2001. "Surveillance of Tax Policies: A Synthesis of Findings in Economic Surveys." OECD Economics Department Working Paper 303, Paris.

Warren, Alvin. 2001. "U.S. Income Taxation of New Financial Instruments." Harvard University, School of Law, Cambridge, Mass. Processed.

Wenger, Ekkehard. 1999. "Taxes on Business Profits." In Manfred Rose, ed., *Tax Reform for Countries in Transition to Market Economies.* Stuttgart: Lucius & Lucius.

Wurts, Brian, and Frankie Fenton. 2002. "Indirect Taxes on Financial Services." *International Tax Review* (April) (www.internationaltax review.com).

7

Seigniorage, Reserve Requirements, and Bank Spreads in Brazil

Eliana Cardoso

In 2001, nominal bank lending interest rates in Brazil reached an annual average of 44 percent for business loans and 73 percent for personal loans. With the inflation rate (measured by the consumer price index) no more than 8 percent, such rates act as a serious constraint on borrowing, especially for longer terms. No wonder then that bank credit was just 28 percent of GDP: not because of a lack of sophisticated credit analysis or even of lending capacity, but essentially from the effect of high interest rates on demand. The cost of funds to banks is high. Money market and wholesale deposit rates averaged almost 18 percent in 2001, and the intermediation margins above these rates must cover the cost of taxes and other impositions—including the cost of high reserve requirements—and government-directed lending, as well as the costs of non-performing loans.

This chapter examines the role of bank-captured seigniorage as well as explicit taxation in influencing spreads. Bank seigniorage revenue depends on the interaction between inflation, the market for demand deposits, and the rate of reserve requirements imposed by the central bank. Bank seigniorage revenue increased with inflation in Brazil until 1989, declined when inflation accelerated above 1,000 percent per year after 1992, and turned negative with the government stabilization *Real Plan* in 1995.

Despite the lack of competition otherwise observed in Brazilian banking, it will be seen that any increase in seigniorage collected by commercial banks has tended to reduce the spread between interest rates on deposits and loans. As a corollary, it can be inferred that reductions in the cost of reserve requirements and directed credit programs can drive down bank spreads and net margins—if supported by sound fiscal and monetary policy. Since inflation stabilized in the mid-1990s, the role of explicit taxation on financial intermediaries has become relatively more important for the explanation of the behavior of bank spreads.

The first section briefly summarizes the topic of financial liberalization in Brazil and follows with a review of the macroeconomics underlying the country's historically high interest rates. The chapter then discusses reserve requirements and bank seigniorage collection. It continues with evidence on the impact on bank spreads of seigniorage collection, inflation, explicit taxation, operational costs, and provisions for non-performing loans. The chapter concludes with some suggestions for strengthening Brazil's banking system.

Financial Liberalization in Brazil

Like many other countries, Brazil has taken extensive steps toward financial liberalization during the past 20 years. Successive governments reduced credit controls, rationalized reserve requirements, removed all interest rate ceilings on deposits in 1979, reduced barriers to entry after 1991, and liberalized controls on international capital flows during the 1990s. The path of reforms accelerated after 1995, when the government closed or privatized 10 state banks. Between mid-1994 and mid-2001, the share of public banks in total assets of the banking sector fell by 65 percent, while the share of foreign institutions increased fourfold. Loans from the financial system to the public sector practically disappeared (figures 7.1 and 7.2).

A variety of tax and quasi-fiscal instruments affect financial institutions and financial intermediation in Brazil. Some are explicit taxes included in the tax code, such as the income tax, the tax on pre-tax corporate income (CSLL), the tax on financial operations (IOF), taxes on gross revenues (PIS and COFINS), and the tax on bank debits (CPMF). Table 7.1 describes the structure of taxes and contributions in Brazil at the end of the 1990s, including the base of the tax, its destination, and the share of revenues in the relevant variable.

Other taxes on financial intermediation are not defined explicitly and are not treated as taxes in budget accounting. These include nonremunerated reserve requirements on demand deposits and di-

Figure 7.1. Loans from the Private Financial Sector as a
Percent of GDP, Brazil, 1989–2000

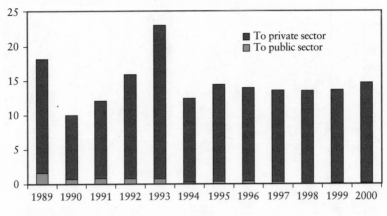

Source: Table 7.2.

Figure 7.2. Loans from the Public Banking Sector as a
Percent of GDP, Brazil, 1989–2000

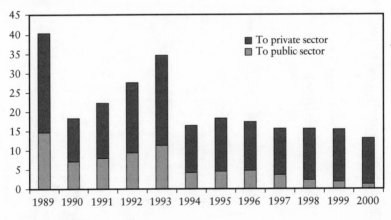

Source: Table 7.2.

rected credit at subsidized interest rates. Implicit taxes (discussed
later) secure credit for the government itself or for preferred sectors
at lower than market interest rates.

Brazil has a shallow intermediation system, whether measured by
the ratio of liquid liabilities or private credit to GDP—no better than
the Latin American averages and well below that of upper-middle

Table 7.1. Taxes and Contributions at the End of the 1990s, Brazil

Taxes and contributions	Base	Value in 1997 (R$)	Share in relevant variable	Destination
Federal Taxes				
Income tax	Personal and business income	35.6	4.6% of GDP	Federal, 53%; states, 21.5%; municipalities, 22.5%; development funds, 3%.
Import tariffs	CIF imports	5.1	8.3% of imports	Federal
Industrial products (IPI)	Industrial value-added	16.6	9.8% of manufacturing GDP	Federal, 43%; states, 21.5%; municipalities, 22.5%; development funds, 3%; export fund, 10%.
Financial operations (IOF)	Loans, insurance, Foreign investment	3.8	6.7% of financial GDP	Federal
Rural land	Land values	0.2		Federal, 50%; local, 50%
Fees	Various	0.3		Federal
Federal Contributions				
Social security	Private wage bill	44.1	20.1% of non-government wages	Social security benefits
COFINS	Gross revenues	18.3	2.4% of GDP	Social security benefits
CPMF	Check debits	6.9	12.1% of financial GDP	Health
CSLL	Pre-tax corporate income	7.2	2% of operational surplus	
PIS/Pasep	Gross revenues	7.3	0.9% of GDP	FAT: Deposits at federal financial institutions
Federal employee contributions	Federal wage bill	2.6	6.1% of federal wages	Payment of federal pensions

Other social contributions	Various	0.6	5.9% of non-government wages	Severance benefits, housing
FGTS	Wage bill	12.9		
Economic contributions	Various	0.9	0.8 of wages	FNDE
Salário-Educação	Wage bill	2.8		
State Taxes				
Value-added (ICMS)	Value added	59.8	7.7% of GDP	States, 60%; local, 25%; FUNDEF, 15%
Vehicle (IPVA)	Vehicle value	3.8		States, 50%; local, 50%
Inheritance (ITCD)	Inheritance value	0.3		States
Social security contributions	Wage bill	1.5	1.9% of state government wages	States
Municipal Taxes				
Urban property (IPTU)	Assessed value	3.1	2.6 of rental income	Municipalities
Transfer of fixed assets (ITBI)	Value of asset	0.8	0.9% of services GDP	Municipalities
Services (ISS)	Value-added	4.4		Municipalities
Fees	Various	2.0		Municipalities
Other	Various	0.1		Municipalities

Source: Carrizosa 2000.

income countries (see Beck, Demirgüç-Kunt, and Levine 1999). The loans made by private commercial banks have short maturity and even short-term credit is scarce. In 2000, the average stock of credit by the private financial sector to the private sector represented just 14.6 percent of GDP (table 7.2). The wide bank spreads are undoubtedly a contributing factor, associated as they are with the extremely high lending rates noted above. One causal factor in these wide spreads is certainly the low ability of creditors to enforce claims.[1] But it is the other tax-like factors on which this chapter focuses.

The Macroeconomics behind Brazil's High Interest Rates

This section looks at some of the major macroeconomic developments that formed the backdrop against which bank interest rates have been determined.

Real Interest Rates in the 1980s and 1990s

In Brazil, the negative real interest rates that characterized the financial repression in the 1960s and 1970s are long gone. On average over the ten years between 1975 and 1984, real interest rates on deposits were negative because of interventions, unexpected changes in inflation, and imperfect indexation (table 7.3). Thereafter, with increasing financial liberalization, real interest rates on time deposits rose sharply averaging 10 percent between 1985 and 1989, though with huge fluctuations (table 7.4). With the acceleration of inflation in the mid-1980s, indexation intervals became shorter and a share of deposits was held in accounts linked to the daily behavior of overnight interest rates.

Between 1984 and 1994, the annual rate of inflation exceeded 100 percent in all years except 1986. Yet though confidence in the financial system was damaged by a spectacular series of failed stabilization plans, involving six monetary reforms in ten years,[2] together with a moratorium on external debt in 1987 and the 1990 deposit freeze,[3] inflation did not destroy the Brazilian economy. Indexation, the adaptive policy response, became pervasive throughout the economy and its capacity to accommodate inflation may partially explain Brazil's failure to engage in serious structural change before 1995.

By 1992, when President Fernando Collor was ousted from power in a corruption scandal, inflation reached 1,000 percent per year and exceeded 2,000 percent in December 1993. With daily indexation of

Table 7.2. Loans as Percent of GDP, Brazil, 1989–2000

Year	Loans from the public financial sector		Loans from the private financial sector		To the public sector	Loans from public and private financial sectors			
	To the public sector	To the private sector	To the public sector	To the private sector		Personal loans	Business loans	Total to the private sector	Total loans
1989	14.7	25.7	1.6	16.5	16.3	1.5	40.8	42.3	58.6
1990	7.1	11.2	0.7	9.3	7.9	0.6	19.9	20.5	28.4
1991	8.0	14.3	0.8	11.3	8.8	0.9	24.7	25.6	34.4
1992	9.4	18.2	0.8	15.1	10.2	1.4	31.9	33.3	43.5
1993	11.3	23.4	0.7	22.3	12.0	2.3	43.4	45.7	57.8
1994	4.3	12.2	0.3	12.2	4.5	2.3	22.1	24.4	28.9
1995	4.6	13.8	0.4	14.1	4.9	2.4	25.5	27.8	32.8
1996	4.8	12.6	0.4	13.6	5.2	2.4	23.8	26.2	31.4
1997	3.7	12.0	0.3	13.3	4.0	3.2	22.0	25.3	29.2
1998	2.3	13.3	0.2	13.3	2.5	3.7	22.9	26.7	29.1
1999	1.8	13.6	0.1	13.5	2.0	3.9	23.2	27.1	29.1
2000	1.2	11.9	0.1	14.6	1.4	4.6	21.8	26.4	27.8

Note: Loans as percent of GDP were calculated by dividing the average stock of credit (between December of current year and December of previous year) by GDP.

Source: Central Bank of Brazil.

247

Table 7.3. Real Interest Rates, Brazil, 1970–2001 (percent per year)

| | Passive real rates | Active real rates | | |
| | Certificate of | Commercial | Working | Average of |
Period	time deposit	paper	capital	active rates
1970–74	3	24	—	—
1975–79	–3	14	10	—
1980–84	–6	20	20	—
1985–89	10	*	*	—
1990–94	19	—	42	—
1995–98	22	—	74	92
1999–2001	6	—	—	45

— Not available

* Information for active rates between 1985 and 1989 from different sources is inconsistent.

Note: Real interest rates are defined as $r = [(1 + i)/(1 + \pi)] - 1$ where i is the annualized average monthly interest rates and π is the general price index (IGP-DI). Calculations use the general price index because current consumer price indices are not available for earlier periods. Real interest rates between 1999 and 2001 are higher when consumer price indices are used in place of the general price index.

Sources: Central Bank of Brazil, Institute of Economic Research (IPEA), Andima, and Broadcast.

Table 7.4. Spreads between Active and Passive Annual Interest Rates, Brazil, 1970–2001 (percent)

Period	Between rates on commercial paper and certificate of time deposit	Between rates on working capital and certificate of time deposit	Between average active rates and certificate of time deposit
1970–74	20	—	—
1975–79	18	13	—
1980–84	28	28	—
1985–89	—	—	—
1990–94	—	19	—
1995–98	—	43	57
1999–2001	—	—	37

— Not available

Note: Spreads are defined as $s = (1 + rl)/(1 + rd) -1$, where rl is the real interest rate on loans and rd is the real interest rates on time deposits, as defined in table 7.3.

Source: Table 7.3.

Figure 7.3. Passive Real Interest Rates before the *Real Plan,* Brazil, January 1970–June 1994 (percent)

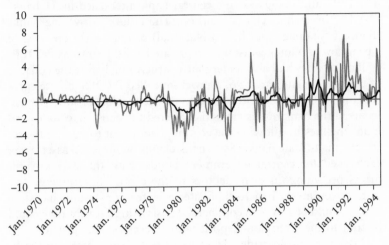

Note: Gray = actual monthly rates; black = moving average.
Source: Instituto de Pesquisa Econômica Aplicada (IPEA), Rio de Janeiro.

financial assets, real interest rates on time deposits jumped to 19 percent on average in the first half of the 1990s (table 7.3, figure 7.3).

Launched in 1994, the *Real Plan* combined a brief fiscal adjustment, a monetary reform, and the use of the exchange rate as a nominal anchor. Stabilization was supported by very tight monetary policy: real deposit rates averaged 22 percent per year between June 1995 and December 1998 and the authorities sharply increased reserve requirements (see discussion below). The plan brought inflation under control with remarkable speed: measured by consumer prices, it fell from four digits in 1994 to two digits in 1995 and to less than two percent in 1998. Nevertheless, the real exchange rate appreciated sharply.

The difference between domestic and foreign interest rates resulted in increased external borrowing and helped finance the current deficit resulting from real appreciation, providing apparent stability. To avoid a monetary expansion induced by capital flows, inflows were partly sterilized, and this entailed sizable fiscal costs, given the international interest differential that had opened up.

Banking Problems

By increasing the cost of debt servicing, high real interest rates not only complicated fiscal adjustment but also contributed to the deterioration of bank portfolios, particularly those of public banks, further straining the fiscal resources needed for restructuring. Between mid-1994 and mid-1997, the central bank intervened in 51 banks and 140 other financial institutions. The failure of two big banks (Banco Econômico and Banco Nacional) prompted the creation of a program providing assistance to private banks, known as PROER.

Public banks had also undergone restructuring before the collapse of the *real*. In August 1996, a program called PROES (a sister program to PROER) was introduced to reduce the role of state governments in the banking system and curb credit expansion to states and municipalities by allowing the central government to finance the restructuring of state banks. State bank claims on impaired assets were exchanged for central government bonds, with the state governments becoming, in turn, debtors to the central government. The state governments had to liquidate, privatize, or ensure that state banks would be run on a commercial basis. Alternatively, they could be transformed into non–deposit-taking development agencies.

After the restructuring, the share of state banks assets in the financial system fell sharply, though the largest financial institutions in the country are still the federally owned Banco do Brasil and Caixa Econômica Federal. In 2000, the average stock of credit from public banks to the private sector was 12 percent of GDP, compared to 14.6 percent from private banks (table 7.2).

After the Real Plan

During these years, the general lack of confidence in the ability of the regime to sustain the exchange rate anchor and to meet its obligations was reflected in the increasing use of dollar-denominated and floating rate debt. By early 1999, 21 percent of domestic public debt was dollar-denominated and 70 percent was indexed to the overnight interest rate. Moreover, maturities fell; the interest due on domestic debt in January 1999 alone exceeded 6 percent of GDP. Given the lack of fiscal consolidation, external international shocks to confidence in 1997 and especially in 1998—combined with strong resistance by the domestic business community to the record high interest rates that were being employed in an attempt to stem capital outflows—forced the government to float the *real* on January 15, 1999; six weeks later it had depreciated by 35 percent.[4]

Charting the appropriate course of monetary policy in subsequent months required balancing the risk of a return to the old story of persistent inflation (if interest rates were left too low) against the danger of pushing the economy into a severe recession—not only costly in itself but a threat to the government's counter-inflationary

Figure 7.4. Real Interest Rate, Brazil, 1992–2001 (Selic rate deflated by the consumer price index, percent per year)

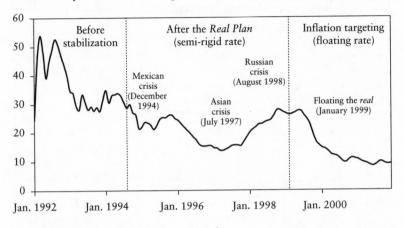

Source: BBV Bank.

resolve. In any event, the timing and scale of the interest rate increases in the early months of the float were successful in shifting the economy from a potentially explosive situation to a path of steadily declining inflation, allowing real interest rates to fall gradually. A formal inflation-targeting policy was adopted in June 1999 and succeeded in meeting the stringent targets of 8 and 6 percent for 1999 and 2000. Interest rates and reserve requirements were also reduced (table 7.3, figure 7.4).

Despite this success, lending rates and bank spreads continue to be very high (tables 7.4, 7.5). The central bank calculates that op-

Table 7.5. Spreads between Active and Passive Monthly Interest Rates and Net Margins of Commercial Banks, Brazil, 1995–2000 (percent)

Period	Spread between the average active interest rates per month and the rate on certificate of deposits per month	Commercial bank margin net of administrative expenditures, expenditures with bad loans, and explicit taxes
1995	5.3	0.90
1996	3.6	0.77
1997	3.1	0.76
1998	3.3	0.90
1999	3.2	1.01
2000	2.5	1.01

Source: Central Bank of Brazil.

Figure 7.5. Monthly Spread between Loan and Deposit
Rates and Net Margin of Banks, Brazil, 1995–2001
(12-month moving average, percent)

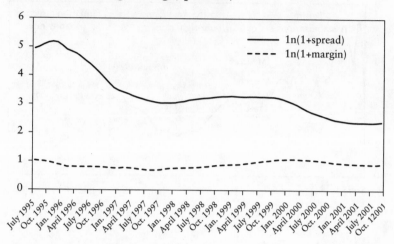

Source: Central Bank of Brazil.

erational expenses and provisions for non-performing loans account
for 35 percent of the total spread between deposit and lending rates;
direct and indirect taxes explain an additional 30 percent and the
net bank margin the remaining 35 percent (Central Bank of Brazil
2001).

The sharp decline in spreads between 1996 and 2001, shown in
figure 7.5, derives in part from the decline in operational costs; the
end of inflation forced banks to merge and reduce the numbers of
branches and staff. Other factors also contributed to this decline:
the tax on financial operations (IOF) was cut from 6 to 1.5 percent
in October 1999. Reserve requirements also declined between 1996
and 2000, as discussed in the next section.

Reserve Requirements and Commercial
Bank Seigniorage

The central bank requires each bank to hold a minimum amount of
specified reserve assets, including cash deposits, with the central
bank, in proportion to deposit liabilities (tables 7.6, 7.7). The difference between the market interest rates on short-term securities
and the interest rate paid on required reserves represents a tax. As
in the case of currency, the government is borrowing at below mar-

Table 7.6. Rates of Required Reserves before the *Real Plan*
Brazil, 1969–93 (percent of deposits)

Month and year	Demand deposits[a]		Time deposits	
	Region A[b]	Region B[b]	Region A[b]	Region B[b]
April 1969	27	18	9	4.5
May 1971[c]	27	18	9	4
January 1973	27	18	0	0
March 1973[d]	27	18	0	0
July 1973[e]	27	18	0	0
July 1974[f]	27	18	0	0
February 1975[g]	27	18	0	0
July 1975[h]	27	18	0	0
April 1976	33	18	0	0
July 1976	35	18	0	0
October 1977	40	18	0	0
July 1979[i]	40	18	0	0
December 1984	40	18	22	22
June 1985	40	18	20	20
January 1992	40	18	0	0
November 1993	40	40	0	0

[a]The periods and formula for calculating average deposits on which required reserves were to be based changed many times between 1969 and 1993.

[b]Region B: Acre, Alagoas, Amazonas, Bahia, Ceará, Espírito Santo, Goiás, Maranhão, Mato Grosso, Pará, Paraíba, Pernambuco, Piauí, Rio Grande do Norte, Sergipe. Region A: All other states.

[c]A reduction of one-half percentage point in required reserves will make up resources from demand deposits destined to loans to small and medium enterprises.

[d]A reduction of 2 percentage points in required reserves will make up resources from demand deposits to be destined to loans to exporters.

[e]Percentage of demand deposits destined for rural credit increased from 10 percent to 15 percent.

[f]Amount to be destined to loans to small and medium enterprises increased to 4 percent of demand deposits.

[g]Mandatory loans for working capital of small and medium enterprises increases to 8 percent of demand deposits.

[h]55 percent of required reserves to be held in government bonds (LTN or ORTN).

[i]Percentage of demand deposits destined for rural credit increased from 15 percent to 17 percent.

Source: Central Bank of Brazil.

ket interest rates. Commercial banks collect seigniorage (or an inflation tax) on non–interest-bearing demand deposits (Brock 1989). Non–interest-bearing reserve requirements reduce this revenue. Commercial banks can pass this loss of revenue on to depositors, who will receive lower interest rates on deposits, and to borrowers, who will face higher interest rates on loans. The spread between deposit and loan rates will increase. How much the deposit rate will fall and how much the loan rate will increase depends on the elasticity of demand for loans compared with the elasticity of supply of deposits, assuming that both markets clear. The inflation rate will also interact with reserve requirements to increase the spread between the two rates, depending on how depositors allocate their money holdings between currency, demand deposits, and time deposits (McKinnon and Mathieson 1981).

For most of the period between 1969 and 1993, reserve requirements on time deposits in Brazil were zero (table 7.6). In the poorest regions of the country (Acre, Alagoas, Amazonas, Bahia, Ceará, Espírito Santo, Goiás, Maranhão, Mato Grosso, Maranhão, Pará, Paraíba, Pernambuco, Piauí, Rio Grande do Norte, and Sergipe), required reserves on demand deposits were 18 percent from 1969 to 1993, when they were increased to 40 percent. In the richest regions, reserve requirements on demand deposits increased from 27 percent in 1969 to 40 percent between 1977 and 1993.

Reserve requirements were seen as a way of taxing the profits that would accrue to the banks during periods of high inflation. Restricted competition prevented interest competition for deposits, allowing banks to earn high profits on non–interest-bearing demand deposits. Reserve requirements represented a tax on these profits. But after 1975 and until mid-1994, 55 percent of reserve requirements on demand deposits could be held in government securities.

Between 1969 and 1993, a percentage of demand deposits were earmarked for rural credit, loans to exporters, and loans to small and medium enterprises (see notes to table 7.6). Although the situation has improved since 1995, banks are still required to allocate 25 percent of average demand deposit balances to rural credit and 60 percent of savings deposits to real estate finance. In principle, the impact of forced investments on spreads is similar to reserve requirements. But the interest paid on government directed lending contributes to meeting the interest cost of deposits. Currently there are no ceilings on the rates commercial banks can charge for loans mandated for the rural sector. For real estate lending, the gross yield matches the cost of funding of savings deposits.

In mid-1994, the *Real Plan* increased reserve requirements on demand deposits to 100 percent (60 percent on other liquid resources, and 20 percent on time deposits (table 7.7). The required reserves-to-deposit ratio rose from an average of 26 percent during January–June 1994 to 64 percent during November 1994–April 1995. This increase in reserve requirements and the decline of inflation led to a substantial loss of seigniorage revenue for deposit banks.

Table 7.7. Rates of Required Reserves after the *Real Plan,* Brazil, 1994–2001 (percent)

Period	Demand deposits	Time deposits	Saving deposits	Credit operations	FIF-CP	FIF-30 days
Before the Real Plan	40	0	15	0	0	0
July 1994	100	20	20	0	0	0
Aug. 1994	100	30	30	0	0	0
Oct. 1994	100	30	30	15	0	0
Dec. 1994	90	27	30	15	0	0
April 1995	90	30	30	15	0	0
May 1995	90	30	30	12	0	0
June 1995	90	30	30	10	0	0
July 1995	83	30	30	10	35	10
Aug. 1995	83	20	15	8	40	5
Sept. 1995	83	20	15	5	40	5
Nov. 1995	83	20	15	0	40	5
Aug. 1996	82	20	15	0	42	5
Sept. 1996	81	20	15	0	44	5
Oct. 1996	80	20	15	0	46	5
Nov. 1996	79	20	15	0	48	5
Dec. 1996	78	20	15	0	50	5
Jan. 1997	75	20	15	0	50	5
Dec. 1998	75	20	15	0	50	5
March 1999	75	30	15	0	50	5
May 1999	75	25	15	0	50	5
July 1999	75	20	15	0	50	5
Aug. 1999	75	20	15	0	0	0
Sept. 1999	75	10	15	0	0	0
Oct. 1999	65	0	15	0	0	0
March 2000	55	0	15	0	0	0
June 2000	45	0	15	0	0	0
Sept. 2001	45	10	15	0	0	0

Source: Central Bank of Brazil.

Bank seigniorage revenue (or inflationary revenue) is the increase in non–interest-bearing demand deposits (ΔDD) minus the increase in non–interest-bearing required reserves (ΔRR).[5]

Figure 7.6 shows commercial bank seigniorage revenue divided by loans. Between 1970 and 1989, bank seigniorage was high relative to more recent periods. It reached a peak immediately after the *Cruzado Plan* in 1985, when prices were frozen and money growth increased ahead of inflation. It turned temporarily negative in 1987, when inflation accelerated ahead of money growth.

Between 1990 and mid-1994, a period of extremely high inflation, bank seigniorage declined as people economized on their hold-

Figure 7.6. Seigniorage Collected by Commercial Banks as
Share of Loans, Brazil, 1971–2001 (12-month moving
average, percent)

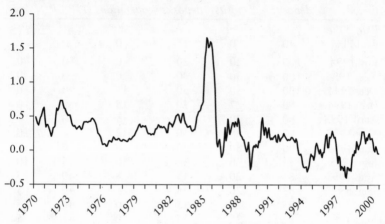

Source: Central Bank of Brazil and IPEA.

ings of nonremunerated real demand deposits. In 1995, bank seigniorage revenue turned negative. The *Real Plan*'s sharp increase in
reserve requirements reduced bank seigniorage.

Under the *Real Plan*, the share in total seigniorage seized by the
central bank increased from an average of 60 percent in the first
half of 1994 to 84 percent a year later. As a consequence, the share
in GDP of seigniorage seized by deposit banks fell from 2 percent to
close to zero and seigniorage collected by the central bank rose from
1.8 percent of GDP in 1993, the peak inflation year, to 3 percent in
1994, the year of the *Real Plan* (Cardoso 1998).

This appropriation of seigniorage from the banking sector to the
central bank helped finance government spending as inflation
ebbed, but it also put the banking sector at risk. Lending interest
rates and bank spreads increased sharply, as did non-performing
loans. As already mentioned, these elements exposed the weaknesses of the Brazilian banking sector in the mid-1990s. After 1998,
as reserve requirements declined, bank seigniorage recovered.

The data suggest that there is a Laffer curve for bank seigniorage
in relation to inflation. Seigniorage increases with inflation but as
inflation continues to increase, the demand for real money, including interest-free demand deposits, declines more than proportion-
ally with the increase in inflation, and bank revenue from seigniorage declines (table 7.8).

Table 7.8. Ratio of Bank Seigniorage to Loans, Inflation
Rate, and Required Reserves, Brazil, 1970–2000

Period	Bank seigniorage divided by loans (percent)	Average inflation rate (IGP-DI) (percent per year)	Range of required reserves on demand deposits (percent)
1970–74	0.485	21	18 to 27
1975–79	0.223	46	18 to 40
1980–84	0.364	143	18 to 40
1985–89	0.500	507	18 to 40
1990–June 1994	0.189	1,660	18 to 40
July 1994–1998	–0.118	16	60 to 100
1999	0.086	20	60 to 65
2000	0.225	10	45 to 55

Sources: Central Bank of Brazil and IPEA.

The objective of the next section is to determine the impact of
seigniorage on bank spreads and margins.

Empirical Evidence on the Link between Seigniorage and Spreads

Bank spreads and margins reflect the cost of intermediation. According to Ho and Saunders (1981), banks are risk-averse dealers in
loan and deposit markets where loan requests and deposit funds arrive randomly. Bank interest margins are fees charged by banks for
the provision of liquidity. Allen (1988) extends the model to account for cross-elasticity of demand between bank products and
Angbazo (1997) extends it for default risk. Wong (1997) confirms
the results of the earlier models and predicts that bank interest margins are positively related to the banking sector's market power, operating costs, credit risk, and interest rate risk.

Explicit and implicit taxes on financial intermediation can also
raise spreads. Taxes on financial transactions drive a wedge between
what borrowers pay and lenders receive, thus increasing the spread
(Chamley and Honohan 1993). The wedge will reduce the total
amount of resources passing through the financial system and raise
the rate paid by borrowers or lower deposit rates, depending on the
elasticity of demand for credit and on the elasticity of supply of deposits (Hanson and Rocha 1986).

Reserve requirements can also drive a wedge between borrowing
and lending rates and thus act as an implicit tax on financial intermediation, if the interest rate on required reserves is lower than the

interest rate on deposits. The wedge develops because the reserve requirement allows only a fraction of the deposits to be loaned. Therefore the lending rate must exceed the deposit rate in order to cover the total interest due on deposits.

In the case where both deposits and required reserves are interest-free, an increase in required reserves would transfer seigniorage revenue from commercial banks to the central bank and act as an increase of taxes on bank profits.

Koyama and Nakane (2001) find a positive long-run relationship between bank spreads in Brazil and operational costs, indirect taxes, and country risk. They use the Johansen co-integration test and find a positive but nonsignificant relationship between bank spreads and the required rate of reserves. But the co-integration test might not be appropriate, inasmuch as the rates of required reserves and indirect taxes are not known to be nonstationary.

This section takes a different approach to test the impact of reserve requirements on bank spreads. The effect of reserve requirements on bank spreads depends on the interaction with inflation and deposit demand and its ability to affect bank seigniorage revenue and spreads. Thus this section tests the hypothesis that a gain in bank seigniorage revenue reduces bank spreads and margins.

Table 7.9 reports results of regressions of the spread between average lending rates and the interest rate on time deposits after the *Real Plan*. The lagged inflation rate, lagged operational costs, lagged provisions for overdue loans, and lagged direct and indirect taxes are included in regressions 3 and 4 in table 7.9. The ratio between seigniorage revenues and loans appear with different lags in all specifications. Table 7.10 reports results of regressions of the bank margin net of explicit taxes, operational costs, and provisions for bad loans. Table 7.11 reports results of regressions of the spread between the interest rate on loans to working capital and the interest rate on time deposits from 1990 to 2000. Definitions of variables and data sources are listed in the appendix. The estimation technique is ordinary least squares.

In all the regressions, bank seigniorage revenue has the expected negative sign and is significant. An increase in seigniorage collected by commercial banks reduces the spread between deposit and loan rates. The variable measuring bank seigniorage revenue is defined as a single-month value of bank seigniorage relative to loans with four lags in regressions 1 and 4. It is defined as the six-month moving average of bank seigniorage relative to loans in regressions 2 and 4, again with a lag of four months. As expected, the effect of the average seigniorage is bigger than the effect of a single month. A 100 percent increase in the six-month average bank seigniorage four months earlier reduces spreads between 15 and 30 percent in differ-

Table 7.9. Determinants of the Spread between Active and Passive Rates after the *Real Plan*

Variable	Regression 1 (1994:12– 2001:09)	Regression 2 (1994:12– 2001:09)	Regression 3 (1995:01– 2001:09)	Regression 4 (1995:01– 2001:09)
Constant	0.001 (1.08)	0.001 (1.23)	0.012 (15.97)	0.013 (20.01)
Bank seigniorage revenue $(t–4)$	–0.074 (–2.05)	—	–0.070 (–2.53)	—
6-month average bank seigniorage revenue $(t–2)$	—	–0.148 (–1.64)	—	—
6-month average bank seigniorage revenue $(t–4)$	—	—	—	–0.305 (–4.45)
Inflation rate $(t–1)$	0.047 (1.54)	0.053 (1.80)	0.058 (2.83)	0.041 (2.49)
Direct taxes $(t–1)$	—	—	0.97 (23.42)	0.93 (19.57)
Indirect taxes $(t–1)$	—	—	0.997 (8.08)	0.94 (8.28)
Operational costs $(t–1)$	—	—	0.517 (4.39)	0.543 (5.15)
Provisions for overdue loans $(t–1)$	—	—	0.785 (7.88)	0.749 (8.37)
Spread $(t–1)$	0.95 (29.24)	0.94 (25.98)	—	—
Number of observations	82	82	81	81
Adjusted R^2	0.95	0.95	0.95	0.96
Durbin-Watson	1.90	1.88	1.66	1.83

Notes: All variables expressed as natural logarithms (see appendix for definitions). Estimation by OLS with Newey-West HAC Standard Errors and Covariance
(t statistics in parentheses)
(lag truncation = 3)
Source: Author's calculations.

ent specifications, while a 100 percent reduction in bank seigniorage four months earlier reduces the spread by 7 percent.

Regressions 9 and 10 reported in table 7.11, including years before the *Real Plan,* show a bigger impact of bank seigniorage on spreads. A 100 percent increase in the six-month average of the ratio between bank seigniorage and loans two months earlier re-

Table 7.10. Determinants of the Commercial Bank Net Margin after the *Real Plan*

Variable	Regression 5 (1994:12– 2001:09)	Regression 6 (1994:10– 2001:09)	Regression 7 (1994:11– 2001:09)	Regression 8 (1994:11– 2001:09)
Constant	0.0025 (2.94)	0.0024 (2.93)	0.002 (1.72)	0.0025 (3.11)
Bank seigniorage revenue (t–3)	–0.023 (–2.25)	—	—	—
Bank seigniorage revenue (t–4)	–0.027 (–1.95)	—	—	—
6-month average of bank seigniorage revenue (t–2)	—	–0.056 (–1.34)	—	—
6-month average of bank seigniorage revenue (t–3)	—	—	–0.094 (–2.57)	–0.063 (–1.82)
Inflation (t–1)	0.011 (0.81)	—	0.025 (2.02)	—
Inflation (t–2)	0.021 (0.96)	—	—	—
February 95 dummy (Mexico's contagion)	0.001 (3.76)	0.001 (2.67)	0.0015 (2.40)	0.001 (3.75)
February 99 dummy (the *real* floats)	0.002 (2.65)	0.003 (15.59)	0.0023 (11.48)	0.003 (17.71)
Margin (t–1)	0.687 (6.98)	0.734 (8.34)	0.662 (7.90)	0.722 (8.39)
Trend	—	—	0.0003 (1.05)	—
Number of observations	82	84	83	83
Adjusted R^2	0.63	0.61	0.62	0.61
Durbin-Watson	1.99	2.03	2.04	2.00

Notes: All variables expressed as natural logarithms (see appendix for definitions). Estimation by OLS with Newey-West HAC Standard Errors and Covariance
   (t statistics in parentheses)
   (lag truncation = 3)
Source: Authors' calculations.

duces the current bank spread by 73 percent. Results in table 7.11 have to be looked at with a grain of salt because data for interest rates before 1995, compiled from different sources, are not based on large samples such as the information published by the central bank for the period after September 1994.

Table 7.11. Determinants of the Spread between Interest Rates on Working Capital Loans and Interest Rates on Time Deposits

Variable	Regression 9 (1990:03–2000:12)	Regression 10 (1990:03–2000:12)
Constant	0.0195	0.0196
	(10.23)	(8.48)
Bank seigniorage revenue	–0.268	—
(t–2)	(–1.84)	—
6-month average of bank	—	–0.727
seigniorage revenue (t–2)	—	(–2.99)
Inflation	–0.070	–0.061
	(–6.69)	(–6.11)
March 1990 Dummy	0.171	0.166
(Collor Plan)	(12.87)	(28.31)
July 1994 Dummy	0.192	0.192
(Real Plan)	(15.81)	(17.96)
Spread (t–1)	0.244	0.236
	(5.40)	(3.34)
Number of Observations	130	130
Adjusted R^2	0.79	0.80
Durbin-Watson	1.91	2.03

Notes: All variables expressed as natural logarithms (see appendix for definitions).
(t statistics in parentheses)
Source: Authors' calculations.

Inflation Costs

The reasons usually given for intermediation costs to rise with inflation are the following: Inflation decreases the maturity of contracts and thus requires more frequent interest rate transactions per unit of assets. Chronic inflation leads to an expansion of the branch network as banks compete for low-cost deposits by offering more services and branches. The variable measuring operational costs in regressions 3 and 4 probably captures both effects better than the inflation rate variable.

In regressions 1 to 8 in tables 7.9 and 7.10, the coefficient of lagged inflation rate, following the *Real Plan*, is positive but small. In regressions 9 and 10 in table 7.11, covering a period of high and volatile inflation rates, the inflation rate has a negative and significant coefficient that perhaps reflects inflationary revenue not fully captured by the bank seigniorage revenue.

It is also worthwhile observing that in regressions 3 and 4, covering the period of low inflation after the *Real Plan*, the response of spreads to changes in inflation and bank seigniorage revenue is smaller than the response to other variables such as explicit taxes on financial intermediation and the costs of provisioning for non-performing loans.

Explicit Taxes

The results in table 7.9 (regressions 3 and 4) suggest that both indirect and direct taxes pass through completely to bank customers. Thus the evidence does not support the notion that corporate income taxes, as opposed to indirect taxes on financial intermediation, are not a distorting tax on bank profits.

The complete pass-through of income taxes in a context of growing capital mobility is also consistent with the assumption that international investors demand a net-of-tax return on capital invested in the country.

Non-Performing Loans

Non-performing loans are often seen as a source of upward pressure on bank spreads and real lending rates because bankers try to offset their losses on their non-performing loans by charging higher interest rates to their performing borrowers.

The evidence in table 7.9 is consistent with this hypothesis. A 100 percent increase in the ratio of provisions for overdue loans to credit increases the spread between deposit and lending rates by 80 percent.

The evidence for Brazil is consistent with the evidence from industrial countries where non-performing loans are associated with higher spreads. It contradicts the evidence for Latin America in Brock and Rojas-Suarez (2000).

It is also meaningful to observe that while average bank spreads between monthly deposit and loan rates fell between 1996 and 2000, the ratio of the interest rate on working capital loans to non-prime borrowers relative to the interest rate on working capital loans to prime borrowers increased (figure 7.7). High lending rates may reflect financial distress among non-prime borrowers.[6]

Operational Costs

Figure 7.8 shows a dramatic decline in operational costs of banks between 1996 and 2001. According to regressions in table 7.9, only

Figure 7.7. Risk Spread and Average Intermediation Spread, Brazil, 1995–2000 (percent)

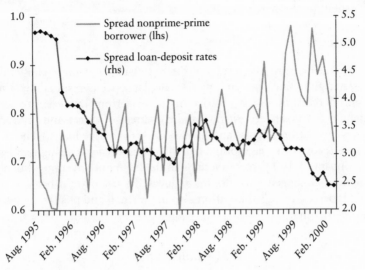

Source: Published interest rates.

Figure 7.8. Operational Costs Relative to Credit, Brazil, 1995–2001 (percent)

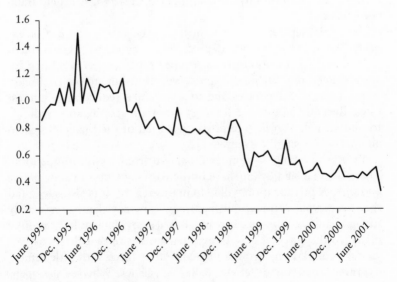

Source: Central Bank of Brazil.

half the decline in operational costs is passed through to a decline in bank spreads. This points to less-than-perfect competition in the Brazilian banking sector.

Net Margin

Table 7.10 reports the results of the regression of commercial bank net margin. Bank net margin is calculated as a residual by the Central Bank of Brazil (2001). (It deducts from interest rates on loans the deposit interest rate and the effect of direct and indirect taxes, operational costs, and provisions for overdue loans.) The coefficient for bank seigniorage has the expected negative sign and is significant. A 100 percent increase in the six-month average of bank seigniorage lagged two months reduces the net margin between 6 and 9 percent. Lagged inflation also has a small and positive impact on the net margin.

Conclusion

Brazil's financial development is still lacking: it has all the basics, but depth and term finance are absent. Term credit in the free segments of the market does not exist because of very high real interest rates and uncertainty linked to a history of high inflation. Recent demonstrations of commitment to low inflation, an important element of the inflation targeting adopted since 1999, will help build confidence.

Domestic deposit rates remain high even in the absence of expected large exchange rate depreciation because high government debt coupled with political uncertainty raises concerns among investors. Persistent fiscal adjustment will contribute to the credibility of macroeconomic policies and to a sustained reduction in interest rates. Recently adopted technology for credit scoring and credit information will also help improve the reach of the financial system and access for small entrepreneurs.

Brazil's banking system can benefit from more competition. There is still a significant share of the banking sector in state hands and further privatization will help in this regard. It is also suggested that promoting competition from new, low-cost banks, especially foreign banks, can reduce spreads. Brazil's government has carefully managed the entry of new foreign banks, aware that their cost advantage could derive from a low-cost labor force with little seniority, rather than any difference in real efficiency. Whereas the opening of the domestic banking sector spelled disaster for local banks in other emerging economies, the major Brazilian banks have increased their market share and margins.

Concentration of the banking sector continued to increase in 2001. To judge from the data, the banks seem to have chosen to earn high profits rather than compete vigorously. Year-end results for 2001 shows that Brazilian banking sector profitability contrasted sharply with the modest results of the vast majority of nonfinancial enterprises. The net profits of the 31 largest banks more than doubled between 2000 and 2001.

The analysis in this chapter suggests that reducing reserve requirements and directed credit could reduce bank spreads and net margin. Yet experience suggests that these measures can succeed only if supported by adequate fiscal policy.

Appendix. Definition of Variables

The *spread between active and passive rates* is defined as the natural logarithm of the ratio between one plus the average interest rate on loans in the segment of free loans and one plus the interest rate on time deposits of 30 days.

Operational costs are defined as the natural logarithm of one plus the ratio of operational costs and the volume of credit (calculated from a sample of 17 large banks, Central Bank of Brazil 2001, annex I).

Provisions for overdue loans are defined as the natural logarithm of one plus the ratio of provisions for overdue loans and the volume of credit (based on a sample of 17 large banks in Central Bank of Brazil 2001, annex I).

Direct taxes are defined as the natural logarithm of one plus the ratio between the burden of the Income Tax and the Pre-Tax Corporate Income (the CSLL) in a 30-day loan financed by a 30-day time deposit based on tax rates and simulations (Central Bank of Brazil 2001, annex I).

Indirect taxes are defined as the natural logarithm of one plus the indirect tax rates. Indirect taxes include the tax on financial operations (IOF), taxes on gross revenues (PIS and COFINS), and the tax on bank debits (CPMF).

Commercial bank seigniorage revenue is defined as the natural logarithm of one plus the ratio of bank seigniorage and the credit of banks to the private sector.

Bank margin is the natural logarithm of one plus the net margin calculated as a residual after deducting from lending rates: the passive rate and the expenses with administration, bad loans, and taxes.

Data and Sources

Interest rates on time deposits are from the Central Bank of Brazil and from the Institute of Applied Economic Research (IPEA) in Rio de Janeiro, Brazil. Consistent interest rates on loans do not exist for the whole period between 1970 and 2001.

For the period between September 1994 and September 2001, the Central Bank of Brazil has published the average of interest rates on different instruments calculated from large samples.

Interest rates on loans between 1990 and 2000 are interest rates on working capital loans from Andima until 1991, from DIESP until 1993, and from the Central Bank between 1994 and 2000.

Interest rates on loans between 1970 and 1980 are interest rates on commercial paper (*ao mutuário*) from the website of Instituto de Pesquisa Econômica Aplicada (IPEA). Data on credit, monetary base, and demand deposits are from the IPEA data bank.

The general price index, IGP-DI, from Fundação Getúlio Vargas, Rio de Janeiro, is also available on the IPEA website.

Notes

1. Courts are inefficient: Dakolias (1999) shows that there are 2,975 cases pending per judge in Brasilia and 3,129 in São Paulo, compared to 58 in Singapore and 244 in Hungary. The time taken to resolve a case (number of cases pending at the start of the year divided by the number of cases resolved during this year) is 1.9 years in Brasilia and 1.6 years in São Paulo, compared to 0.04 years in Singapore and 0.5 years in Germany. Pinheiro and Cabral (1999) estimate that a judicial execution to recover a creditor claim can take between one and ten years. The government is working to improve these conditions. Congress is examining the creation of a Bank Credit Bill (cédula de crédito bancário), a credit instrument that allows the collection of debt under commercial law instead of civil law and thus increases the speed with which a loan claim can be executed. Among measures adopted to reduce costs of financial intermediation, the central bank modernized the payment system and introduced a Credit Risk Data Center. The central bank now makes available on its website standardized information on credit operations, including interest rates for each type of operation, degree of arrears, and average term differentiated by financial institution.

2. In the 20th century, Brazil had eight monetary reforms that removed zeros from the previous currency and changed the name of the currency, as follows: Mil-Réis (1900–42), Cruzeiro (1942–66), Cruzeiro Novo (1967–69), Cruzeiro (1970–86), Cruzado (1986–89), Cruzado Novo (1989–90), Cruzeiro (1990–93), Cruzeiro Real (1993–94), and Real (1994–2000).

3. In early 1990, when inflation reached close to 3,000 percent per year, the Collor Plan of March 1990 drastically cut liquidity. An arbitrary freeze was imposed for 17 months on nearly two-thirds of the money supply (M4), broadly defined to include demand deposits, mutual funds, federal bonds, state and municipal bonds, saving deposits, and private bonds. Although Brazilians eventually managed to circumvent some of these controls, the financial freeze took over personal assets and was wildly unpopular.

4. Because the PROER program had restored bank balance sheets to health, and because many had anticipated the devaluation and positioned themselves to benefit from it through the holding of dollar-denominated government bonds and financial derivatives, the banking system survived the devaluation and did not become a destabilizing factor, as in other countries.

5. Observe that $\Delta DD - \Delta RR \equiv \Delta M1 - \Delta H$: that is, the difference between total seigniorage and the seigniorage collected by the central bank. $\Delta M1$ is total seigniorage: the sum of the increase in currency, ΔC, and ΔDD. ΔH is the seigniorage collected by the central bank: $\Delta C + \Delta RR$. Thus

$$\Delta DD - \Delta RR \equiv \Delta DD + \Delta C - \Delta C + \Delta RR \equiv \Delta M1 - \Delta H$$

In figure 7.6, the ratio between commercial banks seigniorage and loans is $(\Delta M1 - \Delta H)/L$, where $\Delta M1$ is the increase in the monthly average stock of $M1$; ΔH is the increase in the monthly average stock of high powered money; and L is outstanding credit to the private sector, average between current and previous month.

6. Patrick Honohan suggests that the widening spread on non-prime over prime rates could instead reflect changing competitive conditions in banking, with the top firms getting increased access to competitively supplied finance so that banks have to squeeze poorer risks harder to cover their costs.

References

Allen, Linda. 1988. "The Determinants of Bank Interest Margins: A Note." *Journal of Financial and Quantitative Analysis* 23 (2): 231–35.

Angbazo, Lazarus. 1997. "Commercial Bank Net Interest Margins, Default Risk, Interest-rate Risk, and Off-Balance-Sheet Banking." *Journal of Banking and Finance* 21 (1): 55–87.

Beck, Thornsten, Aslı Demirgüç-Kunt, and Ross Levine. 1999. "A New Database on Financial Development and Structure." Policy Research Working Paper 2146. World Bank, Washington, D.C.

Brock, Philip. 1989. "Reserve Requirements and the Inflation Tax." *Journal of Money, Credit and Banking* 21 (1): 106–21.

Brock, Philip, and Liliana Rojas-Suarez. 2000. "Understanding the Behavior of Bank Spreads in Latin America." *Journal of Development Economics* 63 (1): 113–34.

Cardoso, Eliana. 1998. "Virtual Deficits and the Patinkin Effect." *IMF Staff Papers* 45 (4): 619–46.

Carrizosa, Maurício. 2000. *Brazil: Structural Reform for Fiscal Sustainability*. Washington D.C.: World Bank.

Central Bank of Brazil. 2001. *Juros e Spread Bancário no Brasil: Avaliação de Dois Anos do Projeto*. Brasília, DF: Central Bank of Brazil.

Chamley, Christophe, and Patrick Honohan. 1993. "Financial Repression and Bank Intermediation." *Savings and Development* 17 (3): 301–08.

Dakolias, Maria. 1999. *Court Performance Around the World: A Comparative Perspective*. World Bank Technical Paper 430. World Bank, Washington, D.C.

Hanson, James, and Roberto Rezende Rocha. 1986. "High Interest Rates, Spreads, and the Costs of Intermediation." Industry and Finance Series 18. World Bank, Washington, D.C.

Ho, Thomas S., and Anthony Saunders. 1981. "The Determinants of Bank Interest Margins: Theory and Empirical Evidence." *Journal of Financial and Quantitative Analysis* XVI (4): 581–99.

Koyama, Sérgio Mikio, and Márcio I. Nakane. 2001. "Os determinantes do Spread Bancário no Brasil." In Central Bank of Brazil, ed., *Juros e Spread Bancário no Brasil*. Brasília, DF: Central Bank of Brazil.

McKinnon, Ronald, and Donald Mathieson. 1981. "How to Manage a Repressed Economy." *Princeton Essays in International Finance* 145. Princeton University, International Economics Section, Princeton, N.J.

Pinheiro, Armando Castelar, and Célia Cabral. 1999. *Credit Markets in Brazil: The Role of Judicial Enforcement and Other Institutions*. Ensaios BNDES 9. Rio de Janeiro: Banco Nacional de Desenvolvimento.

Wong, Kit Pong. 1997. "On the Determinants of Bank Interest Margins under Credit and Interest Rate Risks." *Journal of Banking and Finance* 21 (2): 251–71.

World Bank. 2001. *Finance for Growth: Policy Choices in a Volatile World*. New York: Oxford University Press.

8

Taxation of Financial Intermediaries as a Source of Budget Revenue: Russia in the 1990s

Brigitte Granville

Control over the instruments of monetary policy, conventionally seen as a means of maintaining price stability, can also be employed as a means of providing implicit subsidies and imposing implicit taxes. The degree to which—and the manner in which—this can happen depends on how the banking system is structured, and on the political and statutory role of the central bank. In turn, the effectiveness of both the banking system and of monetary policy in achieving its conventional goal is strongly affected by the degree to which government spending, tax, and deficit policies are operated through the use of monetary policy instruments, such as the minimum reserve requirement and the interest rate on central bank lending.

Russia provides a dramatic case study of a dysfunctional quasi-fiscal role for finance. Russia began its reform efforts in January 1992 not only with budget and banking systems inherited from the centrally planned economy, but also in the wake of de facto insolvency. After all, in December 1991, the Soviet Vneshekonombank (which had been responsible for the country's external and foreign currency obligations) had defaulted on all its liabilities, including short-term trade debt.

The subsequent decade can be divided into three main periods for the purposes of this study. For most of the 1992–95 period, seigniorage coming from the nominal growth in the monetary base (including required and excess reserves) provided financial support to fiscal and quasi-fiscal expenditures. At the same time, high inflation in 1992–94 allowed taxpayers to exploit time lags between the calculation and payment of tax liabilities. This in turn adversely affected real tax revenues, already depleted by the adverse effects on compliance of the erosion of private income through recession, as well as through inflation itself. The revenue decline increased the fiscal pressure for monetary financing of the budget deficit, given the lack of any alternative.

Seigniorage declined between 1995 and 1997, reflecting efforts to reduce and stabilize inflation. The primary budget deficit was reduced and there was a shift in the financing of the budget deficit away from central bank credits in favor of Treasury bills.[1] In addition, the independence of the Central Bank of Russia (CBR) was increased[2] and the floating exchange rate was replaced in July 1995 with a (crawling) peg regime. Nevertheless, the ratio of domestic debt to GDP and the burden of servicing that debt grew so fast that financing the debt became unsustainable, resulting in the August 1998 default.

Considerable progress has been achieved in the fiscal position since 1998, reducing government recourse to the CBR, as well as to foreign borrowing and other forms of domestic financing. Thanks to high oil prices, the CBR has been able to build up its foreign exchange reserves. The monetary base expanded—now reflecting a growth in real money demand rather than inflation. Thus seigniorage again became an important source of revenue, though it is now being used to ensure external debt servicing capacity, and hence solvency.

The next section describes several features of the system, especially the directed credits of the 1992–95 period and the high bill yields of 1995–98. The banking system benefited from these conditions, at least for a while, though others were taxed, whether through the inflationary consequences of the credit expansion or the collapse of 1998, which was the culmination of the high-yield bill period. The chapter then analyzes the extent and role of two important implicit financial sector taxes: the inflation tax on currency (which fell disproportionately on lower-income households), and unremunerated reserve requirements (which were largely passed through to banking customers in the extremely high banking spreads). The chapter concludes by discussing the persistent lack of depth in the Russian banking system, partly a consequence of the implicit taxes discussed in the previous sections.

The Central Bank and the Banking System

The Soviet State (Central) Bank was formally liquidated on December 25, 1991 and the Central Bank of Russia (CBR)—subsequently called Bank of Russia (BOR)—took over its responsibilities. Until 1994, the CBR remained a passive institution charged with financing a budget deficit that was large but at the same time difficult to measure, due the extent of fiscal and quasi-fiscal expenditures.

At least until 1994, the financing of explicit fiscal expenditures, including the servicing of external debt, accounted for a relatively low proportion of money creation. In contrast, a large proportion was attributable to subsidies or transfers to the enterprise sector: in other words, to quasi-fiscal expenditures.

This is reflected in the balance sheet of the CBR by the fact that the sizeable growth in domestic assets (NDA) was dominated until mid-1993 not by *credits to government* but by *credits to commercial banks*. These credits were designed not only to provide liquidity to banks through the normal refinance mechanism; they also included subsidized credits funded by the budget and the central bank and channelled through commercial banks to state enterprises. Only after mid-1993 did credits to government—that is, explicit monetary financing of the budget deficit—become the main source of domestic asset growth.

Directed Credits

The quasi-fiscal activities of the central bank were financing activities that were not purely monetary in nature.[3] Their typical form was the provision of subsidized credit. The legacy of the central planned economy was visible here in the difficulty of distinguishing between budget and credit financing, with both banks and enterprises being state-owned. Enterprises would receive subsidies either from the government budget or from a bank in the form of subsidized credits. These credits were designated "directed credits" or centralized credits because they originated from the center—whether from the central bank or the government—but were channelled through commercial banks. A Federal Treasury Department was not introduced until 1994 and became operational only in 1998.[4] Meanwhile, budgetary funds were being distributed partly by the CBR and partly by designated commercial banks. Directed credits were used both to provide liquidity to banks and support specific enterprises, sectors, and regions in Russia and in the Former Soviet Republics (FSRs).

One of the reasons that state enterprises had the political weight to obtain credits at subsidized interest rates was that they traditionally undertook a large amount of the social expenditures (housing, kindergartens, medical care, and so on) benefiting their employees, as well as implicit unemployment insurance (Boycko and Shleifer 1994). These credits were directly funded by the CBR and did not appear in the budget. This confusion of fiscal and monetary policy made the system of transfer to enterprises complex and nontransparent.

A principal justification offered for this kind of support to enterprises was the need to keep the level of employment stable. It was difficult to re-deploy workers, not least because of repressive policies preventing workers from moving to where they could gain employment (migration between cities was not allowed without a residence permit). Unemployment was kept at artificially low levels through such "directed" credits and other subsidies. During the period 1992–98, registered unemployment remained between 1.1 and 2.6 percent of the labor force.[5] Even under the more rigorous International Labour Organization (ILO) definition, it varied between 4.8 and 11.9 percent for the same period. Low unemployment figures, however, had their counterpart in a dramatic fall in labor productivity. Indeed, the nonpayment of wages to workers meant that many jobs were in fact fictitious (Commander and Tolstopiatenko 2001). This policy aggravated the shrinking of the tax base. It would have been cheaper—because more effectively directed—to have financed direct provision of welfare benefits to workers.

Directed credits were allocated following requests from enterprises to the Supreme Soviet (or legislature), the government, and even in some cases directly to the CBR.[6] The commercial banks were left as little more than the passive instruments of such decisions, reminiscent of their position under the old command-administrative system. The credits themselves were rarely reimbursed.[7]

As for supplying liquidity to the banks, faster change in the commercial banking system could have been promoted by introducing a straight discount window. Instead, credit auctions were introduced only in February 1994 and even then represented a small share of refinancing to banks. (The first Lombard credit auctions were not until April 1996.)

The Pattern of Credit Outlays in Detail

Central bank credits to enterprises fell into two categories (table 8.1), those channelled through commercial banks, and those that began as credits to the Ministry of Finance but were on-lent to enterprises.

Table 8.1. Central Bank of Russia Credit Allocations, 1992–93

Allocation	1992		1993	
	In Rbn	% of GDP	In Rbn	% of GDP
Total CBR credits[a]	5,703	31.6	24,790	15.3
Budget	1,189	6.6	11,276	6.9
Enterprises	3,608	20.0	11,111	6.8
Via commercial banks	2,804	15.5	8,150	5.0
Agriculture and Roskhleboprodukt	1,300	7.2	3,616	2.2
Energy	400	2.2	193	0.1
Northern Territories	300	1.7	2,134	1.3
Industry	500	2.8	466	0.3
Other	304	1.7	421	0.3
Regions with urgent need	—	—	1,320	0.8
Via Ministry of Finance	804	4.5	2,961	1.8
Working capital	600	3.3	—	—
Investment	105	0.6	700	0.4
Military conversion[b]	77	0.4	—	—
Roskhelboprodukt	22	0.1	1,566	1.0
Other budget loans	—	—	695	0.4
Other republics	906	5.0	2,403	1.5

— Not available.

[a]The ratio of CBR directed credit over the total stock of CBR gross credit to banks amounted to 99 percent in 1992 and in 1993.

[b] In 1993, conversion credits for military-industrial enterprises classified as subsidies in fiscal accounts.

Sources: Based on data from CBR, Ministry of Finance, and IMF (1995, table 35, p. 96).

The credits channelled through commercial banks totalled Rbs 2,804 bn or 15.5 percent of GDP in 1992, and Rbs 8,150 bn or 5 percent of GDP in 1993. They were directed or "centralized" credits in the sense that through its regional branches, the central bank informed the commercial banks (usually former state banks specialized in the sector chosen for the credit) which state enterprises were to receive the credit and at what interest rate. The credits were concentrated on the agriculture[8] and energy sectors. Most of these credits were to compensate for the price controls that stayed in force in those sectors. For instance, bakery enterprises were subsidized for any producer price above Rbs 12/kg. The sizeable energy subsidy represented, broadly speaking, the difference between the value of potential energy exports restricted through quotas and domestic prices of primary energy sources.[9]

The Central Bank's credits directed to enterprises via the Ministry of Finance amounted to Rbs 804 bn or 4.5 percent of GDP in 1992, and 1.8 percent of GDP in 1993. Such credits were allocated off-budget to enterprises. They enabled the Ministry of Finance to borrow a greater amount from the CBR than the ceiling imposed by the Supreme Soviet, since special credit lines had been secured for these operations separate from the overall credit ceiling. These credits included *military conversion* and *working capital* credits.

Military conversion credits were subsidies to the Military-Industrial Complex (MIC) used to maintain employment in a sector that would otherwise have been left crippled by the collapse of state defense procurement orders. Civilian products represented only some 44 percent of the output of the MIC enterprises in 1988. Rbs 77 bn were allocated during 1992.[10]

The origin of working capital credits lay in the central planning system, when enterprises had automatically obtained working capital from the budget. During the second half of 1992, the government faced an increasing number of complaints from firms claiming that they could not borrow from commercial banks, the interest rate being too high (although it was negative in real terms) and the term too short (usually three months or less). The government agreed to extend working capital loans through the central bank. These loans were usually for two years at subsidized interest rates. The sum allocated—Rbs 600 bn—was meant to restore the 1992 real value of working capital.

Scale and Subsidy Element

By the end of 1992, credits to state enterprises allocated either by the Central Bank or by the government amounted to almost 20 percent of GDP; while another 25 percent of GDP had been allocated in explicit subsidies through the budget (table 8.2). Financial transfer to state enterprises thus amounted to 45 percent of GDP in 1992. In 1993 and 1994, directed credits programs were decreased, mostly in the areas of social expenditures and unemployment insurance. Centralized credits were officially ended by a presidential decree (no. 244) in February 1995.

The problem of credits was not confined to their size. They were, in addition, allocated largely at concessional interest rates substan-

Table 8.2. Explicit Subsidies to State Enterprises, Russia, 1992

	Value (Rbn)	% of GDP
Explicit subsidies	4,454	24.7
Agriculture	308	1.7
Coal	180	1.0
Local budgets	585	3.2
Other	30	0.2
Interest rates of which	630	3.5
CBR credits	495	2.7
Government credits	135	0.7
Centralized imports	2,721	15.1

Source: IMF (1993, table A1, p. 139).

tially below the CBR refinance rate (which was already highly negative in real terms), the difference being paid by the federal budget. For instance at the beginning of 1993, agricultural credits were allocated at an annual rate of 25 percent (plus a 3 percent commission for the commercial bank), while the refinance rate stood at an annual 100 percent (as of March 30, 1993). The subsidy covered the 75 percent difference, which was supplied by the federal budget at the end of the fiscal year. Total subsidies on interest rates—whether from the CBR or from the government—amounted to 3.5 percent of GDP in 1992.

Theoretically, the responsibility for these credits and their repayment lay with the commercial banks, which became the distributing intermediaries. The credits were provided for one year, although normal commercial credits were granted for no more than three months. Firms supposedly had an incentive to repay them in order to get more funds. But the negative interest rates effectively meant that directed credits amounted to grants. And no action at least until the end of 1994 was taken against a bank or a firm that failed to reimburse such a loan. Banks for their part showed no reluctance to handle such credits, especially because banks usually did not immediately channel the money to the earmarked firm.[11] On October 1, 1993, subsidized credits were cancelled.

Rouble Zone

Another important counterpart to the expansion of the monetary base during 1992 and 1993 was *credits to Former Soviet Republics*. The CBR provided both non-cash and cash credits to these countries of the "near-abroad" to allow their enterprises to continue trading with Russian enterprises. The credits financed these countries' imports from Russia and thus had much the same effect as direct subsidies to Russian industries. The main difference was that with pure subsidies, the products might not even have been sold but instead might simply have piled up at the factory.

The Rouble zone was especially costly in 1992. Central bank credits to the Former Soviet Republics alone reached 8.5 percent of Russian GDP if delivery of cash is excluded, and 11.6 percent if cash is included (Granville 1997). At the same time, the FSRs' own central banks were themselves able to issue rouble credits to be spent in Russia, thus further contributing to the growth of Russia's money supply and inflation.

In 1992–93, conflict between President Boris Yeltsin and the Supreme Soviet was reflected in conflicting policy stances of the Ministry of Finance and the central bank on the question of resolving the rouble zone issue. The Executive wanted to end the Rouble zone, a policy opposed by the central bank, which was constitutionally subordinate to, and politically protected by, the Supreme Soviet. While the Ministry of Finance managed in July 1992 to regulate the expansion of non-cash credit, cash transfers remained beyond its control. The CBR exploited the failure to bring cash transfers under Ministry of Finance control by making transfers in cash, in the form of pre-1993 banknotes: that is, without the Russian flag. This loophole was stopped abruptly in July 1993 with the removal from circulation in Russia of the pre-1993 roubles, an action that precipitated the collapse of the Rouble zone.

The Market for Government Bills

If banks benefited from their role as passive intermediaries in the process of directed credits, they profited even more—at least for a time—from treasury operations in foreign exchange and government bills.

Whereas private banks actively speculated in foreign exchange gains during the earlier phase from 1992 to 1995, they changed their strategy after the floating exchange rate was replaced with a (crawling) peg regime in July 1995. From 1995 to 1998 they switched their holdings from foreign exchange to rouble Treasury bills (GKOs), the market for which had been introduced in May 1993. Central bank data show that income on GKOs accounted for 41 percent of the earnings of the top 100 banks as of September 1997. Thanks to the high yield on GKOs, Sberbank (Russia's oldest bank), with about 35 percent of the market, returned pre-tax profits of $US2 billion in

1996. Since around two-thirds of Sberbank's liabilities consisted of household deposits, Sberbank acted as a conduit for channelling housing liquid assets into government debt. In contrast to Sberbank, the large commercial banks relied for their build-up of GKO holdings on the profitability of GKOs themselves and on various forms of foreign borrowing. The balance sheet position that resulted was a mirror image of that which had prevailed in the period up to mid-1995; instead of large foreign currency holdings matched by rouble liabilities, there were now GKO holdings matched by foreign currency liabilities.[12]

During this period, the majority of banks derived their profitability from the spread between deposit rates and government bond yields. In other words, instead of being taxed, banks were subsidized and protected by the CBR policy by artificially maintaining high yields on GKOs. This policy had several elements. First access to foreigners was restricted until 1996; then foreign investors were forced under the terms of the "S-account" system to purchase dollars forward at artificial prices in order to cap the covered GKO yields.[13] De facto full liberalization came only months before the default, in January 1998.

In August 1996, foreign investors were allowed to enter the market by opening a specially created new category of accounts, known as "S" accounts, in authorized Russian banks. The bank would then transfer the funds to its account at the Moscow Interbank Currency Exchange (MICEX), where it would buy and sell GKOs according to its foreign client's instructions. Foreigners investing in the GKO-OFZ market (OFZ were Treasury bonds) through "S" accounts could thus trade freely in the secondary market. To prevent rapid outflows of foreign money, however, the central bank required foreign investors to tie up their investment for three months before repatriating their returns. At the beginning of this three-month period, foreigners had to enter a forward contract with CBR, with the rouble/dollar exchange rate being artificially set to ensure a fixed dollar return of 15 percent.[14] Such a massive transfer to the banks was economically harmful across the board, not least to the fiscal position and the sound development of the Russian banking system itself.

Forms of Taxation

The private sector (households, enterprises, and banks) suffers from inflation because of the heightened costs attached to holding non–interest-bearing monetary assets, specifically currency and bank reserves. Currency is mainly held by households, while other central bank liabilities are held by the banking industry in the form of required reserves.

Inflation Tax on Currency

In terms of its distributional effect, inflation is clearly regressive. This is not only because of the limited ability of pensioners and low-wage earners to shelter their income against inflation, but also because access in practice to foreign currencies or other inflation-proof assets is generally restricted to higher-income groups and more mobile groups. The wealthiest sections of the population have easier access to income-bearing, indexed, or otherwise protected assets. In Russia although the minimum sum required to open a deposit account at the saving bank Sberbank[15] was, until October 1, 1993, just 10 roubles—and as such, a small barrier to this form of saving—this minimum was increased in dramatic steps; by August 1995, it was 300,000 Rbs—equivalent to more than half the then-prevailing monthly average wage rate. By effectively precluding deposits by small savers, this increased the regressivity of the inflation tax.[16]

Tables 8.3 and 8.4 present some data on the inflation tax on currency (C) and bank reserves. Seigniorage on currency is measured as a flow (ΔC). Seigniorage has been divided into an inflation component measured on a stock basis ($\pi_t MB_t$) and a residual reflecting changes in velocity of currency. In both cases, revenue from the inflation tax on currency was initially very important, but declined steeply over the period. From table 8.4 it can be seen that seigniorage from bank reserves was at a higher level during the more inflationary quarters: for instance, from 1994Q I to 1995QII, 1998QIV to 1999QII, and 2000QI to 2000QIII.

Minimum Reserve Requirements

From the beginning of 1992 minimum reserve requirements were increased sharply: from 2 to 15 percent on short-time deposits (term less than one year) and 10 percent on long-term deposits. In April 1992 the requirements were further raised to 20 percent and 15 percent for short-term and long-term deposits, respectively.[17] They stayed at this high level until May 1996, when they were decreased to 18 percent and 14 percent, respectively (table 8.5).

Note, however that these rather high ratios were not achieved in practice. The actual requirement in practice worked out at a much lower proportion of deposits. Thus minimum required bank reserves as reported by the BOR at the end of December 1992 amounted to no more than 11 percent of total deposits reported for the same date,

Table 8.3. Seigniorage on Currency, Russia, 1993–2001 (percent)

Year and quarter	Inflation consumer prices (1)	Seigniorage from currency % GDP (2)	Inflation component from currency %GDP (3)	Residual component % GDP (4) = (2) – (3)	Currency %GDP (5)
93 IV	68.9	—	—	—	13.4
94 I	46.6	5.0	8.0	–3.1	17.2
94 II	25.2	. 5.8	4.4	1.4	17.4
94 III	18.5	3.2	3.1	0.1	16.7
94 IV	42.3	2.9	6.5	–3.6	15.3
95 I	50.0	–0.7	6.4	–7.1	12.7
95 II	27.6	5.5	4.0	1.5	14.6
95 III	17.8	2.7	2.5	0.3	13.8
95 IV	13.8	2.8	2.1	0.8	14.9
96 I	10.9	1.3	2.0	–0.8	18.7
96 II	6.4	3.5	1.3	2.1	20.4
96 III	2.1	–1.6	0.3	–1.9	16.2
96 IV	3.1	1.3	0.5	0.8	15.1
97 I	4.9	0.2	0.9	–0.7	17.4
97 II	4.0	5.2	0.9	4.3	21.8
97 III	1.8	–0.3	0.3	–0.7	19.2
97 IV	0.6	–0.6	0.1	–0.7	17.6
98 I	3.2	–1.5	0.7	–2.2	21.1
98 II	1.5	1.9	0.3	1.6	20.5
98 III	16.1	3.9	3.6	0.3	22.1
98 IV	39.9	4.8	8.8	–4.0	22.2
99 I	22.9	–1.6	4.6	–6.2	20.1
99 II	8.6	4.9	1.7	3.2	19.5
99 III	6.2	–0.3	1.0	–1.8	15.7
99 IV	4.0	4.0	0.8	3.2	18.7
00 I	4.5	–1.1	0.8	–1.8	17.2
00 II	3.7	4.8	0.7	4.1	19.6
00 III	5.3	1.8	0.9	0.9	17.5
00 IV	4.9	3.4	1.1	2.4	21.4
01 I	6.7	–1.0	1.4	–2.4	21.2
01 II	5.6	4.0	1.3	2.7	22.5

—Not available.

Source: Calculated from IMF, *International Financial Statistics,* March 1998 and January 2002.

as compared with the 17.5 percent average of nominal required ratios. There is no one obvious explanation for the difference between minimum percentage reserve requirements imposed by law and the actual minimum reserves held by banks. Various hypotheses may be advanced.

Table 8.4. Seigniorage on Bank Reserves, Russia, 1993–2001 (percent)

Year and quarter	Inflation consumer prices % per year	Bank reserves as % deposits	Seigniorage from bank reserves as % GDP	Seigniorage from bank reserves as % government revenue
93 IV	68.9	71.1	n.a.	n.a.
94 I	46.6	60.1	0.9	n.a.
94 II	25.2	51.5	2.7	20.3
94 III	18.5	60.5	5.1	44.7
94 IV	42.3	49.8	1.2	8.7
95 I	50.0	49.9	2.9	21.3
95 II	27.6	46.4	3.1	22.7
95 III	17.8	39.3	−0.6	−3.9
95 IV	13.8	35.3	0.9	6.8
96 I	10.9	35.2	1.1	9.9
96 II	6.4	33.4	0.0	−0.2
96 III	2.1	35.3	1.4	11.4
96 IV	3.1	33.9	0.2	1.1
97 I	4.9	33.7	0.8	10.1
97 II	4.0	32.7	0.4	3.4
97 III	1.8	28.5	−0.8	−6.8
97 IV	0.6	33.6	2.2	13.1
98 I	3.2	29.7	−1.3	−16.0
98 II	1.5	27.3	−1.1	−9.2
98 III	16.1	27.6	−1.5	−14.9
98 IV	39.9	31.3	3.0	19.7
99 I	22.9	41.3	4.6	44.3
99 II	8.6	44.8	3.6	22.9
99 III	6.2	42.3	0.4	3.1
99 IV	4.0	41.6	1.6	9.8
00 I	4.5	50.1	4.7	29.9
00 II	3.7	51.3	2.8	14.6
00 III	5.3	52.0	2.4	14.2
00 IV	4.9	45.6	0.0	0.1
01 I	6.7	41.5	−0.9	−5.4
01 II	5.6	37.3	−0.2	−1.0
01 III	2.3	35.6	—	—

n.a. Not applicable.
— Not available.
Source: Calculated from IMF, *International Financial Statistics,* March 1998 and January 2002.

A first hypothesis is that the method of calculating minimum reserve requirements permitted a certain amount of manipulation. Banks were allowed to choose the deposit base on which reserve requirements were calculated. Two different methods were available: the average of the balances at the end of consecutive five-day periods

Table 8.5. Minimum Reserve Requirements, Russia, 1995–98 (percent)

Dates in effect:	Less than 1 month[a]	Type of account 1–3 months[b]	Over 3 months[c]	FX[d]	Sberbank individual accounts[e]
Feb. 1–April 30, 1995	22	15	10	2	—
May 1, 1995–April 30, 1996	20	14	10	1.5	—
May 1–June 10, 1996	18	14	10	1.25	—
June 11–July 31, 1996	20	16	12	2.5	—
Aug. 1–Oct. 30, 1996	18	14	10	2.5	—
Nov. 1, 1996–April 30, 1997	16	13	10	5	10
May 1–Nov. 11, 1997	14	11	8	6	9.5
Nov. 12, 1997–Nov. 30, 1998	14	11	8	9	9.5
Dec. 1, 1997–Jan. 31, 1998	14	11	8	9	8
Feb. 1–Aug. 23, 1998	11	—	—	—	8
Aug. 24–Aug. 31, 1998	10	—	—	—	7

— Not available.
[a]Demand accounts and fixed-term liabilities with terms of 30 days and less.
[b]Fixed-term liabilities falling due from 31 days to 90 days.
[c]Fixed-term liabilities falling due from 91 days and more.
[d]Foreign currency accounts.
[e]Individuals' rouble accounts regardless of term (Sberbank).
Source: Central Bank of Russia.

each month; and the average on daily balances for all days in the month. In addition, all banks were required to provide deposit balances on the first day of the month. Provision of deposit balances relating to the sixteenth day of the month was optional. This method allows for two or more banks to collude in shifting deposits in order to obtain a more favorable (lower) reserve requirement.[18] The fact that the calculation took place only once a month gave added opportunity for collusion between banks. This method of calculation was eventually changed in 1995.

A second hypothesis is that banks may have been exempted from reserving against an amount of deposits equal to total centralized credits, which would have reduced the reserve requirement by between one third and one half.

There was a return to the use of high reserve requirements in the immediate aftermath of the August 1998 crisis. The BOR relied again on an increase in (unremunerated) reserve requirements, though this time the intention was mainly to control liquidity, using increased non–interest-bearing reserve requirements to keep control over reserve money and therefore pass the cost of sterilization to commercial banks. From late 1998, reserve requirements were raised on four occasions from 5 percent (for both rouble and foreign currency deposits) to 10 percent on foreign currency deposits and corporate rouble deposits and to 7 percent on household rouble deposits. In 1999, commercial banks' holdings of (unremunerated) free reserves at the CBR increased to the equivalent of more than 10 percent of rouble broad money, well above their pre-1998 crisis level. This increase reflected the fact that the collapse of the GKO market had deprived banks of alternative liquid instruments and that the interbank market remained dormant, as well as the reluctance among banks to increase credits to the economy.[19]

This policy has allowed the BOR to build up external reserves as inflows increased on the back of the upswing in the commodity price cycle.

Excess Reserves

In addition to the required reserves, Russian depositories also hold substantial excess reserves (also non–interest-bearing): that is, reserves above the amount actually reported as minimum reserve requirements. This is especially surprising given that excess reserves are deposited by commercial banks at the central bank on a non–interest-bearing account; they are voluntary and can be withdrawn at any time. The scale of excess reserves is interpreted as being in part due to the inefficiency of the inter-bank payment system effected through the CBR inter-branch clearing system.

The high level of excess reserves in either nominal or real terms through 1992 and 1993 created a risk of a new acceleration of the money supply, even in the absence of increased credits. In August 1993, for example, compulsory reserves (that is, minimum reserve requirements) stood at Rbs 1,615.1 billion, while funds held in CBR correspondent accounts (that is, excess reserves) amounted to Rbs 4,407 billion. If all the banks with excess reserves had decided to use them at the same time to expand credit, the money supply could have increased by four times.

Impact of Financial Intermediary Taxation

The inflation tax resulting from the consequent increase in the rouble money base has been largely paid by bank depositors. Lately, the abundant rouble liquidity has enabled the government to maintain highly negative real yields on its domestic debt. This, along with the structural distortions caused by tax evasion already mentioned, continues to inhibit the expansion of the long-term deposit base—which, in turn, would enable the banks to reorient their balance sheets to the real sector, thereby evading this latest incidence of the inflation tax.

The Burden of High Reserve Requirements

Raising the rate of required reserves on deposits is a tempting policy tool. By increasing the monetary base and thereby counterbalancing a decrease in the money multiplier, the result is higher government revenues. These additional revenues are ultimately financed by depositors and investors.

The borrowers and depositors pay for the extra expenditure of the budget financed this way. The cost for the economy is the distortion in the level and structure of real interest rates (that is, high real interest rates on borrowers and low or negative real interest rates on depositors).

Table 8.6 presents the actual nominal interest rates on loans and deposits. High reserve requirements impose a tax on bank intermediation in the absence of reserve remuneration at market rates. This tax results in a widening of the spread between lending and deposit rates. While real lending rates were quite high, real deposit rates were negative until the fourth quarter of 1995 and again after August 1998.

Table 8.6. Nominal Interest Rates on Loans and Deposits, Russia, 1994–2001 (percent per year)

Year and quarter	Deposit rate (id)	Lending rate (il)	Spread	Annualized inflation rate	Real deposit rate (rd)	Real lending rate (rl)
94 III	181.3	301.6	120.3	97.05	84.25	204.55
94 IV	125.2	297.3	172.1	309.92	–184.72	–12.62
95 I	142.9	416.3	273.4	406.52	–263.62	9.78
95 II	122.4	378.5	256.1	165.26	–42.86	213.24
95 III	72.9	251.1	178.2	92.83	–19.93	158.27
95 IV	69.6	231.9	162.3	67.60	2.00	164.30
96 I	61.7	187.8	126.1	51.10	10.60	136.70
96 II	55.4	176.4	121	28.26	27.14	148.14
96 III	60.1	142.8	82.7	8.84	51.26	133.96
96 IV	43	80.2	37.2	12.94	30.06	67.26
97 I	29.1	63.9	34.8	21.13	7.97	42.77
97 II	18.2	48.6	30.4	17.12	1.08	31.48
97 III	11	38.4	27.4	7.40	3.60	31.00
97 IV	7.4	33.8	26.4	2.58	4.82	31.22
98 I	11.7	32.8	21.1	13.30	–1.60	19.50
98 II	12.6	42.4	29.8	6.14	6.46	36.26
98 III	18.8	46.8	28	81.94	–63.14	–35.14
98 IV	25.1	45.2	20.1	282.52	–257.42	–237.32
99 I	22	45.1	23.1	128.14	–106.14	–83.04
99 II	13.4	39.8	26.4	38.94	–25.54	0.86
99 III	10.4	38.4	28	27.20	–16.80	11.20
99 IV	9	35.5	26.5	17.03	–8.03	18.47
00 I	9.6	31.7	22.1	19.43	–9.83	12.27
00 II	6.6	25.9	19.3	15.69	–9.09	10.21
00 III	5.4	21.4	16	22.76	–17.36	–1.36
00 IV	4.4	18.8	14.4	21.27	–16.87	–2.47
01 I	4.4	18.8	14.4	29.57	–25.17	–10.77
01 II	4.8	17.9	13.1	24.31	–19.51	–6.41
01 III	5.0	18.0	13.0	9.61	–4.61	8.39

Source: Calculated from IMF, *International Financial Statistics,* March 1998 and January 2002.

The Lack of Monetary Depth: A Problem of Trust

A long-term consequence of the erosion of savings through the inflation tax (especially the destruction of real savings balances in the Sberbank during the inflationary burst of 1990–92) and the wide intermediation spreads is the failure of the banking system to grow (table 8.7). The abrupt destruction of savings in August 1998 added to the malaise by creating a widespread popular distrust of private banks after the events of August 1998. Adding this to the state's

Table 8.7. Deposits in the Banking System, Russia, 1993–2000 (percent of GDP)

	Demand deposits	Time and saving deposits	Foreign currency deposits	Total deposits
1993	7.3	2.9	7.0	17.3
1994	5.3	3.9	6.1	15.4
1995	4.5	4.5	3.6	12.6
1996	4.1	4.4	3.2	11.8
1997	6.6	3.2	3.2	13.0
1998	5.5	3.5	7.1	16.1
1999	5.5	3.7	6.4	15.5
2000	6.3	3.7	5.9	15.9

Source: Calculated from IMF, *International Financial Statistics,* March 1998 and January 2002.

long track record of monetary confiscation through inflation and (in recent years) by successive devaluations of the rouble, it is easy to explain why Russian citizens prefer to save in foreign currency (in practice, U.S. dollars) rather than roubles. It does not fully explain the weak deposit base, however. Foreign currency deposit accounts have been legal since 1992. Sberbank deposits carry an implicit state guarantee, which was honored in practice after the financial crash of August 1998. It should follow that a large volume of U.S. dollar savings should be kept in the Sberbank.[20] Instead, such savings amount to only 6 percent of GDP, with at least a further 15 percent of GDP kept in the form of cash U.S. dollar savings at home.

The reason for this is that the distrust of the state extends to fear of state expropriation of wealth, given that virtually all personal wealth has been accumulated without full payment of tax, and so is vulnerable. Russian households therefore prefer to hide cash dollars under the mattress rather than place them in a bank deposit account where they might be discovered by law enforcement officials.

With the personal tax reform (including a low 13 percent flat rate of personal income tax) in force from January 2001, the state aims to encourage households and businesses to abandon the gray economy. With time, it is hoped that people will obtain a track record of legality and gradually become inclined to place their savings in deposit accounts.

Turning to the assets side of the banking system's balance sheet, long-term lending to enterprises is constrained by the weak deposit base. Lending to the private sector was about 9 percent of GDP in 1997 and 12 percent in 2000. Twenty-five percent of total banking system credit to the banking sector is accounted by Sberbank. Only about 4 percent of private sector investment is financed by domestic borrowing, while 63 percent is financed by the enterprise's own funds. But the absence of intermediation also stems from structural failings that extend beyond those of the banking system itself. Chief among these is the lack of functioning commercial land and housing markets. As a result, firms and households have been deprived of the most obvious source of collateral for borrowing. Just as tax reform is a key to restoring a normal deposit base, so another key structural reform can help solve this problem of collateral: namely, land reform. Important steps were taken in 2001 with the adoption of the Land Code (signed into law on November 8, 2001), and then in 2002, when a separate law on agricultural land was adopted by the federal parliament. This code gives enterprises the right to buy freehold title to the land on which they sit, and it defines a reasonable price scale to prevent the exercise of this right falling victim to predatory local officialdom.

Notes

1. 1995 Federal Budget Law.
2. The "Central Bank Law" enacted in April 1995.
3. This section draws on materials contained in Granville (1995).
4. Diamond (2002, pp. 12–13).
5. The Russian definition excludes all job seekers who have an alternative income, such as students and pensioners.
6. Freinkman (1994, p. 7) reports that "the CBR itself initiated special subsidized directed credit programs in 1992 (about 30 percent of total CBR directed credits), which were targeted at expanding working capital of enterprises and reducing the burden of the arrears crisis."
7. According to *The Wall Street Journal Europe* (June 6, 1991), "In 1990, the Soviet government wrote off Rbs 93 bn of bad loans to the agricultural sector alone."
8. Amelina, Galbi, and Uspenskii (1993) show that the volume of grain credits from the CBR in 1992 was equivalent to about Rbs 620 bn or 3.4 percent of GDP, which was about half the credits issued to the agricultural sector in 1992.
9. World Bank and International Monetary Fund (1993, p. 7).
10. Gavrilenkov and Koen (1995, p. 11).
11. Freinkman (1994, p. 10) reports that "Three groups of banks are participating in such programs: a/former state specialised banks (Promstroi and Rosselkhoz) are main channel banks for a wide set of enterprises. b/sectoral banks (e.g Neftekhim, Gasstroi, Electro, etc.) founded by enterprises in particular subsectors of industry and being under the control of enterprise associations and concerns, which emerged in place of former line ministries. c/some new commercial banks founded by truly private sector (e.g.

Menatep), which established strong links to the government and are the most successful in extracting various privileges."

12. See Dmitriev and others (2001).

13. See Willer (2001, pp. 239–260).

14. See Granville (2001, pp. 93–130).

15. The Sberbank is the oldest bank in Russia, founded in 1842. It survived the 1917 Revolution by virtue of five years' dormancy, which were followed by resuscitation in 1922 as a national savings institution for the masses. Following passage of the Russian law on banks and banking activities of December 2, 1990, the Sberbank became a joint stock commercial bank on March 22, 1991, registering its license on June 20, 1991. It has the advantage of having inherited an immense geographic coverage in terms of a national branch network. The Sberbank's broad geographical coverage and visibility meant that it enjoyed a degree of trust among ordinary people, far greater than any of the more modern commercial banks.

16. See Granville and Shapiro (1996).

17. In May 1995, minimum reserve requirements were changed as follows: on deposits up to 30 days, 20 percent; between 30 and 90 days, 14 percent; over 90 days, 10 percent.

18. International Monetary Fund (1995, p. 202).

19. International Monetary Fund (2000, p. 13).

20. A draft law on compulsory insurance of household deposits in private banks is under consideration at the time of writing, to supplement the implicit guarantee of deposits in the CBR-owned Sberbank (which helps explain why about 85 percent of household deposits are held in Sberbank). The proposed law would endow a government deposit insurance agency with an initial Rbs 6.5 billion transfer from the government, to be supplemented with contributions from the banks at a rate of 0.15 percent of their deposits. Deposits would be insured up to a ceiling.

References

Amelina, Maria, Douglas Galbi, and A. Uspenskii. 1993. *The Distribution of Central Bank Credits for Grain Procurements.* Macro and Financial Unit (MFU), Moscow.

Boycko, Maxim, and Andrei Shleifer. 1994. "The Russian Restructuring and Social Assets." Paper presented at the conference on Russian Economic Reforms in Jeopardy, Stockholm School of Economics, June 15–16, Stockholm School of Economics, Stockholm, Sweden.

Commander, Simon, and Andrei Tolstopiatenko. 2001. "The Labour Market." In Brigitte Granville and Peter Oppenheimer, eds., *Russia's Post-Communist Economy.* Oxford: Oxford University Press.

Diamond, Jack. 2002. "Budget System Reform in Transitional Economies: The Experience of Russia." IMF Working Paper WP/02/22. International Monetary Fund, Washington, D.C.

Dmitriev Mikhail, Mikhail Matovnikov, Leonid Mikhailov, Ludmilla Sycheva, and Eugene Timofeyev. 2001. "The Banking Sector." In Brigitte Granville and Peter Oppenheimer, eds., *Russia's Post-Communist Economy*. Oxford: Oxford University Press.

European Bank for Reconstruction and Development (EBRD). 1997. "Transition Report." European Bank for Reconstruction and Development, London.

Freinkman, Lev. 1994. "Government Financial Transfers to the Enterprise Sector in Russia: General Trends and Influence on Country Macroeconomic Performance." World Bank, Washington, D.C. Processed.

Gavrilenkov, Evgeny, and Vincent Koen. 1995. "How Large was the Output Collapse in Russia? Alternative Estimates and Welfare Implications." In *Staff Studies for the World Economic Outlook*, Washington, D.C., International Monetary Fund.

Granville, Brigitte. 1995. *The Success of Russian Economic Reforms*. London and Washington, D.C.: Royal Institute of International Affairs, International Economic Programme. Distributed by the Brookings Institution.

———. 1997. "Farewell, Rouble Zone." In Anders Åslund, ed., *Russia's Economic Transformation in the 1990s*. London: Pinter.

———. 2001. "The Problem of Monetary Stabilization." In Brigitte Granville and Peter Oppenheimer, eds., *Russia's Post-Communist Economy*. Oxford: Oxford University Press.

Granville, Brigitte, and Judith Shapiro. 1996. *Less Inflation, Less Poverty, First Results for Russia*. Discussion Paper 68. International Economics Programme, The Royal Institute of International Affairs, London.

Granville, Christopher. 2001. "The Political and Societal Environment of Economic Policy." In Brigitte Granville and Peter Oppenheimer, eds., *Russia's Post-Communist Economy*. Oxford: Oxford University Press.

International Monetary Fund. 1993. *World Economic Outlook*. Washington, D.C.

———. 1995. *Russian Federation. IMF Economic Review* 16. Washington, D.C.

———. 2000. *Russian Federation: Staff Report for the 2000 Article IV Consultation and Public Information Notice Following Consultation*. Washington, D.C.

Willer, Dirk. 2001. "Financial Markets." In Brigitte Granville and Peter Oppenheimer, eds., *Russia's Post-Communist Economy*. Oxford: Oxford University Press.

World Bank and International Monetary Fund. 1993. *Subsidies and Directed Credits to Enterprises in Russia: A Strategy for Reform*. Washington, D.C.

Part III

Particular
Taxes

9

Corporate Income Tax Treatment of Loan-Loss Reserves

Emil M. Sunley

The tax treatment of bank loan-losses has been a contentious issue in a number of developing and transition countries. Banks and bank regulators generally want the tax rules for recognizing loan-losses to conform closely to regulatory accounting in order to encourage banks not to under-provision for loan-losses and to ensure a current tax benefit from loss provisioning. Tax officials often are wary of regulatory accounting, and fear that accepting it for tax purposes will significantly reduce income taxes paid by banks.

The treatment of loan-losses is the central tax policy issue relating to the taxation of banks, given the importance of loans in bank assets and the cost of bad debts. In the United States, for example, loans and leases represented 60 percent of bank assets in 2000, and loan-loss provisioning represented 21 percent of net income before taxes and provisioning (Bassett and Zakrajšek 2001). In many developing and transition economies, loan-losses are an even larger share of net income before taxes and loss provisioning.

This chapter addresses primarily *when* and *how* loan-losses should be recognized as an allowable expense for tax purposes. To address these issues, financial and regulatory accounting of loan-losses first must be considered.

Financial and Regulatory Accounting for Loan-Losses

Loan-losses are an inevitable cost that banks incur in order to earn income, and these losses should be recognized as an expense for both financial and tax purposes.[1] For financial accounting, loans are recorded at their face value until they become fully worthless and are written off. However, a provision or reserve account is established for potential losses *present* in the portfolio of loans. On a bank's financial statement, the value of loans is often shown on a net basis (that is, the face value of the loans corrected by the estimated loss). In particular, International Accounting Standard IAS 30 (IAS 30 2002) provides that:

> The amount of losses which have been specifically identified is recognized as an expense and deducted from the carrying amount of the appropriate category of loans and advances as a provision for losses on loans and advances. The amount of potential losses not specifically identified but which experience indicates are present in the portfolio of loans and advances is also recognized as an expense and deducted from the total carrying amount of loans and advances as a provision for losses on loans and advances.

Thus IAS 30 recognizes both *specific* and *general* reserves.[2] Specific reserves are linked to specific loans and the amount of reserve required usually depends on the length of time that payments of interest and principal have been past due, the value of any pledged collateral, and the financial soundness of the borrower. The general reserve is not linked to specific loans but reflects losses that experience indicates are *present* in the portfolio of loans but not yet specifically identified. Any amounts set aside for *future* losses should be accounted for as appropriations of retained earnings: that is, not recognized as a current expense.[3]

Regulatory accounting for bank loan-losses is very similar to financial accounting required by IAS 30.[4] The Basel Committee on Banking Supervision has outlined sound practices for loan accounting and disclosure (Basel Committee 1999). In particular,

> A bank should identify and recognize impairment in a loan or a collectively assessed group of loans when it is probable that the bank will not be able to collect, or there is no longer reasonable assurance that the bank will collect, all amounts due according to the contractual terms of the loan agreement. The impairment should be recognized by reducing the carrying amount of the loan(s) through an allowance or charge-off and

charging the income statement in the period in which the impairment occurs.

A bank should measure an impaired loan at its estimated recoverable amount.

The aggregate amount of specific and general allowances should be adequate to absorb estimated credit losses associated with the loan portfolio.

Like IAS 30, the Basel Committee recognizes both specific and general reserves. The general reserve is to cover *latent* losses, which are not yet identified but which are known to exist. The general reserve is not supposed to cover future losses.[5]

The assessment of both specific and general reserves "should be performed in a systematic way, in a consistent manner over time, in conformity with objective criteria and be supported by adequate documentation" (Basel Committee 1999). That said, the setting of the appropriate level of allowances "necessarily includes a degree of subjectivity" (Basel Committee 1999).

The additions to specific and general reserves both reduce reported profits. However, they are often accounted for differently on the balance sheet. In Slovenia, for example, the required provision for impaired loans is accounted for on the active side of the balance sheet as an adjustment for doubtful accounts; the provision for performing loans is accounted for on the passive side of the balance sheet as part of "other long-term liabilities." Moreover, general reserves for performing loans are often counted as part of bank capital, generally tier II capital (discussed further below), as these reserves are not "pledged" to cover specific loans that are already impaired.

The bank regulatory agency in many countries specifies a scheme for classifying loans and setting minimum reserves. The guidelines for the various loan categories—for example, special mention, substandard, or doubtful—are often set in terms of past due payments. More forward-looking criteria to reflect expected probability of default (such as the creditworthiness of the borrower) are still uncommon (Laurin and Majnoni 2003).

For example, in broad outline, Turkey requires specific provision of:

- 20 percent of loans with limited potential to be recovered or 90 days in arrears
- 50 percent of loans unlikely to be recovered or 180 days in arrears
- 100 percent of loans deemed irrecoverable or with arrears over one year.

These required provisions are reduced to the extent that doubt-ful or bad debts are covered by guarantees or collateral. The amount of this reduction varies according to the quality of the guar-antee or collateral. In addition, there must be a general provision of 0.5 percent of cash loans and 0.1 percent of contingent liabilities.

The Central Bank of the Philippines requires specific reserves ranging from 5 to 100 percent:

- 5 percent for "loans especially mentioned" (loans that have potential weakness—past due for 30 to 90 days)
- 25 percent for "substandard loans that are unsecured" (loans that involve a substantial and unreasonable degree of risk to the in-stitution because of unfavorable record or unsatisfactory character-istics—past due more than 90 days)
- 50 percent for "doubtful loans" (loans that have the weakness inherent in substandard loans, with the added characteristics that the existing facts, conditions, and values make collection or liqui-dation in full highly improbable and in which substantial loss is probable)
- 100 percent for "loss" loans (loans considered uncollectible and worthless, and that are past due for a period of at least six months).

In addition to the specific reserve, the Central Bank of the Philip-pines requires a general reserve equal to 2 percent of a bank's un-classified loan portfolio.

The rationale for reserve accounting is straightforward. In a port-folio of loans, certain loans are non-performing[6] or otherwise im-paired. Some of these loans will ultimately be uncollectible. If, based on past experience, 25 percent of the loans past due for 6 to 12 months are likely to be uncollectible, a reserve should be established for loan-losses equal to 25 percent of the amount of these loans. These losses are already present in the portfolio of loans past due for 6 to 12 months and should be recognized as an expense for this period, even though it is not possible at this time to identify just which loans will ultimately be worthless.

The reserve for loan-losses is not for *future* losses (that is, losses not yet present or latent in the portfolio of loans).[7] While banks and other companies need to maintain sufficient equity capital to cover unantic-ipated future losses, additions to the company's equity should not be treated as a current expense (for either financial or tax purposes).

Under a normal reserve method, regardless of how the actual re-serve is calculated, any recoveries for loan-losses are credited to the reserve, and any loans charged off the books are debited to the re-serve. The expense item for loan-losses for any year is equal to the amount necessary to bring the reserve up to the end-of-year level, after the beginning-of-year reserve has been adjusted for recoveries and charge-offs. The expense item is computed as follows:

	Reserve at end of year[8]
Less:	Reserve at beginning of year[9]
Plus:	Loans written off
Less:	Actual recoveries for loan-losses previously written off
Equals:	Expense item for loan-losses

Determining the expense for loan-losses based on a reserve method appears to provide a double deduction for losses. Each loss, however, reduces profits only once. There is no double deduction because the actual charge-off is debited against the reserve,[10] and once a loan is charged off, there would be no end-of-year reserve with respect to that loan.[11] The end-of-year reserve relates only to loans outstanding on the bank's books at the end of the year.

There is a closely related issue to the treatment of loan-losses: the treatment of unpaid interest. Most banks, at least large banks, are on the accrual method of accounting[12] and thus accrue interest income on loans as the claim arises and not when the income is received. The Basel Committee recommends that a bank should cease accruing interest when a loan is identified as being impaired. For countries that use a loan classification scheme, a loan would be considered impaired when a specific reserve is required for the loan. In addition, when interest ceases to accrue on a loan, uncollected interest that had been previously accrued should be reversed. This treatment of unpaid interest seems reasonable, as the bank's claim on unpaid interest may be of lower quality than the bank's claim on the principal amount of the loan.

Banks, like other businesses, need to maintain sufficient capital to provide a cushion to cover large, unanticipated future losses. To ensure this, the bank regulatory authority in each country requires banks to meet capital adequacy standards. Under the 1988 Basel Accord, tier I capital (basic equity) must be at least 4 percent of risk-weighted assets. Tier II capital (undisclosed reserves, revaluation reserves, subordinated debt, and general loan-loss provisions) must be at least 8 percent of risk-weighted assets. The general loan-loss provision, however, cannot be greater than 1.25 percent of risk-weighted assets. This, in part, ensures that the regulatory authority does not set a high mandatory general provision to offset the tendency of certain banks to under-provision non-performing loans.

To the extent that the prudential rules for loan-loss provisioning and the capital adequacy standards require banks to maintain more equity capital than is truly needed, the capital cost of the bank is increased and nonbank financial institutions may have a competitive advantage.[13] For example, insurance companies may guarantee bank loans. This may reduce the bank's need for specific reserves as the guarantee will reduce the reserve required for non-performing loans (see the prudential rules for Turkey described above). In addition, the insurance companies may not have to meet capital requirements that are as stringent, giving them a lower cost of capital than banks. Though beyond the scope of this chapter, this all suggests that when prudential rules for loan-loss provisioning and capital adequacy standards are too conservative, banks can be put at a competitive disadvantage.

The Tax Treatment of Loan-losses: An Introduction

The tax treatment of loan-losses varies widely across countries.[14] Some countries (the United States for large banks—those with more than $500 million in assets,[15] Australia, Korea, Malaysia, and the Philippines) allow only the *charge-off method*, under which loan-losses are recognized only when loans become worthless. In determining whether a loan is worthless, all pertinent evidence, including continual non-performance, adequacy of collateral, and the financial condition of the debtor should be considered. Under the charge-off method, if an amount previously charged off as uncollectible is later recovered or the loan again becomes performing, the amount previously written off is restored to income.

In the Philippines, loan-losses are allowed only for worthless and uncollectible loans that have been charged off the books of a bank's account as of the end of the taxable year. The tax authority allows a debt to be written off for tax purposes once it has been written off by the bank with the approval of the Central Bank of the Philippines. Some countries (Japan and Thailand) set limits on the tax deduction for loan-losses. In Thailand, banks can deduct loan-loss provisions from taxable income up to 25 percent of net income or 0.25 percent of total outstanding loans, whichever is less. Loan-losses may be written off for tax purposes only when civil action has been brought against the debtor, the debtor has declared bankruptcy, or died.

Many countries allow a *reserve method* (that is, provisioning) for accounting for loan-losses for tax purposes, in addition to requiring it for regulatory purposes. However, only a few countries attain full conformity between financial and tax accounting for loan-losses. Many countries (such as Canada, France, Kazakhstan, and the United

Kingdom) grant tax deductibility to specific allowances or charge-offs in the year they occur, but not for general allowances. Serbia allows a tax deduction only for the specific allowance, but gives the allowance a "haircut"—that is, reduces its effective value. Under the new Serbian income tax, banks are allowed a tax deduction equal to 90 percent of the addition to the loan-loss provision required by the national bank for non-performing loans. The Russian Tax Code establishes its own reserve rules (related to the rules of the national bank). A reserve is allowed for loans past due only 45 days, and the total reserve cannot exceed 10 percent of the gross receipts of the tax year. In the Kyrgyz Republic, banks may establish a reserve based on the experience of the leading banks of the world. The reserve shall not exceed 10 percent of the loans outstanding. A few countries allow general provisioning for tax purposes (for example, based on a percentage of eligible loans), but limits are usually placed on the general provision. Germany requires that the general provision for tax purposes not exceed 60 percent of average loan-losses over the past five years. Singapore limits the general provision to 3 percent of the amount of qualifying loans (Laurin and Majnoni 2003).

Given this wide diversity in tax treatment, there clearly is no generally accepted international standard as to the appropriate tax treatment of loan-losses. In determining the tax treatment of loan-losses, a country should weigh several considerations. Does the charge-off or the reserve method best measure the income of the bank? Should there be full or partial conformity between the regulatory and tax treatment of loan-losses? Should a tax deduction be allowed for general reserves? If the tax law is changed, for example, to allow a reserve method, how should the transition be treated for tax purposes?

Charge-off vs. Reserve Methods

Both the charge-off and reserve methods recognize that bad debts are costs of earning income, and thus their cost should be a deductible expense for financial and tax purposes. In general, the reserve method accelerates the recognition of the expense compared to the charge-off method. The fundamental question, however, is which method results in a better matching of income and expenses. This is an empirical question.

A test of whether a method for recognizing bad debts results in a proper matching of income and expense is to determine whether it results in the effective tax rate on a portfolio of loans being equal to the nominal tax rate. If the effective tax rate—measured as the percentage reduction in the rate of return due to taxes—is less than the nominal tax rate, the recognition of the losses is too accelerated. If the reverse is true, the recognition of the losses is too delayed.[16]

Consider first the following simple example. A bank makes 1,000 loans for $1,000 each at the end of year 0 (table 9.1). Each year 2 percent of the loans default. If the interest rate on these loans is 12.2449 percent, the interest income will cover the 2 percent loss and provide a 10 percent before-tax return.[17] If each year's loss— the principal amount of the loans that defaulted during the year— is allowed as an immediate tax deduction and the nominal tax rate is 30 percent, the after-tax rate of return is 7 percent. Thus the after-tax rate of return is 30 percent lower than the before-tax rate of return, implying an effective tax rate of 30 percent, which is equal to the 30 percent nominal tax rate.

In this example, the true economic loss[18] in value of the loan portfolio would be permitted as a tax-deductible expense each period. This is the necessary and sufficient condition to ensure that the effective and nominal tax rates are equal (Samuelson 1964).

The key assumption is that the loans default at a constant percentage rate per year (declining balance assumption).[19] Suppose, instead, that all loans remain fully performing until the end of the fifth year (table 9.2). At that time, 9.6 percent of the loans default, which is just equal to the cumulative amount of defaults in the first example. If the bad debts were deductible for tax purposes instantaneously at the end of year 5, the effective tax rate would be 31.4 percent. For the effective tax rate to equal the nominal tax rate, a reserve for future losses would have had to have been established in the earlier years, even though no loans are past due. The annual addition to this reserve would need to be just equal to the decline in the value of the loan portfolio, and this addition would need to be deductible for tax purposes. Over the five-year period, the portfolio would decline in value from $1,000,000 to $903,921 as the end of the five-year period approaches. Put another way, the value of the portfolio at the beginning of year 5 would not be $1,000,000—even though no loans have defaulted as yet.

In contrast to the assumption that loans go bad only in the final year, a bank could originate loans at the end of year 0 and certain loans would instantaneously go bad.[20] All the other loans would remain performing for five years, when the principal amount would be paid in full. Both the charge-off method and the reserve method, by permitting the loan-losses to be written off in year 1, would provide too generous tax treatment of the bad debts in that the resulting effective tax rate would be less than the nominal tax rate. The loan-

Table 9.1. Income and Cash Flow from Loan Portfolio (constant rate of default)

Year	Principal	Interest	Before-tax cash flow	Present value (r = .10)	Taxable income	Tax (30%)	After-tax cash flow	Present value (r = .07)
0	1,000,000	—	-1,000,000	-1,000,000	—	—	-1,000,000	-1,000,000
1	980,000	120,000	120,000	109,091	100,000	30,000	90,000	84,112
2	960,400	117,600	117,600	97,190	98,000	29,400	88,200	77,037
3	941,192	115,248	115,248	86,588	96,040	28,812	86,436	70,558
4	922,368	112,943	112,943	77,142	94,119	28,236	84,707	64,623
5	903,921	110,684	1,014,605	629,990	92,237	27,671	986,934	703,670
Total	—	—	—	0	—	—	—	0

Note: At the end of year 0, the bank makes $1,000,000 of five-year loans. At the end of each year, 2 percent of the loans default. The interest rate is 12.2449 percent per year on the outstanding principal amount at the end of each year. The portfolio yields a 10 percent before-tax rate of return (fifth column). Taxable income is equal to interest income for the year less the amount of loans that defaulted during the year. The after-tax rate of return is 7 percent (last column). The effective tax rate is 30 percent.

Source: Author's calculations.

Table 9.2. Income and Cash Flow from Loan Portfolio (default at term)

Year	Principal	Interest	Before-tax cash flow	Present value (r = .104958)	Taxable income	Tax (30%)	After-tax cash flow	Present value (r = .072034)
0	1,000,000	—	−1,000,000	−1,000,000	—	—	−1,000,000	−1,000,000
1	1,000,000	122,449	122,449	110,818	122,449	36,735	85,714	79,955
2	1,000,000	122,449	122,449	100,291	122,449	36,735	85,714	74,582
3	1,000,000	122,449	122,449	90,765	122,449	36,735	85,714	69,571
4	1,000,000	122,449	122,449	82,143	122,449	36,735	85,714	64,896
5	903,921	110,684	1,014,605	615,982	26,270	7,881	1,006,724	710,997
Total	—	—	—	0	—	—	—	0

Note: At the end of year 0, the bank makes $1,000,000 of five-year loans. At the end of year 5, 9.6 percent of the loans default. The interest rate is 12.2449 percent per year on the outstanding principal amount at the end of each year. The portfolio yields a 10.4958 percent before-tax rate of return (fifth column). Taxable income is equal to interest income for the year less the amount of loans that defaulted during the year. The after-tax rate of return is 7.2034 percent (last column). The effective tax rate is 31.4 percent.

Source: Author's calculations.

losses in year 1 are a cost of earning income not only in year 1 but also over the life of the portfolio. Thus these losses should be spread over the five-year period and not deducted solely in the first year.

These examples are admittedly artificial, but they allow one to determine the effective tax rate on a portfolio of loans, given the pattern of loan-losses. One conclusion from these examples is that if the loans were expected to go bad at a constant rate per year, the charge-off method would, in theory, produce the appropriate matching of income and expenses. There is an important proviso, however. These examples assume that all past due loans are ultimately worthless and there is no recognition lag between when past due payments occur and when the charge-off is allowed. The reserve method, by accelerating the tax deduction compared to the charge-off method, may provide a reasonable solution for the recognition lag and take into account that all past due loans do not become worthless.

If banks are required to go to court or await the bankruptcy or death of the debtor before writing off debts that clearly are not recoverable, then the charge-off method is overly restrictive. Depending on the bankruptcy laws and court practices, the charge-off delays in some countries could go on indefinitely. At minimum, bad debts should be charged off for tax purposes in the year they are classified as worthless for regulatory purposes.

The Case for Conformity

A major advantage of having a high degree of conformity between loan-loss provisioning for financial and tax purposes is that the tax authority would not have to assess the reasonableness of the provision. Instead, the tax authority could rely on the bank regulatory authority to "audit" the loan-loss provision. This would provide banks with greater certainty by reducing disputes between the banks and the tax authority. However, a high degree of conformity does not necessarily require full conformity. Administrative simplification would still be obtained if only specific provisions are deductible for tax purposes or if the specific provision is given a "haircut," as in Serbia.

Conformity between financial and tax accounting for loan-losses also would ensure that the tax system does not provide a disincentive for banks to adequately provide for loan-losses.[21] Each dollar added to the reserve for financial or regulatory purposes would reduce taxable profits by a dollar and provide a current tax benefit, so long as the bank has positive taxable income. Once a bank is in a tax loss position, additional tax deductions from additional reserving only increase the loss carry forward, and this may provide no tax benefit if the bank ultimately fails.

The tax treatment of loan-loss provisioning also affects capital adequacy ratios. If a bank sets a specific provision of 100, tier I capital and profits are reduced by 100, absent taxation. As a result, stockholders' equity is also reduced by 100. However, if the provision is deductible for tax purposes, after-tax profits, stockholders' equity, and tier I capital are all reduced by $(1-t)100$, where t is the corporate tax rate. Thus a tax deduction for the loan-loss provision cushions the effect of the provision on the amount of the bank's tier I capital. All other things equal, this should reduce the disincentive for banks, already constrained by the need to meet capital adequacy ratios, to adequately provide for loan-losses.

If there is no current tax deduction for the loan-loss provision (for example, the country is on the charge-off method for tax purposes), the effect on tier I capital may still be cushioned if a deferred tax asset[22] is recognized for financial accounting, and this asset is counted toward tier I capital. Admittedly, this asset is a non-earning asset, and therefore not as valuable as an asset that can generate income.

The Case against Full Conformity

There are several considerations that can be used to argue against full conformity between financial and tax accounting in this context.

Financial vs. Tax Accounting

Both financial and tax accounting are based upon the premise of measuring income, but their goals are somewhat different. Financial accounting—and prudential rules, in particular—is based on conservatism: that is, to delay recognition of income as long as possible and to anticipate expenses and losses as soon as possible. Notwithstanding the bankruptcy of Enron, such a system is designed to ensure that the profits and the net worth of the company are not overstated.

The objective of tax accounting is the opposite: that is, to ensure that income is not understated. Therefore, income is taxed as soon as it belongs to the taxpayer. Thus it would be normal to tax prepayments of rent as soon as they are received, regardless of the fact that they relate to a period beyond the tax year. Similarly, tax accounting defers deductions until it is clear that the liability will actually be incurred. Various reserves allowed for financial accounting generally are not allowed for tax accounting.[23]

General Reserves

From the tax accounting point of view, the general reserve for loan-losses looks quite suspect. Although the general reserve is for "present" or "latent" losses, it is, by its nature, "speculative," and involves a great deal of judgment by bank managers (Laurin and Majnoni 2003). The fact that the general reserve is often included as part of tier II capital suggests that this reserve may be for future losses. At the very least, it is for current losses that have not yet been identified. Consistent with tax accounting, generally, a liability should not be recognized for tax purposes until it is certain (that is, it can be identified) and can be reasonably estimated. Moreover, recognizing general provisions for tax purposes can be very expensive in terms of foregone tax revenue, as many banks would have general provisions that are larger than their specific provisions.[24] It is not surprising, therefore, that tax authorities are wary of allowing banks to deduct general reserves for unidentified, but arguably "present" losses.

Specific Reserves

There is also a suspicion, at least among tax officials, that the specific reserves are set on the high side to be conservative, to protect the capital of the banks, and to reduce overly risky behavior.[25] If the bank regulator fears that banks may not properly classify loans, the required provisions for each category may be set at a higher rate in order to partially offset the tendency to misclassify loans. Moreover, required reserves for regulatory purposes are minimums, as the bank regulatory authority wants to make certain that banks do not understate their losses.[26] The tax authority, however, wants to ensure that banks do not overstate reserves. Instead of being minimums, the regulatory reserves should be maximums, if allowed for tax purposes.

To counteract the bias that regulatory reserves are too conservative, it may be appropriate to reduce the provision level for tax purposes—say to 80 or 90 percent of the regulatory rate. If the loans actually do go bad, they will ultimately be completely written off; this is therefore a timing issue.

Tax Treatment of Borrowers vs. Bank Lenders

From the tax policy perspective, there is an additional concern regarding a reserve method for accounting for loan-losses: namely, the asymmetric treatment of banks and their business borrowers. In general, when interest is an expense of the borrower, it is at the same time income of the lender, just as when a business pays wages and deducts the expense, the worker is taxable on the wage income. Similarly, when a bank has a loan-loss, the borrower has income—forgiveness-of-indebtedness income. However, this income is recognized only when the debt is forgiven: that is, written off. If a bank recognizes the loan-loss through provisioning, it may be able to claim the loss in an earlier tax year than when the borrower must recognize income. This timing difference between the expense of the bank and the income of the borrower works to the disadvantage of the fiscal authorities. This is probably more of a theoretical problem than a real one, however. When borrowers are unable to make the debt payments, they likely are in economic difficulty and have tax losses. In this situation, it may not matter in which year the forgiveness-of-indebtedness income is recognized for tax purposes, as no tax liability will accrue in any event.

Transition Rules

If a country is going to switch from the charge-off to the reserve method, one needs to be concerned about how the transition is handled. Suppose, for example, the effective date of the switch is January 1, 2003. Suppose further that for a particular bank, the beginning-of-the-year reserve is $100, and the required end-of-year reserve is $120. If the country had always been on the reserve method, the tax deduction for 2003 would be $20, ignoring any write-offs and recoveries. However, the beginning-of-the-year reserve of $100 has never been allowed as a tax deduction. How should this $100 be treated for tax purposes?

One possibility would be to allow an additional deduction of $100 in 2003 on the grounds that $100 would have been an expense in earlier years if the country had been on the reserve method. This could be quite expensive in terms of foregone tax revenues. Also, a special rule (such as a longer loss carryover period) may be needed to cover the situation where the one-time deduction creates a large loss carryover that likely will not be used during the carryover period.

An alternative and the preferred approach for handling the transition would be to treat the switch from the charge-off to the reserve method as a change in the method of accounting. The effect of the change—an additional deduction of $100—would be spread over three to five years.[27] For countries that are concerned about the revenue cost of switching to the reserve method, the allowable deduction could be further limited in the first year to, say, 25 percent of taxable income before the reserve deduction. This percentage would increase to 100 percent over several years. Any amount disallowed in one year as a result of this limit would be carried over to subsequent years until allowed.

Conclusions and Recommendations

There is no standard international practice as to the treatment of bank loan-losses for tax purposes. Some countries use the charge-off method; other countries allow provisions for loan-losses along the lines of the provisions required for regulatory accounting. Only rarely do countries have full conformity between book and tax provisions for loan-losses. It is much more common for countries to disallow general provisions for performing loans.

The widespread practice of under-provisioning in many developing countries, and the importance of ensuring that tax rules do not unduly discourage the establishment of needed provisions, means that there is much to be said for ensuring an adequate tax deductibility for loan-loss provisions. Some conclude that all provisions should be tax-deductible. But on the assumption that banks are following prudent provisioning practice, this chapter takes the position that the tax rules for loan-losses should be closely tied to (but not necessarily the same as) the prudential rules for provisioning. However, no tax deduction should be allowed for a general provision for performing loans. Also, it may be appropriate to reduce the specific provisioning allowed for tax purposes to 80 or 90 percent of the regulatory rate, in order to reflect the real income of banks as accurately as possible. When countries using the charge-off method for tax purposes switch to a reserve method, this change should be treated as a change in the method of accounting and the effect of the change spread over three to five years.

Appendix A9.1. Soviet-style Accounting

Whether loan-losses should be an allowable expense was an issue under Soviet-style accounting, which was developed to provide fiscal data to the state, rather than information for shareholders, creditors, and managers. In practice, an enterprise was required to *offset* all its expenses with revenues it earned from the sale of its products and services (Ash and Strittmatter 1992).

There were no private banks in the Soviet economy before a transition period just before the break-up of the Soviet Union. All enterprise loans (or cash transfers) came from the State Bank (Gosbank) after the Ministry of Finance had approved the budget, which contained a breakdown by individual enterprise. State-owned companies did not go bankrupt, in part, because the plan for each enterprise was set to ensure that revenues (including transfers from the State Bank) offset expenses. Once private banks appeared, loans were guaranteed by the state. If a business defaulted on its loan, the guarantee would be called. Bank bad debts generally were unknown.

The income taxes first adopted by various states of the former Soviet Union reflected Soviet-style accounting: revenue offsetting allowable expenses. Thus private banks were not allowed tó claim a tax deduction for loan-losses, which were not considered an allowable expense. Instead, these costs were accounted for as direct charges against the bank's equity.

Western-style accounting for the earnings of an enterprise is premised on a *matching* of expenses to the revenues to which they relate. With respect to the accounting treatment of bad debts, it is recognized that when a bank originates a portfolio of loans, it is not known which loans in the portfolio will default, but some inevitably will. A loan-loss is considered a cost that a bank incurs in order to earn income on performing loans. Loan-losses therefore should be a deductible expense.

The various states of the former Soviet Union have all adopted income tax laws that now recognize bad debts as costs of earning income. For these countries, the major policy issue—and the primary focus of this chapter— is when and how the cost of loan-losses should be recognized for tax purposes.

Appendix A9.2. Insurance Reserves and Investment Income

The financial and tax treatment of insurance companies has been a contentious issue in a number of developing and transition countries. If the regular corporate income tax is going to apply, two major policy issues need to be addressed: the appropriate reserves to allow for tax purposes, and the allocation of investment income.[28]

Insurance companies operating in a country are usually subject to regulation by an insurance authority that requires the maintenance of reserves against the contingent liabilities that are insured. These contingent liabilities may require expenditures to be made in the current year or in future years. In determining the appropriate reserve, the regulatory authority should require discounting of expected future expenditures, using a pre-tax discount rate, in order to reflect the time value of money.

The reserves appear to be an ordinary and necessary cost of doing insurance business, and additions to these required reserves are commonly allowed as deductions in determining taxable income. These reserves involve quite complex actuarial computations, which cannot be effectively audited by the tax authority in most countries. They may exaggerate the contingent liabilities—for example, assuming high mortality or accident rates or low discount rates—reflecting the concern of the insurance regulators to give policyholders confidence in the company's solvency.

If the reserves are too conservative, then allowing a tax deduction for the full amount of the addition to reserves results in an understatement of the company's income. One possible counteraction would be to give the reserves required for regulatory purposes a "haircut" (or a reduction in their effective valuation) before allowing them as a deductible expense for tax purposes.

In developing and transition countries, insurance policies are often written by international companies. The accumulated reserves may be invested offshore, as the domestic capital market is quite limited. The associated investment income, however, would normally be foreign-source income and thus not taxable in the country in which the policies are written. This mismatching of income and expenses can lead to insurance companies reporting little or no taxable income in the country where the policies are written. A possible counteraction would be to require that the investment income of an insurance company operating across international borders be allocated based upon liabilities insured in each country.

Because of the complexity of determining income of an insurance company and the appropriateness of its reserves, some authorities recommend a gross premium tax in lieu of imposing the regular income tax on insurance companies (Hussey and Lubick 1996). Non-insurance activities such as financial leasing would be treated as conducted in a separate entity subject to the regular corporate income tax.

Notes

1. That bank loan-losses should be recognized as an expense for both financial and tax purposes is not controversial, at least under Western market-oriented accounting. However, under Soviet-style accounting, banks were not allowed to claim a tax deduction for loan-losses. Soviet-style financial and tax accounting and whether loan-losses should be allowed as an expense are discussed further in appendix A9.1.

2. In this chapter, the terms "reserves" and "provisions" will be used interchangeably.

3. Reserves of an insurance company recognize current and future expenditures that are necessary to settle current obligations. According to IAS 37 (2000), where the effect of the time value of money is material, insurance reserves (or provisions) should be discounted using a pre-tax discount rate. Appendix A9.2 elaborates on insurance reserves.

4. By excluding the word "future," the 1991 amendments to the Basel Accord aligned regulatory accounting with financial accounting. See Beattie and others (1995, p. 20).

5. The definition of specific and general provisions and their uses vary across countries (Laurin and Majnoni 2003).

6. The term "non-performing loans" most commonly refers to loans on which the payments are past due by 90 days or more, but practices vary across countries. Non-performing loans are usually subject to a specific reserve. Loans that are past due for only a short period of time are not considered to be non-performing (Cortavarria and others 2000).

7. It may well be that next year the oil sector will go sour and bank loans to the oil sector will become impaired. These losses are a future expense and they should be recognized in future periods.

8. Based on the classification of loans at the end of the current year.

9. Based on the classification of loans at the end of the prior year.

10. In some countries, worthless loans are charged directly against income (and not debited against the reserve). When this approach is followed, the necessary addition to the reserve to bring the reserve up to the end-of-year balance would be correspondingly reduced.

11. If 75 percent of the loan had been reserved at the end of the prior year, then charging the loan against the reserve will give a tax deduction in the current year for 25 percent of the loan. The tax deduction would be equal to the reserve at the end of the year minus the reserve at the beginning of the year plus the bad debt written off (0 − 75 + 100).

12. Under the International Accounting Standards (IAS), the accrual method is a fundamental accounting policy. Transactions and events are recognized when they occur and they are recorded in the accounting records and reported in the financial statements of the periods to which they relate. Expenses are recognized in the income statement on the basis of a direct association between the costs incurred and the earning of specific items of income (matching). Under the accrual method, the timing of the actual payment or transfer of consideration is not relevant.

13. Also, differences in loan-loss provisioning and the capital adequacy standards across countries will impact the competitiveness of banks (Beattie and others 1995).

14. For an international comparison of the tax treatment of loan-losses in developed countries, see Escolano (1997) and Beattie and others (1995).

15. Although the United States requires large banks to use the charge-off method, it allows banks a partial write-off of debts, mitigating the harsh effects of the charge-off method (Dziobek 1996).

16. Calculation of effective tax rates on theoretical portfolios of loans buttressed the case for the United States switching from the reserve method to the charge-off method (Joint Committee on Taxation 1985).

17. $(100)(1 - .02)(.122449) - 2 = (100)(.10)$.

18. The economic loss in the value of the portfolio would be measured by comparing the present value of the future before-tax cash flows, discounted at 10 percent, at the end of year, compared to the value of the end of the prior year.

19. Another key assumption is that the loan-loss is charged off immediately.

20. By analogy, when oil companies drill dry holes in seeking oil reserves, the cost of these unsuccessful wells could be viewed as capital costs incurred in order to find producing wells. The costs of the dry holes would be capitalized and written off over the life of the producing wells. Most countries, however, permit dry holes to be expensed for tax purposes.

21. This may be particularly important in times of fiscal stress when banks have high rates of non-performing loans and defaults. It is somewhat ironic that during periods of fiscal stress, countries, mainly in Latin America, have often adopted bank debit taxes, which tend to encourage disintermediation (Coelho, Ebrill, and Summers 2001).

22. Some countries, including the United States, determine the income tax expense for financial accounting purposes based on the reported profits for financial purposes adjusted for permanent differences between financial and taxable income (such as tax credits and exempt income). If financial income is greater than taxable income due to timing differences, the tax on this income, which is not currently payable, is considered a deferred tax asset on the balance sheet. Thus even though the provision does not result in a current tax benefit, after-tax financial profits and stockholders' equity are reduced by only $(1-t)$ times the amount of the provision. To illustrate, if financial profits are $100 and the tax rate is 20 percent, the tax expense for financial purposes would be $20. If taxable income is $150 due to greater provisioning allowed for financial purposes than for tax purposes, the $10 tax liability payable now on the $50 difference would be treated for financial purposes as a deferred tax credit. Thus the additional provision of $50, not recognized for tax purposes, reduces the net worth of the firm by only $40, as the $10 future tax savings generated by the provisioning is considered an asset on the balance sheet.

23. The two exceptions would be loan-loss provisions for banks—the focus of this chapter—and the required reserves of insurance companies. In both cases, the tax authority can rely on the regulatory authority for banks and insurance companies to determine the reasonableness of the reserve.

24. For example, if a bank had classified loans equal to 3 percent of total loans and had set specific reserves averaging 40 percent of the classified loans, the specific provision would be only 1.2 percent of total loans—less than a general provision of 1.25 percent applying to the other 97 percent of loans.

25. Even if this is so, bank managers (with the concurrence of regulators) may under-provide for reserves at times of distress, whether or not additions to reserves are tax-deductible. Tax policy probably cannot correct this.

26. The regulatory authority is also concerned that banks do not have "hidden reserves" in order to smooth income. Any reserve for future losses should be accounted for as an allocation of retained earnings: that is, below the line.

27. Spreading the effect of a change in the method of accounting is quite common practice when a business switches from cash to accrual accounting or changes its method of accounting for inventories. When the United States went from a reserve method to the charge-off method for large banks, the existing reserve at the end of 1986 was brought back into income over four years.

28. There are also important issues related to how policyholders and beneficiaries should be treated. Generally, businesses should deduct premiums accrued or paid to insure business risks. Any benefits paid under the insurance policies to businesses would be included in taxable income. If the benefits are paid to employees or other persons, they generally are not taxable. However, if the benefit payment replaces income that otherwise would have been taxed (such as lost earnings), the benefit probably should be taxable. In the case of life insurance provided by an employer, it would be unseemly to tax life insurance proceeds but it would be appropriate to tax employees on the value of company-provided insurance. In the United States, for example, employees are required to include in income the cost of company-provided group life insurance in excess of $50,000 of such insurance.

References

Ash, Ehiel, and Robert Strittmatter. 1992. *Accounting in the Soviet Union.* Westport, Conn.: Greenwood.

Basel Committee on Banking Supervision. 1988. *International Convergence of Capital Measurement and Capital Standards.* Basel, Switzerland: Bank for International Settlements.

———. 1999. *Sound Practices for Loan Accounting and Disclosure.* Basel: Bank for International Settlements.

Bassett, William F., and Egon Zakrajšek. 2001. "Profits and Balance Sheet Developments at U.S. Commercial Banks in 2000." *Federal Reserve Bulletin* 87 (June): 367–93.

Beattie, Vivien A., Peter D. Casson, Richard S. Dale, George W. McKenzie, Charles M. S. Sutcliffe, and Michael J. Turner. 1995. *Banks and Bad*

Debts: Accounting for Loan-Losses in International Banking. New York: John Wiley & Sons.

Coelho, Isaias, Liam Ebrill, and Victoria Summers. 2001. "Bank Debit Taxes in Latin America: An Analysis of Recent Trends." IMF Working Paper WP/01/67. International Monetary Fund, Washington, D.C.

Cortavarria, Luis, Claudia Dziobek, Akihiro Kanaya, and Inwon Song. 2000. "Loan Review, Provisioning, and Macroeconomic Linkages." IMF Working Paper WP/00/195. International Monetary Fund, Washington, D.C.

Dziobek, Claudia. 1996. "Regulatory and Tax Treatment of Loan-Loss Provisions." IMF Paper on Policy Analysis and Assessment, 96/6. International Monetary Fund, Washington, D.C.

Escolano, Julio. 1997. "Tax Treatment of Loan-Losses of Banks." In William E. Alexander, Jeffrey M. Davis, Liam P. Ebrill, and Carl-Johan Lindgren, eds., *Systemic Bank Restructuring and Macroeconomic Policy.* Washington, D.C.: International Monetary Fund.

Hussey, Ward M., and Donald C. Lubick. 1996. *Basic World Tax Code and Commentary.* Arlington, Virginia: Tax Analysts.

International Accounting Standards Committee. 2002. "IAS 30: Disclosures in the Financial Statements of Banks and Similar Financial Institutions." In *International Accounting Standards 2002.* London: International Accounting Standards Board.

———. 2002. "IAS 37: Provision, Contingent Liabilities and Contingent Assets." In *International Accounting Standards 2002.* London: International Accounting Standards Board.

Joint Committee on Taxation. 1985. *Tax Reform Proposals: Taxation of Financial Institutions.* Report JCS 38-85, U.S. Congress, Washington, D.C.

Laurin, Alain, and Giovanni Majnoni, eds. 2003. *Bank Loan Classification and Provisioning Practices in Selected Developed and Emerging Countries.* Washington, D.C.: World Bank.

Samuelson, Paul A. 1964. "Tax Deductibility of Economic Depreciation to Insure Invariant Valuations." *Journal of Political Economy* 72 (6): 604–06.

10

Bank Debit Taxes: Yield Versus Disintermediation

Andrei Kirilenko and Victoria Summers

In the past 15 years, a number of countries, mostly in Latin America, have imposed taxes on banking transactions. These taxes are usually levied on withdrawals from or other debits to bank accounts, including check clearance, cash withdrawals, and payments of loan installments.

Since 1988, bank debit taxes have been introduced in Argentina, Brazil, Colombia, Ecuador, Peru, and Venezuela. With the exception of Brazil, bank debit taxes were introduced at the time of crisis with the objective of quickly generating a burst of revenue.

These taxes have the support of many policymakers and virtually no organized popular opposition. Collection and administration costs of these taxes are minimal. In addition, the government gains an immediate and continuous revenue stream, since the taxes are collected from transactions in real time.

However, since bank debit taxes are levied on intermediated financial transactions, their imposition is likely to result in financial disintermediation. Broadly speaking, disintermediation is the withdrawal of funds from financial intermediaries, with the payments being made in some other way (for example, in cash, by barter, or through accounts not subject to tax). Disintermediation results not only in the reduction of the tax base, but also in a possible misallocation of financial resources.

This chapter presents a first formal attempt to estimate the scale of disintermediation resulting from the introduction of a bank debit tax. Drawing on a model of financial intermediation by Kirilenko and Summers (2001), this study derives a relationship between the disintermediation resulting from introduction of a bank debit tax and the deadweight welfare loss attributable to the tax.

Using data from four Latin American countries, this study estimates the scale of disintermediation attributable to the tax and deduces the welfare loss. The calculations rely on two key assumptions: namely that the entire burden of the bank debit tax falls on bank borrowers, and that the impact of the tax on financial intermediation does not yet arise in the first full month after its introduction.

The study finds that bank debit taxes have coincided with significant welfare losses, especially at higher rates. Expressed as a percentage of revenue, deadweight losses following the introduction of the tax reached up to 30 percent in Venezuela, up to 35 percent in Colombia, and up to 45 percent in Ecuador. However, the study does not find significant deadweight losses in Brazil.

Introduction of a bank debit tax resulted in disintermediation of up to 28 percent in Venezuela, up to 41 percent in Colombia, and up to 47 percent in Ecuador. This means that for every dollar in revenue raised by a bank debit tax, there was a loss of financial intermediation equal to 28 cents in Venezuela, 41 cents in Colombia, and 47 cents in Ecuador. Again, no significant disintermediation was found in Brazil. Both the deadweight losses and disintermediation effects cumulate as the taxes remain in place.

While bank debit taxes can be used as a quick and effective way to generate revenue, pending the implementation of improvements in the arrangements for collecting more efficient taxes (Tanzi 2000), this study confirms that, as time passes, and especially at higher rates of tax, debit taxes may lead to significant welfare losses and financial disintermediation.

The rest of the chapter is organized as follows. After a brief description of bank debit taxes and a discussion of their productivity, the chapter points out the relationship between deadweight loss and disintermediation. It then describes the data and estimation results and presents selected descriptive evidence. The chapter concludes that at higher rates or over an extended period of time, bank debit taxes may lead to significant financial disintermediation.

Bank Debit Taxes in Latin America

Bank debit taxes are currently in effect in Argentina, Brazil, Colombia, and Venezuela, and were in place previously in Ecuador and Peru. With the exception of Brazil, bank debit taxes were introduced at a time of, and in response to, general economic crisis, as an emergency means of raising government revenue. In all cases the tax was explicitly introduced on a temporary basis, though in some cases it was then extended.

- In Argentina when a bank debit tax was introduced as a temporary measure in 1988, tax revenues were declining dramatically because of hyperinflation, increased evasion, and depressed economic activity. The tax was reintroduced under similar circumstances in April 2001.
- In Peru, when the Impuesto a los Débitos Bancarios y Financieros was introduced as a temporary and extraordinary revenue measure in 1989, the nation was immersed in a deep economic crisis and central government revenues had fallen from 14.9 percent of GDP in 1985 to 6.1 percent of GDP in 1989.
- In Colombia, when a temporary Impuesto a las Transacciones Financieras (known as the "dos por mil") was adopted in November 1998, the health of the financial sector had already deteriorated markedly and the government had declared an economic emergency.[1]
- In Ecuador, the tax was introduced in 1999, at a time when the economy plunged into a major economic and financial crisis.
- In Venezuela, a temporary bank debit tax was collected from May to December 1994 and from May 1999 to May 2000. The tax was reintroduced in Venezuela for 12 months beginning March 2002.

There is a considerable diversity in the design of these taxes from country to country.[2] Transactions subject to or exempt from the tax as well as tax rates differ significantly. Tax rates have ranged between 0.2 and 2.0 percent.[3] In all cases, the rates have varied both across countries and across time, without any discernible trend.

The taxes have been imposed on debits to (withdrawals from) checking, savings, and term accounts in banks and other financial institutions, and on loan withdrawals (in Brazil, Colombia, and Venezuela). In Colombia, the tax is also imposed on credits of bank interest to accounts and on repurchase agreements (repos). In Ecuador, the base of the tax was somewhat different; the tax was imposed not only on withdrawals but also on credits to checking, savings, term, loan, and other accounts at financial institutions, as well as on remittances abroad and on payments abroad by exporters and importers. Thus both deposits to and withdrawals from the same accounts were subject to the tax. The taxation of both debits and credits is also a feature of the tax introduced in Argentina in 2001.

Most countries provided exemptions for transactions by certain types of institutions (for example, government agencies) and some specific transactions, including repos and transactions with the central bank. In Argentina (through 1992 and between April and December 2001) and in Ecuador, a portion of the bank debit tax has been creditable against the income tax or the VAT.

Tighter anti-avoidance measures have been introduced in the more recent taxes. The measures included restrictions on the use of cash for settlements, prohibition of multiple endorsements of checks, and application of the tax to all but the first endorsement upon final settlement.

Revenue Productivity

As can be seen from table 10.1, the short-term revenue performance of transactions taxes, particularly in Brazil, Colombia, and Ecuador, has been quite strong. In Brazil and Colombia, the taxes have produced revenues in the range of 0.60 to 1.45 percent of GDP for ad valorem tax rates in the range of 0.20 to 0.37 percent. The revenue performance of the tax in Ecuador was exceptionally strong in its first year, reflecting its application to a broader base including both debits and credits, though part of the gross revenues were creditable against other taxes. The taxes imposed in Argentina and Peru in the late 1980s and early 1990s were significantly less productive, as gauged by the ratio of revenues as a percent of GDP to the average statutory rate.

Overall, the more recent taxes have been more productive than those introduced a decade ago. In Brazil, a high revenue yield has been sustained over several years. However, in Colombia and Ecuador, monthly real revenues from the tax were on a declining trend. In Venezuela, revenues held up through the end of 1999 from the tax's introduction earlier in that year, but declined rapidly in 2000. It should also be noted that revenue productivity appears to decline with higher tax rates. For example, while the tax base in Ecuador was much broader than in the other cases, revenue productivity was considerably lower in Ecuador than in Brazil and in Colombia, where the tax rates are lower.

Calculating Disintermediation and the Deadweight Welfare Loss

Kirilenko and Summers (2001) formulate a model that focuses on the intermediation role of banks and postulates that the debit tax with the rate τ is perceived by the depositor as, in effect, a reduction

Table 10.1. Bank Debit Taxes, Selected Latin American Countries, 1989–2002

Country and year introduced	Effective tax rate	Gross revenue[a]	Productivity[b]
Argentina			
1989	0.70	0.66	0.94
1990	0.30	0.30	0.99
1991	1.05[c]	0.91	0.86
1992	1.20	0.92	0.77
2001	0.99[c]	1.08	1.10
Brazil			
1994	0.25	1.06	4.24
1997	0.20	0.80	4.00
1998	0.20	0.89	4.44
1999	0.24[c]	0.83	3.46
2000	0.33[c]	1.34	4.02
2001	0.37[c]	1.45	3.97
Colombia			
1999	0.20	0.69	3.45
2000	0.20	0.60	3.00
2001	0.30	0.75	2.50
Ecuador			
1999	2.00	3.38[d]	1.69
2000	1.60	2.37[d]	1.48
Peru			
1990	1.42[c]	0.69	0.49
1991	0.81[c]	0.57	0.70
Venezuela			
1994	0.75	1.30	1.73[e]
1999–2000	0.50	1.12	2.24
2002	0.85	1.57	1.85

[a]Gross revenue in percent of GDP.
[b]Gross revenue in percent of GDP divided by average statutory rate.
[c]Average of rates, adjusted for the period tax was in effect.
[d]Tax was levied on both debit and credit transactions.
[e]Adjusted for the period tax was in effect.
Source: National authorities and authors' estimates.

in the yield of bank deposits from r_b, say, to $r_b/(1 - \pi)$.[4] The model predicts that after the introduction of the tax, the equilibrium amount of funds intermediated by the banks declines by a fraction β of their initial value N, where β is a function of the tax rate τ.

While disintermediation is an intuitive economic concept, it is quite difficult to estimate. At the same time, since Harberger (1964), there exist standard techniques to estimate a deadweight welfare loss due to taxation.[5] The deadweight welfare loss L caused by the tax is the area of the "Harberger triangle" that can be calculated as one half of the tax times the change in the tax base βN:

$$2L = \tau\beta(\tau)N$$

This can be compared with tax revenues T, which are equal to the tax rate times the new tax base:

$$T = \tau[1 - \beta(\tau)]N$$

The deadweight loss as a fraction of revenues is thus

$$l = \frac{L}{T} = \frac{1}{2}\left(\frac{\beta(\tau)}{1 - \beta(\tau)}\right),$$

or equivalently, $\beta = 2l/(1 + 2l)$.

A zero deadweight loss implies that the bank debit tax has no impact on financial intermediation. Alternatively, infinite deadweight loss corresponds to complete disintermediation.

Data and Estimation

This study uses monthly series of bank debit tax revenues for four countries: Brazil (June 1999–December 2001); Colombia (January 1999–December 2001); Ecuador (January 1999–December 2000); and Venezuela (May 1999–May 2000). The revenue data comes from the authorities of these countries.

Indices of bank debit tax revenues were constructed by expressing the real value of each month's revenue as a percentage of the revenue flow in the first full month of the operation of the tax. The real value is obtained by deflating each month's nominal revenues by the corresponding month's consumer price index (CPI) drawn from *International Financial Statistics*, a monthly publication of the International Monetary Fund. The base month for the indices is January 1999 for Colombia, January 1999 for Ecuador, and June 1999 for Venezuela. For Brazil, two base dates are used: July 1999 and May 2000, thereby treating the sizable change in tax rate from the latter month as if it were a new tax.[6]

The revenue indices are then divided by the statutory tax rate to obtain a measure of trends in the revenue productivity or yield of the tax. Thus while the revenue index for Colombia in December 2000 is 85, jumping to 120 in January 2001, the fact that the tax rate increased from 0.2 percent to 0.3 percent between the same two months means that the productivity index declined from 85 to 80 (=120 × 0.2/0.3).

In order to calculate the deadweight loss, one needs an estimate of the revenue that would have resulted had there been no disintermediation. The model assumes that during the first month after the introduction of the tax, there is minimal change in the behavior of borrowers and depositors. This assumption allows one to use actual bank debit tax revenues collected during the first full month following the introduction of the tax as an estimate of τN.[7]

Estimates of deadweight loss l for each country and each month after the first full month for which data are available are expressed as a percentage of tax revenues and shown in figure 10.1 as three-month moving averages. Deadweight losses following the introduction of the tax reached up to 30 percent in Venezuela, up to 35 percent in Colombia, and up to 45 percent in Ecuador.

The study does not find significant deadweight losses in Brazil. However, because the tax was already being collected in Brazil between February 1997 and February 1999, it is likely that most of the behavioral changes in response to the tax had already taken place before July 1999. As a result, the method used in this model, which assumes no behavioral response before July 1999, would likely result in an underestimate of the impact of the tax. In contrast, Albuquerque (2002) estimates the deadweight loss in Brazil to be 21.7 percent of the net tax revenue in 2000.

Using the relationship between the deadweight loss and disintermediation derived above, the estimates for deadweight losses as a fraction of revenues, l, can be translated into measures of disintermediation β for each country and month, also expressed as a percentage of tax revenues and shown in figure 10.2 as three-month moving averages. Introduction of a bank debit tax resulted in disintermediation of up to 28 percent in Venezuela, up to 41 percent in Colombia, and up to 47 percent in Ecuador. Again, the study does not find significant disintermediation effects in Brazil. It does find that both the deadweight losses and disintermediation effects increase as the taxes remain in place.

Descriptive Evidence

Anecdotal evidence suggests that bank debit taxes are distortionary and have contributed to significant financial disintermediation. First, following the introduction of the tax, individuals and businesses substitute away from bank-intermediated transactions into

Figure 10.1. Deadweight Loss from Bank Debit Taxes, Selected Latin American Countries, 1999–2001

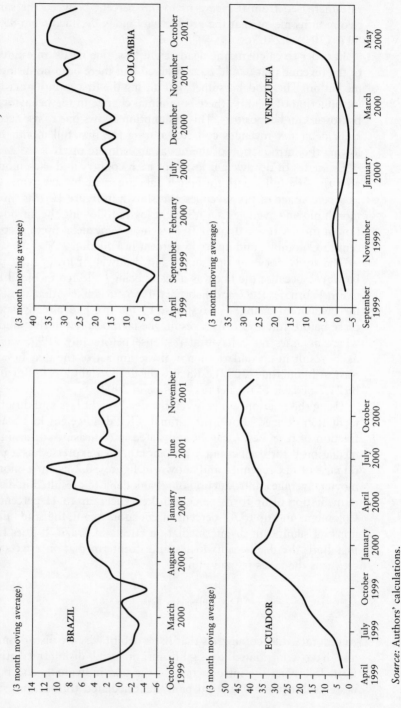

Source: Authors' calculations.

Figure 10.2. Disintermediation Caused by Bank Debit Taxes, Selected Latin American Countries, 1999–2001

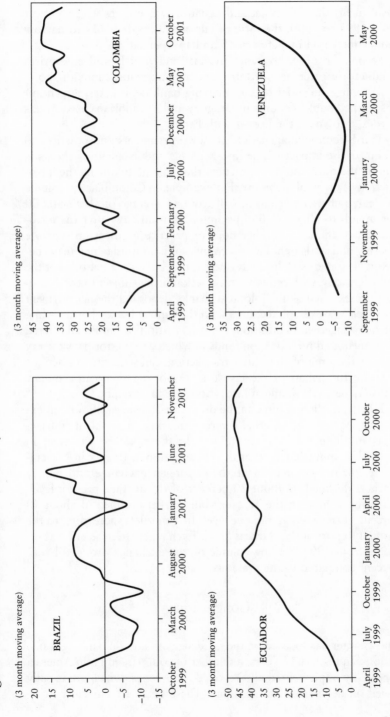

Source: Authors' calculations.

cash. In Brazil, Colombia, and Ecuador where taxes were in effect from 1998 to 2000, the ratio of currency outside banks to narrow money increased by between 15 and 150 percent.[8]

Second, in order to avoid the tax, individuals and enterprises conduct a greater proportion of their bank transactions offshore. For example, in order to avoid paying bank debit taxes, Argentinians opened bank accounts in Uruguay and Ecuadorians used Aquas Verdes, a town on the border with Peru.

Third, economic agents create new instruments and practices to minimize the impact of the tax. Multiple endorsement of checks is among the most common practices that emerge following the introduction of the bank debit tax. For example, in Colombia, the volume of cleared checks was cut in half from an average of about 60,000 per month to about 30,000 per month within days after the introduction of the tax. Another popular practice is to set up separate clearing and settlement bank accounts so that intraday payments between customers can be aggregated and debited on a net basis at the end of the day, with only that transaction being subject to the tax. In some cases, such as in Colombia, banks deposited the net payment into their tax-exempt accounts with the central bank, thus avoiding the tax altogether. In addition, financial institutions in Brazil offered investment and privatization funds in which an investor pays the tax only at the time of the initial transaction. Subsequent transactions done on the behalf of the investor are not taxed, because money transfers between financial institutions are tax-exempt.[9]

Finally, trading volume in the domestic Treasury bill, foreign exchange, equity, and interbank money markets may fall if transactions in these markets are subject to the tax. For example, in Colombia, immediately after the introduction of the tax in November 1998, the volume in interbank foreign exchange and money markets declined to about 20 percent of the average pre-tax level, while the volume in the Treasury bill market declined to about 10 percent of the average pre-tax level. In Venezuela, according to the Annual Report of the Caracas Stock Exchange, after the tax was introduced in 1999, trading volume on the exchange dropped by 47 percent compared to the previous year.

Conclusion

This chapter has focused on the incidence of taxes on banking transactions. In the last 15 years, a number of countries in Latin America repeatedly implemented and revoked these taxes, which are usually levied on debits to bank accounts. These taxes are currently in effect in Argentina, Brazil, Colombia, and Venezuela, where they have been quite effective in generating revenue in the short run.

This has been the first formal attempt to estimate deadweight losses and disintermediation following the introduction of bank debit taxes, using data from Brazil, Colombia, Ecuador, and Venezuela. The study finds that, especially at higher rates, these taxes have coincided with significant welfare losses and financial disintermediation. Deadweight losses following the introduction of the tax reached up to 30 percent in Venezuela, up to 35 percent in Colombia, and up to 45 percent in Ecuador.

The study also derives a relationship between deadweight welfare losses and disintermediation. Using this relationship, it shows that the introduction of a bank debit tax resulted in disintermediation of up to 28 percent in Venezuela, up to 41 percent in Colombia, and up to 47 percent in Ecuador. The analysis does not find significant disintermediation or deadweight losses in Brazil, for which the data series is not really long enough to allow effective use of the study's method. The study also finds that both the deadweight losses and disintermediation effects cumulate over time as the taxes remain in place.

These findings support a view that at low rates and for a limited time, bank debit taxes can be used as a quick and effective way to generate revenue, while the implementation of more traditional taxes is being improved. However, at higher rates or over an extended period of time, the taxes may lead to significant financial disintermediation.

Notes

1. In December 2000, the tax was made permanent and its rate was increased to 0.3 percent.

2. See Coelho, Ebrill, and Summers (2001) for a comprehensive description of bank debt taxes in Latin America.

3. The 2 percent tax rate was applicable in Peru from April to September 1990.

4. This insight comes from Caminal (1997).

5. See Hines (1999) for a discussion of Harberger's contribution to the estimation of deadweight welfare losses.

6. In Brazil, the tax was not collected during the first half of 1999, while the tax rate remained at 0.38 percent. In June 2000, the tax rate was lowered to 0.3 percent. To compensate for a potential bias in the estimates because of a reduction in distortions followed by the lowering of the tax rate, this study re-based the index of tax revenues to May 2000.

7. For example, if the tax became effective on May 15, 1998, this study uses tax revenues for the month of June 1998.

8. This substitution can sometimes lead to a systemic crisis. For example, the introduction of a 1 percent tax on any bank transaction in Ecuador in December 1998 led to a widespread preference for cash, which seriously exacerbated the ongoing liquidity crisis in the banking system. A blanket deposit insurance guarantee, introduced at the same time as the financial transaction tax, was not sufficient to restore confidence in the banking system. In the three months after the introduction of the tax, amidst a run on the currency, six small banks and the second largest bank had to be closed. In March 1999, fearing a run on the whole banking system, the government froze all demand and savings deposits for six months and all time deposits for one year.

9. Such funds were authorized by the central bank in order to minimize the disintermediation effects of the tax.

References

Albuquerque, Pedro H. 2002. "How Bad Is BAD Taxation? Disintermediation and Illiquidity in a Bank Account Debits Tax Model." Presented to the 2002 North American Meeting of the Econometric Society, Los Angeles. Processed.

Caminal, Ramon. 1997. "Financial Intermediation and the Optimal Tax System." *Journal of Public Economics* 63 (3): 351–82.

Coelho, Isaias, Liam Ebrill, and Victoria Summers. 2001. "Bank Debit Taxes in Latin America: An Analysis of Recent Trends." Working Paper 01/67. International Monetary Fund, Washington, D.C.

Harberger, Arnold C. 1964. "The Measurement of Waste." *American Economic Review* 54 (3): 58–76.

Hines, James R., Jr. 1999. "Three Sides of Harberger Triangles." *Journal of Economic Perspectives* 13 (2): 167–88.

Kirilenko, Andrei A., and Victoria Summers. 2001. "Bank Debit Taxes: Productivity vs. Financial Disintermediation." International Monetary Fund, Washington, D.C. Processed.

Tanzi, Vito. 2000. "Taxation in Latin America in the Last Decade." Working Paper 76. Stanford University, Center for Research on Economic Development and Policy Reform, Stanford, Calif.

11

Securities Transaction Taxes and Financial Markets

Karl Habermeier and Andrei Kirilenko

This chapter argues that transaction taxes can have negative effects on price discovery, volatility, and market liquidity in securities markets. These effects can lead to a reduction in market efficiency and may contribute to increased asset price volatility.

Financial markets transform latent demands of investors into realized financial transactions. Securities transaction taxes (STTs) alter this transformation. Proponents of STTs argue that such taxes can reduce market volatility, help prevent financial crises, and reduce excessive trading.[1] Opponents believe that STTs are difficult to implement and enforce and that they can do great damage to financial markets.

This chapter considers the impact of transaction taxes on financial markets in the context of four broad questions. How important is trading? What causes price volatility? How are prices formed? How valuable is the volume of transactions? These questions are at the core of the debate on the role of transaction taxes. The arguments here draw on research on market microstructure, asset pricing, rational expectations, and international finance.

Market microstructure studies suggest that trading is essential for price discovery—the process of finding market clearing prices. A large number of markets rely on dealers to provide price discovery, as well as liquidity and price stabilization. Levying STTs on the

This chapter is printed by permission of *IMF Staff Papers,* where an earlier version appeared.

dealers inhibits their ability to assist investors with the transformation of latent demands into realized transactions. The literature also finds that much of the volatility is caused by informed traders as their information is aggregated into transaction prices. Taxing financial transactions does not reduce the volatility due to "noise" trading.[2] Rather, it introduces additional frictions into the price discovery process.

The literature on option pricing under transaction costs shows how frictions on the trading in one asset affects prices and volumes of that and other assets. Using a simple framework based on this literature, this chapter demonstrates how volume can migrate to the assets that are not subject to the tax. That is to say, there will be an increase in the use of these assets for the purpose of risk or liquidity management. The chapter also argues that it is very difficult to design and implement a tax that does not favor one portfolio of assets over another portfolio with exactly the same payoff.

Recent studies on rational expectations question the traditional view that volume is just an outcome of the trading process and is not valuable per se. These studies find that volume can play an informational role. Consequently, if transaction taxes cause volume to migrate, then they can hamper the informational efficiency of markets.

International finance provides other interesting examples of market fragmentation, where essentially the same security is traded in distinct markets, as well as of market segmentation, involving persistent price differentials for different groups of purchasers. Volume fragmentation can occur because of restrictions on trading of substitutable securities, such as different classes of company shares. This leads to market segmentation and inefficient price discovery.

This chapter is organized as follows. After reviewing the literature on STTs, the chapter provides a brief description of the Swedish experience with such taxes. It then deals with the four broad questions specified above. The next-to-last section reviews international finance evidence on market segmentation and execution costs in different markets. The final section observes that transaction taxes can have a substantial effect on investment. Overall, the finding is that securities transaction taxes can create unexpectedly large distortions.

Literature on Securities Transaction Taxes

Opinion is divided on the merits of securities transaction taxes. Many proponents of STTs advance the following propositions.[3]

• The contribution of financial markets to economic welfare does not justify the resources they command. During a given time period, the resources that change hands in financial markets far exceed the value of the underlying or "real" transactions.

• Many financial transactions are highly speculative in nature, and may contribute to financial or economic instability.

• Market instability, including crashes, enriches insiders and speculators, while the costs are borne by the general public.

• Financial market activity increases inequalities in the distribution of income and wealth.

From this perspective, some argue that governments ought to tax financial transactions to discourage destabilizing speculation that can threaten high employment and price stability, as well as to raise revenue. The massive volume of financial transactions in well-developed modern markets would—they reason—allow substantial revenue to be raised by imposing low tax rates on a broad range of transactions. Higher rates, it is argued, should be levied on short-term transactions, since these seem to benefit primarily market intermediaries and not "real" users.

Opponents of STTs have more faith in the ability of markets to allocate resources efficiently without direct intervention from public policy. However, the opponents also lack a convincing argument to justify the volume of resources flowing through financial markets. In addition, numerous documented anomalies, as well as a history of market crashes, do not lend themselves easily to the idea that financial markets are fully efficient. Neither does the fact that market participants devote considerable resources to analyzing previous transaction prices and volumes. Thus instead of showing that the allocation of resources to the financial sector is justified on efficiency grounds, or that observed market volatility is optimal, the opponents of STTs have focused on practical shortcomings of the taxes themselves.[4]

There are two dimensions to the difficulties in implementing STTs. First, if an STT is applied in one financial market but not in others, the volume of transactions tends to migrate from the market that is taxed to markets that are not. Effective enforcement of STTs thus requires either a cross-market and perhaps even a global reach or measures to segregate markets. For example, tax authorities in one country may attempt to require payment of the tax on transactions made by their residents not only in financial markets within their own borders, but in other markets as well. Alternatively, they may impose controls on cross-border financial transactions.

Second, financial assets promise certain payoffs at different times and under different relevant circumstances (the latter often summarized as "states of the world"). Since the composition of the assets used in financial transactions matters less than the distribution of payoffs over time and in different states of the world, the tax base must be defined as a function of the final payoff, rather than the assets employed. A securities transaction tax would be considered neutral if it did not favor one portfolio of assets over another portfolio with exactly the same pattern of payoffs. Since payoffs can be replicated by portfolios consisting of different types of assets, the imposition of an STT can create a greater distortion than it is trying to mitigate. Instead of trading less because of the tax, investors may transact more in assets that are taxed at a lower rate or not taxed at all. As a result, real resources devoted to financial transactions may in fact increase rather than diminish following the imposition of an STT.

Given the lack of a consensus on the theory, there have been many attempts to resolve the debate empirically. However, empirical studies undertaken so far have not been able to decisively resolve the debate on the effects of transaction taxes on financial markets.[5]

Empirical research has encountered three major problems. First, the effects of taxes on prices and volume are hard to disentangle from other structural and policy changes taking place at the same time. Therefore, estimates based on the assumption that everything else in the economy is held constant are potentially biased.

Second, it is difficult to separate transaction volume into stable (or "fundamental") and destabilizing (or "noise") components. Thus it is hard to say which part of the volume is more affected by the tax.

Third, it is hard to differentiate among multiple ways in which transaction taxes can affect asset prices. These ways include changes in expectations about the impact of the taxes, the cost of creating and trading in close substitutes not covered by the tax, and changes in market liquidity.

Empirical studies seek answers to three main questions. The first question is whether transaction taxes have an effect on price volatility. Roll (1989) studies stock return volatility in 23 countries from 1987 to 1989. He finds no evidence that volatility is reliably related to transaction taxes. Umlauf (1993) studies equity returns in Sweden from 1980 to 1987, before and during the imposition of transaction taxes on brokerage service providers. He finds that the volatility did not decline in response to the introduction of taxes. Saporta and Kan (1997) study the impact of the U.K. stamp duty on volatility of securities' prices. They also find no evidence of a relationship between the stamp duty and volatility. Jones and Seguin (1997) examine the effect on volatility of the introduction of negotiated commissions on U.S. national stock exchanges in 1975, which resulted in a permanent decline in commissions. They argue that this event is analogous to a one-time reduction of a tax on equity transactions. They reject the hypothesis that the lowering of commissions increases volatility. Hu (1998) examines the effects on volatility of changes in transaction taxes that occurred in Hong Kong, Japan, Korea, and Taiwan from 1975 to 1994, and does not find significant effects. Finally, Hau and Chevallier (2000) examine the effect on volatility of minimum price variation rules in the French stock market. They argue that minimum price variation rules resulted in a doubling of transaction costs for stocks priced above a certain threshold (500 francs). They argue that this is analogous to the application of a transaction tax on the stocks above the threshold. They find that the increase in transaction costs results in "a statistically significant, but economically insignificant" reduction in the volatility of returns on a daily, weekly, and monthly basis.

The second question is whether transaction taxes affect trading volume. Umlauf (1993) reports that after Sweden increased its transaction tax from 1 to 2 percent in 1986, 60 percent of the volume of the 11 most actively traded Swedish stocks migrated to London. The migrated volume represented over 30 percent of all trading volume in Swedish equities. By 1990, that share increased to around 50 percent. According to Campbell and Froot (1995), only 27 percent of the trading volume in Ericsson, the most actively traded Swedish stock, took place in Stockholm in 1988. Hu (1998) examines 14 tax changes in four Asian markets and finds that differences in turnover before and after changes in the tax level are not statistically significant.

Third, empirical studies seek to find out whether transaction taxes have an impact on the prices of securities. Umlauf (1993) reports that the Swedish All-Equity Index fell by 2.2 percent on the day a 1 percent transaction tax was introduced and again by 0.8 percent on the day it was increased to 2 percent. Saporta and Kan (1997) find that on the day stamp duty in the United Kingdom was increased from 1 to 2 percent, the stock market index declined by 3.3 percent. Hu (1998) finds that on average the return on the announcement date is –0.6 percent in Korea and –1.6 percent in Taiwan, with the result for Taiwan being highly statistically significant.

One of the main reasons for the dispersion and inconclusiveness of results is the lack of appropriate data. Since the questions are essentially of the market microstructure-type, an ideal dataset would consist of transaction frequency data for individual financial instruments. In order to take revisions in expectations into account, the data should start well before the announcement of the transaction tax and include a sufficient number of observations following its imposition. Furthermore, in order to separate volume into meaningful categories, the data should be broken down according to the type of investor: for example, institutional investors, hedge funds, and mutual funds. In contrast, most empirical studies rely on weekly equity index returns.

The Swedish Experience

To illustrate the arguments that follow, this section presents a brief description of the Swedish experience with STTs. The Swedish experiment lasted for more than eight years. The first measure was announced in October 1983 and the last one was abolished in December 1991. The analysis in this section is based on the studies by Umlauf (1993) and Campbell and Froot (1995).

The initiative to impose financial transaction taxes came from the Swedish labor sector in 1983. The labor sector did not claim that trading in financial markets led to inefficient outcomes. Rather, according to Umlauf (1993), in the opinion of the labor sector, "the salaries earned by young finance professionals were unjustifiable . . . in a society giving high priority to income equality," especially given the seemingly unproductive tasks that they performed. On this basis, the Swedish labor sector proposed to levy taxes directly on domestic brokerage service providers.

Despite the objections of the Swedish Finance Ministry and the business sector, popular support led to the adoption of taxes by Parliament. The taxes became effective on January 1, 1984. They were levied on domestic stock and derivative transactions. Purchases and sales of domestic equities were taxed at 0.5 percent each, resulting in a 1 percent tax per round trip. Round-trip transactions in stock options were taxed at 2 percent. In addition, exercise of an option was treated as a transaction in the underlying stock and thus was subject to an additional 1 percent round-trip charge. The tax coverage and rates reflected a popular perception about the "usefulness" of transactions in different financial instruments, with those involving equity options being the least "useful."

Continuing pressure from the labor sector compelled the Parliament to double the tax rates in July 1986 and broaden its coverage in 1987. Furthermore, following large losses in interest futures and options (most notably by the City of Stockholm, which lost SEK 450 million), the tax was extended to transactions in fixed-income securities, including government debt and the corresponding derivatives in 1989.[6] The maximum tax rate for fixed-income instruments was set at 0.15 percent of the underlying notional or cash amount. In addition, the tax was designed to be "yield-neutral," with longer maturities instruments being taxed at progressively higher rates.

The revenue performance of the tax was disappointing. According to the Finance Ministry of Sweden, the government collected SEK 820 million in 1984, SEK 1.17 billion in 1985, and SEK 2.63 billion in 1986. This accounted for 0.37, 0.45, and 0.96 percent of the total revenue for the corresponding years. After doubling the tax rates the government was able to collect SEK 3.74 billion in 1987 and SEK 4.01 billion in 1988. This accounted for 1.17 and 1.21 percent of the total revenue.[7] Thus a 100 percent increase in the tax rate resulted in a 22 percent increase in revenue.

Widespread avoidance was one reason for the weak performance of the tax. Foreign investors avoided the tax by placing their orders with brokers in London or New York. Domestic investors avoided it by first establishing offshore accounts (and paying the tax equal to three times the round-trip tax on equity for funds moved offshore) and then using foreign brokers.

The scale of avoidance was manifested by a massive migration of stock trading volume from Stockholm to other financial centers. Since the brokerage business is highly competitive, finding a close substitute for brokerage services offshore was not costly. According to Umlauf (1993), following the doubling of the tax, 60 percent of the volume of the 11 most actively traded Swedish stocks migrated to London. The migrated volume represented over 30 percent of all trading volume in Swedish equities. By 1990, that share increased to around 50 percent.

However, the market does not necessarily move off shore, if close substitutes are available domestically. For example, trading in bonds did not move offshore, but shifted to debentures, forward contracts, and swaps.

Application of the tax to fixed-income instruments did result in a sharp drop in trading volume in Swedish government bills and bonds and in fixed-income derivatives contracts. Campbell and Froot (1995) estimate that during the first week of the tax, bond trading volume dropped by about 85 percent from its average during the summer of 1987 and trading in fixed-income derivatives essentially disappeared. This significantly undermined the ability of the Bank of Sweden to conduct monetary policy, made government borrowing more expensive, and eroded both popular and political support for the tax. Taxes on fixed-income instruments were abolished in April 1990. Taxes on other instruments were cut in half in January 1991 and abolished altogether in December 1991.

Following the abolition of the tax, some trading volume came back to Sweden. According to Campbell and Froot (1995), 41 percent of the trades in Ericsson took place in Stockholm in 1992. Overall, the proportion of the trading volume in Sweden increased for almost all equities in 1992. That year, 56 percent of all trading volume in Swedish equities took place in Stockholm.

The most striking features of the Swedish experience are the extent to which investors avoided the tax by finding or creating close substitutes, the extent to which market activity suffered, and the reversibility of the effect once the tax was removed.

How Important Is Trading?

The Swedish labor sector believed that trading in financial markets is an essentially unproductive task. Just how important is trading? The answer to this question depends on how the trading is conducted. In Sweden, investors had to carry out financial transactions mostly through dealers.

However, trading does not have be conducted exclusively through dealers. It can be done through other mechanisms. For example, in continuous electronic auctions, buyers and sellers trade directly with each other, bypassing the dealers. Why didn't such an auction develop in Sweden? In fact, under the law, transactions executed without dealers were exempt from taxes.

According to the market microstructure literature, under some circumstances, dealers offer services that cannot be provided by other types of market designs at lower cost. It is especially true for infrequently traded assets, such as most of the Swedish stocks. Perhaps for that reason the order flow migrated not to another trading design, but to dealers in London and New York.

Dealers provide several important services. They provide liquidity and assume substantial risks by contributing their own capital. Accordingly, they demand adequate compensation for the provision of liquidity and the capital that they put at risk. The dealer's compensation is higher for illiquid assets.

In addition, dealers who act as market makers in particular securities must furnish competitive bid and offer quotations on demand and be ready, willing, and able to effect transactions in reasonable quantities at the quoted prices. In other words, a buyer does not have to wait or look for a seller, but can simply buy from a dealer who sells from his inventory. According to Pagano and Roell (1990), "this implies that, in contrast with what happens on auction markets, traders are insured against execution risk, i.e., the risk of finding few or no counterparties to trade." The dealer's compensation is higher for assets with a higher execution risk.

This highlights another important function that dealers play: namely, the provision of price stability. According to Madhavan (2000), "the presence of market makers who can carry inventories imparts stability to price movements through their actions relative to an automated system that simply clears the market at each auction without accumulating inventory."

The provision of liquidity, price discovery, and price stabilization requires inventory management. Inventory management is achieved through the buying and selling of securities. Hasbrouck and Sofianos (1993) examine a set of quote, trade, and inventory data for market makers (specialists) on the New York Stock Exchange (NYSE). According to their data, the market maker's activity (both purchases and sales) averages about 26 percent of the total transaction flow (also both purchases and sales). For the most frequently traded stocks, this number is 20 percent, while for the least frequently traded stocks, it rises to 38 percent.[8] Thus dealers become much more important as liquidity providers in less frequently traded stocks.

Inventory management can involve both customer and inter-dealer trading. When a competitive inter-dealer market is available, dealers can adjust their inventory without waiting for a public order flow to arrive. According to the empirical evidence, dealers trade in the inter-dealer market when they want to manage large inventory positions. Lyons (2001) suggests that inter-dealer trading in the foreign exchange market currently accounts for about two-thirds of the total volume. Hansch, Naik, and Viswanathan (1998) show that the average size of an inter-dealer trade on the London Stock Exchange is much larger than the average size of a trade with the general public. They also show that inventory levels at which dealers trade among themselves is about twice as large as those at which they trade with the general public. They find that 38 percent of the variation in inter-dealer trading is explained by variation in inventory levels. They conclude that "inter-dealer trading is an important mechanism for managing inventory risks in dealership markets."

Thus trading is important. It helps manage risks. Dealers demand compensation for the services that they provide and the risks that they take. If trading becomes costly as a result of transaction taxes, dealers cannot manage their risks effectively. Accordingly, they become less willing to put their own capital at risk in order to provide liquidity. Investors cannot carry out their desired trades, their latent demands are not fully satisfied, and resources are not allocated to their best uses.

What Causes Volatility?

The previous section argued that trading is important. But can it also be the cause of volatility?

French and Roll (1986) conduct an empirical study of the variability of stock returns over trading and nontrading periods. Using data for all stocks listed on the NYSE and American Stock Exchange (AMEX) for the period 1963 to 1982, they find that on an hourly basis, the variance of stock returns is between 13 and 100 times larger when markets are open for trading than the variance when the markets are closed, depending on the definition of nontrading period.

They investigate three possible causes for the higher volatility during trading hours. First, higher volatility may be caused by the arrival of more public information during trading hours. Second, it may be caused by informed investors as their private information is incorporated into prices. Finally, higher volatility may be caused by the process of trading itself as prices fluctuate because of market frictions and transaction costs.

They also find that the process of trading accounts for at most 12 percent of the daily return variance. The rest of the variance is attributable to the arrival of public and private information during trading hours. While they cannot directly decompose the effects of public and private information on volatility, they conduct a test that suggests that most of the variability in stock returns can be attributed to the arrival of private information during trading hours.

Later studies have relied on much more refined transaction-level data to further decompose transaction price volatility. Madhavan, Richardson, and Roomans (1997) develop a stylized, reduced-form model of price volatility and use transaction-level, intraday data on 274 NYSE-listed stocks during 1990 to estimate it.

They argue that price volatility can be explained by the variability of four components: public information, private information, transaction costs, and other market frictions (price discreteness). They estimate that the impact of public information accounts for 46 percent of volatility at the beginning of the trading day and 35 percent at the end. The impact of private information (including the interaction between cost and private information effects) drops from 31 percent in the morning to 26 percent at the closing of trading. Variability in transaction costs increases from 22 percent at the opening to 35 percent at the end of the trading day. Finally, price discreteness accounts for the remaining 1 to 4 percent at the beginning and the end of the trading day, respectively.

Transaction costs in the Madhavan, Richardson, and Roomans (1997) model capture dealer costs for supplying liquidity on demand. They include compensation for inventory costs, putting their capital at risk, and other transaction costs. The model implies that other things being equal, higher transaction costs increase volatility. If transaction costs also include transaction taxes, then introduction of STTs can result in higher rather than lower volatility of transaction prices.

How Are Prices Formed?

In perfect, frictionless markets, asset prices immediately reflect all available information. As the new information arrives, investors rebalance their portfolios of assets. The rebalancing results in an updated set of prices. In the absence of transaction costs, the rebalancing can be done continuously and price discrepancies are eliminated instantaneously. However, in real markets, agents face transaction costs. The presence of even small transaction costs makes continuous rebalancing infinitely expensive. Therefore, valuable information can be held back from being incorporated into prices. As a result, prices can deviate from their full information values.

The dissatisfaction with the assumption of continuous portfolio rebalancing was the starting argument for the literature on the replication of assets under transaction costs. The literature recognizes that continuous rebalancing is not feasible and formulates discrete rebalancing under transaction costs.

This section presents a simple theoretical framework based on the literature on option pricing with transaction costs. It is assumed that securities taxes are a source of transaction costs. The framework studies the impact of STTs on portfolio rebalancing and price formation.

A Simple Example

Consider a simple two-period example (following Hull 1985). There are three assets in the market: a risk-free bond yielding 3 percent per year, a non–dividend-paying stock, and a call option on the stock. The starting price of each share of stock is equal to $20. After a year, assume that the stock price will either have increased to $22 or have fallen to $18, with equal probability. The strike price of the option at the end of the year is taken to be $21.

Simple option pricing theory can be employed to compute in what proportions a call option and a risk-free bond must be held in order to be equivalent to 100 shares of stock. As shown in the appendix, on the assumptions given, this portfolio requires exactly 400 options (worth $0.63 each) and $1,747 of the bond.

But a 1 percent transaction tax on buying or selling the stock greatly lowers the value of the option, as the tax of $0.22 must be incurred twice if the option is exercised and the stock then sold. Working through the arithmetic reveals that the option is only worth $0.39 and that now 694 options must be bought (along with $1,728 worth of bonds) to match 100 shares.

If the transaction tax is also levied on option transactions or on bonds, there is a further change in the required number of options in the portfolio to replicate the shares—but in these cases, the changes are very small. Thus extending the transaction tax to all three assets certainly does not restore neutrality.

Note that even in this simple example, it is quite difficult to design and even more difficult to implement a tax that does not favor one portfolio of assets over another portfolio with exactly the same payoff (such as a stock versus a bond and a call option). A uniform transaction tax is not payoff-neutral. For a tax to be payoff-neutral, the tax rates must be such that a change in the value of a replicating portfolio is exactly equal to the change in the price of the underlying asset. In other words, the tax rates must depend on what is known as the "delta" of the replicating portfolio.[9] But it is known that, in practice as in theory, "delta" changes as more information is revealed about the (unknown) underlying stochastic process. Therefore, a payoff-neutral tax would have to be frequently adjusted. This would make it difficult to implement.

A Generalized Model

Boyle and Vorst (1992) have generalized the simple two-period example to a multi-period case. They use a method proposed by Cox, Ross, and Rubinstein (1979), who assumed a dynamic price process according to which, during each subperiod of length Δt, the stock price increases by a factor $\theta = \exp\{\delta\sqrt{\Delta t}\}$, with probability p; otherwise it decreases by the same multiplicative factor.

Boyle and Vorst show that, if this binomial multiplicative price is itself unaffected by transaction costs—that is, if the response of agents to transaction taxes does not lead to a change in θ—the call option can still be priced after the introduction of transaction costs by increasing the variance by an amount that is positively related to the rate of the transaction cost or tax and inversely related to the length of the rebalancing period.[10] Specifically, if δ^2 is the original variance, the modified variance, $\hat{\delta}^2$ is given by,

(11.1)
$$\hat{\delta}^2 = \delta^2 \left(1 + k \frac{2}{\delta\sqrt{\Delta t}} \right)$$

where k is the rate of transactions cost.[11]

How Valuable Is the Volume of Transactions?

According to the example presented in the previous section, demand for assets changes following the introduction of a transaction tax on a stock. The demand for derivatives goes up and the demand for both stocks and bonds decreases. Changes in demand translate into changes in the volume of realized transactions. Was anything lost as a result of this change in volume? Does it matter if transaction volume migrates to other instruments, markets, or countries? It does not, if the volume is not valuable. But how valuable is the volume of realized transactions?

According to standard rational expectations models with supply uncertainty, trading orders have both informational (or "signal") and "noise" components. Without the noise, aggregate supply uncertainty is resolved, and prices adjust to their full information level. Otherwise, the informational component is aggregated into prices and the "noise" is left in volume. Consequently, volume is just an outcome of the trading process. It does not have any information about the fundamentals or the trading process and, therefore, lacks value.

According to this view, the migration of volume to other instruments, markets, or countries does not result in any loss of value or efficiency. It just means a reallocation of supply uncertainty. In other words, if transaction volume moves from Stockholm to London, investors in Stockholm become exposed to less uncertainty associated with "noise" trading and investors in London to more of it. Thus after a transaction tax is imposed, if volume migrates away from the taxed asset, the policymakers should perhaps just change their revenue projections and not worry about any fundamental market effects.

The long-held view that volume is not valuable per se has recently come under scrutiny. Blume, Easley, and O'Hara (1994) investigate the informational role of volume. In their model, the source of "noise" is not supply uncertainty, but the precision of private information about the signal. Prices aggregate information about the average level of private information. Trading volume contains information about the precision of individual private signals. Thus volume does not just contain "noise," but has a nontrivial informational role to play. Price-volume sequences are more informative than prices alone. This role becomes especially important for infrequently traded stocks that often do not get much analyst coverage.

In addition, Easley, O'Hara, and Srinivas (1998) investigate the informational role of transaction volume in options markets. They develop a model where informed traders can trade in stock or options markets. They empirically test the model and find that option volume data contain information about future stock prices. Thus they conclude that "volume plays a role in the process by which markets become efficient." Consequently, a migration of volume from the derivative market may also result in the loss of informational efficiency.

This new view represents a fundamentally different perspective on the role of volume. It can be summarized as saying that "volume matters." The migration of volume results in lower informational efficiency of instruments and markets from which it migrated. If transaction taxes cause the volume to migrate, then they do affect the ability of markets to aggregate information and prevent a more efficient allocation of resources.

Evidence from International Finance

The international finance literature provides examples of market segmentation and execution costs in different markets. Market segmentation can result from direct restrictions on foreign ownership, exchange and capital controls, and regulatory and accounting aspects including disclosure rules, settlement practices, and investor protection rights. Bekaert (1995) studies 19 emerging markets and finds that exchange and capital controls (and taxes that have a similar effect), as well as regulation and accounting practices, are significant in explaining market segmentation. Restrictions on foreign ownership are apparently being circumvented by the closed-end country funds.

Domowitz, Glen, and Madhavan (2000) use a comprehensive database of execution costs (including transaction taxes) for 42 countries from September 1996 to December 1998. They use panel data techniques to study the interaction between cost, liquidity, and volatility across countries and through time. They find that except for North America, explicit equity trading costs such as brokerage commissions, taxes, and fees account for about two-thirds of total execution costs. In the United States, average explicit one-way trading costs are the smallest for the countries in their study, accounting for 8.3 basis points or a fraction of 2.2 percent of mean return (374 basis points) for the period 1990–98. In other words, a complete rebalancing of the portfolio once a year results in an average explicit cost of 2.2 percent of its annual mean return. The largest explicit cost of 106 basis points is in Ireland, which has a stamp duty of 1 percent. In Ireland, the explicit costs of turning over a portfolio of equities just once a year accounts for a full 25 percent of the annual mean return.

They also find that over time, with the exception of transition economies, costs have generally declined, and that higher trading costs are positively related to increased volatility and lower volume.

Summary and Conclusions

This chapter examines recent research relevant to assessing the impact of securities transaction taxes on financial markets. This research includes work on market microstructure, asset pricing, rational expectations, and international finance. The study concludes that in most circumstances, transaction taxes can have negative effects on price discovery, volatility, and liquidity and lead to a reduction in market efficiency.

The arguments made in this chapter may be summarized as follows. First, in dealership markets, trading facilitates the provision of liquidity, price discovery, and price stabilization. Trading also helps to manage risks. If investors cannot carry out their desired trades, their latent demands are not fully satisfied and resources are not allocated to their best use.

Second, price volatility can be explained by the variability of four components: public information, private information, transaction costs, and other market frictions. Other things being equal, higher transaction costs increase volatility. Consequently, the introduction of STTs can increase the volatility of transaction prices.

Third, a simple theoretical framework based on the literature on option pricing with transaction costs shows that following the introduction of a transaction tax, the demand for derivatives can increase substantially. Moreover, it is difficult to design and implement a tax that does not favor one portfolio of assets over another portfolio with exactly the same payoff.

Fourth, if transaction volume has an informational content, then a migration of volume would result in lower informational efficiency of instruments and markets from which it migrated. If transaction taxes are the cause of volume migration, then they can inhibit the informational efficiency of markets.

Finally, the international finance evidence on market segmentation and execution costs in different markets suggests that except for North America, explicit equity trading costs such as brokerage commissions, taxes, and fees account for about two-thirds of total execution costs. The study concludes that higher trading costs, some of which are due to STTs, are positively related to increased volatility and lower volume.

Transaction taxes can thus have a substantial effect on the transformation of investor demands into transactions. STTs can obstruct price discovery and price stabilization, increase volatility, reduce market liquidity, and inhibit the informational efficiency of financial markets.

Appendix. Working through the Numerical Example

In order to compute the portfolios presented in the fifth section, begin by choosing a number of shares δ so that holding that number of shares and selling 100 call options provides a risk-free portfolio: that is, one that has the same value whether the share goes up or down. Since the value of option at maturity when it is "in the money" is exactly 1 (since then the option allows the share to be bought at the strike price of 21 and sold at 22), δ must satisfy:

(A11.1) $22 \, \delta - 100 = 18 \, \delta.$

The solution to this equation is $\delta = 25$. The value of this portfolio at the end of the year will be $18 \, \delta = 450$, which equals $437 discounted to the present at 3 percent per year. This, then, must be the value of the risk-free portfolio at the outset. Therefore since the 25 shares will then cost $500, one can conclude that the price of the 100 options is $500 − $437 = $63.

Rearranging, one can conclude that a portfolio consisting of 100 call options and $437 of bonds will exactly replicate the payoff on 25 shares. Equivalently, to replicate 100 shares requires exactly 400 options and $1,747 of bonds.

Suppose now that a transaction tax of 1 percent is introduced on all period-one transactions in the stock. Once more, when the stock price is equal to 22, the option gives a right to buy the stock at 21 and sell it at 22. But now this round-trip transaction is subject to transaction taxes. To buy the stock, the option's holder must pay an additional $0.21 when buying the stock and $0.22 when selling it. Accordingly, the net terminal value of an in-the-money option is now just $0.57.

Let δ^* be the amount of stock in the risk-neutral valuation portfolio adjusted for the transaction tax. Then, subtracting 1 percent transaction tax from the price of the share in each case,

(A11.2) $21.78\ \delta^* - 57 = 17.82\ \delta^*.$

The solution is now $\delta^* = 14.4$ and the value of the portfolio at the end of the year will be $17.82\ \hat{\delta} = \$257$. The present value of this amount is equal to 249. Since the 14.4 shares will the cost 288, the price of the 100 options is $288 - \$249 = \$39$.

Rearranging, one can conclude that a portfolio consisting of 100 call options and $249 worth of bonds replicates just 14.4 shares. Replicating 100 shares requires 694 options (plus $1,728 of bonds).

Notes

1. For example, Eichengreen, Tobin, and Wyplosz (1995) argue that "transaction taxes are one way to throw sand in the wheels of superefficient financial vehicles."

2. By this term is meant trading by those who have poor information, or whose trades are based on liquidity needs. It could also include trading automatically generated by portfolio balancing programs.

3. See, for example, Tobin (1984); Summers and Summers (1989); Stiglitz (1989); and Eichengreen, Tobin, and Wyplosz (1995).

4. See, for example, Campbell and Froot (1995).

5. Hammond (1995) reviews most of the empirical research on financial transaction taxes. Empirical studies since 1995 have sought to address similar issues by using other data sets.

6. Officially, the extension of the tax to fixed-income instruments was supposed to achieve "neutrality" with the tax on equity transactions. See Campbell and Froot (1995).

7. By contrast, tobacco taxes accounted for 1.26 and 1.37 percent of the total revenue collected in 1987 and 1998, respectively.

8. The statistics are calculated by taking the participation rates reported in the paper as a fraction of 50 percent, the rate which implies that the market maker is a counterparty to all trades.

9. "Delta" is conventionally defined as the response of the value of a derivative portfolio with respect to the price of the underlying asset.

10. Reinhart (2000) argues that the introduction of STTs may also make asset prices more variable in the general equilibrium setting.

11. Leland (1985) develops an extension to the Black-Scholes continuous-time model and shows how to modify the variance to price call options in the presence of transaction costs. In Leland's model, the variance increases in the presence of transaction costs, reflecting the discontinuous rebalancing of portfolios necessitated by transaction costs.

References

Bekaert, Geert. 1995. "Market Integration and Investment Barriers in Emerging Equity Markets." *World Bank Economic Review* 9 (1): 75–107.

Blume, Lawrence, David Easley, and Maureen O'Hara. 1994. "Market Statistics and Technical Analysis: The Role of Volume." *Journal of Finance* 69 (1): 153–81.

Boyle, Phelim P., and Ton Vorst. 1992. "Option Pricing in Discrete Time with Transaction Costs." *Journal of Finance* 47 (17): 271–94.

Campbell, John Y., and Kenneth A. Froot. 1995. "Securities Transaction Taxes: What About International Experiences and Migrating Markets?" In Suzanne Hammond, ed., *Securities Transaction Taxes: False Hopes and Unintended Consequences.* Chicago: Catalyst Institute.

Cox, John C., Stephen A. Ross, and Mark Rubinstein. 1979. "Option Pricing: A Simplified Approach." *Journal of Financial Economics* 7 (3): 229–63.

Domowitz, Ian, Jack Glen, and Ananth Madhavan. 2000. "Liquidity, Volatility, and Equity Trading Costs Across Countries and Over Time." International Finance Corporation, Washington, D.C. Processed.

Easley, David, Maureen O'Hara, and P. S. Srinivas. 1998. "Option Volume and Stock Prices: Evidence on Where Informed Traders Trade." *Journal of Finance* 53 (2): 431–65.

Eichengreen, Barry, James Tobin, and Charles Wyplosz. 1995. "Two Cases for Sand in the Wheels of International Finance." *Economic Journal* 105 (428): 162–72.

French, Kenneth, and Richard Roll. 1986. "Stock Return Variances: The Arrival of Information and the Reaction of Traders." *Journal of Financial Economics* 17 (1): 5–26.

Hammond, Suzanne, ed. 1995. *Securities Transaction Taxes: False Hopes and Unintended Consequences.* Chicago: Catalyst Institute.

Hansch, Oliver, Narayan Y. Naik, and S. Viswanathan. 1998. "Do Inventories Matter in Dealership Markets? Evidence from the London Stock Exchange." *Journal of Finance* 53 (5): 1623–56.

Hasbrouck, Joel, and George Sofianos. 1993. "The Trades of Market Makers: An Empirical Analysis of NYSE Specialists." *Journal of Finance* 68 (5): 1565–93.

Hau, Harald, and Anne Chevallier. 2000. "Evidence on the Volatility Effect of a Security Transaction Tax." INSEAD, Fontainebleau Cedex, France. Processed.

Hu, Shing-yang. 1998. "The Effects of the Stock Transaction Tax on the Stock Market: Experiences from Asian Markets." *Pacific-Basin Finance Journal* 6 (3–4): 347–64.

Hull, John C. 1985. *Options, Futures, and Other Derivatives.* Upper Saddle River, N.J.: Prentice Hall.

Jones, Charles M., and Paul J. Seguin. 1997. "Transaction Costs and Price Volatility: Evidence from Commission Deregulation." *American Economic Review* 87 (4): 728–37.

Leland, Hayne E. 1985. "Option Pricing and Replication with Transaction Costs." *Journal of Finance* 60 (5): 1283–1301.

Lyons, Richard K. 2001. *The Microstructure Approach to Exchange Rates.* Cambridge, Mass.: MIT Press.

Madhavan, Ananth. 2000. "Market Microstructure: A Survey." *Journal of Financial Markets* 3 (3): 205–58.

Madhavan, Ananth, Matthew Richardson, and Mark Roomans. 1997. "Why Do Securities Prices Change? A Transaction-level Analysis of NYSE Stocks." *Review of Financial Studies* 10 (4): 1035–64.

Pagano, Marco, and Alisa Roell. 1990. *Auction Markets, Dealership Markets and Execution Risk.* London: CEPR Financial Market Paper Series.

Reinhart, Vincent R. 2000. "How the Machinery of International Finance Runs with Sand in its Wheels." *Review of International Economics* 8 (1): 74–85.

Roll, Richard. 1989. "Price Volatility, International Market Links, and their Implications for Regulatory Policies." *Journal of Financial Services Research* 3: 211–46.

Saporta, Victoria, and Kamhon Kan. 1997. "The Effects of Stamp Duty on the Level and Volatility of UK Equity Prices." Working paper. Bank of England, London.

Stiglitz, Joseph E. 1989. "Using Tax Policy to Curb Speculative Short-term Trading." *Journal of Financial Services Research* 3: 101–15.

Summers, Lawrence H., and Victoria P. Summers. 1989. "When Financial Markets Work Too Well: A Cautious Case for a Securities Transaction Tax." *Journal of Financial Services Research* 3: 261–86.

Tobin, James. 1984. "On the Efficiency of the Financial System." *Lloyd's Bank Review* 153: 1–15.

Umlauf, Steven R. 1993. "Transaction Taxes and the Behavior of the Swedish Stock Market." *Journal of Financial Economics* 33 (2): 227–40.

12

Consumption Taxes: The Role of the Value-Added Tax

Satya Poddar

This chapter considers the application of expenditure or consumption-type taxes to the financial sector, with special emphasis on the role of the VAT. Most financial services are exempt from value-added taxation (VAT) in virtually all the countries employing this form of broad-based consumption tax. This means that financial institutions do not charge tax on the supply of exempt financial services, but they do pay tax on their own purchase of taxable goods and services acquired for use in making the exempt supplies. The decision to exempt financial services from VAT has revolved around conceptual and administrative difficulties associated with measuring the value of financial services on a transaction-by-transaction basis, rather than social or economic policy reasons. The nonneutral treatment of financial services relative to other taxable goods and services leads to a number of economic distortions and administration and compliance difficulties. While historically, tight regulation of most such services limited the impact of these nonneutralities and complexities, globalization and deregulation have significantly increased the importance of those situations where the exemption system does not perform well.

Confronted with growing problems, policymakers are seeking alternative approaches that treat such services in a more neutral fashion. This chapter looks at the issues raised by the exemption system, and describes and evaluates alternative approaches that have been identified and, in some cases, tried in certain countries. Following a discussion of how financial services can be categorized for the purposes of taxation, the chapter turns to the current tax treatment of financial services and its drawbacks. The next section pauses to consider some theoretical considerations as to the ideal tax base. The chapter then looks at the main alternatives that are available, whether under the rubric of the VAT, or in terms of compensatory taxes. The study concludes with observations specifically relevant to developing countries.

Categories of Financial Services

To understand the current treatment of financial services under consumption tax systems and to undertake tax policy analysis of potential options, five categorizations of financial services are useful. These are by type, by provider, by economic function, by the form of service provided, and by the nature of the consideration.

An obvious place to start in looking at categories of financial services is by reference to the *type of the services* provided. Financial services are also usually identified in this manner in the market place. They are referred to as being banking services, life insurance, and so on. Table 12.1 sets out one classification of the main types of financial services on this basis. The taxing statutes generally use

Table 12.1. Five Main Categories of Financial Services

1. Deposits, borrowing, and lending
a. Banking operations
b. Credit card operations
2. Purchase, sale, and issuance of financial securities
a. Bonds, shares, options, guarantees, and foreign currencies
b. Gold and precious metals
3. Insurance
a. Life
b. Property and Casualty
4. Brokerage and other agent services
a. Buying and selling of financial securities
b. Underwriting and other transactions where agents act as principals
5. Advisory, management, and data processing
a. Asset management and investment advice
b. Administrative and information services, incidental or supplementary to financial services
c. Other

type of service as the means of identifying financial services in order to specify the tax treatment applicable. For example, the Sixth VAT Directive of the European Community (EC) exempts insurance and reinsurance from VAT under article 13(B)(a), and a list of other financial services under article 13(B)(d). The types of services cited may be broad, as in table 12.1, or much more detailed and disaggregated into many subcomponents, as is done in some countries under their tax regulations or administrative guidelines.[1]

Second, in some instances financial services may be associated with a particular *type of provider*, such as an insurance company or a bank. Some types of indirect taxes on financial services may specify that the tax is to be collected by or imposed on only a particular type of business. For example, premium taxes may be collected only on services provided by companies that are registered as insurance companies. This approach may be workable only in cases were there is regulation of the activity involved and the service being taxed is available only from a financial institution of a particular type. Deregulation and disintermediation make it difficult to link the application of tax to a service by type of provider.

Third, financial services can also be categorized by the *economic function* that is being performed that leads to creation or addition of value. Financial services can be categorized under functions such as:

• Intermediation between borrowers and lenders
• Pooling of savings
• Pooling of risks
• Provision of liquidity
• Transaction clearing services
• Creation and making of markets, and
• Agency services.

These are functions that consumers of financial services are willing to pay for. Categorization by economic function is primarily useful as an analytical tool in addressing fundamental questions about what should be the proper indirect tax base for a financial service. They also draw attention to certain characteristics of financial services that may be important in designing and analyzing tax structures. For example, management of risk is a fundamental ingredient in many types of financial services. Under Canadian legislation, presence of financial risk is used as an important determinant for distinguishing financial services from non-financial services. While useful analytically, services are not typically provided on a function-by-function basis, and this type of categorization is of limited use in the design of tax structures.

A fourth categorization of financial services is according to the role played by the service providers. They may be involved in financial transactions *as principals or as agents* arranging for transactions between principals. When providers of financial services act as principals, they will be entering into financial contracts under their own name and assuming any risks in the transaction (although the risks may be hedged). For example, an insurer will always be acting as a principal. When providers of financial services act as arrangers for transactions, they act as agents or in some other facilitating role for third parties that are the principals in the transaction. An asset manager or adviser would always be playing the role of arranging for transactions. As discussed later, this distinction has some important implications in understanding the current systems and designing alternative approaches. It is also a prime factor in terms of the fifth categorization of financial services: that is, by the nature of consideration. While the distinction between the role of the provider as a principal and as an agent or arranger is relatively clear in most cases, the same institution may act in both capacities. For example, an investment dealer may arrange for transactions of clients as a broker and may also be involved in the market as a principal in a market-making capacity.

The fifth categorization of financial services of relevance is the *nature of consideration.* Consideration for the supply of a financial service can take two basic forms, an explicit fee or commission, or a financial margin. In the case of explicit fees or commissions, financial services are charged for in the same way as other services, such as those of an electrician or a barber. The fee or commission measures the consideration for the supply of the service. It is relatively straightforward to apply the tax to such fees or commissions.

This is not the case where the consideration is implicit, in the form of a financial margin. In a loan and deposit business of a bank, for example, financial transactions give rise to a series of cash flows representing principal, payment of interest, and payment of risk premiums. The consideration for the service in these cases is the margin that remains with the bank, after all cash inflows and outflows have been taken into consideration. Such a margin represents a consideration for a bundle of transactions (such as deposits and loans) and cannot be readily attributed to individual transactions. Therefore it is difficult to identify the appropriate tax base in such cases, an issue that is returned to in detail later.

It was mentioned earlier that the categorization by the role of the service provider was closely associated with the categorization by the nature of consideration. This is because an arranger for a financial transaction is constrained to collecting consideration in the form of a readily observable fee or commission. On the other hand, where the provider is a principal, it will often obtain consideration for the service in the form of a margin. However, this is not necessarily the case. For example, a bank may charge explicit fees for services to depositors and borrowers, or it may earn its consideration in the form of the margin between interest received on loans and paid on deposits, or by a combination of fees and commissions, and margin. Therefore there is an element of substitutability between the two basic forms of considerations that will be seen to have had important implications for the current manner in which financial services are treated in consumption tax systems.

Current Approaches to the Taxation of Financial Services

The most common approach to financial services under a VAT or other general consumption taxes is to exempt them from tax, for reasons shortly to be considered. However, the scope of the exemption may vary somewhat from one jurisdiction to another. In addition, certain jurisdictions have adopted compensatory taxes to obtain additional revenues where the exemption applies.

The exemption system in the European Union provides a useful case for discussing the rationale for the exemption. Article 13 of the Sixth VAT Directive provides for certain exemptions from VAT for supplies of financial services made within the territory of a member state.[2] The exemptions apply for supplies within the member states or to residents of other member states. Two broad rationales have been suggested for VAT exemptions, one dealing with the economic or social characteristics of a good or service, the other with operational issues in the application of the tax to the good or service.

The economic rationale for special treatment is the perception, whether factual or not, that it will make a consumption tax system less regressive. Exemptions (and lower tax rates) for certain goods and services supplied by public bodies and nonprofit organizations would fall into this category. The social reason for exemption would be that the good or service in question is so meritorious that it deserves to be tax-free. The treatment of medical care or education would be examples of the social rationale. It is important to note that neither of these two arguments applies in the case of financial services. Indeed, attempts to tax specific financial services in developing countries often appear to be founded on the view that such taxes would be progressive. There is even a view that some activities, such as currency trading, may be related to undesirable speculation and thus constitute demerit transactions.

The rationale for exemption of financial services thus must be found in the operational aspects of applying the tax to these types of transactions. At the advent of the VAT in Europe, there was not always conceptual clarity and consensus about the appropriateness of some transactions being subject to VAT and about the definition of the base, if those transactions were to be taxable. Issues could involve whether a transaction was related to consumption or investment, or what the conceptually correct measure of consideration was. As was noted earlier in the discussion of the nature of consideration for supplies of financial services, the consideration for financial services may be of an implicit form that is hidden in the margin left after a series of monetary flows. In such cases, there is no readily available measure of consideration on a transaction-by-transaction basis that can serve as a basis for the application of VAT. While one can only speculate, as there is no explicit statement of the rationale for exempting financial services, the main reason for the exemption was likely this lack of an explicit measure of consideration.[3]

While the discussion above dwelled on operational difficulties of applying VAT where consideration is received in the form of margin, it would have been possible to apply VAT to fees and commissions, and restrict the exemption solely to margin activities. However, full use of this approach has been rejected in the past because, to some extent, consideration for financial services provided by principals to a transaction can be in the form of either explicit fees or commissions, or margin. For example, as noted earlier, charges for deposit account services may take the form of either low or zero interest being paid on deposits, or explicit fees per transaction or per month. It was believed that there would be too much of an incentive to substitute margin charges for explicit fees and commissions, and too many competitive distortions created under this approach. As a result, many financial services for which consideration is typically in the form of explicit fees and commissions are also exempted. However, there are some exceptions. For example, safety deposit box fees are taxable in almost all countries with a VAT.

Financial services are thus exempted under virtually all general consumption tax systems around the world, with some taxation of such services that involve explicit fees and consideration. The extent of taxation varies from country to country, but presumably reflects judgments about the substitutability of margin for fees and commissions in given instances. As a broad generalization, the more recently designed VATs tend to tax a somewhat broader selection of financial services than the older systems. For example, Australia, Canada,

New Zealand, and Singapore, which have more recently introduced VATs, extend the taxation of financial services in various ways beyond the European coverage of financial services. This may reflect, in part, the fact that the degree of substitutability between fees and margins may be declining under the pressures of certain economic developments. This issue is returned to later as the options available for extending the base for taxation are identified and evaluated.

Once the operational difficulty of taxing financial services is accepted, the options that are fully consistent with a credit-invoice VAT approach are exemption and zero-rating. Under zero-rating, no tax is charged on the supply of financial services, but the service provider is allowed to recover input tax credits related to the supply. Given this choice, exemption can be justified as somewhat of a compromise solution that applies some tax (by denying input credits) and thus collects some revenue. From these perspectives, exemption is a less extreme approach than zero-rating, which would be more appropriate in situations where regressiveness or merit arguments are the key policy rationales.

Finally, it needs to be acknowledged that the current system in many countries places considerable reliance on compensatory indirect taxes applied to financial services or financial institutions that operate outside broad-based consumption tax structures. These taxes may be introduced primarily for revenue reasons, but may also be rationalized as being responses to the incomplete taxation under the VAT due to exemption. For example, the compensatory taxes on the payroll of financial institutions in France and the Province of Quebec (Canada), both discussed later, are directly linked to the exemption (or zero-rating) for financial services and are an alternate form of tax on value-added in financial transactions. However, it should be recognized that, in some instances, compensatory taxes on financial services have also been introduced in response to perceived weaknesses in the taxation of the income of financial service providers. Compensatory taxes in these cases are viewed as being in the nature of a minimum tax for income tax purposes. For example, the Canadian federal government and several Canadian provinces have taxes on the capital of financial institutions that owe their existence to a perceived failure to tax the income of such institutions appropriately in the past. The relationship of compensatory taxes to the exemption for financial services under VAT is thus often obscure or complex.

Assessment of the Current System

The discussion now turns to the problems and distortions arising under the current treatment of financial services. These can be grouped under three broad headings: economic, definitional, and allocation of input tax credits.

It should be noted that, in general, these problems would have counterparts for any type of an exempt supply and thus are not unique to financial services. However, the significance of the resulting economic problems caused by the exemption may be greater in the case of financial services than for other supplies. The financial sector plays an important role in national economies and has linkages with other sectors throughout the economy. The impact of the distortions can thus extend to almost all other registrants. In addition, competitive pressures in the financial sector are quite significant as a result of globalization and increasing international trade, meaning that distortions may translate into significant shifts in economic behavior and relative market position of individual products and their suppliers.

Economic Distortions

There are three types of economic distortion created by the exemption structure. First, the effective tax rate falls below the statutory rate where the services are received by consumers. Second, there is tax cascading (a tax on a tax) where the services are received by businesses. Third, there is an incentive for financial institutions to produce inputs by themselves that would more efficiently be produced by external suppliers (the self-supply bias) to take advantage of the exemption. There are also international trade implications and government revenue effects.

Underlying each of these is the effect of exemption on the effective tax rate of financial services. An exemption under a VAT is really a two-edged sword, providing for a nil tax rate on supplies of the exempt good or service, but denying the deduction of input taxes related to the supply. This can have dissimilar results depending upon where in the chain of supply the financial service is provided. If the exempt good or service is supplied to a final consumer, the effective tax rate must take into account the input taxes paid by financial institutions that are not credited to them. In general, the effective tax rate is less than the standard rate for supplies to consumers, but it is not "zero." For the effective tax rate to be truly zero, the supply would need to zero-rated, which allows for the full deduction of input tax credits. It is this fact that explains the choice of exemption as a compromise solution in the case of financial services, where the traditional rationales for nontaxation of regressiveness and merit do not apply, but full taxation is not feasible on administrative grounds.

The effect is qualitatively different where the exempt good is supplied at some point in the supply chain before the final sale to consumers. In this case, the blocked input tax credits become embedded in the price paid by business purchasers, and tax cascading or tax on tax occurs. The prices of goods and services sold to final consumers would reflect not only the tax applicable at the point of final sale, but also the embedded, non-creditable input taxes. In this case, the exemption, rather than providing any relief, results in a net tax penalty. If full taxation is the desired objective, the system overshoots this result, and the extent of the bias is determined by the size of the non-creditable input taxes. It also violates a fundamental tenet of VAT that tax should apply only on final consumption, not on intermediate transactions.[4]

The exemption applicable to financial services creates an incentive for financial institutions to self-supply inputs. This self-supply bias extends not only to direct labor services, but also to goods that require significant labor input. For example, in-house production of computer software by the financial institution will avoid the VAT that would otherwise apply if the software (treated as a good in certain jurisdictions) were acquired from another supplier. This bias creates inefficiencies in the production and delivery of services by the financial sector.

Imported financial services are generally not taxed by the destination country, while the same service is usually zero-rated by the country of origin. Where the service is provided from a country without a VAT, it could effectively be zero-rated if there is no tax on the inputs to the financial service.[5] As a consequence, imported supplies of financial services are typically free from VAT altogether. Because domestic supplies of exempt financial services have embedded VAT, competitive inequities and economic distortions take place in the destination country. In other words, domestic financial institutions providing similar services will be less competitive than foreign suppliers, as their cost structure includes VAT. This creates a tax-based incentive for foreign supply of financial services that is undesirable from the domestic perspective. For example, financial institutions in Europe are concerned about the effect on competition from the United States, which does not impose the burden of non-creditable input taxes on its financial institutions.

While this may not have been perceived as a major problem in the past, it is an increasing concern as innovations in the delivery of services make foreign supply more feasible. The financial sector is a growth industry whose structure is changing through institutional consolidation such as mergers, new forms of alliance, and outsourcing. To accommodate these structural changes and support growth in the sector, many countries have taken steps to lower regulatory barriers to improve market access to international supplies of such services (for example, through foreign branch banking). Market developments such as telebanking and internet banking have further facilitated this development. The supply of financial services without a physical presence in an economy is thus becoming common in many countries.

Financial institutions are increasingly outsourcing the processing of their financial transactions to large service providers that can realize significant economies of scale by pooling the processing of transactions for several institutions. The service providers have successfully argued before the courts that these processing services in themselves constitute financial services and should not be subject to tax (for example, in the Danish case *Sparekassernes Datacenter v. Slatteministeriet,* and the U.K. case *U.K. Customs and Excise Commissioners v. FDR Ltd*). This exemption would be of limited consequence where the processing services are provided locally. The services would continue to incur non-creditable input taxes. However, where they are provided from a foreign jurisdiction without a VAT or from one where they are zero-rated, they will enjoy a tax advantage, relative to domestic services, which, assuming a VAT rate of 15 to 20 percent, could be as large as 5 to 10 percent of the total value of the services.

The EC system of treating supplies of financial services between member states as exempt, as opposed to zero-rated, minimizes such competitive distortions, but only for trade within the Community. Moreover, even the trade within the Community is affected by the lack of uniformity in the tax rates and application of the exemption across the Community. As the Sixth VAT Directive is not directly applicable to member states, each member state has been required to define the boundaries of certain key terms and phrases within the confines of its tax legislation—which is closely bound up with national civil and commercial law while respecting the Community law. The European Commission has been steadily trying to harmonize the categories of transactions that are exempt since the Sixth VAT Directive was implemented, but with only mixed success.

Financial institutions operating at the Community level must contend with practical application of the VAT legislation in different member states. This creates legal uncertainty and barriers to intra-Community trade, while at the same time introducing potential planning opportunities that distort behavior. In addition, tax authorities in individual member states must try to ensure that the tax is correctly applied and collected with this distortionary force at work.

An important policy consideration in moving away from the exemption system is the potential impact on government revenues. Under a reform that introduced full taxation of financial services, the price of financial services to households would rise and the price to business registrants would fall. The net effect on revenues is thus an empirical question reflecting the extent of these offsetting effects. Huizinga (2002) has prepared estimates for the EC of the effect of introducing full taxation of financial services in the banking sector. This analysis found that revenues would rise by some 9.5 billion euros to 15.0 billion euros (about 0.1 percent of GDP), depending upon certain assumptions relating to potential economic responses to the change and the current level of taxation. An important consideration in this result for banking in the EC is that the tax collected on business services appears to be significantly lower than would be surmised by looking only at the size of the current tax base in respect of business services. Huizinga (2002, p. 516) observes that, "The main reason must be that tax administrations currently provide banks with almost full VAT input credits—against the spirit of the exemption system." Overall, the indications are that under the exemption system the reduction in tax on consumer services is larger than the additional tax on business services. This means that there is a government revenue loss relative to full taxation. However, this result may not necessarily hold in countries that currently levy significant compensatory taxes, which would be eliminated upon the introduction of full taxation.

Definition of Financial Services

For the exemption system to operate, there must be a definition of what constitutes a financial service. There are number of difficulties and ambiguities involved in setting out and applying the necessary dividing lines.

- *Exempt versus taxable financial services*: The VAT base typically includes most supplies of goods and services on a broad basis and then excludes financial services as defined in the legislation. Whatever the definitions chosen, the actual system must make fine distinctions between taxable and exempt services in a large number of potential situations. For example, the Canadian Customs and Revenue Agency lists some 240 types of transactions for trust companies alone and divides them into taxable and exempt categories.

This issue has become even more of a problem area because of deregulation and globalization. Traditional products are being unbundled into their component parts and bundled into new products.

As part of this process, financial transactions are being out-sourced to third parties, creating difficult questions as to whether these supplies are taxable or exempt. The dividing line between exempt financial services and taxable activities is thus becoming more problematic and blurred. It is useful to note that virtually all the problematic cases are those in which the fee for services is explicit, rather than implicit in the form of the margin. The latter are always financial services that are exempted from tax, with the possible exception of property and casualty insurance, which is taxable in certain jurisdictions (such as New Zealand). The former can include a wide variety of services, including financial advisory services, wealth management services, trustee services, safekeeping and custodial, share registry, data/transaction processing, appraisals, debt collection, financial counseling, actuarial, legal, accounting services, and insurance evaluation. Many of these services are taxable when provided in isolation (financial advice), but exempt when provided in conjunction with a financial transaction (such as financial advisory services during the course of purchase or sale of financial securities). It is this dual treatment of these services that leads to complexity in the determination of their status.

• *Financial services supplied by non-financial businesses*: Non-financial businesses often provide financial services as part of their activities. For example, retail stores may operate credit operations. For neutrality, such operations should receive the same treatment as similar operations carried out by financial institutions. However, to avoid complexity and allocation problems, some de minimis threshold will usually be used to ignore some incidental financial service activities, such as payment of interest and dividends. In applying the trade-off between neutrality and compliance simplification objectives, there will inevitably be some problems.

• *Services incidental or supplementary to financial services*: The provision of a particular financial service will often have attached to it services of a taxable nature, or vice versa. For example, banks will often provide a combination of taxable payroll services, and exempt checking and other banking services. VAT systems must have rules in place to deal with these types of situations as they create difficulties in compliance or administration and provide opportunities for tax planning.

• *Mixed supplies*: Financial services and non-financial services may be provided together for a single consideration. For example, credit card services, in addition to the basic credit authorization services, may include such features as "air mile" entitlement for redemption on travel or goods, extended warranties for goods purchased, and rental car collision insurance. For comparable treatment to the underlying components being purchased separately, there would need to be an allocation of the price among the components of the supply. Lawmakers and administrators must decide where to strike a balance in such situations between complex allocation requirements and formulaic allocations that leave open possibilities for tax planning.

Input Tax Credit Allocation

Wherever there is a co-mingling of exempt financial services with either taxable or zero-rated activities, registrants for the tax will need to allocate sales as to type in order to determine the extent of input tax credit entitlement. The two broad approaches used are direct attribution, in which the actual use of inputs is used to determine eligibility for input credits, and formula allocation, in which some readily available measure of exempt versus taxable or zero-rated revenues is used to determine right of deduction. However, there is considerable variation in the specifics of the input tax credit allocation, even among countries using the same broad approach. Whatever the rules used, allocation is the source of considerable complexity.

In order to carry out the allocations, financial businesses may need to collect information and modify accounting systems that would not otherwise be required. In addition, planning opportunities will inevitably exist that may cause changes in behavior. Change-of-use rules to handle changes in the use of fixed assets between exempt versus taxable activity also necessitate considerable additional record-keeping. Sales between related parties become problematic when the tax collected may not be creditable. The incentive is to minimize prices in sales between related parties and there are normally arm's length pricing rules to prevent this practice. However, as with transfer pricing issues under the income tax, the application of such rules introduces difficult administrative issues. Problems with non-deductible input tax credits on sales among affiliates within a corporate group provide an incentive for in-house supply. This may lead to tax-induced reorganizations or tax authorities may allow some form of group relief or consolidation in response to the issue.

Financial Services: What Should the Tax Base Be?

Like any other business, the provision of financial services requires the input of purchased goods and services, labor, and capital. A value-added tax is designed to tax final consumption expenditures that reflect the value-added through labor and capital inputs at each stage in the production of a final consumer good or service. It is important to be very clear as to what this tax base consists of, in the case of financial services.

As noted, where the consideration for a financial service does not take the form of explicit fees or commissions, it is hidden in a set of cash flows and is not readily observable. The cash flows under a financial transaction can have four elements: the principal amount of a financial instrument, the pure time value of money, the risk premium, and the charge for intermediation services.

The principal amount represents the capital value in the transaction. For example, it would be the amount deposited by a customer in a bank account or the amount loaned by a bank to the borrower. It is an amount that does not represent a permanent inflow or outflow to the intermediary. It is a cash flow that is expected to reverse eventually at the conclusion of the transaction (for example, the deposit will eventually be withdrawn or the loan repaid).

The pure time value of money is that component of cash flows that reflects the opportunity cost of funds in the absence of any credit, market, or other such risks. It is the element in financial transactions that must be excluded to maintain the fundamental property of a consumption tax: namely, that the pre-tax and post-tax ratio of current to deferred consumption be maintained.

The risk premium is a charge reflecting compensation to the intermediary for the risks inherent in the transaction (such as an interest charge on a loan over and above the pure time value of money, reflecting the expected value of default by the borrower in loan repayments) or an outflow on account of risks (such as claim payments by an insurer). This risk premium should also be excluded from the base for a consumption tax, as it does not represent a net value added in the economy. To the extent that the expected risk premium reflects actual future loan losses or insurance claims, the financial flow associated with the risk premium will not be realized or will be paid out later. They thus do not represent consideration that will be retained by the financial service provider as a payment for value-added. It is a form of redistribution of wealth, either between the financial institution and its customers, or among various participants in a risk-pooling arrangement.

The intermediation charge is the residual component of any cash flows from a financial transaction. As the name suggests, it is only this last component that represents a consideration for financial services and that should attract VAT. The challenge lies in isolating this component for each individual transaction, in a manner that makes it practical to apply the VAT to it, and that is consistent with the application of VAT to other goods and services. Methods for doing this and further observations about the pure time value of money and measurement of risk in this context are presented in the later section on methods of full taxation.

The discussion in the previous section identified a variety of economic, definitional, and input tax credit allocation problems that can be associated with the current exemption system. Financial institutions have raised concerns about the detrimental impact of the exemption on their competitiveness because of the large volume of blocked input tax credits associated with financial services provided to business customers. If the rationale for the exemption relates to difficulties in application of the tax rather than considerations of regressivity and social policy needs, and the current exemption system is perceived to be distortionary, it would appear that taxation would be desirable—if a practical approach to taxation could be identified. Indeed the European Commission has been seeking to identify and analyze taxation options that could replace the current system. The objective is to identify solutions that move toward full taxation of financial intermediation services as much as possible, consistent with other policy and operational concerns.

However, some of the underlying premises in the rationale for full taxation of financial services are being debated, as implied in the above discussion. This debate is diverse and contains several strands. Before getting into options for revised approaches to taxation of financial services, it is useful to identify the underpinnings of these arguments, if only briefly. Since the considerations involved are varied, complex, and open to dispute, no attempt is made to provide a complete description or firm conclusions. However, the issues raised do provide some background relevant for the discussion of options.

The most extreme form of challenge to full taxation as an option is the argument that financial intermediation services do not affect the consumer utility function, acting only to facilitate a change in the time profile of other consumer goods and services that do enter the utility function.[6] Under this viewpoint, if only final consumption goods should be taxed under a VAT, and financial services are intermediate goods that do not provide any utility in themselves, financial services should be exempt from tax. This view has been challenged by Auerbach and Gordon (2001), who argue that a VAT is equivalent to a tax on the income of all primary factors that enter into the production of final consumer goods. For neutrality under this tax base, all income of primary factors, such as labor, that enter into the provision of financial services must also be taxable. An argument reaching a similar conclusion as to the fallacy of nontaxation based on financial services not entering directly into the utility function is provided in the discussion of aspects of optimal taxation of financial activities by Boadway and Keen (chapter 2, this volume).

Jack (2000) has argued that the requirement that the price of all consumer goods should increase by the same percentage under a VAT may not require imposition of VAT on certain financial services. If the prices of other goods rise by the percentage of the VAT, and the prices of financial services are proportional to the size of nominal transactions, neutrality would require no direct taxation in such cases. On the other hand, where the financial services are of a fixed amount, taxation is appropriate. Building on this viewpoint, it can be argued that a modified system of exemption or zero-rating for margin services coupled with taxation of fees or commissions may be more appropriate than full taxation.[7]

Auerbach and Gordon show that this is erroneous if the tax is viewed as being equivalent to one on all primary factors of income. However, the discussion by Boadway and Keen (chapter 2) lays out the argument that, if the objective is an optimal consumption tax, the approach suggested by Jack may have some validity.

In line with this, a final set of arguments expressed in Chia and Whalley (1999) and discussed by Boadway and Keen (chapter 2) is that an optimal consumption tax might apply low tax rates to financial services, but not necessarily zero tax rates. As this argument is really one for a different consumption tax base than contemplated under a VAT, it goes beyond the scope of the discussion here.

Support for retaining the exemption system may also be based on the view that certain costs involved in the operation of full taxation may more than offset any benefits gained by elimination of the distortions discussed earlier in this chapter.[8]

The discussion in the remainder of this chapter is based on the more conventional view that the VAT is designed to be a tax consistently applied to all the inputs that contribute to value-added. In this case, the objective of the tax is to fully tax financial services supplied to nonregistrants, and to ensure that taxation of supplies of financial services to business registrants does not result in tax cascading. The issue then is the identification of options that achieve the desired results without excessive administration or compliance costs, and the introduction of new distortions that may offset any benefits from improvements on the exemption structure.

Taxation of all financial services to nonregistrants is consistent with the practice for non-financial goods and services. It does not matter if the nonregistrant is using these goods in some productive activity. As long as the person is not registered, the supply is taxable and there is no recovery of input tax credits available. The fact that the financial supply is supporting rearrangement of consumption patterns should not matter. Other services of a real nature such as transportation and storage costs also help in rearranging consumption patterns, but are subject to tax. The key identifier is that supplies to households that are not registered as businesses are taxable, whatever their nature or subsequent use.[9] This is a fundamental characteristic of credit-invoice VAT systems.

Policy Options

Against this background, three general approaches to policy options to replace the current exemption system can be considered. The first, the full taxation approach, would attempt to isolate the financial intermediation consideration where it is hidden in financial margins and apply tax to it, as well as to any explicit fees and commissions charged in respect of financial services. The second approach involves alternatives modifying the exemption system by extending full tax to selected financial services. The final option attempts to apply the tax to value-added in financial services through compensatory taxes by use of the addition method of value-added taxation.[10]

The options that will be reviewed here include the following *full taxation* options:

- Basic cash flow tax
- Tax Calculation Account (TCA) system
- TCA system with zero-rating of business transactions

Also considered will be a variety of modified exemption systems:

- The option system
- Taxation of explicit fees and commissions
- Taxation of agency services only
- New Zealand system
- Exemption with input credits
- Australian system

Finally, the French, Israeli and Quebec systems of compensatory taxes using the addition method will also be discussed.

In modifying the exemption system, a question arises as to how one can evaluate whether an extension of coverage is "good" or "bad." It is possible to enumerate some principles or benchmarks that can aid in this process. These principles and benchmarks are also relevant in assessing ad hoc systems of indirect taxation being adopted by developing countries for financial services for their revenue needs.

First, the base for the tax should be no more than the financial intermediation service. Ad hoc levies are particularly prone to violate this benchmark. For example, a premium tax on gross insurance premiums has an aggregate base of total premiums, rather than the intermediation service base, which is premiums less claims. Second, modifications to the exemption system should lessen the tax on business inputs (that is, avoid tax cascading). This is one of the principles that the exemption system and certain of the options being considered fail to satisfy. Third, new approaches should lead to broader coverage of financial services. The narrowing of the tax base is one important source of the economic distortions and other problems with the exemption approach. Fourth, any new approach will raise compliance/administration issues of its own and may introduce new types of distortions. Only new approaches that are improvements in this respect should be adopted. Finally, new approaches must not be susceptible to tax planning or behavioral changes that effectively undo any improvements in respect to the other objectives. For example, extending taxation to a particular fee or commission may appear to broaden coverage and not run afoul of any of the other guidelines. Nonetheless, it is undesirable if the tax can easily be circumvented by converting the fee into a nontaxable financial margin.

Full Taxation

The earlier discussion described the fundamental problem with the application of VAT to financial services: the difficulty in identifying the appropriate consideration hidden in the margin created by a set of four different types of cash flows (principal, time value of money, intermediation services, and risk premium). The consideration for financial services can still be measured by the *net* cash flows received by a financial institution in respect of any given transaction. However, for purposes of applying a VAT, this value must be computed on a transaction-by-transaction and customer-by-customer basis to allow input credits where claimable. Under the normal VAT system, there is no apparent mechanism for allocating this aggregate measure of the value of financial services to individual transactions.

It has generally been accepted, following from the discussion in the Meade Committee Report (Institute for Fiscal Studies 1978), that the basic cash flow method provides a means of measuring the value of margin services on a transaction-by-transaction and customer-by-customer basis. This report, which fully developed the so-called F-base for taxation of business services, is considered to supply the necessary conceptual definition of a tax base for transactions in financial instruments. The Tax Calculation Account (TCA) methods described below are operational approaches to achieving the results of the basic cash flow method, while avoiding certain problems associated with it.

Basic cash flow tax   Under the basic cash flow method, all cash inflows from financial transactions (whether of income or capital nature) received by a financial institution would be treated as consideration in respect of taxable sales, on which VAT must be remitted to the government by the financial institution. All cash outflows (whether income or capital) paid by a financial institution would be treated as taxed purchases, for which the financial institution would be entitled to a refund of VAT from the government.

Under this approach, transactions with nonresidents can be readily zero-rated simply by applying the zero rate of tax to cash inflows and outflows from and to nonresidents. Where the customer is a business that is a VAT-registrant, all cash inflows received by the business customer would be treated as taxable sales, on which VAT would be remitted to the government by the customer. All cash outflows paid by the business customer would be treated as taxed purchases, for which the customer would be entitled to a refund of VAT from the government.

The cash flow method automatically arrives at an appropriate treatment of risk on an ex post basis. For example, on a loan, the cash outflows generate a refund of VAT. If the loan leads to a bad debt, there is never any inflow of cash and there is no offsetting tax collected. In effect, there is full loss offsetting in respect of the actual losses associated with credit risk under the cash flow method. Interest payments on the loan are fully included in the tax base, even though they include a risk premium. This system of recognition of risks obviates the necessity of having to estimate the risk premium included in cash inflows and taken out of the tax base. Risks are removed from the base by giving a deduction for the losses or cash outflows (for example, in the form of insurance claim costs) suffered by the financial institution because of risks. If actual risks turn out to be smaller than the anticipated risks built into the pricing of the financial services, the excess is taxable as profit, which is a component of the value-added by the financial institution. In the same manner, any excess of actual risks over anticipated risks gives rise to a reduction in profits and is treated as a reduction in value-added.

The basic cash flow method would result in VAT being applied to financial services in a manner that is consistent with the normal VAT system and would correctly allocate the VAT base between depositors and borrowers. However, several problems have been identified with respect to the application of the basic cash flow method to financial services, as noted below:

• Since the principal amount of a loan would be subject to tax at the time the loan is made, borrowers would have to be able to find financing for the tax, in addition to the original loan requirements. This could create additional borrowing requirements and present cash flow problems.

• Significant transition problems would arise under the basic cash flow method upon implementation of the system and whenever the tax rate changed. The correct amount of tax is levied under the basic cash flow method only where all of the cash flows associated with a loan or deposit are subjected to tax. If cash flows arising before the date of implementation are not subject to tax, then the appropriate amount of VAT will not have been collected. For example, if a deposit is received before the implementation date, no VAT would be remitted in respect of the deposit. If the deposit is withdrawn after the date of implementation, then VAT would be refunded on the deposit even though VAT was not paid when the deposit was accepted.

• Due to the volume of cash inflows and outflows between financial institutions and their customers, applying VAT to all capital and income cash flows could be burdensome to both financial institutions and their customers.

These problems have generally been perceived as rendering the basic cash flow method nonoperational, despite its theoretical attractions. Despite these difficulties, the cash flow method is a relatively simple way of applying VAT to a variety of financial transactions, such as insurance and financial derivatives. It is also the most akin to the normal VAT for non-financial goods and services. If full taxation were introduced, it is likely that financial institutions would choose to use this method, if available, for certain of their transactions that are not subject to the transitional issues: that is, those transactions that do not straddle the commencement of the system or a change in the tax rates.

Tax Calculation Account system The Tax Calculation Account (TCA) system was developed as an option that would mirror the results of the cash flow system, while providing mechanisms to surmount the transition and liquidity problems associated with the full cash flow system.[11] It essentially works via a tax suspension account for margin transactions, with all the necessary calculations handled by financial institutions.

Under the TCA system, the collection or crediting of tax on cash inflows or outflows of a capital nature is suspended. The amount of the tax or credit suspended accrues interest at a rate (referred to as the indexing rate or the cost-of-funds rate) reflecting the pure time value of money. The suspended amount of tax or credit generally reverses at the end of the transaction when the capital flows reverse:

for example, when a loan is repaid or the deposit is withdrawn. The net tax payable at the end of the transaction is thus the tax (credit) applicable on the interest received (paid) minus (plus) the interest at the indexing rate on the deferred tax (credit) amount. This system is equivalent to defining the consideration for the principal financial services as interest (or other forms of income or expense flows) received (or paid) minus the interest calculated at the indexing rate, which is the pure time value of money.

The tax calculation account provides a means to make the necessary adjustments to avoid the transition problems referred to earlier. Under this system, an opening entry is created in the TCA for the tax (credit) amount for any balances outstanding for principal transactions (for loans and deposits, for example) at the time of commencement of the system. The opening entry is equal to the tax that would have been collected or credited on the principal amount, had that transaction taken place at the commencement of the system. Once this opening entry is created, all subsequent calculations for the existing transactions would be identical to those for new transactions.

The TCA calculations are needed for only those activities in which the financial institution is acting as a principal and the consideration takes the form of margin. Where the consideration takes the form of an explicit fee or commission, the tax could be applied to it directly, in a manner identical to that for other goods and services.

Risks under the TCA system are handled in the same manner as under the cash flow system: that is, they are recognized on an ex post basis when they occur. The taxable margin for a loan is reduced by any bad debts. As and when a loan becomes a bad debt, the taxable margin becomes a negative amount, for which the financial institution claims a tax credit.

During 1995–96, the TCA system was tested at ten large financial institutions in six countries in Europe, under a project sponsored by the European Commission. The pilot tests involved a review of virtually all the major financial products and services offered by the institutions, their input tax credit allocation systems, and administration and compliance costs of the current and the TCA system.[12] A number of design issues received special consideration during the testing of the system, and two key ones can be summarized here.

First, under the TCA system, the indexing rate plays a critical role in the measurement of consideration for financial services. Should the indexing rate be a single indexing rate for financial transactions of all maturities or one that is matched to maturity? After extensive deliberations, use of a single, short-term, interbank rate was found to be appropriate in all cases. This allowed tremendous simplification of the system, which would have otherwise been unworkable.

The second issue related to the impact of risk on the measurement of consideration. As was indicated earlier, an element included in the margins of financial institutions is a risk premium, and a pure risk premium should not attract a value-added tax. The risk premium does not reflect any added value in an economy; rather it reflects a redistribution of value among the market participants as market risks play out. While the existence of a risk consideration in pricing is not unique to financial services, it is a much more fundamental and pervasive consideration in pricing for many such services than it is for real goods and services. The appropriate treatment of the risk premium can be achieved under the TCA system by including all interest charges in the tax base, and allowing the financial institution a tax credit for the bad debts realized by it. This gives the same loss offsetting result as is provided under the full cash flow method that was discussed earlier. The pilot tests confirmed that negative balances in the TCA account should be treated symmetrically to positive ones in applying the VAT: that is, they should give rise to a VAT refund or credit.[13]

Overall, the tests confirmed that the TCA system was conceptually robust and resulted in proper application of VAT to all financial products and services. Financial institutions, however, did identify a number of concerns and apprehensions about the system. The main concern identified in the tests was the newness of the concept and the time and effort that would be required by financial institutions to familiarize their staff and customers with it and to modify their computer system for the TCA computations. Another major concern was that the computed tax amount on a given transaction would reveal information on margins earned by financial institutions. This information would affect market competition, be subject to misinterpretation, and lead to time-consuming explanatory discussions with customers.

TCA system with zero-rating of business transactions To address the concern noted above about the implementation costs of the TCA system, an option was identified that would involve zero-rating of principal financial transactions with other VAT registrants. This approach obviates the necessity of any TCA calculations for transactions with business customers, who account for the vast bulk of transactions for many financial institutions. For the remaining transactions with final consumers (or VAT nonregistrants), the TCA computations could be done on a global basis, assuming that such customers would not need any statement of the VAT included in their charges to the financial institution. The method would maintain the overall conceptual integrity of the TCA system, while resulting in simplification of compliance and administration. The zero-rating of financial transactions with business customers would not result in revenue loss to the government, assuming that any tax otherwise collected on such transactions would have been fully deductible by the customers. The principal compliance issue beyond the calculation of the necessary TCA in respect of services provided to nonregistrants would be the need to determine the tax status of customers in order to assign the appropriate tax status. This approach would also mean that pricing would need to be done on a tax-exclusive basis for business customers and a tax-inclusive basis for nonregistrants, which could lead to some confusion among customers.

Modified Exemption Systems

Another general approach that could be taken would be to maintain the exemption system, but to modify it in ways that are designed to improve its operation. The two principal avenues for improving the operation of VAT for financial services are to reduce the degree of taxation of related business inputs and to broaden the range of financial services to consumers that are taxable. Several options in both these regards can be identified. One possibility to reduce the taxation of business inputs would be to make the "option" that is in place in certain countries in the European Union more widely available. The tax coverage can also be broadened by extending the tax to agency services—as is done in Singapore—or to all explicit fees and commissions. Another type of approach is to make selected use of cash flow tax methods to tax selected types of financial services most amendable to this treatment, as is done for property and casualty insurance in New Zealand. Ad hoc methods to reduce the level of blocked input tax credits in respect of business customers are also being tried in Singapore and elsewhere. The Australian system, under its Goods and Services Tax (GST), is briefly described at the end of the section as a system that has adopted a set of these approaches.

The option system In the EC, member states are allowed to extend an option to financial institutions to be taxable. The option is potentially of interest to financial institutions that deal largely with commercial clients where the customers will be able to claim input tax credits.

Currently, Belgium, France, and Germany provide for this option. The details for the option vary from country to country. In France, banks, financial institutions, and persons performing finan-

368
SATYA PODDAR

cial transactions may elect to be subject to VAT. The election is irrevocable and covers all revenues that fall into the scope of the election. The election mainly covers revenues from credit transactions (other than interest), such as filing charges; revenues from securities transactions undertaken for the benefit of the client; and particular commissions and brokerage fees.

The option has not been widely used. It also has not been developed systematically. For example, the concept of the base has not been well defined. Lacking a measure of financial intermediation in margin transactions, the base is usually considered to be some gross amount of cash flow.

The option does meet the criteria of removing tax from business inputs, but the conditions for its use have tended to be restrictive and it is attractive only to firms with mainly business customers. Its uneven availability and variations in its structure have been a source of intra-Community distortions. In its current form, it is thus only a modest and partial solution to the problem of taxation of business inputs, but it does move in the right direction.

Taxation of explicit fees and commissions   Another approach results from a reexamination of the issue of substitutability of consideration in the form of margin for explicit fees and commissions. This substitutability was noted at the outset as a reason for exempting many services primarily priced as a fee or commission. If concerns about substitutability are no longer valid, taxation of all explicit fees and commissions for financial services would be feasible.

The two key factors forcing financial institutions into operating on a fee or commission basis are disintermediation and deregulation. At one time, a bank would offer a deposit account with low or zero interest rates to customers. The low interest rate would yield a margin, which would cover the costs of a set of financial services to customers. Under disintermediation, customers who do not require certain services are reluctant to sacrifice interest on their deposits. They choose to earn interest via financial products offering more competitive rates and pay for only those services they need on a separate basis. Similar pressures exist to unbundle services related to borrowing with lower interest rates charged and specific services paid for separately. Less regulated markets have added to the pressures on the use of margin pricing by fostering competition and allowing the development of efficient, stand-alone services provided by third parties that can be priced only on an explicit fee basis. As a result of disintermediation and the unbundling of prices for financial products and services, fees and commissions account for an increasing proportion (as much as 80 percent) of total revenues of financial institutions. These same forces mean that there may be a more limited risk of substitution of margin for fees than was assumed to be the case in the past.

If one accepts that such substitution has become a less serious threat, alternative approaches can be identified that reduce the overall distortions in the system markedly. One such approach would be the taxation of all explicit fees and commissions. This would significantly increase the breadth of coverage of taxation of financial services, and, to the extent the preceding observations are correct, would lead to little tax-induced switches to margin pricing. Under this approach, exemption for financial services would be limited to consideration received in the form of a principal amount, interest, dividends, and other similar amounts (such as blended cash flows from financial derivatives) from transactions undertaken by a principal. Exemption would thus be strictly limited to consideration received in the form of margin.

This option can be seen to score very well in relationship to the principles for assessing alternative approaches enunciated earlier. It applies only where the value of the service is identified in explicit form and thus applies to the appropriate base. It would reduce tax cascading where financial services are provided to businesses on a fee or commission basis. Indeed, it could encourage the trend to conversion of financial service margins into fees for business customers, which would lead to less cascading. It would provide a substantial increase in the taxable coverage of financial services under VAT.

Of course, there would be an incentive to shift consideration for services supplied to consumers into still-exempt margins. However, this will be no worse than the status quo, although it would mean that revenues that might be anticipated from the tax on fees and commissions would not materialize. It would also be possible to exclude specific types of transactions from tax where conversion to margins is most problematic, such as foreign exchange dealings. Alternatively, the conversion of fees to margin could be discouraged by deeming the margin earned on certain types of transactions (such as securities bought and resold to fulfill prior customer orders) to be fees.

It would also provide significant benefits in reducing or eliminating several of the distortions under the exemption system identified earlier. Assuming that explicit fees account for a significant portion of total revenues of financial institutions, the quantum of input taxes blocked as a result of the remaining exempt supplies should be reduced to a modest fraction. As a result, the self-supply bias for financial institutions would not be as serious under this approach. With the taxation of all explicit fees and commissions, a simplified formula for input tax allocations could be devised for financial institutions that would be less complex and distortionary than the current structure. In the case of the EC, intra-Community biases would be reduced, as the list of exempt services and the input tax allocation formulae would be more consistent across member states.

Another advantage of this system is that it would eliminate virtually all disputes about the taxable or exempt status of certain services, such as for contracting-out arrangements for financial transaction processing services. The potential tax in individual outsourcing contracts can amount to tens of millions of dollars annually. Examples of contracting out of financial services by financial institutions to specialized providers of services can be found for brokerage, advisory, and processing and management services, such as credit card processing data centers. This issue, as illustrated in the court cases *Sparekassernes Datacenter v. Slatteministeriet* and *U.K. Customs and Excise Commissioners v. FDR Ltd.* has assumed considerable importance. Before these cases were filed, outsourced services were generally held to be subject to VAT. European jurisprudence in these cases invoked the principal that the characteristic of the service should not be changed by the contracting out of the service to a third party. While this removed the bias against outsourcing to local suppliers, treating them as exempt creates a huge incentive to outsource them from countries without VAT or in countries where the supply of exported services are zero-rated.

Because such contracting out arrangements invariably involve the use of agents, the consideration is inevitably in the form of fees and commissions. Therefore taxation of all fees and commissions would address this issue.

Taxation of explicit fees and commissions could be supplemented with an option given to financial institutions to apply the tax to the margin services as well. The application of tax to the margin services could be based on the TCA system.

This approach could be viewed as an intermediate step to transition to the full taxation system, as under the TCA system. Again, to minimize compliance burden of TCA calculations for each individual transaction, principal financial transactions with VAT registrants could be zero-rated under this option-to-tax approach. This would allow financial institutions to compute the tax on their retail transactions on a global basis at the end of a tax period. In return, they would be able to claim full deduction of their input taxes. For those financial institutions that do make use of the option, this system will result in elimination of virtually all economic distortions (including tax cascading) that arise under the current exemption system.

Once financial institutions become familiar with the TCA system, consideration could be given to making its use mandatory. This would be a nonintrusive way of bringing financial services fully within the VAT system.

Taxation of agency services only   Singapore has adopted a variant of the previous approach under which it taxes only agency services. Examples of taxable services are brokerage for executing transactions for the sale and purchase of securities on behalf of customers; brokerage for life or general insurance; premiums of general insurance; and merchant banks' fees on corporate restructuring. All principal services remain exempt, regardless of whether consideration is explicit or implicit.

As far as agency services are concerned, this approach merits many of the same comments as the taxation of all fees and services. Where it applies, it employs the correct tax base and broadens the coverage. It also reduces certain distortions. For example, it addresses disputes about the status of certain contracting out arrangements. Finally, it restricts additional taxation to those areas where substitutability of margins for fees is least likely.

The main drawback of this approach is its limited coverage; it leaves the exemption system in place for all principal transactions. In these cases, it does not respond to tax cascading, broaden coverage, or deal with the distortions of the exemption system. This approach is an improvement on the current system and would be attractive for countries where it is believed that substitutability is likely to be a serious problem in the case of principal transactions. Relative to the taxation of all fees and commissions, the desirability of this approach depends upon whether the distortions associated with substitutability outweigh the new distortions arising from the differential treatment of principals and agents identified in the previous paragraph.

New Zealand system   New Zealand applies its Goods and Services Tax to a comprehensive base, but again excluding financial services. The tax applies to general insurance but does not extend to life insurance, creditor protection policies, and other financial intermediation services. For general insurance, the New Zealand system is in most respects modeled after the basic cash flow structure.[14]

Overall, the New Zealand system for financial services is not much different from the basic exemption system prevailing in Europe and other jurisdictions, and is subject to the same economic distortions and concerns as elsewhere.

Exemption with input credits   Conceptually, input credits are appropriate in a VAT where a good or service is taxed at the normal rate or a zero rate. However, in order to eliminate or alleviate the cascading effect of the exemption method, countries such as Singapore and Australia are allowing input credits in certain cases even under the exemption system.

As has been described, fee-based financial services provided by financial agencies in Singapore are taxed, while most principal financial services remain exempt from VAT. However, in order to reduce the cascading effect of the exemption method, Singapore allows financial institutions to claim input tax credits under either of two approaches: the "special method" or "fixed input tax recovery method."

Under the special method, financial services that were provided to VAT registrants are treated as if they were eligible for application of a zero rate. Therefore, in order to get this benefit, financial institution needs to segregate the eligible financial services out of the total services that have been provided to all customers. This approach is equivalent to the zero-rating of financial services provided to registrants, which was described earlier as an adjunct to the TCA method to make it less of a compliance burden.

Under the other method, the fixed input tax recovery method, a financial institution can claim a credit for a fixed percentage of total input taxes. The recovery percentages are differentiated according to the type of financial institution involved. While this method does provide some relief for tax cascading in respect of services provided to business customers, it moves the coverage of the tax even further from full taxation in respect of services provided to nonregistrants. This fixed input recovery method is not seen as being a permanent part of the system. Presumably, it is intended that as experience is gained with the special method, input credit recovery may eventually be limited to that approach.

Australian system   The Australian GST is a broadly based value-added tax that provides an exemption for financial services. However, it extends taxation to financial agency services and to non-life insurance and provides for some recovery of input credits in regard to financial services.

The definition of financial services is restricted to transactions performed by principals. Therefore such services as brokerage not undertaken as a principal are subject to tax. Insurance, other than life insurance, is also taxed.

The strict exemption approach is modified somewhat by allowing a 75 percent credit for GST paid on a defined list of services acquired for use in making exempt financial supplies. This was done in an attempt to counter the self-supply bias created through the exemption of financial services. The percentage for the credit allowed was chosen so that the noncreditable tax on acquired services was approximately equivalent to the noncreditable tax that would have applied on self-supplied services.

Conceptually, the Australian system does address many of the problems of an exemption system. However, it is yet to be determined how the complexity of its design (attributable primarily to the definition of services that are eligible for the 75 percent credit) would affect its operation.

Compensatory Taxes Using the Addition Method

The aggregate financial intermediation services of a financial institution can be measured readily. This can be done by using any of the addition, subtraction, or cash flow systems. However, only the cash flow or the TCA systems can function on a transaction-by-transaction basis and be compatible with a credit-invoice VAT. Nevertheless, in the absence of an operational method to tax financial services fully, it is possible to use one of the aggregate methods to bring some or all elements of such services into the tax net. Systems of this type, employing different forms of an addition tax, exist in France, Israel, and the Province of Quebec in Canada. This section looks at the features of these types of compensatory taxes as adjuncts to a VAT in the real sector.

Compensatory taxes using the addition method are designed to tax the full value of financial services, or at least, a larger proportion of the full value than an exemption system. A major objective of compensatory taxes is to raise revenue in respect of activities that are seen as not being subject to full taxation. Conceptually, if non-labor inputs are already taxed under the exemption system, then supplementary taxation of labor used to supply financial services and the profits from supplying such services will achieve full taxation of the value of financial services.[15] However, these compensatory tax systems have major implications for tax cascading, incentives for self-supply, and many of the other issues that have been discussed in respect of the taxation of financial services. The following discussion highlights the structure of three such taxes and briefly explores key implications of the approaches taken.

French system   Employers established in France must pay a payroll tax if at least 90 percent of their turnover (including any turnover that is outside the scope of VAT) is not subject to VAT. Therefore most financial institutions are subject to this payroll tax on all or a part of their gross salaries. The taxable portion of their salaries is equal to the difference between 100 percent and the percentage of the turnover that is either subject to VAT or zero-rated. Rates of payroll tax vary from 4.25 to 13.6 percent.

The payroll tax is designed to bring the labor component of value-added into the tax base. As far as financial services supplied to households are concerned, the combination of blocked input taxes and the payroll tax on labor means that the tax base moves closer to the full taxation of financial services. It also eliminates the self-supply bias for financial institutions.

A major disadvantage of the approach is that it increases the extent of tax cascading in respect of business inputs, because the quantum of tax collected at the financial institution level now includes both blocked input taxes and the payroll tax on labor inputs. The French system does have the "option" in place that can provide relief in certain cases, but its reach is limited.

Another undesirable feature of compensatory taxes is that they are applied and collected at the time the costs are incurred and not when the consumption takes place. If the labor being taxed is used to support financial services that will be delivered to consumers in future periods (as for example when it relates to manufacture of capital goods, such as computer software), tax is collected in the current period, rather than at the future time when consideration is actually received for delivering the service to the final consumer. This is tantamount to collecting tax on the time value of money, a characteristic of an income tax, not a consumption tax.

Israeli system Israel applies an addition-method VAT to insurers and deposit-taking institutions. These institutions cannot claim a credit for input VAT. Credits are also not available to registered customers purchasing financial services from financial institutions. The Israeli system is thus similar to the French system, but also includes the profit component of value-added in the tax base. The comments about the implications of the Israeli system largely mirror those of the French system, but apply with even greater force because of the taxation of profits.

A further issue that arises in this form of addition-method compensatory tax is the compatibility of the profit measure with a consumption tax base. Taxation of the time value of money will occur if an income tax measurement of profits is used to determine the base. To prevent this, the profit component must be adjusted in a number of ways to reflect consumption tax principles. Most notably, it must be recomputed on the basis of immediate expensing of capital.

Quebec system   The Province of Quebec in Canada has adopted a different approach for taxation of financial services under its provincial VAT. Quebec zero-rates financial services, but applies supplementary taxes on labor and capital of financial institutions (and on insurance premiums).

Revenue considerations are certainly an important rationale for this approach. In Quebec, the government explicitly stated that the taxes were being imposed to offset, at least in part, the revenue loss from zero-rating. The resulting system is a unique one with unusual features. The design neither tries to capture the full value of financial services (due to zero-rating) nor does it attempt to fully implement a zero-rating system.

As far as the taxation of labor and capital is concerned, the comments are similar to those for the French and Israeli systems. However, the combination of zero-rating of financial services and the application of the payroll tax has the unique effect of creating a strong incentive for outsourcing of internal processing and administration functions of financial institutions. By outsourcing these functions, they incur no additional non-creditable VAT, and avoid the payroll tax.

Overall, the Quebec system is essentially one that zero-rates financial services. However, the compensatory payroll and capital taxes could be viewed as replacing partial taxation under the exemption system with another form of partial taxation.

The Choices for Developing Countries

Developing countries that introduce VAT will want to adopt models that draw on experience elsewhere, and that do not incorporate untried features and approaches. In the case of financial services, this means that an exemption system will need to apply in the case of some financial services. The question at this point becomes how broad the exemption should be. Should it be quite inclusive, as in the EC, or be limited to principal activities, as in Singapore, or apply only to margin activities? Should compensatory taxes be employed? In answering these questions, policymakers will have to balance the demands of certain competing objectives, and take into account certain characteristics of their financial system and economy.

Developing countries will typically have an objective of applying taxation to financial services as a progressive source of revenue, as well as to avoid the distortions associated with an exemption described earlier. Taxation of financial services is viewed as progressive because such services as banking, brokerage, property and casualty insurance, and foreign exchange transactions are connected closely with those with income and wealth. This has certainly been a major consideration in the decision of the Government of India to extend its service tax to a variety of financial and other services, including share brokerage and insurance. Generally, where an exemption is in place under a VAT, there will likely be less revenue than under full taxation. The progressive revenue objective thus dictates as wide an application of VAT to financial services as possible. It will also lead countries to consider compensatory taxes where an exemption must be provided and even additional ad hoc taxes for revenue purposes.

In deciding how far taxation can proceed, certain characteristics of the economy and the financial sector will need to be taken into consideration. Some factors found in developing countries may make it easier to apply taxes to financial services without adverse effects, while others may make it more difficult. The relevant considerations will vary from country to country and careful consideration will be needed to determine what specific approach should be taken among the alternatives described earlier.

Factors that may dictate a conservative approach relying heavily on exemption are the importance of not retarding development of the financial sector, and not diverting financial activity into the informal sector where tax is not collected. It is paramount to recognize that financial markets are crucial for a well-functioning economy. A characteristic of developing economies may be that consumers and businesses make relatively little use of financial services. Developing the sector allows transaction costs to be reduced and capital markets to develop. If taxation is likely to cause financial activity to move underground or offshore at the expense of local institutions, there may be little revenue gain from taxation and significant economic cost. Blockages to the development of the sector as a result of excessive or badly designed taxes can do significant damage that cannot be justified by short-term revenue considerations.

If significant levels of financial services to households are provided by small, largely unregulated, and untaxed entities in the informal sector, taxation may drive consumers toward this segment of the economy. Attempts to apply full taxation on financial services in this case will not increase tax revenues and may not be desirable on economic development grounds.

Yet, in some instances, characteristics of financial services in developing countries may make it possible to adopt models that tax a broader range of financial services more fully. If the financial sector is concentrated and highly regulated, approaches that tax most fees and commissions or agency services could be feasible. Regulatory controls may mean that there is little behavioral change associated with these approaches. However, substitution of margin for fees and commissions is likely to be an issue in respect of at least some services even in these cases. For example, attempts to tax fees and commissions on foreign exchange transactions have proven unsuccessful in some countries such as Russia, as the form in which consideration was earned was rapidly changed to margins or moved into the untaxed, informal economy. Where substitution is likely to be feasible, it will probably be better to introduce an exemption for the service in question.

Moving further along the spectrum to full taxation is also likely to be more feasible where competition is limited in the financial sector. This would be the case if the potential for international competition from competing sources of supply is minimal because of foreign exchange controls, or if these services are provided by government monopolies, or both.

In making the choice, it is important to consider compliance and administration issues and the extent to which taxation versus exemption will create competitive distortions and significant behavioral changes. Some factors that are problematic in developed economies may raise less difficulty in developing countries. For example, outsourcing may not be as feasible as in developed countries.

If revenue and other policy considerations dictate further taxation of the financial sector than would be available under a broad system of exemption, then the best option would appear to be an extension of tax to those financial services for which an explicit fee is charged. Compensatory taxes would be a less satisfactory alternative because, as noted, they raise their own distortions and difficulties.

Notes

1. One type of financial service identified in table 12.1 that is somewhat unusual is the purchase and sale of gold and precious metals. Gold and certain other precious metals play a dual role in the economy in that they are traded both as consumer and industrial commodities, and also for investment purposes. As a result, gold bullion, in particular, has often been singled out for treatment that to some degree mirrors the treatment of financial products under consumption tax systems.

2. Other exemptions specified include goods and services supplied by certain public bodies, sale of land and buildings, and leasing of immovable property. For useful perspectives on the current system of exemptions see European Economic Commission (1995) and OECD (1988). McLure

(1987) provides a description and analysis of VAT exemptions in the European Community, as well as other OECD-member countries.

3. For another discussion of the rationale for exemption, see Ebrill and others (2001, pp. 94–97).

4. See the discussion of this issue in chapter 2.

5. One response to importation biases, self-assessment, is not very effective in the case of financial services. Another approach, requiring registration by foreign institutions, has been more effective where it has been applied because, in an industry that requires considerable trust to operate, registrants and consumers are often reluctant to deal with nonregistered parties.

6. See Grubert and Mackie (2000).

7. See chapter 2 for a more complete discussion of the underlying issue. Edgar (2001) also surveys this issue and considers alternatives to full taxation that might be based on the arguments advanced by Jack.

8. See Cooper and Vann (1999) for an argument of this type—in favor of retaining exemption—until a clear, internationally agreed method of taxation is settled upon.

9. VAT systems and income tax systems differ fundamentally in this regard. Individuals under an income tax are typically taxable on each source of income, consisting of labor income, business income, investment income, rents, and capital gains. There is no registration requirement and the sole test is whether the activity in question is undertaken with a profit motive. In the case of the latter four income sources, associated expenses may be deducted in determining income subject to tax. The allowance of a deduction for investment expenses that are attributable to investment activity means that the income tax does contain a dividing line between deductible and non-deductible expenses, including for financial services. This is a necessary feature of arriving at an appropriate tax base including, of course, the time value of money.

10. The discussion of the options includes a brief description of examples of alternative approaches used in selected countries. However, these examples are illustrative; they do not constitute a broad survey of country-by-country approaches. For a more inclusive discussion of systems of taxing financial services, see Tait (1988).

11. The TCA system was developed by Ernst & Young in a set of studies on cash flow taxation done for the Commission of the European Communities. It is described in Ernst & Young (1996a). The system as it would apply to deposit or loan transactions is also described in Poddar and English (1997). The system was further developed and analyzed in a series of pilot studies carried out at selected European financial institutions under the auspices of Commission of the European Communities. A complete description of the system indicating how it would apply to various types of financial services drawing on the results from these pilot projects is available in the Customs section of the European Commission website (http://europa.

eu.int/comm/taxation_customs/publications/reports_studies/report.htm #financial).

12. See previous note.

13. A detailed discussion of this issue can be found in Ernst & Young (1996b). The actual occurrence of risk is recognized for each individual transaction separately. This leads to situations in which the net cash flows or margins earned from certain transactions become negative. Even though each individual contract is priced to yield a positive anticipated margin (a positive ex ante price) to the financial institution, the actual margin (the ex post price) for a subset of transactions would necessarily be smaller or negative because of the occurrence of risk. There is no operational mechanism that allows an ex ante isolation of the pure risk premium for tax purposes with precision or objectivity.

14. The exact structure adopted does vary in some ways from the ideal cash flow system. See, for example, Ernst & Young (1996a, pp. 156–57).

15. Value added should also include financing costs for capital: that is, interest on funds borrowed to acquire business assets. In the case of financial institutions, one needs to draw a distinction between this interest component and the interest costs for deposits and other funds acquired during the course of borrowing and lending business. The former are a component of value added, but not the latter. A portion of profits, which represents a pure rate of interest on shareholders' funds used in lending business, should also be excluded from the VAT base. This is achieved under the TCA system by defining the base as interest received less an indexing adjustment that represents cost of funds at the pure rate of interest.

References

Auerbach, Alan, and R. H. Gordon. 2001. "Taxation of Financial Services under a VAT." University of California, Berkeley, Department of Economics. Processed.

Boadway, Robin, and Michael Keen. 2003. "Theoretical Perspectives on the Taxation of Capital Income and Financial Services" (chapter 2, this volume).

Chia, N. C., and J. Whalley. 1999. "The Tax Treatment of Financial Intermediation." *Journal of Money, Credit and Banking* 31 (4): 704–19.

Cooper, Graeme S., and Richard J. Vann. 1999. "Implementing the Goods and Services Tax." *Sydney Law Review* 21: 337–436.

Ebrill, Liam, Michael Keen, Jean-Paul Bodin, and Victoria Summers. 2001. *The Modern VAT.* Washington, D.C.: International Monetary Fund.

Edgar, Tim. 2001. "Exempt Treatment of Financial Intermediation Services under a Value-Added Tax: An Assessment of Alternatives." *Canadian Tax Journal* 49 (5): 1133–1219.

Ernst & Young. 1996a. "Value-Added Tax: A Study of Methods of Taxing Financial and Insurance Services." Prepared for the European Commission, Directorate General XI, Customs and Indirect Taxation. Brussels. Processed.

————. 1996b. "Negative TCA Balances under the TCM/TCA Cash-flow Method." Prepared for the European Commission, Directorate General XI, Customs and Indirect Taxation. Brussels. Processed.

European Economic Commission. 1995. "Options for a Definitive VAT System." Working Paper E-5. Directorate-General for Research, Brussels.

Grubert, Harry, and James Mackie. 2000. "Must Financial Services be Taxed Under a Consumption Tax?" National Tax Journal 53 (1): 23–40.

Huizinga, Harry. 2002. "A European VAT on Financial Services?" Economic Policy 35: 499–534.

Institute for Fiscal Studies. 1978. The Structure and Reform of Direct Taxation. Report of a Committee Chaired by Professor J. E. Meade (The Meade Committee Report). London: George Allen & Unwin.

Jack, William. 2000. "The Treatment of Financial Services under a Broad-based Consumption Tax." National Tax Journal 53 (4): 841–51.

McLure, Charles E. 1987. The Value-Added Tax, Key to Deficit Reductions? Washington, D.C.: American Enterprise Institute for Public Policy Research.

OECD (Organisation for Economic Co-operation and Development). 1988. Taxing Consumption. Paris.

Poddar, Satya, and Morley English. 1997. "Taxation of Financial Services under a Value-Added Tax: Applying the Cash Flow Approach." National Tax Journal 50 (1): 89–111.

Tait, Alan. 1988. Value-Added Tax: Practices and Problems. Washington, D.C.: International Monetary Fund.

13

The Accidental Tax: Inflation and the Financial Sector

Patrick Honohan

Although first and foremost a monetary phenomenon, inflation has wider implications for macroeconomic stability, competitiveness, and contracting, notably because many contracts, especially wage contracts, are fixed in terms of money. Two particular features of inflation—and their interaction—are the focus of this chapter: the potential to ease the government's budget constraint and the impact on financial sector performance.

Inflation is nowadays often an "accidental tax," with surprisingly little use of direct monetary financing of the government. Inflation has two contrasting impacts on the financial sector. On the one hand, by increasing the risk and cost of payments and maintaining liquid transactions balances, it increases the demand for certain financial services, swelling the value-added and profitability of banks. On the other hand, the interaction of inflation with a nonindexed tax system often results in an effective rate of taxation on financial intermediation that is super-sensitive to the inflation rate. The high and volatile effective tax rates are associated with wide intermediation margins and a reduced scale of intermediation.

For society, both effects are costly distortions. Even if banking activity and profits are increased by the additional demand for efficient payments services, this is a socially costly diversion of resources from more productive activities. The costs of tax-inflation interactions can be reduced by avoiding particular tax designs, including taxes on gross interest receipts, off-market interest ceilings, and unremunerated reserve requirements.

This chapter is organized as follows. The next section reviews the underlying theory of inflation as a tax, asking whether it could form a part of the optimal set of taxes, especially bearing in mind its impact on the financial system. The section that follows examines the mechanics of how inflation generates revenue for the government, uncovering evidence suggesting that, in most countries recently, most of the fiscal benefit flows through the profits of the central bank, rather than in the form of direct financing. The chapter then presents empirical evidence of the impact of inflation on banking activity and profits, showing that, while the financial system shrinks with inflation—stock markets, apparently, more than the banking sector—inflation tends to be associated with a boost to bank profitability and value-added. The chapter shows how highly sensitive the effective rate of other taxes (especially those on interest) can be to inflation, and proposes a measure of that sensitivity. After offering some remarks on incidence, the chapter concludes with a call to improve the indexation of the tax system so far as the computation of interest is concerned.

Could Inflation Be a Good Tax—Even for the Financial Sector?

If inflation is always and everywhere a monetary phenomenon, then the inflation tax too is inherently a monetary phenomenon. But, as with the causes of inflation itself, it is often necessary to look behind the money creation in order to understand the processes that create and sustain the conditions for monetary expansion. Rather than being the consequence of a measured policy decision to impose an "inflation tax," inflation is more often the result of quite different policy dynamics. For example, it may result from monetary accommodation of a wage bargaining process, or of exchange rate depreciation caused by non-monetary factors.

Genuine Tax or Analytical Construct?

To some extent, the concept of inflation tax is an analytical construct rather than a recognized and managed source of revenue for the state. It is clear enough that inflation and the associated money creation can represent a transfer of resources to the state, but measuring the resources so transferred, or even identifying the tax base, is a matter of analysis on which authors differ. No government budget contains a line entitled "inflation tax" or "seigniorage." That is not to say that the implicit revenue comes as a surprise at the end of the year; estimates of the revenue and expenditure of the various channels through which inflation will affect the budget will normally be taken into account in budgetary forecasts. Thus only if the inflation is unexpected will there be surprises.

It is the increased demand for holdings of nominal base money associated with inflation that will create the conditions for the budget to profit from the government's monopoly pricing of base money.

It is not even the case that inflation will always be associated with a net gain to the budget. Existing conventions and contracts may greatly erode, or even reverse, the gains. Thus as was famously pointed out by Tanzi (1977), if government wage rates are indexed or quickly adjust to changing price levels while tax receipts, struck in nominal terms, arrive at the Treasury in arrears, an engineered expansion in the money supply may not provide enough resources to cover the additional net outlays that are required because of the change in prices.

Few governments, then, set out consciously to exploit the inflation tax. If there is monetary financing of the budget, it is seen as a financing, rather than as a tax device, albeit one that is likely to have the politically costly side effect of inflation. Nevertheless, once governments are benefiting from the implicit revenue of a steady rate of inflation, they will quickly feel the loss of this revenue from a stabilization, as was pointed out in respect of some potential Exchange Rate Mechanism and European Monetary Union members (Grilli 1989a, b; Repullo 1991).

Should an Inflation Tax Be Used?

Some have argued that perhaps governments *should* consciously exploit the inflation tax. Of course, Bailey (1956) and Friedman (1953, 1971) argued that in an essentially partial equilibrium steady state context, the optimal rate of inflation tax was zero, to be achieved (absent any way of paying interest on currency notes) by a steady proportionate contraction in the money supply and the associated deflation. But, as noted in this context by Phelps (1973), taxes without distortions are not generally available, so that in order to finance socially desirable government expenditure, the optimal set of taxes might easily include the inflation tax. An unresolved debate has raged since over this issue. Among theorists, the question has been whether the inflation tax is one of those taxes (following the argument of Diamond and Mirrlees 1971) that should optimally be omitted from the set of taxes, in preference to taxes that can achieve the desired impact on consumption without distorting production structures. An increasingly refined literature has pinpointed that, in order to sustain the original Friedman proposition, it must be the case that the role of money is essentially reducible to that of an intermediate good.[1]

If higher inflation induces less reliance on money balances in household portfolios, instead channeling more of savings into capital formation, the result could be more rapid growth. This proposition, advanced long ago by Tobin (1978) and retaining theoretical support in some models of endogenous growth, remains controversial and rather heterodox.[2] Certainly, empirical studies cited below show a negative cross-country correlation between inflation and growth.

The existence of non-trivial collection costs for formal taxes may provide another rationale for use of the inflation tax. Some authors have gone so far as to suggest that the presence of currency substitution may in this respect be harmful, in that it limits the scope for using the inflation tax for such reasons (Sibert and Liu 1998).[3]

The base of the inflation tax includes not only currency, but also unremunerated or partly remunerated required banking reserves. It is hardly disputed nowadays that the primary rationale for sizable unremunerated reserves is fiscal. (Even if some techniques of monetary stabilization involve the imposition of required reserves, little if any fiscal penalty is needed to ensure their effectiveness in this role.)[4] Noting that bank depositors are more prosperous than those whose liquid assets are wholly in the form of currency notes, some scholars have argued that the major political economy motivation for using partially remunerated reserve requirements instead of relying on seigniorage from currency is only to discriminate between income groups. In these models, a partly remunerated reserve requirement will be preferred (to an unremunerated one) by a government supported by the rich.[5] As to the distinct question of whether reserve requirements or a tax on deposit interest is a preferable steady state way of raising government revenue, the majority view among theoreticians, since the work of Freeman (1987) and Brock (1989), has been that the two are equivalent. Some authors argue that the deposit tax is preferable, to the extent that it allows the banks to make more use of any special abilities to earn higher returns on loanable funds, thereby better facilitating the transfer of needed fiscal resources to the government.[6]

Some have taken this reasoning to imply that the rate of inflation tax, if optimally chosen, should be correlated with other rates of tax (the tax smoothing argument).[7] While the tax smoothing argument may seem plausible in theory, the difficulty in practice of controlling inflationary psychology and expectations means that a given target for the rate of inflation tax may not be as easily hit as with other taxes.

Without doubt, recourse to monetary financing is often much easier and quicker than adjusting tax rates and schedules in order to raise additional revenue.[8] Therefore, on a time-series basis, after taking account of adjustment costs, one would expect optimally chosen inflation financing to be correlated, not with other tax rates, but with unanticipated fluctuations in spending or in the government deficit (the residual financing argument). This does appear to be the case, but in a systematic way only for high inflation countries (Fischer, Sahay, and Vegh 2002; Boyd, Levine, and Smith 2001).[9]

Response of the Financial System to Inflation

The monetary and financial system does not remain passive in response to inflation. Countless studies document the substitution away from non–interest-bearing monetary assets in favor of interest-bearing or indexed assets, or to those denominated in foreign currencies, or to non-monetary assets. It is this substitution that has the most important impact on the performance and functioning of the financial system. On the one hand, the volume of funds that it is able to mobilize and intermediate may shrink. On the other hand, its capacity to provide the instruments to insulate economic agents from the effects of high or volatile inflation is an important aspect of its social contribution.

The average rate, the variability, and the predictability of inflation are three key elements contributing to the impact of the inflation tax. These in turn are linked to the rate of monetary expansion, but not in a neat or mechanical way. Over the long term, the rate of inflation can be expected to equal the rate of base money growth less the rate of growth in the real economy, with some allowance for technical change in the demand for base money. In practice, this relation is a good predictor only at high rates of money growth (and it is very good for hyperinflation). This means that there is a disconnect between the rate of tax as measured by the opportunity cost of holding interest-free base money (which will be related to the expected inflation rate) and the flow of financing to the budget from money creation (Honohan 1996).

Costs of Inflation

What are the social costs of the inflation tax and how big are they? This broad and much discussed question takes us beyond the sphere

of the financial sector (Cukierman 1984; Feldstein 1999). Broad, reduced form calculations have compared how growth rates vary with
inflation across countries.[10] But such calculations do not consider
the channels of effect and what aspects of the financial system may
be involved. The early study by Bailey (1956) adopted a simple approach by measuring the lost consumer surplus under an estimated
demand for money function. Several more specific channels of effect
have been studied theoretically, including the considerations that, in
the face of steady inflation, agents will over-economize on the holding of transactions balances (Cooley and Hansen 1991)[11] and that
they will hold too few precautionary balances, resulting in unneeded
fluctuations in consumption (İmrohoroğlu and Prescott 1991).[12]

It is often noted that—as agents will adjust only to the expected
part of inflation, with perhaps some allowance for the variability—
unexpected inflation is, to some extent, like a lump-sum tax. However, it could contribute to the market's future allowance (risk-
premium) for surprises entailing a long-lasting deadweight loss
effect—which could even be larger than if each period's inflation
were fully anticipated in advance.

How Does the Government Get Hold of the Inflation Tax Revenues?

In simple textbook models, the role of money creation in influencing the government's budget constraint is typically expressed in
terms of a balance sheet identity that must be satisfied at all times,
such as:

$$(13.1) \qquad G - T = B - (1 + r)B_{-1} + M - M_{-1}$$

where G and T represent spending and taxation, B is the stock of
bonds (perpetuities), r the rate of interest paid on the bonds, and M
the stock of base money. This is all fine and perfectly consistent, but
do the implicit institutional arrangements correspond to reality?
Curiously, this question does not appear to figure prominently in
the theoretical literature, although it is important in empirical
analyses, especially for particular countries.[13]

Almost all countries now have an articulated accounting system
that clearly distinguishes the central bank from the government. An
increase in the central bank's monetary liabilities (currency and the
deposits placed, mainly by banks and other financial institutions—
known as the money base) need not have as its counterpart an in-

crease in central bank credit to the government. (The empirical facts on this are examined later.)

If the central bank does not "lend" newly created money to the government, is there still seigniorage, and if so how does the government receive the seigniorage? The short answer to this is that the seigniorage does exist, and comes through the assets that are acquired by the central bank in return for issuing money base. These are either foreign exchange, claims on the banking system, or claims on other sectors of the domestic economy.

These assets in turn are not usually handed over to the government to be liquidated in aid of the budget.[14] Instead they are typically held on the central bank's balance sheet, where they earn interest until redeemed, and that interest accrues to the benefit of the central bank's income statement. Most central banks are owned by the government or, if they are not, the government nevertheless is usually entitled to the bulk of the central bank's profits in due course. In this case, it is through the distribution of the central bank's profits that the government's budget finally receives the seigniorage in the form of cash.

Other demands on the revenues of the central bank can intervene, with the result that some of the seigniorage never reaches the government's budget. For one thing, the operational expenses of the central bank will often be paid out of its interest revenues; also, the central bank may undertake lending or similar activities at below-market interest rates.[15] Such schemes are, in effect, off-budget subsidies; although they reduce the flow of seigniorage to the budget, they do relieve the budget from alternative spending programs that would have been required to achieve the same goals as the subsidized lending by the central bank. Improved transparency and fiscal control argue against such hidden subsidies paid for out of seigniorage before it is transferred to the government, but they do continue to be observed, although less often than before.

The often delayed and opaque nature of the link between monetary expansion and the budget in regimes where relatively little of the base money liabilities of the central bank are backed by its lending to government contrasts sharply with the consolidated budget identity of equation 13.1. An expansion in non–interest-bearing base money that is fully backed by an increase in foreign bills, for example, will yield only the interest rate in the first year. There may even be a further delay in transmitting this to the government, depending on the accounting and dividend procedures of the central bank.[16]

Dividend and accounting policies of central banks are changeable and often rather opaque. Nonetheless, the balance sheet structures can be examined to detect which central banks back their base money liabilities with net claims on the government, which with net foreign assets, and which with other net claims on domestic sectors. The institutional arrangements where mostly government backing is used (corresponding to equation 13.1) may be termed "Mode I," and where mostly foreign exchange is used may be termed "Mode II."

An analysis along these lines was carried out for 153 central banks using data in *International Financial Statistics* (IFS).[17] A caveat needs to be added in regard to this data inasmuch as the stated composition of assets reported by central banks to IFS could differ from the effective composition after account is taken of swaps and other derivative activities.[18] Strikingly, the mean (and median) percentage of foreign exchange backing of base money in the world's central banks (in 2000) was more than 100 percent (table 13.1). Far from the picture implied by equation 13.1, which implicitly allocates all of the annual increase in base money to advances to government, the overall picture suggests a predominance of Mode II-type institutional arrangements. Clearly there is also a wide variation from

Table 13.1. Backing of the Money Base by Foreign Exchange or Claims on Government

Proportion backed by:	Quartile	2000 %	Change 1998–2000 %
Foreign exchange	Lower quartile	45.0	28.8
	Median	100.4	115.5
	Upper quartile	154.5	237.2
Government	Lower quartile	−12.8	−70.4
	Median	11.7	−1.1
	Upper quartile	53.8	63.7
Government less central bank capital	Lower quartile	−1.6	−13.0
	Median	21.3	14.1
	Upper quartile	60.7	71.4
Currency share in money base	Lower quartile	42.3	30.8
	Median	56.7	54.8
	Upper quartile	72.9	81.2

Note: Based on calculations for 153 countries of the end-2000 level (and for 130 countries of the 1998–2000 change) in money base as a percentage of the end-2000 level (and the 1998–2000 change) in foreign exchange reserves, net claims on government, and net claims on government less central bank capital. Also currency as a percentage of the money base.

Source: Author's calculations, based on *International Financial Statistics.*

country to country, with some countries relying heavily on net credit to government as the main backing for base money. The calculations were also carried out for 1998 and 1999 and for the change from 1998 to 2000. While the mean foreign exchange backing was lower in those years, it was still very high.

Analysis of the change shows even greater reliance on foreign exchange backing at the margin in 1998–2000. Of the 130 countries that increased their money base between 1998 and 2000, 80, or 38 percent, fully backed all of the new money base with foreign exchange. All but 20 had at least 25 percent foreign exchange cover at the margin. Far from routinely adding to the government's indebtedness to the central bank, in well over half the countries (72 cases), central bank credit to government actually declined. In only 30 cases did such credit increase by as much as half the increase in the money base.

An alternative calculation (the third row in table 13.1) nets out the capitalization (and other items) of the central bank on the grounds that an increase in net credit to the government that is funded by an increase in central bank capitalization does not represent monetary financing. The results of the calculation are qualitatively similar and indicate even less of a link between monetary financing of the government and increases in base money.

If this analysis reveals that the timing and mechanisms of budgetary finance through money creation and the inflation tax are most commonly closer to Mode II than Mode I—and as such, quite different from the textbook model—it is natural to ask whether there is a clear statistical link between inflation and the institutional mode of seigniorage transmission, or between monetary depth and the institutional mode, in each case measuring the mode by the degree to which money base increase is backed by foreign exchange or by net credit to government. Figure 13.1 presents the relevant scatterplots. Because of the wide range of values for the explanatory variable, no strong relationship is evident. Regression analysis confirms the theoretically plausible negative correlation between inflation and the degree of foreign backing (and a positive correlation with net government credit), but the finding is not statistically significant, even after excluding the largest outliers.

The Impact of Inflation on the Financial Sector

How does inflation affect the scale and profitability of financial intermediation and real rates of return? In addition to reviewing some cross-country evidence from the literature, this section contributes

Figure 13.1. Alternative Sources of the Monetary Base and Their Correlation with Monetary Depth and Inflation

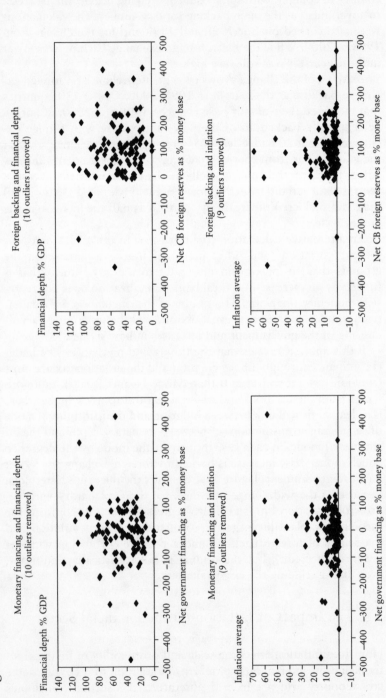

Source: Author's calculations, based on *International Financial Statistics.*

some new empirical evidence on these issues. Inflation is found to be positively associated with profitability and especially with the value-added of the banking system. But the balance sheet size of the banking system shrinks with inflation, though the effect may be smaller at higher rates of inflation. Stock market liquidity also diminishes with inflation, apparently to a greater extent. The Fisherian link between inflation and nominal interest rates—only weakly evident in the cross-country data at low rates of inflation—is clear at higher rates.

Since the rate of inflation is endogenous to macroeconomic policies and financial sector structures, it would be unwise to assert too strongly that the relationships detected are causal ones. Furthermore the impact of inflation on financial sector magnitudes is highly dependent on administrative, legal, and tax characteristics for which no good statistical controls are available. Therefore the statistical associations should be regarded as indicative of general tendencies, rather than immutable laws.

Bank Profitability

First, consider the impact of inflation on bank profitability. This question was addressed by the major studies of Demirgüç-Kunt and Huizinga (1999) and Claessens, Demirgüç-Kunt, and Huizinga (2000). Although exploring the role of inflation was not the main focus of these papers, the authors concluded that the impact of inflation on profitability, while not very significant, is positive. Looking again at this issue with more recent data confirms and reinforces their finding. In addition, this study finds that inflation has a stronger and more consistent positive association with the value-added of the banking system.

The above-mentioned authors used data from the income statements of about 3,000 banks in 80 countries from 1988 to 1995. They examined a large range of potential determinants, both bank-specific and country-specific, of bank profitability. The bank-specific determinants included equity capitalization (which not surprisingly increases the ratio of before tax profits to total assets),[19] the average tax rate paid (estimated to pass-through 100 percent to before tax profits), and a dummy for foreign ownership (helps a bank's profitability by as much as 50 basis points in low-income countries, and hinders it in large). A bank with high overhead costs as a share of total assets does not, on average, recover these fully, although the point estimate suggests that the shortfall is very slight.[20] The other bank-specific explanatory variables represent the shares in total assets represented by loans and non-interest earning assets, respectively, and of deposits in total liabilities. Relative to the excluded balance sheet categories, a heavy reliance on non-interest earning assets hits the bottom line, especially in rich countries; access to sources of funding other than deposits boosts profitability. Loans contribute to profits somewhat more than the excluded category.

These are the only bank-specific variables used in the Demirgüç-Kunt and Huizinga (D-H) analysis, but they are augmented by a series of macro, tax, and institutional variables. It is here that the effect of inflation is measured. In fact, inflation is nowhere significant at the 10 percent level, but the coefficient is positive, its size implying that a 10 percent rate of inflation boosts bank profitability by about 10 basis points of total assets. The significant macro variables in these regressions are per capita income and the real wholesale interest rate, both of which are estimated to add to profits.[21] GDP growth is not significant.

Demirgüç-Kunt and Huizinga include the economy-wide average reserve holdings as a proxy measure for this form of quasi-taxation.[22] Interestingly, average reserve holdings (as a share of total assets) in poorer countries sharply reduce before-tax profits, whereas they increase them in richer countries. One would expect that unremunerated reserve requirements might have an especially severe impact where inflation is high, but this was not tested by the authors.

If the focus is on the overall impact of inflation, it needs to be borne in mind both that inflation may be jointly determined with some of the other variables included in the regression (notably the real interest rate). Also, the wide variation of inflation rates (and in particular the inclusion of Brazil, which in the sample period reached 2,300 percent inflation) and the use of country dummies may mask a genuine impact of inflation on bank profitability. This prompts a revisit to the data and a closer look at inflation effects (though without retaining the micro aspects). With cross-sectional data covering some 70 countries, then, it seems appropriate to pursue a loose specification search to try to assess the scale and robustness of any link between inflation and average profitability.

As shown in figure 13.2, a bivariate scatterplot of the country-average values of the two variables suggests a positive relationship. This is confirmed by regression analysis on these averaged figures (table 13.2). The reported regressions use log-inflation instead of the level and include all of the other cross-country variables that were significant in the D-H study: namely, per capita GDP, real interest rates, and the level of reserves. Even including all these variables, inflation remains highly significant when the equation is estimated in log form or, if Brazil is excluded, even in level form.[23]

Upon further examination, the interesting fact emerges that inflation strongly interacts with reserve holdings—not to reduce prof-

Figure 13.2. Bank Profitability and Inflation, 1988–95

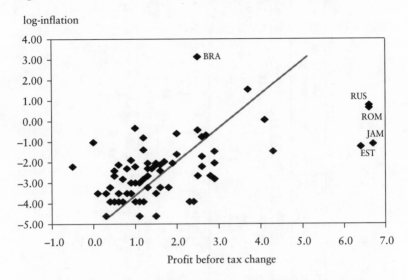

Notes: See note to table 13.3; BRA Brazil; EST Estonia; JAM Jamaica; ROM Romania; RUS Russia.

its, but instead to increase them! Rather than the reserve holdings being involuntary, in countries with high reserve holdings and high inflation the banks are likely finding ample remuneration at least on their marginal reserve holdings. A look at some of the high-profit countries in the scatterplot shows Russia and Romania to be prominent, no doubt pointing to special features of these transition economies' systems in the early 1990s.[24]

For the second half of the 1990s, figure 13.3 presents a similar scatterplot of average country banking profits (measured here by the rate of return on assets) against log-inflation. The same approach to equation specification is adopted. Once more, a clear upward-sloping relation appears in the simple regression (table 13.3, equation 1). In this case, a 10 percentage point increase in inflation from the sample median of 6 percent per year to 16 percent is associated on average with an increase in return on assets of 0.4 percentage points—compared with a median value of 1.1 percent.[25] The relationship appears strongly significant, and survives the addition of per capita income and real interest rates (neither of which are significant in this later data set, as shown in table 13.3, equation 2). Once again, the pattern of outliers (more than three standard errors away) is interesting: Moldova, with high measured profitability and inflation; and Thailand, with very low profitability (reflecting the crisis of 1997–78) and moderate inflation. These outliers do

Table 13.2. Inflation and Bank Profitability, 1988–95

Equation	1		2 Exclude Brazil		3 Log form		4	
Variable	Estimate	(t stat)	Estimate	(t stat)	Estimate	(t stat)	Estimate	(t stat)
Constant	2.262	(9.6)	1.941	(8.4)	3.518	(11.8)	3.544	(12.1)
Inflation	0.066	(1.1)	−0.972	(3.9)	0.685	(5.0)	0.727	(6.9)
GDP per cap × 10^{-4}	−0.863	(3.5)	−0.689	(3.0)	−0.122	(0.5)	—	—
Real interest	0.001	(0.1)	0.001	(0.1)	—		—	
Countries	All		Not Brazil		Not Brazil		Not Brazil	
Functional form	level		level		log		log	
Method/no. obs	OLS	67	OLS	66	OLS	72	OLS	72
RSQ/DW	0.188	1.46	0.338	1.82	0.409	1.91	0.741	1.76

Note: Dependent variable is profit before tax as a percentage of total assets (country average). Equation 1 includes the same variables as in D-H's equation 1.

Table 13.2. (continued) Inflation and Bank Profitability, 1988–95

Equation	5		6		7 Exclude Brazil		8	
Variable	Estimate	(t stat)	Estimate	(t stat)	Estimate	(t stat)	Estimate	(t stat)
Constant	3.217	(11.8)	1.748	(3.2)	1.475	(3.1)	2.657	(6.9)
Inflation	0.609	(6.2)	−0.074	(1.2)	0.976	(4.2)	0.526	(5.1)
GDP per cap × 10^{-4}	—		−0.503	(0.7)	−0.384	(0.6)	—	
Real interest	—		0.000	(0.0)	0.002	(0.1)	—	
Reserve requirements	—		3.165	(1.6)	2.986	(1.8)	2.152	(1.8)
Res. requirements × GDP/cap.	—		−2.780	(0.6)	−2.070	(0.5)	—	
Tax rate	—		−0.364	(0.4)	−0.643	(0.7)	—	
Tax rate × GDP/cap	—		0.016	(0.1)	0.191	(0.1)	—	
Countries	All		All		Not Brazil		Not Brazil	
Functional form	log		level		level		log	
Method/no. obs	OLS	73	OLS	55	OLS	54	OLS	58
RSQ/DW	0.355	1.92	0.265	0.86	0.409	1.91	0.560	1.77

Notes: Dependent variable is profit before tax as a percent of total assets (country average). Equation 6 includes the same variables as in D-H's equation 2. For each equation is shown the number of observations, the method (ordinary least squares), and the R-rated and Durbin-Watson statistics.

Source: Author's calculations. The banking data is from Demirgüç-Kunt and Huizinga (1999).

Figure 13.3. Bank Profitability and Inflation, 1995–99

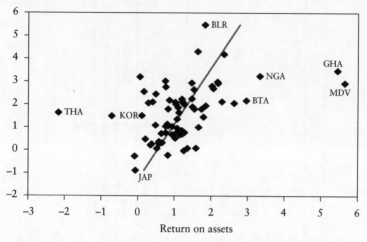

Notes: See note to table 13.3. BLR Belarus; BTA Botswana; GHA Ghana; JAP Japan; KOR Korea; MDV Moldova; NGA Nigeria; THA Thailand.

not, however, strongly influence the simple regression with log-inflation. Here the link with reserve ratios no longer applies.

As a control against under-specification, the analysis also checked to see whether some of the other variables employed by D-H but not significant for the earlier period remain insignificant here. The only one that is consistently significant is the bank concentration ratio, as shown in table 13.3, equations 5, 6, and 7. It should be borne in mind that this variable is available only for about three-quarters of the countries. Overhead as a share of total assets is only marginally significant, but when included tends to reduce the significance of inflation (equation 5). However this effect is diminished when the main outliers, Moldova and Thailand, are removed. Overall then, inflation does seem to be positively associated with bank profitability in the more recent period, as well.

We conclude that although the link is far from mechanical, in both the early and the late 1990s, higher inflation has tended to yield substantially greater profit opportunities in at least some countries.

Banking Value-Added

Widening the focus to include all the value-added of the banking system reinforces the message that inflation tends to offer possibilities for the financial sector to generate more value-added per unit of total

Table 13.3. Inflation and Bank Profitability, 1995–99

Equation	1		2		3		4	
Dependent Variable	ROA		ROA		VA		VA	
	Estimate	(t stat)	Estimate	(t stat)	Estimate	(t stat)	Estimate	(t stat)
Constant	0.529	(2.6)	0.212	(0.4)	2.422	(6.8)	2.234	(5.9)
Inflation	0.410	(4.1)	0.513	(2.9)	1.462	(8.3)	1.648	(7.4)
GDP per cap $\times 10^{-4}$	—	—	−0.065	(0.4)	—	—	—	—
Real interest	—	—	0.023	(1.1)	—	—	—	—
Res. reqt. $\times$ inflation $\times 10^3$	—	—	—	—	—	—	−0.510	(1.4)
Countries	All		All		All		All	
Functional form	log		log		log		log	
Method/no. obs	OLS	71	OLS	67	OLS	71	OLS	71
RSQ/DW	0.194	2.23	0.217	2.23	0.501	2.25	0.514	2.30

Note: Dependent variable is percent return on assets (country average), except equations 3 and 4, which use value-added as a percentage of total assets.

(Table continues on next page.)

397

Table 13.3. *(continued)* Inflation and Bank Profitability, 1995–99

Equation	5		6		7	
Variable	Estimate	(t stat)	Estimate	(t stat)	Estimate	(t stat)
Constant	-0.590	(1.6)	0.269	(0.9)	-0.328	(1.1)
Inflation	0.092	(0.7)	0.251	(2.8)	0.287	(1.5)
Overheads	0.151	(1.6)	—		0.085	(1.1)
Concentration	1.638	(3.5)	1.535	(3.3)	1.456	(3.8)
Countries	All		All		Not MDA, THA[a]	
Functional form	—		log		log	
Method/no. obs	OLS	54	OLS	53	OLS	52
RSQ/DW	0.360	1.00	0.310	0.923	0.409	1.35

Notes: Dependent variable is percent return on assets (country average). For each equation is shown the number of observations, the method (ordinary least squares), and the R-rated and Durbin-Watson statistics.

[a] Moldova and Thailand.

Source: Author's calculations. The banking data is updated from that in Demirgüç-Kunt and Huizinga (1999). Thanks to Luc Laeven for assembling and making available the 1995–99 data, which is also used in Demirgüç-Kunt, Laeven, and Levine (2003).

Figure 13.4. Bank Value-Added and Inflation, 1995–99

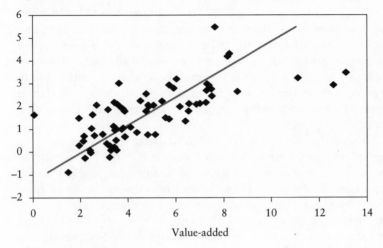

log-inflation

Value-added

Note: See note to table 13.3.

assets. Figure 13.4 shows that the simple correlation between value-added[26] and inflation is even stronger than with just profits. Once again, inflation is the major variable of those discussed above that remains significant in the analysis under different specifications.[27]

A number of alternative specifications parallel to those discussed above for profitability were explored, with value-added as the major explanatory variable. The cross-product of reserve holdings and inflation (also mentioned above for bank profitability) proved to be the most consistently significant variable in the specifications that included a lot of explanatory variables. Removing the least significant variables one by one however, left the (log of the) inflation rate as the only significant variable, with a very high t statistic of over 8 (table 13.3, equation 3). The significance of the cross-product term between reserves and inflation progressively weakens as other explanatory variables are removed, to the point where it is no longer significant when included only with inflation (table 13.3, equation 4).

Finding a strong relation between value-added and inflation should not be any surprise. Banks offer liquidity and transactions services that may be more highly valued in a period of high inflation or in countries where inflation is often high. In addition, these profitability and value-added figures are calculated as a share of total assets, and these, as is well-known, are prone to shrink in real terms in inflationary times.

Bank Asset Size

What then, of the impact of inflation on the overall balance sheet size of the financial sector and its major components? Here the picture is unambiguous. As clearly documented by Boyd, Levine, and Smith (2001), inflation reduces both the size of the banking sector and measures of stock market activity (value traded and turnover). According to their estimates, however, beyond an inflation rate of 15 percent or so, the financial sector does not shrink any further. It appears that inflation has done "all the damage it can" by the time it reaches 15 percent.

Actually, the suggestion that "all the damage has been done by 15 percent" requires close scrutiny in the context of the inflation tax.[28] For one thing, it may seem to fly in the face of a long-held view that reliance on the inflation tax is limited by substitution away from money, and that there is a maximal rate of inflation tax[29] (that is, that there is an inflation tax Laffer curve). The idea of an inflation tax Laffer curve can be made consistent with the finding that the size of the financial sector does not shrink much as inflation increases beyond 15 percent if at high rates of inflation the sector switches to reliance on interest-bearing instruments structured in such a way as to insulate the participants from fluctuations in inflation. Indeed, the same authors, as well as Barnes, Boyd, and Smith (1999), find that nominal financial asset yields tend to be much more strongly correlated (across countries) with inflation at high rates of inflation (again they use the 15 percent cutoff).

Stock Market Activity

Measures of stock market activity also decline with inflation, according to the estimates presented by Boyd, Levine, and Smith. Once again, they identify a slowing of the decline around 15 percent inflation, though here the cutoff is much less distinct and may reasonably be questioned.[30] As both components are hit by inflation, it is important to know which of the two declines by more. For instance, if one takes the ratio of bank assets to market capitalization, does this decline with inflation or not? Somewhat surprisingly, the data and estimates assembled by Boyd, Levine, and Smith strongly suggest that the bank-to-market ratio tends to increase with inflation, at least if market capitalization or value-traded are used as market indicators (figure 13.5).[31] That the effect of inflation on the stock market would be greater than on banking is particularly surprising when one considers that stocks are commonly considered a hedge against inflation (though a most imperfect one, as the

Figure 13.5. How Bank-to-Market Ratios Change with Inflation

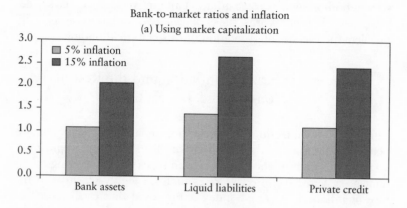

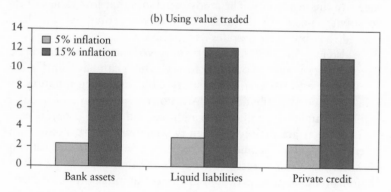

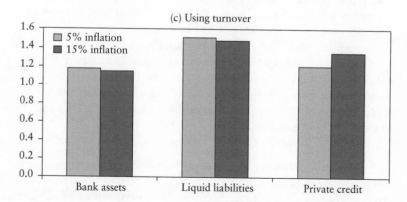

Note: Shows the ratio of various measures of the size of the banking system relative to the size or activity of the stock market.

Source: Based on data in Boyd, Levine, and Smith (2001), using the interquartile gradient for each component.

evidence shows). It seems likely that here especially a common path effect is apparent, with weak macroeconomic policy conditions resulting both in high average inflation and in weak stock market development. In other words, the endogeneity of inflation is especially problematic for the interpretation of this empirical finding.

Interactions between Inflation and the Rest of a Non-indexed Tax System

This study now introduces considerations relating to the interaction between inflation and the remainder of the explicit and implicit tax system. The analysis shows that certain types of tax affecting the financial system have effective rates that are highly sensitive to the rate of inflation. A simple index is proposed that can be used to measure this sensitivity. The study concludes that low values of the sensitivity index are desirable, especially in countries that have proved susceptible to episodes of inflation.

Feldstein (1983, 1999) has aptly observed that the interaction between inflation and a non-indexed tax system can have sizable and unexpected effects—even in a country with single-digit inflation. As inflation increases, the double distortions of inflation and taxation can be multiplicative rather than additive, with severe consequences.

The effects are mainly through two channels. First, nominal interest is treated as income (or an expense), without any adjustment for inflation. Thus it receives a tax charge that depends on the inflation premium that may be built into the interest rate. Alternatively, it might be said that the capital gain on nominal liabilities due to inflation is not chargeable to income tax. Second, depreciation allowances are calculated according to historical cost and not to a realistic replacement cost in line with rising prices.

There is a further effect of taxation in the case where the tax schedule is progressive (with lower rates of tax imposed on lower values of the base). If the thresholds of the progression are not indexed to the price level, rising prices will push the average rate of tax on any real sum higher.

Among the behavioral effects of a non-indexed tax system:

• The real after-tax rate of return to investors in real projects is generally lower. This is because the second effect, usually, and on average, outweighs the first. Accordingly, investment in productive activity is penalized at the expense of investment in land, consumer durables, and other assets not yielding a taxable nominal return, such as gold.

- There may be a shift in the relative advantage of bond and equity finance, even though, for the individual tax-paying shareholder, the fact that bond interest is tax deductible for the corporation may be offset by the fact that it is taxable as shareholder's income.
- Judging monetary policy is complicated. In an inflationary environment, a given gross-of-tax nominal rate of interest may look to be high enough not to be judged expansionary. But for the investing company, the deductibility of nominal interest payments may mean that the net-of-tax real interest rate is very low or negative, and that the stance of monetary policy is not tight enough to dampen spending.

Feldstein notes an important distinction between steady inflation and changes in inflation. Comparing two different steady rates of inflation, equity prices can be expected to rise faster in the higher inflation environment. But when inflation jumps from one steady rate to a higher one, equilibrium price-earnings ratios are damaged by the higher effective tax rate to which they are subject. Accordingly, equity prices will fall at first, before beginning to increase at the faster rate.

What about the influence on the financial services industry? Clearly, the effects can be significant here, too. Some of the same considerations arise, but the relative importance is altered. In addition, there are some new considerations. For one thing, the financial services industry is obviously affected by shifts in the relative reliance on different financing instruments. Thus while the impact of inflation on demand and supply conditions for other industries will be chiefly affected through whatever overall impact there is on the economy at large, inflation will have a first-order or direct influence on the demand for different financial services. The impact of inflation on the scale and activity of financial services firms needs to be considered alongside the effect on their tax-inclusive cost structures.

The degree to which the effective tax rate on financial institutions varies with inflation differs as between different non-indexed taxes. Three degrees may be distinguished:

- tax burdens that increase, but not in proportion to the rate of inflation (first-order non-indexation);
- an increase in the effective tax rate that is approximately proportional to the rate of inflation ("second-order non-indexation," or "supersensitivity"); and
- an even greater (third-order) sensitivity to inflation.

First-order non-indexation is associated, for example with a simple failure to index the thresholds (such as the tax-free allowance and the point at which a higher rate of tax applies) in a progressive tax on non-interest income. In this case, a rise in prices has the effect of pushing more of the tax base into the higher rate of taxation. But to the extent that the rates of taxation are fixed, there is a ceiling on the rate of taxation regardless of the rate of inflation or of the degree to which adjustment of the nominal thresholds lags inflation.

When it comes to taxes on interest income, however, supersensitivity can often arise, implying a potentially volatile inflation rate. Where this arises will obviously depend on the precise specification of the taxes and quasi-taxes involved. This study cannot hope to model every possible tax structure and thus will focus on some simple canonical cases.

If a financial intermediary is thought of as adding value to investable funds by repackaging them for users of funds—thereby increasing both the risk-return profile and liquidity of the provider and the cost and availability of funds for the users—then it is relative to that value-added that the impact of taxation can best be measured.

The three forms in which non-indexed taxes arise most frequently for financial intermediaries are taxes on nominal interest income, nominal interest ceilings, and unremunerated reserve requirements.

One way of looking at the role of inflation in increasing the burden of these taxes is to express the tax taken as a percentage of the real interest income that would otherwise be involved.

Thus a fixed rate of taxation t on nominal interest income, a reserve requirement at a fixed percentage θ of deposits remunerated at rate r^a, or a fixed nominal interest ceiling $\bar{r}$, all represent forms of non-indexed taxation. Their effective rate varies with inflation. All three have higher effective rates as inflation increases. But the degree of variation differs as between the three taxes. As will be shown below, the effective rate for the first two rises rapidly but less than in proportion to inflation (figures 13.6–13.8). The effective tax rate corresponding to the interest ceiling increases more than in proportion to the inflation rate; a doubling of inflation more than doubles the effective rate of tax. As such, the interest ceiling may be described as a third-degree, non-indexed, inflation-supersensitive tax.

These assertions are now substantiated under the familiar assumption that the nominal wholesale interest rate equals a fixed real interest rate ρ plus the expected inflation rate π.[32]

Fixed Tax Rate on Nominal Interest Income

Then if the nominal deposit interest rate r^d equals the nominal wholesale rate less a provision μ^d for deposit-related services, the nominal interest income per dollar deposited will be:

$$r^d = \rho + \pi - \mu^d$$

Figure 13.6. Tax Rates at Different Rates of Inflation

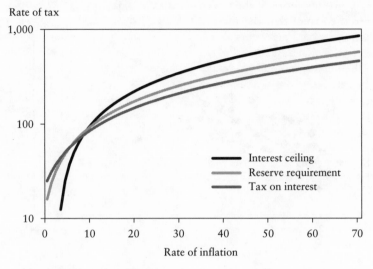

Source: Based on formulas in text.

Figure 13.7. Elasticity of Tax Rates at Different Rates of Inflation

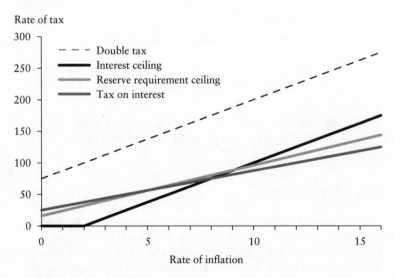

Source: Based on formulas in text.

Figure 13.8. Net Interest Rates and Inflation, 1995–99

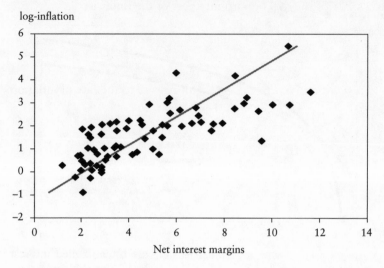

log-inflation

Net interest margins

Note: See note to table 13.3

whereas the real interest income will be $\rho - \mu^d$. Thus the tax collected expressed as a share of the pre-tax real interest income is:

$$z = t\frac{\rho + \pi - \mu^d}{\rho - \mu^d}.$$

The elasticity of the rate of tax with respect to π is:

$$\eta = \frac{\pi}{\rho + \pi - \mu^d}$$

It is easily seen that $\eta < 1$ if $\rho > \mu^d$ and that $\eta \to 1$ as $\pi \to \infty$. Thus the tax on interest income is supersensitive and non-indexed of the second degree.[33]

Reserve Requirement

For the reserve requirement, the nominal opportunity cost of the funds raised in deposits is the nominal wholesale interest rate $r^m = \rho + \pi$. Instead of receiving this amount, the bank receives only the reserve remuneration rate r^r on a fraction θ of the funds raised.[34]

Thus the implicit tax can be written as $\theta \, (r^m - r^r)$, which, expressed as a share of the real opportunity cost of the funds is:

$$z = \theta \frac{\rho + \pi - r^r}{\rho}$$

The elasticity of this tax rate with respect to the rate of inflation π is:

$$\eta = \frac{\pi}{\rho + \pi - r^r}.$$

For $\pi = 0$, $\eta = 0$; and $\eta \to 1$ as $\pi \to \infty$.

Tax-through Interest Ceiling

In this case the basic assumption is that the uncontrolled interest rate on lending, r^a, exceeds the wholesale rate by a fixed provision, μ^a, for credit appraisal and loan-losses. By controlling the lending interest rate at $\bar{r}$, the government is providing an implicit transfer (tax from lender, subsidy to borrower) per dollar lent of $r^a - \bar{r}$, if this is nonnegative. Expressed as a share of what would be the share of the pre-tax real interest income, the implicit tax rate can be written:

$$z = \max\left\{ \frac{\rho + \pi + \mu^a - \bar{r}}{\rho + \mu^a}, 0 \right\},$$

and the elasticity of this tax rate with respect to π is:

$$z = \max\left\{ \frac{\pi}{\rho + \pi + \mu^a - \bar{r}}, 0 \right\}.$$

In this case, for $\bar{r} > r^a$, $\eta > 1$ and $\eta \to 1$ as $\pi \to \infty$. This is a supersensitive tax with non-indexation of the third order, given that the elasticity of the effective tax rate with respect to inflation remains greater than one: much greater, over a certain range of values of inflation.

These patterns are illustrated in figures 13.6 and 13.7 for particular parameter values: $\rho = 0.05$; $t = 0.25$; $\mu^d = 0.01$; $\mu^a = 0.03$; $\theta = 0.25$; $\bar{r} = 0.1$; $r^r = 0.03$. It can be seen clearly from these plots that the effective rate of taxation expressed as a percentage of the real rate of return (or opportunity cost) of the funds involved can quickly exceed 100 percent. Indeed for the parameters chosen, which are not unrealistic, this point is passed for quite modest inflation rates in the range of 10 to 12 percent.

Where the providers of funds to the intermediary are also taxed on the nominal interest received, without deduction for tax already paid by the intermediary, the burden is increased once again. This typically just increases the *rate* of tax without much altering the *elasticity* substantially. If the depositor has the alternative of receiving non-intermediated interest income that is not taxed, it may be more appropriate to see the base of the double tax as being simply the intermediation margin. For the numerical example used in figure 13.6, a double interest tax (already representing a very high rate of tax on the intermediation margin even at zero inflation) also increases rapidly, and, though its elasticity with respect to the inflation rate is lower, this also converges to unity.

The calculations suggest summary ways of quantifying the degree of non-indexation of the various financial sector taxes with respect to inflation. The increase in the effective rate of tax as inflation goes from zero to ten percent could be one measure, which can be called the tax's inflation *gradient*. The *limiting elasticity* of the effective tax rate with respect to inflation as inflation becomes very large could be the other. All taxes in a perfectly indexed tax system would have a zero gradient and zero limiting elasticity.

The three interest taxes discussed have, for the parameters shown, gradients of 63, 80, and 100 percent, respectively. The double taxation (expressed as a percentage of intermediation margin) has a gradient of 125 percent. All have limiting elasticities of 1. The gradients are obviously high. A value of 100 implies that inflation fluctuating between zero and ten percent results in an effective tax rate that fluctuates by 100 percent of the base. The limiting elasticity of 1 implies that the tax rate is unlimited as inflation grows. Actually any limiting elasticity greater than zero has the same implication (and even if the limiting elasticity is zero, the effective tax rate might still increase without limit, though more slowly as inflation increases). The chaotic conditions caused by an unlimited rate of inflation tax as hyperinflation kicks in strongly suggests that any economy prone to surges of high inflation should ensure that its tax system has a limiting elasticity with respect to inflation no greater than zero.

Optimal Degree of Supersensitivity

Supersensitivity implies a high variation of effective tax rates where inflation is variable. Could this be good? It seems unlikely from the point of view of a stable and healthy development of human and organizational capital in the financial services industry. If monetary financing is primarily used in response to unanticipated deficits (the residual financing argument), then an induced volatility in the tax pressure on financial intermediation can hardly be a desired side effect. Equally, if fluctuations in inflation tax are seen as optimally programmed in line with fluctuations in the burden of other taxes (tax smoothing arguments), an induced amplification of some of those other taxes seems equally unlikely to be optimal. (After all, such arguments imply that inflation tax may optimally take up some of the pressure when other taxes are also high and as such causing distortions. Increasing a tax that exacerbates the distortions of existing taxes is not helpful in that context.) Above all, it can be assumed that governments do not anticipate the indirect impact on financial intermediation that this study is considering.

Thus even if setting zero as the optimal value of the gradient may be asking for a lot, a figure near 20 percent might be a realistic policy ceiling.

Incidence of Inflation Tax Interactions

Absent behavioral responses, the increase in the tax take will fall on the legal person liable to pay. In the case of the reserve requirement tax, for example, the shareholders of the bank will bear the entire burden. Especially with such high effective tax rates, however, the assumption of no behavioral response is hopelessly unrealistic.

For banks, it may be assumed that the main burden of the tax will be divided among depositors, borrowers, and bank shareholders. There could also be a burden on employees and suppliers of the banks. In a reasonably full employment context with smooth adjustment of the labor market, however, they would be affected only to the extent that they had sector-specific human capital deployed in the industry.

Whatever behavioral assumptions are made, it is clear that sizable behavioral responses can be expected to supersensitive taxes at high inflation. Naturally, the effects will be larger the closer the untaxed substitutes. Thus in particular, the extent to which dollarization has developed ready onshore alternatives to local currency banking products will be an important factor in the scale of the behavioral response (and the revenue impact of a particular supersensitive tax). Also crucial is whether there are untaxed near-bank financial intermediaries competing with the taxed banking sector.

Table 13.4. Inflation and Net Interest Margins, 1995–99

Equation	1		2		3		4	
Variable	Estimate	(t stat)	Estimate	(t stat)	Estimate	(t stat)	Estimate	(t stat)
Constant	1.105	(2.4)	3.658	(4.0)	-0.000	(0.0)	0.008	(0.0)
Inflation	0.011	(2.3)	0.011	(2.7)	0.418	(2.7)	0.101	(2.5)
Inflation$^2\times10^3$	—	—	—	—	—	—	-1.932	(2.8)
Inflation$^3\times10^6$	—	—	—	—	—	—	6.630	(2.9)
log (GNP/Cap)	-0.426	(3.1)	-0.360	(4.1)	—	—	—	—
Return on assets			0.456	(3.7)	0.570	(4.4)	0.559	(4.4)
Overheads	1.099	(11.2)	0.950	(11.1)	0.937	(8.7)	0.970	(9.1)
Res. requirement × inflation	—	—	—	—	—	—	—	—
Countries	All		All		All		All	
Functional form	level		level		log		log	
Method/no. obs	OLS	68	OLS	68	OLS	71	OLS	71
RSQ/DW	0.813	2.07	0.872	2.23	0.845	2.22	0.864	2.09

(Table continues on next page.)

Table 13.4. (*continued*) Inflation and Net Interest Margins, 1995–99

Equation	5		6		7	
Variable	Estimate	(t stat)	Estimate	(t stat)	Estimate	(t stat)
Constant	4.716	(4.9)	5.573	(3.1)	2.076	(5.9)
Inflation	−0.463	(5.0)	1.324	(5.6)	1.637	(9.4)
log (GNP/Cap)	—		−0.351	(2.0)	—	—
Return on assets	—		—		—	—
Overheads	1.055	(11.9)	—		—	—
Res. requirement × inflation × 10^3	0.473	(2.5)	—		—	—
Countries	All		All		All	
Functional form	log		log		log	
Method/no. obs	OLS	68	OLS	68	OLS	71
RSQ/DW	0.844	2.05	0.587	2.42	0.563	2.35

Note: Dependent variable is net interest margin of banks as a percentage of total assets (country average). For each equation the number of observations, the method (ordinary least squares), and the R-rated and Durbin-Watson statistics.

Source: Author's calculations. See note to table 13.3.

Offshore finance, non-depository onshore finance, and informal finance are also obviously important substitutes for banking, though to a lesser extent.

If inflation merely passed through to all nominal interest rates on banking assets and liabilities on a one-for-one basis, then there would be no impact on net interest margins and no inflation tax at all. The interaction with the tax system is likely the major reason why instead one observes a clear sizable impact of inflation on bank net interest margins expressed as a share of total assets (figure 13.8, table 13.4). Here, as with the other tables, a selection only of the most significant results is shown. (For example, the table does not report a regression including *both* inflation and the interaction of inflation with reserve requirements as they are not both significant when included together.)[35]

The point estimate in the simplest of the regression equations reported in table 13.4 suggests that a doubling of inflation (say, from 5 to 10 percent, or from 10 to 20 percent) can widen the net interest margin by 115 basis points. Considering that the median net interest margin in the 70 countries used was just over 400 basis points, this a sizable effect. Not all of this need be through a tax effect—for instance, it is easy to think of reasons why the average risk of a bank's portfolio would increase with inflation—but the results indicate the potential magnitudes involved.

Even if the tax interaction with inflation can be passed through to the intermediary's customers through the net interest margin, this contributes to the reduced scale of intermediation and the resulting fluctuations in real intermediation activity discourage the development of specialized human capital in loan appraisal skills.

Improving the Indexation of the Tax System

The fiscal authorities are rarely set up to consider, in an explicit way, the impact of inflation on the budget or the interactions between an imperfectly indexed formal tax system and the rate of inflation.

Understanding the fiscal impact of inflation and how it impacts the financial system is important for developing good policies. Nowadays, fewer and fewer governments rely on printing money; the fiscal benefits of inflation come in more indirect forms.

Although inflation shrinks the financial system, it can be associated with increased bank profitability. Yet because interest forms the bulk of their gross revenue, the distortions caused by the interaction between inflation and other non-indexed taxes can be particularly severe for banks and other financial intermediaries.

Our proposed measures of non-indexation (the tax gradient and the limiting elasticity) can help capture some of the most potentially damaging aspects of tax—inflation interaction. Improving the indexation of the tax system so far as the computation of interest is concerned would reduce the sensitivity of effective tax rates on intermediation.

Notes

1. For instance Chari, Christiano, and Kehoe (1996) show that, whether the role of money is characterized in terms of "cash or credit in advance of payment" or in terms of "money in the utility function," the optimality of a zero inflation tax depends on homotheticity and separability properties of the relevant utility functions. Essentially, the assumptions required are those that relegate the role of money to being an intermediate good in the production of utility. See also Correia and Teles (1997).

2. See Alogoskoufis and van der Ploeg (1994), which presents conditions under which inflationary financing of an increase in government spending will be better than tax-financing for growth.

3. The existence of an otherwise untaxed underground economy could be another justification, although perhaps not a strong one (Nicolini 1998).

4. According to Goodfriend and Hargreaves (1983), even in the United States, revenue was the original motive for introducing reserve requirements.

5. See Espinosa-Vega (1995); Espinosa-Vega and Russell (1999, 2001); and Chang (1994).

6. See Espinosa-Vega and Yip (2000) and Mourmouras and Russell (1992). Looking at it from another perspective, the deposit tax equals a reserve requirement *plus* an open market operation (Bacchetta and Caminal 1992).

7. The positive correlation between seigniorage and conventional taxes predicted, for example, by Trehan and Walsh (1990), is based on the idea that the shocks come from spending. But other patterns of shock are possible. Click (2000) shows empirically how interaction between exogenous shocks to any debt, seigniorage, or taxation feed through to the others contemporaneously and over time. See also Mankiw (1987) and Poterba and Rotemberg (1990).

8. This is especially the case where the efficiency of the tax system is underdeveloped—a consequence perhaps of a polarized society where each side is reluctant to improve the permanent arrangements for tax collection in case the other side misuses the revenue. See Cukierman, Edwards, and Tabellini (1992), who provide some evidence that reliance on seigniorage is higher in politically polarized societies.

9. The volatility of inflation tax revenues or, more specifically, the degree of unpredictable fluctuation, does appear to be similar to that of deficits (Calvo and Guidotti 1993).

10. See Sarel (1996); Bruno and Easterly (1998); Fischer, Sahay, and Vegh (2002); and Khan and Senhadji (2000).

11. For Cooley and Hansen's calibration, the welfare costs of this over-economizing on transactions balances is less than the saving made by being able to reduce income tax rates.

12. Using a calibrated model of precautionary balances, İmrohoroğlu and Prescott deduce that the key impact of inflation or other financial sector taxes is their impact on the real rate of return on deposits. As it is, this influences the degree to which agents will over-economize on precautionary balances. A tax that lowers the real rate of return by 5 percentage points is estimated to be equivalent to a loss of about 0.5 percent of average consumption. The model is subject to the criticism that precautionary savings may in the real world be held in other forms not subject to inflation tax. Interestingly, despite fully simulating the stochastic dynamic programming problem of the household, this model does not predict any adverse effect of variations in inflation: only the mean effect on rate of return matters.

13. See Anand and Wijnbergen (1989); Fry, Goodhart, and Almeida (1996); and Goff and Toma (1993). See also Drazen (1985); Honohan (1991); and Robinson and Stella (1993).

14. Sometimes, as with the United Kingdom's Exchange Equalization Account, the foreign exchange received may be transferred to the ownership of the government.

15. Discount window lending by the Deutsche Bundesbank was, until recently, a prominent example. The below-market interest rates charged on this reflected the low remuneration on banks' deposits with the Bundesbank.

16. The process is seen in sharp outline in the European Monetary Union as different member central banks are faced with the question of how to account for unredeemed legacy currency notes. One approach is to recognize that some of these notes are "dead" (lost or destroyed) and as such will never be presented. Of course making an assumption on these lines gives an accounting windfall to the central bank. Should this windfall be transferred as a special dividend to the government, or would that be inflationary?

17. The analysis requires considerable regrouping of categories in IFS, as the breakdown of the accounts of the monetary authority are presented in widely differing ways for different countries.

18. I am indebted to Klaus Schmidt-Hebbel for stressing this point. This could be especially relevant where a central bank wishes to conceal the true scale of its support to the market. Certainly, some central banks have been found in several celebrated instances to have undertaken future commitments of one sort or another that had the effect of reducing their usable for-

eign exchange reserves. And some central bank lending to local banks will have supported onlending to government. It seems less likely that much *direct* lending to government has been concealed in such ways, and it is this direct lending that our data purport to measure.

19. The effect is small, however: about 5 basis points in additional profit for each percentage point of total assets backed by equity, seemingly implying a marginal rate of return on equity of just 5 percent.

20. For a country with a per capita GDP of $1,000, for example, all but about 3 to 5 percent of overhead costs are recovered, on average. For a country ten times richer, however, the estimated recovery rate is much lower; in rich countries, high overheads mean lower profits.

21. Per capita income becomes wholly insignificant if an institutional dummy measuring the quality of contract enforcement in the economy (BERI) is included. Another factor included is bank concentration, which could well influence the banking system's ability to capture some of the inflation tax (see Baltensperger and Jordan 1997).

22. This contrasts with the approach of Saunders and Schumacher (2000), who instead use each bank's non-interest earning assets as an approximation to required reserves. Evidently both are imperfect proxies. Overall reserves include non-compulsory reserves, and in some countries some compulsory reserves are interest-earning even if at an off-market rate.

23. Equations 1-5 in table 13.2 display the cross-country correlation of return on assets (profit before tax) with inflation in the 1988–95 period. Using the significant macro indicators of D-H (1999), equation 1 finds (as they did) an insignificant, though positive, coefficient on the rate of inflation. Brazil is an outlier in the inflation data, however, and removing it (equation 2) uncovers a strong and significant positive relationship. Actually, a more plausible functional form is to use the log-inflation (as the impact of a 1 percentage point change in inflation is unlikely to be the same at high inflation rates). Substituting this results in the per capita income variable becoming insignificant (equations 3 and 4). Inflation is significant with this functional form even if Brazil is included (equation 5).

24. Equations 6 and 7 of table 13.2 explore the tax variables examined in D-H, again using country averages. Dropping Brazil again allows inflation to become significant. The significance of the reserve holdings is amplified if interacted with inflation (equation 8). This result appears to be driven at least partly by the high reported profitability of Russian and Romanian banks.

25. This impact is somewhat smaller than obtained in table 13.2, equations 4 or 5 in the earlier period, but is in line with equation 8.

26. Measured as return on assets plus overheads as a percentage of assets.

27. This is in line with the theoretical predictions of Aiyagari, Braun, and Eckstein (1998), who emphasize the function of the banking system in supplying transaction services in times of inflation.

28. It should be noted that the alternative harmonic functional form for inflation, which embodies a more gradually slowing influence of inflation on financial sector size, actually fits the data better than the threshold regression emphasized by Boyd, Levine, and Smith.

29. Estimates by Bali and Thurston (2000); Easterly, Mauro, and Schmidt-Hebbel (1995); Kiguel and Neumeyer (1995); and others—of the rate of inflation that maximes the inflation tax—tend to be much higher than 15 percent.

30. Actually, the piecewise linear regressions estimated by Boyd, Levine, and Smith for market size and activity have significant discontinuities at the imposed break-point. Thus this study prefers to rely on the harmonic regressions they report, or simply on the interquartile differences in the data sorted by inflation.

31. There is some ambiguity here, depending on which estimates are used. Figure 13.5 is based on simple interquartile differences. Using the regression results suggests that market capitalization does not decline as fast, but that turnover declines more quickly. This study prefers to use the interquartile differences, as the regression estimates risk being extrapolated beyond the range where they can be regarded as trustworthy.

32. Actually, this Fisher relationship is itself quite controversial in the tax context. A partial equilibrium argument can be made to the effect that the nominal interest rate may increase *more* than one-for-one with the rate of inflation because of the need to compensate savers for the fact that nominal interest income is fully chargeable to personal income tax. On the other hand, as has been stressed by Feldstein, the ability of borrowers to pay interest, and hence their demand for funds, may be reduced in times of inflation by other aspects of non-indexation of the tax system (notably lack of indexation of depreciation allowances). Empirically there is no strong evidence of such a tax effect, at least for industrial countries where (because of the greater effectiveness of income tax collection) one would expect the effect to be strongest.

33. An alternative, suggested by Klaus Schmidt-Hebbel (personal communication), would be to specify these expressions in terms of the inflation factor $\pi/(1 + \pi)$, which has the advantage of being bounded by unity and its limiting elasticity with respect to π is zero.

34. Many authors have made the simplifying assumption that all reserve holdings of banks are unremunerated, but this is far from being the case. In many countries the central bank remunerates excess reserves (those in excess of the compulsory requirement). In some, even the required reserves are remunerated (see Fry, Goodhart, and Almeida 1996).

35. Of course, even in an indexed system, such as that of Chile, unremunerated reserve requirements would be expected to affect margins (see Basch and Fuentes 2000).

References

Aiyagari, S. Rao, R. Anton Braun, and Zvi Eckstein. 1998. "Transactions Services, Inflation and Welfare." *Journal of Political Economy* 106 (5): 1274–1301.

Alogoskoufis, George, and Frederick van der Ploeg. 1994. "Money and Endogenous Growth." *Journal of Money, Credit and Banking* 26 (4): 771–91.

Anand, Ritu, and Sweder van Wijnbergen. 1989. "Inflation and the Financing of Government Expenditure: An Introductory Analysis with an Application to Turkey." *World Bank Economic Review* 3 (1): 17–38.

Bacchetta, Philippe, and Ramon Caminal. 1992. "Optimal Seigniorage and Financial Liberalization." *Journal of International Money and Finance* 11: 518–38.

Bailey, Martin. 1956. "The Welfare Costs of Inflationary Finance." *Journal of Political Economy* 64 (2): 93–110.

Bali, Turan G., and Thom Thurston. 2000. "Empirical Estimates of Inflation Tax Laffer Surfaces: A 30-country Study." *Journal of Development Economics* 63 (2): 529–46.

Baltensperger, Ernst, and Thomas J. Jordan. 1997. "Seigniorage, Banking and the Optimal Quantity of Money." *Journal of Banking and Finance* 21 (6): 781–96.

Barnes, Michelle, John H. Boyd, and Bruce D. Smith. 1999. "Inflation and Asset Returns." *European Economic Review* 43 (4–6): 737–54.

Basch, Miguel, and Rodrigo Fuentes. 2000. "Macroeconomic Influences on Bank Spreads in Chile, 1990–95." In Philip Brock and Liliana Rojas-Suarez, eds. *Why So High? Understanding Interest Rate Spreads in Latin America.* Washington, D.C.: Inter-American Development Bank.

Boyd, John H., Ross Levine, and Bruce D. Smith. 2001. "The Impact of Inflation on Financial Sector Performance." *Journal of Monetary Economics* 47 (2): 221–48

Brock, Philip. 1984. "Inflationary Finance in an Open Economy." *Journal of Monetary Economics* 14 (1): 37–53.

———. 1989. "Reserve Requirements and the Inflation Tax." *Journal of Money, Credit and Banking* 21 (1): 106–21.

Bruno, Michael, and William Easterly. 1998. "Inflation Crises and Long-run Growth." *Journal of Monetary Economics* 41 (1): 3–26.

Calvo, Guillermo A., and Pablo E. Guidotti. 1993. "On the Flexibility of Monetary Policy: The Case of the Optimal Inflation Tax." *Review of Economic Studies* 60 (3): 667–87.

Chang, Roberto. 1994. "Endogenous Currency Substitution, Inflationary Finance and Welfare." *Journal of Money, Credit and Banking* 26 (4): 903–16.

Chari, V. V., Lawrence J. Christiano, and Patrick J. Kehoe. 1996. "Optimality of the Friedman Rule in Economies with Distorting Taxes." *Journal of Monetary Economics* 37 (2–3): 203–23.

Claessens, Stijn, Aslı Demirgüç-Kunt, and Harry Huizinga. 2000. "How Does Foreign Entry Affect the Domestic Banking Market?" In Stijn Claessens and Marion Jansen, eds. *The Internationalization of Financial Services: Issues and Lessons for Developing Countries*. Dordrecht, Holland: Kluwer.

Click, Reid W. 2000. "Seigniorage and Conventional Taxation with Multiple Exogenous Shocks." *Journal of Economic Dynamics & Control* 24 (8): 1447–79.

Cooley, Thomas F., and Gary D. Hansen. 1991. "The Welfare Costs of Moderate Inflations." *Journal of Money, Credit and Banking* 23 (2–3): 483–503.

Correia, Isabel, and Pedro Teles. 1997. "The Optimal Inflation Tax." Discussion Paper 123. Federal Reserve Bank of Minneapolis.

Cukierman, Alex. 1984. *Inflation, Stagflation, Relative Prices and Imperfect Information*. Cambridge: Cambridge University Press.

Cukierman, Alex, Sebastian Edwards, and Guido Tabellini. 1992. "Seigniorage and Political Instability." *American Economic Review* 102 (3): 537–55.

Demirgüç-Kunt, Aslı, and Harry Huizinga. 1999. "Determinants of Commercial Bank Interest Margins and Profitability: Some International Evidence." *World Bank Economic Review* 13 (2): 379–408.

Demirgüç-Kunt, Aslı, Luc Laeven, and Ross Levine. 2003. "The Impact of Bank Regulations and Concentration on Bank Efficiency." World Bank, Washington, D.C. Processed.

Diamond, P. A., and J. A. Mirrlees. 1971. "Optimal Taxation and Public Production I: Production Efficiency and II: Tax Rules." *American Economic Review* 61 (1): 8–27 and (2): 261–78.

Drazen, Allen. 1985. "A General Measure of Inflation Tax Revenues." *Economic Letters* 17 (4): 327–33.

Easterly, William R., Paolo Mauro, and Klaus Schmidt-Hebbel. 1995. "Money Demand and Seigniorage-maximizing Inflation." *Journal of Money, Credit and Banking* 27 (2): 583–603.

Espinosa-Vega, Marco A. 1995. "Multiple Reserve Requirements." *Journal of Money, Credit and Banking* 27 (3): 762–76.

Espinosa-Vega, Marco A., and Steven Russell. 1999. "A Public Finance Analysis of Multiple Reserve Requirements." Working Paper 99-19. Federal Reserve Bank of Atlanta.

———. 2001. "Stability of Steady States in a Model of Pleasant Monetarist Arithmetic." Working Paper 2001-20. Federal Reserve Bank of Atlanta.

Espinosa-Vega, Marco A. and Chong K. Yip. 2000. "Government Financing in an Endogenous Growth Model with Financial Market Restrictions." Working Paper 2000-17. Federal Reserve Bank of Atlanta.

Feldstein, Martin. 1983. *Inflation, Tax Rules, and Capital Formation.* Cambridge, Mass.: National Bureau of Economic Research.

———. 1999. "Capital Income Taxes and the Benefit of Price Stability." In Martin Feldstein, ed. *The Costs and Benefits of Price Stability.* Chicago: University of Chicago Press.

Fischer, Stanley. 1982. "Seigniorage and the Case for a National Money." *Journal of Political Economy* 90 (2): 295–313.

Fischer, Stanley, Ratna Sahay, and Carlos A. Vegh. 2002. "Modern Hyper- and High Inflations." *Journal of Economic Literature* 40 (3): 837–80.

Freeman, Scott. 1987. "Reserve Requirements and Optimal Seigniorage." *Journal of Monetary Economics* 19 (2): 307–14.

Friedman, Milton. 1953. *Essays in Positive Economics.* Chicago: University of Chicago Press.

———. 1971. "Government Revenue from Inflation." *Journal of Political Economy* 79 (4): 846–56.

Fry, Maxwell J., 1981. "Government Revenue from Monopoly Supply of Currency and Deposits." *Journal of Monetary Economics* 8 (2): 261–70.

Fry, Maxwell J., Charles A. E. Goodhart, and Alvaro Almeida. 1996. *Central Banking in Developing Countries.* London: Routledge.

Goff, Brian L., and Mark Toma. 1993. "Optimal Seigniorage, the Gold Standard and Central Bank Financing." *Journal of Money, Credit and Banking* 25 (1): 79–95.

Goodfriend, Marvin, and Monica Hargreaves. 1983. "A Historical Perspective on the Rationales and Functions of Reserve Requirements." *Federal Reserve Bank of Richmond Quarterly Review* (April/May) http://www.rich.frb.org/pubs/wpapers/pdfs/wp83-1.pdf

Grilli, Vittorio. 1989a. "Seigniorage in Europe." In M. de Cecco and A. Giovannini, eds., *A European Central Bank?* Cambridge: Cambridge University Press.

———. 1989b. "Exchange Rates and Seigniorage." *European Economic Review* 33 (2–3): 580–87.

Honohan, Patrick. 1991, "Inflationary Effects of Deficit Financing." *Journal of Policy Modeling* 13 (2): 229–40.

Honohan, Patrick. 1996. "Does It Matter How Seigniorage Is Measured?" *Applied Financial Economics* 6 (3): 293–300.

İmrohoroğlu, Ayşe, and Edward C. Prescott. 1991. "Seigniorage as a Tax: An Empirical Investigation." *Journal of Money, Credit and Banking* 23 (2–3): 462–75.

Khan, Mohsin S., and A. S. Senhadji. 2000. "Threshold Effects in the Relation between Inflation and Growth." *IMF Working Paper* WP/00/110. International Monetary Fund, Washington, D.C.

Kiguel, Miguel A., and Pablo Andres Neumeyer. 1995. "Seigniorage and Inflation: The Case of Argentina." *Journal of Money, Credit and Banking* 27 (3): 672–82.

Mankiw, N. Gregory. 1987. "The Optimal Collection of Seigniorage: Theory and Evidence." *Journal of Monetary Economics* 20 (2): 327–41.

Mourmouras, Alex, and Steven H. Russell. 1992. "Optimal Reserve Requirements, Deposit Taxation and the Demand for Money." *Journal of Monetary Economics* 30 (1): 129–42.

Nicolini, Juan Pablo. 1998. "Tax Evasion and the Optimal Inflation Tax." *Journal of Development Economics* 55 (1): 215–32.

Phelps, Edward S. 1973. "Inflation in the Theory of Public Finance." *Swedish Journal of Economics* 75 (1): 67–72.

Poterba, James H., and Julio J. Rotemberg. 1990. "Inflation and Taxation with Optimizing Governments." *Journal of Money, Credit and Banking* 22 (1): 1–18.

Repullo, Rafael. 1991. *Financing Budget Deficits by Seigniorage and Implicit Taxation: The Cases of Spain and Portugal.* CEPR Discussion Paper No. 583. Centre for Economic Policy Research, London.

Robinson, David J., and Peter Stella. 1993. "Amalgamating Central Bank and Fiscal Deficits." In Mario I. Blejer and Adrienne Cheasty, eds., *How to Measure the Fiscal Deficit: Analytical and Methodological Issues.* Washington, D.C.: International Monetary Fund.

Sarel, Michael. 1996. "Nonlinear Effects of Inflation on Economic Growth." *IMF Staff Papers* 43 (1): 199–215.

Saunders, Anthony, and Liliana Schumacher. 2000. "The Determinants of Bank Interest Rate Margins: An International Study." *Journal of International Money and Finance* 19 (6): 813–32.

Sibert, Anne, and Lihong Liu. 1998. "Government Finance with Currency Substitution." *Journal of International Economics* 44 (1): 155–72.

Tanzi, Vito. 1977. "Inflation, Lags in Collection and the Real Value of Tax Revenue." *IMF Staff Papers* 24: 154–67.

Tobin, James. 1978. "A Proposal for International Monetary Reform." *Eastern Economic Journal* 4 (3–4): 153–59.

Trehan, Brian, and Carl E. Walsh. 1990. "Seigniorage and Tax Smoothing in the United States, 1914–86." *Journal of Monetary Economics* 25 (1): 97–112.

Index

Note: *n* indicates note (*nn* more than one note), and italicized numbers indicate figures or tables.

transactions and transaction services
(continued)
costs of, 156, 334–35, 335–37,
341nn9–11
and deposit tax, 92
and inflation, 399, 415n27
and money market funds, 97,
122n15
pricing of, 121n5
stamp duties, 231
taxes on, 313, 315–16
See also financial services and
transactions
transaction taxes, 3, 10–12, 23,
24n10
effect on price volatility, 328–29
effect on trading volume, 329
impact on securities' prices, 329
"noise" trading, 325, 344n2
payment of, 22
Sweden, 330–32, 341nn6–7
taxation model, 85, 121n3
See also securities transaction
taxes (STT)
transparency, 15
Trehan, Brian, 413n7
Trester, Jeffrey, 181
Turkey, 293
two-period life cycle, 34–40, 72–73n2

U.K. Customs and Excise
Commissioners v. FDR Ltd., 354,
370
Umlauf, Steven R., 328, 329, 330, 331
unanticipated deferral, 219, 236n14
unbundling of services, 368
undepreciated capital stock, 50
unemployment, 272, 274, 286n5
uniform tax, 63–64, 76n36
United Kingdom, 65, 203, 328
education, health, and life
protection tax incentives,
150
Exchange Equalization
Account, 414n14
hedging, 224
marginal personal income tax
rate, 201

new financial instruments,
221, 222
reserve requirements, 233
retirement savings, 132
risk capital, 211
tax policy, 202, 224–25
tax treatment of borrowing,
153, 154
United States, 47, 151, 152, 291, 328
bifurcation practice, 225
charge-off accounting, 308n15
competition from financial
institutions, 353
deferred tax income, 309n22
deposit insurance, 25n16
equity ownership, 164n4
marginal personal income tax
rate, 201
new financial instruments,
221, 222–23
reserve accounting method,
308n16
reserve requirements, 232,
233–34
retirement savings, 132, 134
savings for education, health,
and life protection, 149, 150
switch from reserve to charge-
off accounting method,
310n27
tax reform measures, 202
tax treatment of borrowing,
153
universal payments tax, 12
unrealized gains or losses, 219, 222,
226
Uspenskii, A., 286n8
Uruguay, 138, 139, 140, 175
utility of consumption, 84, 121n2
utility functions, 60–61, 65,
74nn34–35, 85–86, 121n3, 359,
413n1

valuation, 227
value-added tax (VAT), 2, 3, 62, 105,
345, 360
applied to financial services,
350–51